D1213166

Myth and National Identity
in Nineteenth-Century Britain

Myth and National Identity in Nineteenth-Century Britain

The Legends of King Arthur and Robin Hood

STEPHANIE L. BARCZEWSKI

OXFORD
UNIVERSITY PRESS

OXFORD
UNIVERSITY PRESS

Great Clarendon Street, Oxford OX2 6DP
Oxford University Press is a department of the University of Oxford.
It furthers the University's objective of excellence in research, scholarship,
and education by publishing worldwide in
Oxford New York

Athens Auckland Bangkok Bogotá Buenos Aires Calcutta
Cape Town Chennai Dar es Salaam Delhi Florence Hong Kong Istanbul
Karachi Kuala Lumpur Madrid Melbourne Mexico City Mumbai
Nairobi Paris São Paulo Singapore Taipei Tokyo Toronto Warsaw
and associated companies in Berlin Ibadan

Oxford is a registered trade mark of Oxford University Press
in the UK and certain other countries

Published in the United States
by Oxford University Press Inc., New York

© Stephanie L. Barczewski 2000

British Library Cataloguing in Publication Data
Data available

Library of Congress Cataloging in Publication Data
Barczewski, Stephanie L.
Myth and national identity in nineteenth century Britain:
the legends of King Arthur and Robin Hood/Stephanie L. Barczewski.
Enlargement of author's thesis (Ph.D.)—Yale University.
Includes bibliographical references (p.) and index.
1. English literature—19th century—History and criticism.
2. Nationalism and literature—Great Britain—History—19th century.
3. Arthurian romances—Adaptations—History and criticism.
4. National characteristics, British, in literature. 5. Medievalism—
Great Britain—Civilization—19th century. 8. Arthur, King—
in literature. 9. Nationalism in literature. 10. Britons in
literature. 11. Outlaws in literature. 12. Myth in
literature. I. Title.
PR468.N293 B37 2000 820.9'358 21—dc21 99-040054
ISBN 0-19-820728-X

3 5 7 9 10 8 6 4

Typeset by J&L Composition Ltd, Filey, North Yorkshire
Printed in Great Britain
on acid-free paper by
Biddles Ltd
Guildford and King's Lynn

Preface

FOR CENTURIES, the legends of King Arthur and Robin Hood have enjoyed a uniquely symbiotic relationship in British culture. They have provided the nation with two of its most important and most popular myths, myths which have been told and retold in a variety of contexts and genres. To this day, there are few stories which are better known to British schoolchildren, and it would be difficult to find someone in the English-speaking world who could not identify the most significant characters and most famous episodes of the two legends. They continue to appear in literature for both children and adults, on television, and in films, and now in the computer age the Internet abounds with websites dedicated to them.

It is this popularity which first attracted me to a scholarly study of King Arthur and Robin Hood. I became interested in the Arthurian legend as a first-year graduate student at Yale University, as I sought a way to combine the literary expertise gained from four years as an undergraduate English major with my newfound love of British history. There had been general surveys of the historical evolution of the legend over the centuries, but no scholarship had focused specifically on the period between the French Revolution and the death of Queen Victoria, which was my chronological area of interest, as well as a time in which Arthur was enjoying a tremendous surge in popularity. As I began looking at nineteenth-century interpretations of King Arthur, however, I noticed that he was being shadowed by an unlikely doppelgänger. Scholars had previously noted the increased interest which the Victorians had displayed in the Arthurian legend, but they had failed to observe a simultaneous fascination with Robin Hood, the medieval outlaw who seemed to represent everything that Arthur opposed. The Arthurian legend is the story of a king, a man at the pinnacle of the political and social hierarchy. The tales of Robin Hood, on the other hand, feature as their protagonist a hero outside of and in many ways subversive to conventional structures of authority.

As I continued to peruse nineteenth-century versions of the two legends, I was struck by the frequency with which King Arthur and

Robin Hood were specifically referred to as national heroes and the constant claims that their legends were somehow relevant to the nation's experience and development. I found it striking that both legends should be described in such a fashion, since they were so very different in terms of their ideological orientation. British national identity in the nineteenth century has only recently come to be a subject of scholarly interest, because it has so often been taken for granted. This was the age, after all, when Britannia ruled the waves and when the sun never set on the British empire, the age of Palmerstonian gunboat diplomacy and jingoistic waving of the Union Jack. National identity was something to be worried about by the nation-building Italians and Germans, or the revolution-plagued French, or the Civil War-torn Americans. British national identity, in contrast, was a relatively simply matter that hardly bore discussion and analysis.

By the 1990s, however, the issues surrounding British national identity in the present were beginning to have an impact on perceptions of that national identity in the past. Most obviously, there were the questions raised by the demands of the Scots and Welsh for greater independence, questions which called to mind the historical relationship of the constituent parts of the United Kingdom. How did the identities of the nations comprising the so-called 'Celtic fringe' fit into the identity of the British nation as a whole? Was it simply a question of a much larger, dominant England swallowing them up, or was the interplay more complex? As I pondered these questions, the distinction between 'Britishness' and 'Englishness' seemed to become more and more crucial in understanding the historical evolution of British national identity. It also seemed to be an issue about which the legends of King Arthur and Robin Hood had something to say, for the nineteenth century saw a concerted effort to transform them both into specifically English heroes, as I explore in Chapters 3 and 4 of this study.

This was not, however, the only point of contention which I saw regarding British national identity in both the present and the past. The modern, postcolonial, democratic world has forced Britain, along with most other western nations, to confront the issue of who—using criteria such as race, class, and gender—is to have full rights of belonging to the nation. Whereas British citizenship, at least when defined in terms of the right to participate in the political process on a national level, was once restricted to upper-class white males, it has over the past two centuries been broadened to take in a much wider range of constituents. This broadening, although it seems natural and inevitable to us today, did not occur without debate and conflict. This, then, is the second main theme which I explore in this study—the way in which the traditional conflict between the legends of King Arthur and Robin Hood paralleled conflicts in nineteenth-century Britain over inclusion and exclusion in the nation. I explore this theme most specifically in Chapters 5 and 6, which focus on gender issues and the British empire respectively, but it weaves in and out of the entire work. There are scholars who feel that such questions do not truly belong in a study of national identity, but I feel that they are crucial. A nation is not so much a 'what' as it is a 'who', and therefore it cannot be understood if its constituent groups cannot be identified.

This study is the product of ten years of my evolution as a scholar of modern British cultural history. It began as a Yale doctoral dissertation, and thus it is there that my acknowledgements must begin as well. Without the financial support which Yale gave me while I was a graduate student, and without the stimulating environment which Yale provided, this book would not exist. There was, at the time I was there, no better institution for the study of British history on this side of the Atlantic. In a practical sense, my debts are large, and I must thank the MacArthur, Mellon, Smith-Richardson, and Whiting Foundations for their support while I was completing my dissertation. My special gratitude goes to the Fox Fellowship, which I was fortunate to receive in my final year of graduate school. This award enabled to complete the writing of my dissertation at Sidney Sussex College of the University of Cambridge and I am certain that my work much benefited from these ideal surroundings. While I was at Cambridge a number of distinguished scholars graciously offered their ideas about and comments on my preliminary drafts, and Professor Jonathan Parry is particularly deserving of thanks for his time and insight.

This brings me to an acknowledgement of my more individual debts. There are four scholars who have had a tremendous impact upon my career, and nothing I have achieved would have been possible without them. Paul Kennedy gave me not only financial but moral support during my time at Yale, and I will never forget his frequent displays of unsolicited kindness. He is a model of how even the brightest academic star can find the time to nurture a future generation of scholars. David Bell simultaneously built my confidence in my abilities and gave my work the most thorough and informed criticism it has ever received, and for that I will always be grateful. My greatest debt, however, is to David Cannadine and Linda Colley. Little did I know that when I wandered into Professor Cannadine's class as a junior at Columbia University that it was a day that would change my life forever. And ever since, his enthusiasm, kindness, and generosity have encouraged me and allowed me to overcome those dark moments that every scholar has when the task before her seems impossible. Linda Colley was a model dissertation advisor whose greatest asset is her ability to teach her students to become independent scholars, even if that process is sometimes a painful or difficult one. There is no one in the historical profession whom I respect more.

The research for and writing of the dissertation upon which this study is based took place at Yale, but the revisions of the manuscript and the completion of the project have been done in the very different, though no less congenial, surroundings of Clemson University. At Clemson I have been given the time and opportunity to transform my dissertation into this book, largely thanks to the efforts of my department chair, Roger Grant. Professor Grant has done whatever I have requested and more to allow me to pursue my research interests, and for that I am extremely grateful. My other colleagues at Clemson have also helped to make the transition from graduate student to assistant professor a happy one.

Finally, no work of scholarship can be completed without the personal support of family and friends. Here, there are three people in particular to whom I owe the greatest debt. My parents have throughout my life given me the opportunity to pursue whatever goals I established, and they barely blinked an eye when I announced my (what to them must have seemed a very sudden and somewhat odd) decision to become a British historian. Their love and faith in me has sustained me through whatever life has dealt me over the last thirty-one years, and I hope that seeing this book in print will repay at least a little of that debt. Finally, my fiancé, Michael Silvestri, has lived with King Arthur and Robin Hood for as long as he has known me. He has guided me through all of the ups and downs of the last five years as only a fellow scholar of British history could do, and I look forward to a lifetime of similar expressions of gratitude in the prefaces of future projects.

Clemson, SC
April 1999

Contents

King Arthur, Robin Hood, and British National Identity

THIS STUDY will examine how the legends of King Arthur and Robin Hood played a role in both displaying and shaping British national identity in the nineteenth century. More specifically, it will focus upon the way in which King Arthur and Robin Hood contributed to, but also challenged, the attempt to build a consensual, celebratory national 'history' based on the notion of Britain's uniquely felicitous political evolution and a related sense of a distinctive national character.[1] Despite what would seem to be a clear relationship between history and national identity, British history-writing in the nineteenth century is often seen as an exception to the European norm. In countries such as France and Germany, it is frequently argued, history writing was crucial to the invention (or post-revolutionary reinvention) of the nation, as these new nations required ancient pedigrees in order to attract popular support and promote political stability. In Britain, by contrast, the story was supposedly different. No such blatant fabrication was necessary, for the nation's political institutions truly were sanctioned by time. All British historians had to do, therefore, was to admire that longevity, rather than create it.[2]

The scholars who have endorsed this point of view, however, have focused almost exclusively on the major works of historical writing, thereby failing to recognize the impact of more popular genres upon the contemporary vision of the past. Outside of the academy, a more romanticized and overtly nationalist history emerged. This view was

---

[1] Stefan Collini, *Public Moralists: Political Thought and Intellectual Life in Britain 1850–1930* (Oxford: Clarendon Press, 1991) 351. See also J. W. Burrow, *A Liberal Descent: Victorian Historians and the English Past* (Cambridge: Cambridge UP, 1981).

[2] Peter Mandler, '"In the Olden Time": Romantic History and English National Identity, 1820–50', in Laurence Brockliss and David Eastwood (eds.), *A Union of Multiple Identities: The British Isles, c.1750–c.1850* (Manchester and New York: Manchester UP, 1996), 78–92.

disseminated throughout British culture, but it was in literature that it made its presence felt most keenly, and therefore this study will concentrate upon that area. In particular, it will focus on how numerous nineteenth-century authors used the legends of King Arthur and Robin Hood as vehicles through which they expressed their ideas about the nation's past, ideas which played a significant role in shaping British national identity in the present.

The purpose of constructing a national past using such legendary material is generally assumed to be the building of a consensus regarding the nation's current status and mission. Indeed, as we shall see, King Arthur and Robin Hood were utilized in literary efforts to identify and promote certain elements considered essential to British national identity. At the same time, however, these efforts reveal some severe cracks in the façade of national unity. In the first place, the past they were used to construct was a narrowly *English* one which left out the other constituent parts of the British Isles. And furthermore, they show that even within this attempt to create a relatively limited 'Englishness', there were tensions and conflicts over what precisely that meant. This study will therefore focus upon the complex nature of British national identity in the nineteenth century, and how in many ways it was shaped by conflict as much as it was by consensus.

Before turning to look specifically at the legends of King Arthur and Robin Hood, however, I must tackle one key question. Any historical study which claims to be about British national identity must first establish precisely with which nation, or nations, it is concerned. If, as it is in this case, the answer to that deceptively simple question is 'Britain', then the next step must be to define what that term means. Does it refer to a single nation, a true 'union', or is it instead a term that describes a precarious political amalgam of several different nations who at best distrust and at worst despise each other? Has 'Britain' ever been anything but an administrative entity created by a series of political acts? And what does it mean and has it meant to be 'British', if it means anything at all?

These are questions with which historians have increasingly grappled in recent years, primarily because the current trend in British politics seems to be pulling away from the Union rather than towards it. Scotland and Wales are shortly to get their own parliaments, and at this point no one can be certain about what sort of implications this will have for the future of Great Britain as a nation. And as the Union seems to be heading towards disintegration, or at least significant alteration, interest has increased in the forces which led to its creation and preservation.[3]

So at which chronological point can we begin to talk about 'national identity' in the context of British history? The scholarship on this subject points emphatically to the sixteenth century. Historians have long recognized that the Tudor period saw the creation of what Geoffrey Elton calls 'the modern sovereign state', in which 'a self-contained national unit came to be, not the tacitly accepted necessity it had been for some time, but the consciously desired goal'. Taking this one step further, Liah Greenfeld has recently asserted that 'it is possible to locate the emergence of national sentiment in England in the first third of the sixteenth century'.[4] Both Elton and Greenfeld, however, focus exclusively upon England, and make no attempt to extend their arguments to the other parts of the British Isles. It seems, therefore, that although there was a form of national identity emerging in the sixteenth century, it was exclusively English in its focus.[5]

But if the rise of the Tudor dynasty gave birth to a new form of national identity, so did its demise. The concept of 'Britishness' first became of serious political relevance in 1603, when King James VI of Scotland became King James I of England. James himself was the most prominent supporter of the new union. 'For even as little brookes lose their names by their running and fall into great rivers,' he declared, 'so by the conjunction of divers kingdoms in one, are all these private differences and questions swallowed up.' Few others, however, shared his enthusiasm, especially in his new English realm. In a speech to the Society of Antiquaries, the historian Henry Spelman complained that 'if the honourable name of England be buried in the resurrection of Albion or Brittania, we shall change the golden beames of the sunne for a cloudy daye, and drownde the glory of a nation triumphant

---

[3] See Kenneth Lunn, 'Reconsidering 'Britishness': The Construction and Significance of National Identity in Twentieth-Century Britain', in *Nation and Identity in Contemporary Europe*, ed. Brian Jenkins and Spyros A. Sofos (London and New York: Routledge, 1996), 83–100.

[4] G. R. Elton, *The Tudor Revolution in Government: Administrative Changes in the Reign of Henry VIII* (Cambridge: Cambridge UP, 1953), 3; Liah Greenfeld, *Nationalism: Five Roads to Modernity* (Cambridge, Mass.: Harvard UP, 1992), 42.

[5] Edwin Jones has recently argued that the Tudor period gave rise to a new, more nationalistic and insular view of England and English history in which xenophobia and a sense of 'specialness' became prominent parts of the English psyche. Edwin Jones, *The English Nation: The Great Myth* (Thrupp, Stroud, Glos.: Sutton, 1998).

through all the worlde to restore the memory of an obscure and barbarouse people'.[6] For the time being, those who shared Spelman's opinion prevailed, and no political union occurred between England and Scotland. Throughout the seventeenth century the two countries maintained separate parliaments and separate identities.[7] There was thus only an extremely limited sense of British national identity prior to 1700. The eighteenth century, however, saw significant changes in the way in which the people of the British Isles perceived themselves and the nation they inhabited. In her study of British patriotism between 1707 and 1837, Linda Colley argues that 'it was during this period that a sense of *British* national identity was forged' (my italics). According to Colley, 'the invention of Britishness' was a direct consequence of a century-and-a-half of successive wars between Britain and France, and its development occurred along lines determined by the nature of this conflict:

It was an invention forged above all by war. Time and time again, war with France brought Britons . . . into conflict with an obviously hostile Other and encouraged them to define themselves collectively against it. They defined themselves as Protestants struggling for survival against the world's foremost Catholic power. They defined themselves against the French as they imagined them to be, superstitious, militarist, decadent and unfree.[8]

Colley's work is an important and revealing one, but even if some form of British national consensus had been achieved by the beginning of the nineteenth century, there still remained a plethora of problems to be solved. In particular, what happened after 1815, when France ceased to be a major military threat? During the remainder of the nineteenth century Britain and France would more often be allies than enemies. Nor, until the rise of Germany at the end of the century, did any other European country pose a real challenge to Britain's military and economic supremacy. If, as Colley claims, the British 'came to define themselves as a single people not because of any political or cultural

---

[6] Claire McEachern, *The Poetics of English Nationhood, 1590–1612* (Cambridge: Cambridge UP, 1996), 158.

[7] See Jenny Wormald, 'James VI, James I and the Identity of Britain', in Brendan Bradshaw and John Morrill (eds.), *The British Problem, c.1534–1707: State Formation in the Atlantic Archipelago* (New York: St Martin's, 1996), 148–71; David Underdown, *A Freeborn People: Politics and the Nation in Seventeenth-Century England* (Oxford: Clarendon, 1996), 5. See also the essays in Steven G. Ellis and Sarah Barber (eds.), *Conquest and Union: Fashioning a British State 1485–1725* (London and New York: Longman, 1995).

[8] Linda Colley, *Britons: Forging a Nation 1707–1837* (New Haven and London: Yale UP, 1992), 1, 5.

consensus at home, but rather in reaction to the Other beyond their shores', how did the removal of that 'Other' affect the trajectory of British nationalism? Did a new 'Other' have to be found? And if so, along what lines did the search for it take place?[9]

Certainly, in the nineteenth century many of the specific elements which Colley identifies as crucial components of British nationalism in the preceding period were called into question. Catholic Emancipation in 1829 had an obvious impact upon a nation which had previously based much of its identity upon a virulent defence of Protestantism. Related to this issue, but also presenting its own set of difficulties, was the incorporation of Ireland into the United Kingdom in 1800. Throughout the nineteenth century the 'Irish question' was to have a profound impact upon Britain's sense of itself and whom it included. Similar, but in some ways even more difficult problems were presented by the steady expansion of the British empire, particularly into areas of the world inhabited by non-white peoples.

At home, another set of issues was raised by the increasingly loud demands of an ever-greater proportion of the British populace for full rights of citizenship. 'Freedom', as opposed to French tyranny and absolutism, had throughout the eighteenth century been a fundamental component of British patriotism. But if everyone could agree that the British were relatively more free than the French, they could not agree on how absolutely free they should be. Did that freedom, defined in its political form as the right to vote, extend to people of all classes? To women? This debate would not be conclusively resolved until after the First World War, when full male and partial female suffrage was finally granted, and it raged with growing intensity for virtually the entire nineteenth century.

The maintenance of British national identity in the face of these new social, political, and cultural conditions was no simple matter. These problems, however, have largely been ignored by historians, who have by and large preferred to leap over the nineteenth century, a period in which they argue that nationalism was so omnipresent and consensual that it can be taken for granted. But by asserting that

---

[9] Ibid. 6. Colley has subsequently argued that the empire replaced France as the source of the 'Other' in nineteenth-century Britain. Linda Colley, 'Britishness and Otherness: An Argument', *Journal of British Studies*, 31 (1992), 325. While agreeing that the empire was an important foundation of British national identity in this period, this study will argue that the elements by which Britons defined themselves were more complex and multifaceted.

British nationalism remained virtually unchanged over the course of the nineteenth century, such arguments ignore the ways in which an otherwise extremely dynamic and vital period had a critical effect on its development. In the early decades, if we accept Colley's argument, a more inclusive 'Britishness' persisted as the preferred means of defining the nation, a definition which permitted new groups to be assimilated with relative ease because it could be altered and expanded to accommodate social and political change. But gradually the stresses to which this recently constructed and in many ways extremely fragile Britishness was subjected threatened at times to destroy it altogether, as the old categories which had distinguished it seemed inadequate for dealing with the new nineteenth-century order, both in a domestic and international context. By the century's end this relatively flexible definition had largely been supplanted by a far more exclusive 'Englishness', which demanded that its constituents adhere to certain ostensibly objective standards.[10] A Briton could be made, but one had to be born English.

This change was not simply due to the increasing dominance of the English centre over the 'Celtic periphery'. To be sure, by the end of the nineteenth century England's population of around 34 million was almost five times that of Scotland and Wales combined. But we should not too readily assume that the 'Anglicization' of Britain was a relentless and uniform process or a matter of forced assimilation, for the attempt to construct such a limited definition of the national community inevitably created dissatisfaction among those excluded from it. It is no coincidence that many of the political tensions which continue to plague Britain to this day, such as increased agitation for independence from the so-called 'Celtic fringe', date from the late nineteenth century, the period in which this new, more assertive 'Englishness' reached its apex. Its proponents were met by a bevy of individuals and groups bent on asserting their 'Scottishness', 'Welshness', or 'Irishness' with equal fervour. Although 'Britishness' continued to exist alongside of and occasionally to overlap these other loyalties, it was no longer the predominant form of national attachment.

---

[10] Laurence Brockliss and David Eastwood, 'Introduction: A Union of Multiple Identities', in Brockliss and Eastwood (eds.), *A Union of Multiple Identities*, 3. It is interesting to note that in discussing the nationalism of the period prior to the accession of Queen Victoria in 1837, Colley writes about 'Britishness', but historians who focus upon the nationalism of the decades after 1880 most often employ the term 'Englishness'. See e.g. Robert Colls and Philip Dodd (eds.), *Englishness: Politics and Culture 1880–1920* (London and Dover, NH: Croom Helm, 1986).

No single explanation will suffice for this alteration in the construction of British national identity. What is clear, however, is that by the end of the nineteenth century the brittle Britishness of its early decades had been shattered, or at least irrevocably altered, by changes in the conditions which had produced it. In many ways, then, the sort of British national identity that Colley discusses may have been only a temporary aberration which was soon challenged by a resurgence of the old internal conflicts among the constituent parts of the United Kingdom, albeit in a modern, nationalist form.

The first four chapters of this study will explore this development in more detail, through the prism of the legends of King Arthur and Robin Hood. The first of these chapters will attempt to put the two legends into cultural context. First, it will provide a brief survey of the previous historical development of King Arthur and Robin Hood, so that we may understand what legacy they carried into the period upon which this study focuses. Then this chapter will turn to the construction of King Arthur and Robin Hood as explicitly national heroes, a process which began during the third quarter of the eighteenth century and culminated during the era of the French Revolution and the Napoleonic Wars. In this period, the selective mobilization of the past—and the medieval past in particular—acted to overcome the tensions created in the present by the often tempestuous relationship among the nation's constituent communities. The Middle Ages could, if manipulated carefully, provide a portrait of a single nation with all its inhabitants marching together towards glory and greatness, rather than one of a hostile group of geographically proximate countries who were constantly warring against one another. Given this cultural context, it is not surprising that the years between 1790 and 1820 saw a literary apotheosis of King Arthur and Robin Hood, two of the nation's greatest medieval heroes.

The second chapter looks at the construction of a new 'national' history in nineteenth-century Britain. Like many other European nations in this period, Britain turned to the past as a potential source of unity in the present, and—again as in those other nations—this process required considerable manipulation and at times blatant fabrication. Ultimately what emerged was a 'British' history that focused almost exclusively upon English actions and accomplishments. I will examine what role the legends of King Arthur and Robin Hood played in this process by demonstrating their popularity in the nineteenth century, for they can have no true cultural meaning without cultural prevalence. Finally, this chapter will offer a general explanation of the meaning of the two legends in a broad sense.

Chapters 3 and 4 will focus on two of the more specific elements in the construction of a new form of British national identity in the nineteenth century. After Napoleon's defeat in 1815, France could no longer serve so readily as the 'Other' against which that national identity was defined. Accordingly, many Britons began to turn to other methods, and a key component of this process was language. The emergence of the study of the English language and its literature as a respected academic discipline was related to the growth of patriotic pride in the nation's culture. In this context, enthusiasm for medieval literature—the earliest expressions of the English 'national genius'— grew steadily in the late eighteenth and nineteenth centuries. Since King Arthur and Robin Hood were two of the most prominent heroes of medieval literature, these efforts frequently involved one or both of them, as Chapter 3 will attest.

During the nineteenth century race, too, came to serve as an increasingly important component of national identity. Influenced by a variety of ideas, including romantic notions of inherent distinctions between peoples from different nations, the claims of anthropologists regarding physical characteristics and their links with nationality, and Darwin's evolutionary theories, nineteenth-century Britons came to support race as the primary explanation for the success of some peoples and the failure of others. More specifically, they came to see themselves as Anglo-Saxons, a race that was destined to dominate the world due to its superior vigour and strength. Literary manifestations of the legends of King Arthur and Robin Hood both reflected and contributed to nineteenth-century attitudes about race. The implications of the racial identity of these two heroes will be examined in Chapter 4.

The final two chapters of this study will examine the tensions created by the new, more specifically *English* form of nationalism which arose during the nineteenth century. Here, the two legends provide excellent windows through which to view nineteenth-century culture, because they offer very different perspectives. King Arthur and Robin Hood have traditionally been diametrically opposed in terms of their ideological orientation. One is a king, a man at the pinnacle of the political and social hierarchy, whereas the other is an outlaw, and thus completely outside of—and potentially subversive to—any conventional hierarchical structure. Arthur represents power and authority, and the tales of his exploits often feature a quest to preserve stability, as he and his knights fight to defend the idyllic social and political world of Camelot. For Robin Hood, on the other hand, the only possible route to power involves taking it away from its current possessors. In the words of Eric Hobsbawm, he is 'the archetype of the social rebel'.[11]

And for the most part, the inherent dichotomy between the social and political orientations of the two legends persisted into the nineteenth century. 'Stories of [Robin Hood's] deeds are the epics of the common people,' wrote J. Walker M'Spadden in his *Stories of Robin Hood and His Merry Outlaws* (1905), 'just as the earlier stories of King Arthur and his knights are the epics of the courtly class.'[12] That two figures so different as King Arthur and Robin Hood could simultaneously function as national heroes suggests that nineteenth-century British nationalism did not represent a single set of values and ideals, but rather a variety of competing points of view. The final two chapters of this work will focus upon this theme by exploring the relationship of the legends to nineteenth-century debates regarding inclusion and exclusion in the British nation.

The Chapter 5 examines the role of female characters in the two legends, and the implications which this had regarding the inclusion of women in the contemporary British state. Much recent literary scholarship has focused upon the misogynist attitude which the Arthurian legend displays towards its female characters in the nineteenth century. Guinevere, for example, came to function as the scapegoat for Camelot's downfall. The legend of Robin Hood, however, demonstrates that Victorian attitudes towards women were not always so one-dimensional. Nineteenth-century authors treated Maid Marian as an extremely positive female character, despite her failure to conform to traditional gender roles. She lives as an equal companion of the Merry Men and takes an active part in their activities, including hunting and other traditionally masculine pursuits. Significantly, she is not criticized for stepping beyond the boundaries of 'appropriate' feminine conduct, but rather praised and even promoted as a role model for contemporary young ladies.

The sixth and final chapter of this study discusses issues of inclusion

---

[11] Eric Hobsbawm, *Primitive Rebels: Studies in Archaic Forms of Social Movement in the 19th and 20th Centuries* (New York: Praeger, 1963), 4.

[12] J. Walker M'Spadden, *Stories of Robin Hood and His Merry Outlaws Retold from the Old Ballads* (London, 1905), p. xii.

and exclusion from an imperial perspective. From the earliest versions of his legend, King Arthur has been depicted as an imperial ruler whose vast domains provide his court with many splendours. Continuing this theme, nineteenth-century authors often used the legend to promote imperial endeavour by drawing comparisons between the knights of Camelot who went upon the quest for the Holy Grail and the modern 'knights of the empire' with dragons of their own to slay in India, Africa, and the Far East. In contrast, Robin Hood has traditionally inhabited a much more circumscribed territory. In fact, his problems, and the problems of his society, have often been attributed to a misguided imperial adventure: Richard I's decision to join the Crusades. This point was not lost on Victorian authors, many of whom used the legend to comment on the foolishness of sacrificing domestic interests to imperial ambitions. This chapter thus displays the complexities of late-Victorian attitudes towards empire by showing that an emphatically pro-imperial figure such as Arthur could function as a national hero alongside the anti-imperial Robin Hood.

How did two national heroes as different as King Arthur and Robin Hood manage to coexist in nineteenth-century Britain? Paradoxically, at the same time as they function as symbols of unity, national heroes can also be sources of division and conflict. For a nation is never a monolithic entity representing a single set of values and ideals, but rather a constantly evolving, precarious consensus which is forced to combine a variety of conflicting attitudes and points of view. And because they are rarely unanimous on what the ideal image of the nation should be, its inhabitants are rarely unanimous on what constitutes a national hero. Instead, different individuals and groups promote various values and attitudes, resulting less in consensus than in competition. Thus, there is always plenty of room for more than one type of national hero in a particular community at a particular time, as this study will show.

CHAPTER ONE

'These two names are national inheritances': The Emergence of King Arthur and Robin Hood as National Heroes

IN EDWARD BULWER LYTTON's epic poem *King Arthur* (1849), the Lady of the Lake takes Arthur to visit the Lords of Time, who ask him to choose from three visions of the future. The first depicts a beautiful valley where Arthur sees himself placidly dozing in the centre of a ring of rose bushes. Objecting to such passivity, he rejects this vision, and is shown a second which features him sitting on a jewel-encrusted throne surrounded by fawning admirers. At first Arthur responds favourably, but when he asks to see images of his subjects, they are revealed to be impoverished and starving. Appalled that a king could live in splendour while his people suffer, he rejects this vision as well. The third vision displays a fresh battleground, with Arthur 'stretch'd lifeless on the sward'. He demands to know the cause for which he has died, and in response he is shown a vision of Britain's future which culminates in Queen Victoria's reign:

> Mild, like all strength, sits Crowned Liberty,
> Wearing the aspect of a youthful Queen:
> And far outstretch'd 'long the unmeasured sea
> Rests the vast shadow of her throne; serene
> From the dumb icebergs to the fiery zone,
> Rests the vast shadow of that guardian throne.[1]

Without hesitation, Arthur chooses this vision, thus opting to sacrifice his own life for the future greatness of his nation.

In 1900 Vivian Matthews and Alick Manley composed an 'original burlesque extravaganza' entitled *Little Red Robin* which compares the

---

[1] Edward Bulwer Lytton, *King Arthur* (London, 1849), 21, 29.

adventures of Robin Hood and his Merry Men to the exploits of the British army in the Boer War. Matthews and Manley depict Robin Hood and his men as stalwart patriots who never fail to respond to their country's call, as this song indicates:

> When the Country's at War and 'To Arms!' is the cry,
> There are plenty of fellows who promptly reply
> That they're ready to fight, and, if need be, to die
> As a true-hearted Englishman should.
> There are others, alas! as we very well know
> Who seize upon every occasion to show
> That their sympathies lie with their countrymen's foe!
> They'd better keep out of the Wood!

These patriotic proclamations are put to the test when King Richard the Lion-hearted pays a visit to Sherwood Forest in order to drum up recruits for the Crusades. True to their word, Robin Hood and his men eagerly agree to follow their king:

> For our swords they swing and our spurs they ring,
> As we ride in the train of our Soldier King;
> Whether by land, or whether by sea,
> Or who is the foeman, what care we?
> 'Here's to the hearts that are brave and true!'
> We sing in a rousing chorus;
> 'Here's to the Red and the White and the Blue
> Of the flag that's waving o'er us!'[2]

These two episodes indicate the close relationship between the legends of King Arthur and Robin Hood and British nationalism in the nineteenth century, a period in which Britons found many heroes worthy of patriotic celebration. Such figures not only provided exemplars of British superiority, but also helped to explain it by displaying its source in the heroic efforts of the great individuals whom the nation had produced. 'The seeds of our national character are to be sought in the lives of the heroes of early England, from whom we trace the beginnings of our best habits and institutions', declared Lady Magnus in her *First Makers of England* (1901).[3] Among the most frequently

---

[2] Vivian Matthews and Alick Manley, *Little Red Robin; or, the Dey and the Knight. Original Burlesque Extravaganza* (London, [1900]), 6, 15.

[3] Lady Katie Magnus, *First Makers of England: Julius Cæsar, King Arthur, Alfred the Great* (London, 1901), p. vii.

invoked of these 'heroes of early England' were King Arthur and Robin Hood.

The 'Once and Future King' Versus the 'Lord of Misrule': The Ideological Contrast Between the Legends of King Arthur and Robin Hood

In 1849 *Sharpe's London Journal* described King Arthur as 'the beautiful incarnation of all the best characteristics of our nation'. Indeed, a plethora of nineteenth-century literary works treat Arthur as a national hero, a man willing to die fighting in his country's glorious cause. In W. J. Linton's 'The Old Legend of King Arthur' (1865), Arthur proclaims:

> I have not flinch'd from peril, nor counted pains;
> What adverse odds, what difficult steps to climb,
> What possible inconvenience or mishap,
> Troubled me never. I ask'd nought but this—
> May it serve thee? my Country! Welcome then.
> Self-care was but a feather in the scale,
> Or as a spark in one vast-soaring breeze—
> The fiery passionate wish to rescue thee.
> Thou wast my sacrificial altar; I
> A bridegroom offering.[4]

At the same time, another medieval hero, Robin Hood, was also elevated into the pantheon of British national heroes. In his poem *The Song of Albion* (1831), Henry Sewell Stokes writes:

> Brave Robin Hood! right honest heart
> And patriot, robber as thou art—
> Yea, Patriot-robber be thy name,
> Spite the false chronicles of Fame!

Robin Hood's status was confirmed in 1859, when a volunteer regiment called the Robin Hood Rifles was formed in Nottingham. In his pantomime *Once upon a Time* (1868), F. R. Goodyer's description of the regiment left no doubt as to the patriotic associations which the legend had come to possess:

---

[4] *Sharpe's London Journal*, 9 (1849), 374; W. J. Linton, *Claribel and Other Poems* (London, 1865), 84.

> They represent a host,
> The pride of Nottingham—their country's boast;
> A thousand gallant hearts like these, I ween,
> Throb proudly underneath the Lincoln green:
> With patriot ardour every bosom glows,
> To guard its native land from foreign foes;
> And whilst all classes mingle in their ranks,
> Their sole reward's a grateful country's thanks.
> An ancient forester their sponsor stood,
> They bear the well known name of Robin Hood.[5]

In the nineteenth century both King Arthur and Robin Hood were thus firmly established as national heroes in British culture. In 1892 F. Mary Wilson declared in the *Temple Bar*, 'Arthur and Robin Hood, these two names are national inheritances'.[6] But how precisely did they attain such lofty positions? In order to gain an understanding of this process, it is necessary to examine the historical evolution of the two legends. We cannot hope to unpack their meaning, or meanings, in nineteenth-century culture without first determining what sort of legacy they carried with them from their respective pasts.

Much of the adaptability—and hence durability—of the legends of King Arthur and Robin Hood stems from the fact that, in both cases, their basis in reality has always been a matter of considerable doubt. From the beginning, interpreters have been free to mould them as they saw fit, reshaping them as current circumstances demanded. In the case of the Arthurian legend, there exist only the most meagre scraps of historical information upon which to base it. No 'King Arthur' is explicitly mentioned in the works of the most important early medieval historians, such as Bede and Gildas, although a few scattered references in the ancient Welsh chronicles point to him as the victor of the Battle of Badon Hill, an encounter between the Celts and invading Saxons which took place about AD 520. Beyond that, there is almost nothing. The gaps in the historical record, however, were quickly filled in by a wealth of fabricated detail. By the early years of the seventh century Arthur was already being depicted as a powerful military

---

[5] Henry Sewell Stokes, *The Song of Albion: A Poem Commemorative of the Crisis* (London, 1831), 18; Ian F. W. Beckett, *Riflemen Form: A Study of the Rifle Volunteer Movement 1859–1908* (Aldershot: Ogilby Trusts, 1982), 301; F. R. Goodyer, *Once upon a Time: or, A Midsummer Night's Dream in Merrie Sherwood* (Nottingham, 1868), 24. I am obliged to Dr Keith Surridge for the reference to Beckett.

[6] F. Mary Wilson, 'England's Ballad-hero', *Temple Bar*, 95 (1892), 411.

chieftain capable of great feats on the battlefield. In the *Gododdin*, a poem attributed to Aneirin describing a battle fought at Catterick in Yorkshire, for example, a warrior is said to have 'gutted black ravens on the rampart of the stronghold, even though he was no Arthur'.[7]

As the centuries passed the Arthurian legend came to be closely associated with the demands and desires of the ruling classes. In the eleventh-century story of *Culhwch and Olwen*, one of eleven Welsh prose tales comprising what is known today as the *Mabinogion*, Arthur's kinsman Culhwch falls in love with the beautiful Olwen and is forced by her father to perform dozens of tasks in order to prove himself worthy of her hand. Beneath this basic narrative lies a revealing commentary on the Welsh elite, who would have sponsored the production and patronized the performances of the story. *Culhwch and Olwen* revolves around a family's failure to reproduce itself, and in a world in which a shortage of sons meant a lack of warriors to defend the family's position and property, such failure translated into disaster. Other threats to the ruling class are present as well, including vassal disloyalty, agricultural infertility, and tribal rivalry. The successful resolution of all of these difficulties at the conclusion of the tale suggests that it may have functioned as a palliative in a harsh world in which elite families constantly struggled to maintain their positions.[8]

In the twelfth century Geoffrey of Monmouth's *Historia Regum Britanniae* transformed Arthur from a Celtic warlord into his more familiar guise as a powerful king. Extremely influential in terms of its impact upon the later legend, Geoffrey's work was the most overtly political treatment of the legend yet. An ambitious cleric seeking royal patronage, Geoffrey concocted an elaborate work of 'history' which linked Arthur genealogically to the Norman rulers of England. As relative parvenus in the European power game, the Normans were extremely eager to justify their new status through various cultural media, and the *Historia* stands as a lasting monument to their success in doing so.[9]

As the twelfth century drew to a close the Arthurian legend was drafted into the emerging literary genre of the courtly romance. The vogue for romance began in France with the tales of Chrétien de Troyes and spread rapidly throughout Europe, flourishing until well

[7] Richard Barber, *King Arthur: Hero and Legend* (New York: Dorset, 1986), 13.

[8] Stephen Knight, *Arthurian Literature and Society* (London: Macmillan, 1983), 34.

[9] Charles Moorman, 'Literature of Defeat and Conquest: The Arthurian Revival of the Twelfth Century', in Valerie M. Lagorio and Mildred Leake Day (eds.), *King Arthur Through the Ages* (New York: Garland, 1990), i. 34.

into the fifteenth century. Functioning essentially as handbooks for knighthood, these romances showed noblemen how to channel their martial energies into more socially useful activities. If their sparkling tone diverged considerably from the violence and brutality of everyday life, so much the better; they depicted an ideal to be striven for, which lent them a real didactic force. The code they expressed may have been inherently elitist, but that was the intention: it served to define the people who followed it as superior and to legitimize their power.[10]

It took the authors of English romances, however, some time to catch up with their continental counterparts, and it was not until the very end of the Middle Ages that an English author produced a genuine masterpiece. Completed around 1470, Sir Thomas Malory's *Le Morte d'Arthur* represents not only the culmination of the medieval romance tradition, but also a tacit admission that the world it depicts was rapidly disappearing. Malory portrays an idealized time in which nobility was not only a birthright but a description of character. By the mid-fifteenth century, however, England was suffering from military defeat abroad, as the Hundred Years' War came to a disastrous end, and civil disorder at home, in the form of the bloody Wars of the Roses.

Malory was personally very much affected by these events, and in fact wrote *Le Morte d'Arthur* while in prison for reasons likely related to the political turbulence of the time. Not surprisingly, his work functions as a commentary upon the contemporary situation. It is no simple allegory, but its connection to the Wars of the Roses is immediate and undeniable, as Malory traces the steady fall of a society into chaos and civil war.[11] In the concluding books he shows the grave consequences which arise from conflicts between noble factions, for this ultimately brings about the destruction of Arthur's realm. The absence of a clear partisan point of view in *Le Morte d'Arthur* suggests that Malory was not so much concerned with achieving victory as with restoring peace and order to the land. It was a noble cause, but one espoused in vain. Malory died in 1471, fourteen years before the Wars of the Roses came to an end.

The Arthurian legend, however, lived on into the sixteenth century, where it came to supply the Tudor dynasty with one of its chief propaganda weapons. Seizing upon the legend as a means of bolstering

---

[10] H. Moller, 'The Social Causation of the Courtly Love Complex', *Comparative Studies in Society and History*, 1 (1958-9), 143.

[11] Knight, *Arthurian Literature and Society*, 137.

his somewhat tenuous claim to the throne, Henry VII proudly proclaimed that the blood of Arthur flowed through his veins, an assertion rendered more plausible by his Welsh ancestry. He even named his eldest son after his legendary 'ancestor'.[12] Following in his father's footsteps, Henry VIII had what was ostensibly Arthur's Round Table (it had actually been made in the thirteenth century) moved to Winchester and repainted in the Tudor colours of green and white. And during the reign of Elizabeth I propagandists frequently employed the Arthurian legend in royal pageantry. During a royal progress to Kenilworth in the 1590s, for example, an elaborate drama was performed in which Merlin was imprisoned in a rock by the Lady of Lake. Elizabeth was summoned to restore order, thereby demonstrating how this sort of pageantry could be used to deliver a political message.[13] The 'cult of Elizabeth' also demanded the development of powerful verbal imagery to complement the visual. In *The Faerie Queene* (1590–6), Edmund Spenser glorifies his monarch for rescuing England from a century of religious strife.[14] Through the character of Prince Arthur, Spenser praises Elizabeth by presenting her with a portrait of the ideal ruler, a portrait he intended her to recognize as her own.

In the early seventeenth century the Arthurian legend continued to be used in royal propaganda. Like Henry VII before him, James I turned to the Arthurian legend to reinforce his uncertain claim to the throne. His supporters declared that his accession fulfilled Merlin's ancient prophecy that England and Scotland would one day be united as they had been under Arthur, and this anagram reflected their hopes for the future of the monarchy and the nation:

> Charles Iames Stuart
> Claimes Arthures seat.

In order to reinforce these notions, James favoured the use of the Arthurian legend in his court masques. In 1588 he himself composed a masque in honour of the Marquis of Huntley's marriage in which the

[12] The Prince of Wales died in 1501 before he could reign as Arthur II.

[13] See Sydney Anglo, *Spectacle, Pageantry, and Early Tudor Policy* (Oxford: Oxford UP, 1969); David M. Bergeron, *English Civic Pageantry 1558–1642* (London: Edward Arnold, 1971); Roy Strong, *The Cult of Elizabeth: Elizabethan Portraiture and Pageantry* (London: Thames and Hudson, 1977).

[14] Michael O'Connell, *Mirror and Veil: The Historical Dimension of Spenser's Faerie Queene* (Chapel Hill: University of North Carolina Press, 1977), 5. See also Robin Headlam Wells, *Spenser's Faerie Queene and the Cult of Elizabeth* (London and Totowa, NJ: Croom Helm, 1983).

court of Scotland was magically transformed into the court of Arthur, and even after abandoning his own literary efforts, he continued to desire the inclusion of Arthurian elements in the masques he commissioned. As the climax of the Christmas festivities of 1609 Ben Jonson composed a masque entitled *The Speeches at Prince Henry's Barriers*, in which Arthur's inclusion was obviously intended to glorify James. In the masque, Arthur praises James for re-creating his empire by reuniting England and Scotland:

> Nor let it trouble thy design, fair dame,
> That I am present to it with my flame
> And influence, since the times are now devolved
> That Merlin's mystic prophecies are absolved
> In Britain's name, the union of this isle,
> And claim of both my sceptre and my style.[15]

The associations of the Arthurian legend with the Stuart dynasty continued into the era of the English Civil War. For a bevy of reasons, Arthur was better suited to representing the royalist than the parliamentary cause. In addition to the repeated attempts on the part of Tudor and Stuart monarchs to proclaim themselves as Arthur's descendants, there is also the traditional puritan antipathy towards chivalric romances to consider. Above all, however, there was the content of the legend itself. The tales of a heroic king undone by treachery and civil strife had implications which most parliamentarians preferred to ignore. John Milton, the leading parliamentarian poet, rejected the Arthurian legend as a suitable subject for a proposed national epic due to its royalist associations. In his youth Milton had been attracted to 'those lofty Fables and Romances', and had even declared his intention to compose an Arthurian epic. By the mid-1640s, however, he had become one of Arthur's most vehement detractors, questioning his deeds, his power, and, ultimately, his very existence: 'But who *Arthur* was, and whether ever any such reign'd in *Britain*, hath bin doubted heertofore, and may again with good reason'.[16] When it came time to write his long-planned epic, he chose as his subject the Book of Genesis rather than the Arthurian legend.

[15] Roberta Florence Brinkley, *Arthurian Legend in the Seventeenth Century* (Baltimore and London: John Hopkins Press, 1932), 7–9; *Ben Jonson: The Complete Masques*, ed. Stephen Orgel (New Haven and London: Yale UP, 1969), ll. 72–7.

[16] James D. Merriman, *The Flower of Kings: A Study of the Arthurian Legend in England between 1485 and 1835* (Lawrence, Ka.: University of Kansas Press, 1973), 58.

For the first thousand years or so of its existence, the Arthurian legend was thus an elite property, for almost all of its interpreters were connected to the highest levels of the social and political hierarchy. Over 500 years after the first appearance of King Arthur in the early Welsh triads, however, another legendary hero emerged from a very different political and social context. Historians once granted the early tales of Robin Hood a prominent place in 'the literature of social discontent' of the late Middle Ages, in which peasant grievances found literary expression for the first time.[17] Although this theory of its origin has largely been discredited, there is still something subversive—or at least strongly anti-authoritarian—about the early legend.[18] In his earliest incarnations Robin Hood is a hero who stands for alternative forms of hierarchy and an egalitarian reaction to oppression.

There is, however, another side to the early legend. Although an outlaw, Robin Hood is at ease among the high-born and displays manners appropriate to a gentleman. Moreover, the principal victim whom he assists is not a lowly serf but a wrongfully impoverished knight, and in hand-to-hand combat he uses a sword, the preferred weapon of the elite, rather than the more humble quarterstaff.[19] Which Robin Hood, then, is the real one? Is he the angry leader of discontented peasants or a displaced gentleman indulging in a bit of harmless sport? There is evidence to support both claims, for Robin Hood's character has always been Janus-faced. The tension between the dangerous outlaw and the good-natured rogue has existed since the inception of the legend, and as we shall see, it continued into the nineteenth century.

First, however, the legend's evolution must be traced. In the fifteenth century Robin Hood came to be associated with the English folk

---

[17] Beatrice Webb, 'Poet and Peasant', in Caroline Barron and F. R. H. du Boulay (eds.), *The Reign of Richard II: Essays in Honour of Mary McKisack* (London: Athlone, 1971), 58–74. See also Maurice Keen, *The Outlaws of Medieval Legend* (London: Routledge, 1961); R. H. Hilton, 'The Origins of Robin Hood', in Hilton (ed.), *Peasants, Knights and Heretics: Studies in Medieval English Social History* (Cambridge and New York: Cambridge UP, 1976), 221–35.

[18] Douglas Gray, 'The Robin Hood Poems', *Poetica*, 18 (1984), 30–2. See also Paul R. Coss, 'Aspects of Cultural Diffusion in Medieval England: The Early Romances, Local Society and Robin Hood', *Past and Present*, 108 (1985), 35–79.

[19] J. C. Holt, 'The Origins and Audience of the Ballads of Robin Hood', in *Peasants, Knights and Heretics*, 236–7. See also his *Robin Hood*, rev. edn. (London: Thames and Hudson, 1989). Keen has since admitted that the views 'expressed by Professor J. C. Holt . . . are much closer to the truth': note to 'Robin Hood—Peasant or Gentleman?', in *Peasants, Knights and Heretics*, 258.

festival known as the May Games. A prominent feature of these revels was the crowning of a mock-king, but in some places that king was replaced by Robin Hood.[20] In small parishes he merely presided over the festivities, but in larger places with greater resources there was often a dramatic performance featuring costumed characters. Robin Hood served a number of different symbolic functions in the May Games. His green clothing and association with the forest made him an appropriate addition to a seasonal celebration of the beginning of summer. He was also, however, an ideal 'Lord of Misrule' who contributed to the inversion of social and political hierarchy that characterized early modern popular festivity.[21] In 1498 Robert Marshall of Wednesbury, Staffordshire, had to defend himself before the Star Chamber against the allegation that, under the name of 'Robyn Hood' at the town fair to celebrate Trinity Sunday, he had led more than a hundred men who had

met . . . at the said town of Willenhall, and then and there riotously assembled themselves, commanding openly that if any of the town of Walsall came therefrom, to strike them down, and in the said town continued their said riotous assembly all the same day, and if any man of Walsall at that day had been seen at that fair, they should have been in jeopardy of their lives.

Equally notorious were the exploits in Nottinghamshire of 'a felowe, whych had renued many of Robin Hodes pagentes', who was arrested for treason in 1502. Robin Hood was thus central to the symbolic repertoire of political subversion in early modern England.[22]

Not surprisingly, the contemporary authorities deplored the Robin Hood plays. In 1536 Sir Richard Morison protested to Henry VIII:

[20] The best description of the May Games can be found in Ronald Hutton, *The Stations of the Sun: A History of the Ritual Year in Britain* (Oxford: Oxford UP, 1996), ch. 24. See also W. E. Simeone, 'The May Games and the Robin Hood Legend', *Journal of American Folklore*, 64 (1951), 265–74.

[21] Ronald Hutton, *The Rise and Fall of Merry England: The Ritual Year 1400–1700* (Oxford and New York: Oxford UP, 1994), 33. The classic study of the links between popular festivity and subversion is Emmanuel Le Roy Ladurie, *Carnival in Romans: A People's Uprising at Romans 1579–1580*, trans. Mary Feeney (Harmondsworth: Penguin, 1981). See also Yves-Marie Bercé, *Fête et révolte: Des mentalités populaires du XVIᵉ au XVIIIᵉ siècle: Essai* ([Paris]: Hachette, 1976), esp. 55–92; Robert Muchembled, *Popular Culture and Elite Culture in France 1400–1750*, trans. Lydia Cochrane (Baton Rouge: Louisiana State UP, 1985).

[22] Holt, *Robin Hood*, 149; and Peter Stallybrass, '"Drunk with the Cup of Liberty": Robin Hood, the Carnivalesque, and the Rhetoric of Violence in Early Modern England', in Nancy Armstrong and Leonard Tennenhouse (eds.), *The Violence of Representation: Literature and the History of Violence* (London: Routledge, 1989), 51.

In summer commonly upon the holy days in most places of your realm there be plays of Robin Hood, Maid Marian, Friar Tuck: wherein, besides the lewdness and ribaldry that there is opened to the people, disobedience also to your officers is taught whilst these good bloods go about to take from the Sheriff of Nottingham one that for offending the laws should have suffered execution.

Such sentiments led to increasing efforts to curb festivities involving Robin Hood. In 1509 the city fathers of Exeter banned Robin Hood plays, and the Lord Warden of the Cinque Ports of Kent and Sussex followed suit in 1528.[23] In 1555 the Scottish Parliament made it illegal to impersonate Robin Hood and imposed the penalty of banishment upon anyone who disobeyed.

At first, however, these reformers experienced little success. In 1549 Bishop Hugh Latimer attempted to preach on a Sunday in a town near London, only to be told upon his arrival that 'the parish are gone a brode to gather for Robyn hoode'. Latimer complained, 'It is no laughynge matter my friends, it is a weepyng matter, a heavy matter, under the pretence for gatherynge for Robyn hoode, a traytoure, and a thefe, to put out a preacher, to have his office lesse estemed, to prefer Robyn hod before the ministracion of Gods words.' By the end of the sixteenth century, however, Robin Hood plays were in decline. All over England in this period popular festivities were coming under attack from evangelical Protestants who associated them with traditional Roman Catholic practices. These sentiments were reinforced by a more general fear of social disorder at a time of growing popular pressure and poverty.[24] In 1579, for example, a Robin Hood play in Lancashire provoked a disturbance, and in consequence a group of Justices of the Peace from near Manchester, the part of the county most noted for Protestant zeal, directed local magistrates to ban the revels. Although such attempts to eliminate popular festivities met with considerable resistance, by the middle of the seventeenth century the May Games survived in only a handful of places.

The campaign to suppress Robin Hood's subversive role in the May Games was only one part of a broader attempt in Elizabethan and Jacobean culture to render him less threatening to the social and political order. This effort also manifested itself on the contemporary

[23] David Wiles, *The Early Plays of Robin Hood* (Woodbridge, Suffolk: D. S. Brewer, 1981), 53; and Hutton, *Rise and Fall of Merry England*, 33.

[24] Stallybrass, 'Drunk with the Cup of Liberty', 64; and Hutton, *Stations of the Sun*, 253–4.

stage, where playwrights set out to create a new, less dangerous Robin Hood. The most famous contemporary dramatic reference to the legend occurs in Shakespeare's *As You Like It*, in which Duke Senior retreats into the forest after he has been banished by his brother, the evil Duke Frederick: 'They say he is already in the forest of Arden, and many a merry man with him; and there they live like the old Robin Hood of England' (I. i. 114–6).

On the surface, Shakespeare's forest is a place where people are free from the constraints of conventional society. There, worldly assets and social rank matter little, and judgements are made only in terms of merit. Ultimately, however, these rebels prove to be no revolutionaries. They contrast the 'antique world' with 'these times', looking back nostalgically to 'better days', when the poor 'have with holy bell been knoll'd to church, | And sat at good men's feasts' (II. vii. 120–2). Shakespeare thus falls back on a conventional solution for a society in chaos: the nobility must restore order by resorting to older modes of behavior based upon mutual responsibility and deference. As the play draws to a close, the Duke and his men prepare for their return to the outside world:

> And after, every of this happy number,
> That have endur'd shrewd days and nights with us,
> Shall share the good of our returned fortune,
> According to the measure of their states.
>
> (V. iv. 172–5)

That last line—'according to the measure of their states'—introduces a jarring note, a sign that conventional social and economic hierarchies are soon to reassert themselves.[25] Shakespeare thus allows his 'outlaws' a certain amount of rejuvenating wildness, but when their actions threaten to become subversive he quickly brings them under control.

As You Like It demonstrates that the elite patrons who exerted a direct and powerful influence over the Elizabethan and Jacobean theatre preferred a less subversive version of Robin Hood. There were two strategies which playwrights pursued in order to carry out their patrons' desires. One was to acknowledge Robin Hood's rebelliousness and then show it being emphatically crushed, thus indicating that such revolts were doomed to failure. In his play *Edward I* (1593), George

---

[25] Richard Wilson, '"Like the old Robin Hood": *As You Like It* and the Enclosure Riots', *Shakespeare Quarterly*, 43 (1992), 14.

Peele's title character must defeat the uprising of the Welsh rebel Lluellen and restore unity to the nation. Peele explicitly compares Lluellen to Robin Hood. The rebel leader tells his men that 'weele get the next daie from Brecknocke the booke of Robin Hood . . . and wander like irregulars vp and down the wildernesse, ile maister of misrule, ile be Robin Hood that once'.[26] As is the case in *As You Like It*, however, the end result is the restoration of the conventional social and political hierarchy. Lluellen's revolt fails, and he is slain and beheaded. Peele thus shows that such rebellions will not succeed; the 'maister of misrule' is brought under control.

Also in 1593 an anonymous play entitled *George a Green, The Pindar of Wakefield* appeared on the stage. Set during the late fifteenth century, it focuses upon the dynastic conflict which sparked the Wars of the Roses. The hero, George a Green, attempts to persuade the townspeople of Wakefield to follow the Yorkist Edward IV against the Lancastrian Henry VI; he argues that 'nature teacheth us duetie to our king'. This presents a sharp contrast to Robin Hood, whose fiercely independent existence in the greenwood represents a threatening alternative to a life of loyal service to the king. When the two characters clash in hand-to-hand combat, the fight symbolizes a struggle between authority and subversion. George wins and persuades Robin to abandon his rebellious ways and pledge his allegiance to the king. Edward, who is present in disguise, reveals himself, and all—including Robin Hood—kneel before him. Royal rule is thus restored, and its challengers are transformed into dutiful servants.[27]

The second strategy which Elizabethan and Jacobean playwrights used to render Robin Hood less subversive was not to defeat him, but to transform him. Anthony Munday's *The Downfall of Robert, Earl of Huntington* (1598) consciously attempts to divest Robin Hood of his associations with the May Games:

> Me thinks I see no feasts of Robin Hoode,
> No merry morices of Frier Tuck,
> No pleasant skippings vp and downe the wodde,
> No hunting songs, no coursing of the Bucke.

Instead of portraying him as a common yeoman, Munday concocted a pseudo-historical title, the Earl of Huntington, for his

[26] *The Dramatic Works of George Peele*, ed. Frank S. Hook (New Haven and London: Yale UP, 1961), 113.

[27] *George a Green, The Pindar of Wakefield* (Tudor Facsimile Texts: London, 1913).

hero.[28] Similarly, in the anonymous play *Looke About You* (*c.*1599), Robin Hood is described as a 'nice choyse faire Earle'.[29] In both of these plays the bold outlaw was gone, replaced by a genteel aristocrat.

In order to make their case for loyalty and obedience, however, authors who would reform Robin Hood were forced to grant a voice to popular political claims.[30] In 1586 William Warner published a long narrative poem tracing English history entitled *Albion's England*. In the section on the reign of Edward II, the poem refers to Robin Hood as a 'county . . . that with a troope of yeomandry did rome', thereby seemingly supporting his transformation from peasant to aristocrat and eliminating much of the levelling sentiment found in the popular tradition. Warner also describes life in the greenwood with no hint of any seditious activities:

> He fed them well, and lodg'd them safe
> In pleasant caves and bow'rs
> Oft saying to his merry men
> 'What juster life than ours?'[31]

Warner's defusion of the political implications of the legend was no accident, because he dedicated *Albion's England* to his patron Henry Carey, first Lord Hunsdon, who was the first cousin of Elizabeth I and a trusted royal advisor. Eager to please both his patron and his monarch, Warner composed a patriotic epic emphasizing loyalty and obedience, and his version of Robin Hood was intended to suit that purpose. Even so, however, Warner could not entirely prevent a note of discord from creeping in. He also refers to Robin Hood and his men as 'malcontents', a term which raises many questions. Why were they malcontented? What sort of grievances could they possibly have had in the midst of Elizabeth's glorious reign, with England in the hands of

---

[28] Anthony Munday, *The Downfall of Robert Earl of Huntingdon* (Oxford: Malone Society Reprints, 1964), ll. 2210–13. Munday's depiction of Robin Hood as an aristocrat may have been derived from a description of the outlaw in the Scottish historian John Major's *Historia Maioris Britanniae* of 1500, in which Major refers to Robin Hood as 'the prince of thieves'. See J. B. Bessinger, Jr., 'Robin Hood: Folklore and Historiography, 1377–1500', *Tennessee Studies in Literature*, 11 (1966), 61.

[29] *A Pleasant Commodie Called Looke About You: A Critical Edition*, ed. Richard S. M. Hirsch (New York: Garland, 1980), 5.

[30] Jonathan Dollimore, 'Introduction: Shakespeare, Cultural Materialism and the New Historicism', in Jonathan Dollimore and Alan Sinfield (eds.), *Political Shakespeare* (Ithaca, NY: Cornell UP, 1985), 12.

[31] *The Poems of William Warner*, The Works of the English Poets, Vol. 4 (London, 1810), 564.

wise men like Hunsdon? Warner makes no attempt to answer these questions, but the mere fact that they are raised at all is significant.

Another example of the difficulty of severing Robin Hood entirely from his popular roots can be found in Anthony Munday's pageant *Metropolis Coronata*, created in honour of London's Lord Mayor's Day in 1615. Commissioned by the Draper's Company, the pageant was intended to serve as a positive commentary on the state of the cloth trade. Its main theme was Jason's quest for the Golden Fleece, but it also featured 'Earle Robert de la Hude, sometime the noble Earle of Huntington'. Munday thus carries over from the stage his notion that Robin Hood was of noble birth. In this instance, however, he embellished the outlaw's genealogy further by transforming him into the son-in-law of London's first Lord Mayor, Henry Fitz-Alwin, thereby linking him to the embodiment of London's civic authority. At the conclusion of the pageant, however, a hint appears that Robin Hood's alliance with the city burghers may be an uneasy one. In the final scene Robin and his men prepare to return to the greenwood, apparently disgruntled with their sojourn in London:

> They will not away from merry Sherwood,
> In any place else to dwell:
> For there is neither City nor Towne,
> That likes them halfe so well.[32]

Once again, Robin Hood had resisted efforts to divorce him completely from his origins in popular tradition. We should thus be cautious about overstating the impact of efforts to remodel the legend in the sixteenth and seventeenth centuries. Despite some degree of success in overlaying him with a veneer of respectability, Robin Hood also retained some of the characteristics of an outlaw who stubbornly refused to bow to authority.

From his origins in the sixth century, King Arthur was thus a hero of the elite who stood for order, authority, and stability. Robin Hood, by contrast, was in at least some of his manifestations an inherently subversive figure, an outlaw who stood for everything Arthur did not: disorder, sedition, and chaos. At times, however, he was alternatively depicted as a model of gentility and good manners, doffing his

---

[32] All citations from *Pageants and Entertainments of Anthony Munday: A Critical Edition*, ed. David Bergeron (New York: Garland, 1985), 85–99.

hood to a passing knight or kneeling before the king. What impact, then, did the respective histories of the two legends have on their future interpretations? And more specifically, what impact did it have on the construction of King Arthur and Robin Hood as national heroes in British culture, a process which, as we shall see, began in the late eighteenth century and culminated in the nineteenth?

'Patriots rise from time to time': The Emergence of King Arthur and Robin Hood as National Heroes

On the surface, medieval heroes such as King Arthur and Robin Hood would seem to have been out of place amidst the steam engines and railways of nineteenth-century Britain. Nothing, however, could have been further from the truth, for this period of modernization was also an age dominated by a fascination with the past, and with the medieval past in particular. The popularity of the Middle Ages in nineteenth-century Britain has been well documented, and there is no need to cover that ground again here.[33] What is more relevant is to explore why such a keen interest in the medieval past flourished in an increasingly industrial and progressive society. The medieval revival was as complex in its origins as it was diverse in its manifestations. In the early nineteenth century medievalism was bound up in the same vast cultural sea-change that produced Romanticism, and more broadly, in the search for new principles of order in a rapidly changing world. The artists and thinkers of the Romantic movement were attracted to the romance, colour, heroism, and beauty of the Middle Ages, qualities that they often found lacking in contemporary life. They also saw the Middle Ages as a potential source of alternative values to those of the industrial capitalist social order, and as a time of moral certainty and religious piety.[34]

In the Victorian age, people continued to contrast the harsh, work-aday realities of modern life with the gentler, romanticized world of the Middle Ages. As change threatened to sweep away everything familiar, Britons turned to the medieval past, which seemed to possess the comforting security and stability their own world lacked. Medievalism

---

[33] The best general study of the medieval revival is Mark Girouard, *The Return to Camelot: Chivalry and the English Gentleman* (New Haven and London: Yale UP, 1981).

[34] Charles Dellheim, *The Face of the Past: The Preservation of the Medieval Inheritance in Victorian England* (Cambridge: Cambridge UP, 1982), 4.

has often been interpreted as a reaction to industrialization. In comparison to modern wage-slaves working in appalling conditions in lint-choked factories and living in filthy hovels in urban slums, many Britons believed the medieval serf had been fortunate.[35] There was more to the medieval revival than mere nostalgia, however. If, on the one hand, it was a protest against modernity, on the other it attempted to address a number of contemporary dilemmas, as authors and thinkers turned to the Middle Ages in search of solutions to the problems plaguing Victorian society.[36]

In Victorian Britain the Middle Ages served as an ideal not only for social reformers, however, but also for the nation as a whole. The vision of a common past helped to transcend class, regional, ideological, and religious barriers, and also to reveal the crucible in which national identity had been forged. In his Romanes Lecture of 1896, entitled 'The English National Character', Mandell Creighton declared that 'no nation has carried its whole past so completely into its present. With us historical associations are not matters of rhetorical reference on great occasions; but they surround the Englishman in everything that he does'. To be sure, in some ways the medieval revival transcended national boundaries. British travellers could admire the great cathedrals of Chartres and Cologne without feeling as if they were committing cultural treason. But at the same time British medievalism involved an equally strong current of national pride. For much of the eighteenth century European culture had emphasized classical history, and Britons had looked specifically to ancient Rome in their search for an appropriate and appealing model of an expanding empire. There were always aspects of this metaphor, however, which made it not entirely satisfactory. After all, Rome had ultimately fallen, a fate which for obvious reasons Britons wanted to avoid, and in consequence they emphasized the differences between the two empires as much as they pointed out their similarities, harping in particular upon the distinction between expansion by destructive arms and expansion by constructive trade.[37]

Moreover, in this period of rapidly burgeoning national self-assertion the British wished to stress the unique qualities which would allow

---

[35] See Alice Chandler, *A Dream of Order: The Medieval Ideal in Nineteenth-Century English Literature* (Lincoln: University of Nebraska Press, 1970), 2–3; Raymond Chapman, *The Sense of the Past in Victorian Literature* (London and Sydney: Croom Helm, 1986), 56.

[36] Dellheim, *Face of the Past*, 15.

[37] Ibid. 70–1; Howard D. Weinbrot, *Britannia's Issue: The Rise of British Literature from Dryden to Ossian* (Cambridge: Cambridge UP, 1993), 147.

them to survive and indeed to thrive where others had failed. And one of the best ways to do this was to construct a glorious and distinctive national history, a history which would show precisely how special they were. Accordingly, in the second half of the eighteenth century many Britons turned to the Middle Ages as they searched for the historical foundations of their nation. There they were able to find the roots of many of the characteristics which they viewed as essential features of their national identity, including the origins of their political system, the foundations of their economic and social order, and the beginnings of their territorial empire.[38]

To be sure, the amount of fabrication involved in this process was considerable. The second half of the eighteenth century saw the increasingly expert production of pseudo-medieval forgeries, such as James Macpherson's Ossian poems and Thomas Chatterton's Rowley ballads. At their crassest level these forgeries were the product of a desire for monetary gain on the part of their creators, but the choice of medieval subjects shows that there was presumed to be an avid audience for these sorts of cultural 'artefacts'. For by this time the British had begun to develop a nationalist history which supported their current aspirations. These efforts led to the gradual construction of a national identity based upon the purported sincerity, honesty, and courage of their medieval ancestors.

The legends of King Arthur and Robin Hood played a prominent role in this construction. As early as the 1690s the physician and poet Sir Richard Blackmore composed two epic poems, *Prince Arthur* (1695) and *King Arthur* (1697), both of which explicitly compare Arthur to King William III. As a staunch Whig and a devout Protestant, Blackmore harboured no doubts about the righteousness of William's cause. In his poetry, Arthur/William's attempt to capture the throne becomes a holy crusade to save both Britain and the true faith:

> At length the suff'ring Britons shall invite
> The fam'd Deliverer to assert their Right,
> And with his Arms the Tempest to repel,
> Which threatning Albion rolls from Rome and Hell.[39]

Although contemporary critics had little patience with Blackmore's heavy-handed moral didacticism, grotesque imagery, and extremely

---

[38] Debra N. Mancoff, *The Return of King Arthur: The Legend Through Victorian Eyes* (New York: Harry N. Abrams, 1995), 22.

[39] Richard Blackmore, *Prince Arthur*, 4th edn. (London, 1714), 170.

purple prose, his two Arthurian epics were significant in that they showed the potential which existed for nationalist treatments of the legend. It would be well over a century before another author would attempt an Arthurian work on such a grand scale, but there were signs throughout the eighteenth century that the possibilities of the legend were becoming increasingly apparent.

At mid-century the Seven Years War produced several patriotic treatments of Arthurian material. Composed in the dark early days of the war, William Hilton's verse drama *Arthur, Monarch of the Britons* (1759) used the legend as a source of hope in an effort to boost sagging British morale. As the play begins, the Britons are in danger of being overcome by their enemies, and Arthur is their only hope. He slays the traitor Mordred, but is mortally wounded in the fight. The final ode offers a vision of Britain's glorious future:

> Heav'nly virtue! now descend,
> Britain's fruitful shores defend.
> Come, O come! and 'stablish here
> Union, lasting and sincere.
> Arts and plenty thence shall grow,
> Peace and freedom thence shall flow.
> Deign but thou this bond to give,
> Arthur's glorious name shall live;
> Warm'd, like him, with worth sublime,
> Patriots rise from time to time;
> Through latest ages, Britons be
> Ever happy, ever free.
> Ever happy, ever free.[40]

Hilton's optimism proved well founded, for the year his drama was published Britain's military fortunes improved dramatically. In one of the more notable successes Admiral Edward Hawke met and annihilated the French fleet at the Battle of Quiberon Bay in November 1759. To commemorate this happy event, Horace Walpole turned to the Arthurian legend. In the spring of 1760 Walpole sent his friend Lord Beauchamp a poem 'on the destruction of the French navy' which referred to the days of King Arthur. The poem has since been lost, but Beauchamp's response reveals much about its nature:

No one objection is raised against the absolute goodness of the piece, but as to the relative goodness of it to the thesis, some alterations and additions it is

---

[40] William Hilton, *The Poetical Works of William Hilton* (Newcastle, 1776), ii. 251.

thought might make considerable improvement. . . . [A] few verses in Arthur's speech touching the nature of the island Britain, might be an improvement. Merlin struck with the particular turn of this inquiry, fired as it were with an instantaneous afflatus of the prophetic spirit, rushes in *media res*; that Britain will be mistress of the world and that every river will swell with the tributary offerings of subject nations. . . .

The following year saw the appearance of Joseph Warton's poem 'To His Royal Highness the Duke of York', in which Arthur's ghost praises those who have volunteered to fight the French:

> With joy your generous toils
> Have I survey'd, who leave your cultur'd fields,
> And pleasant villas, for the din of arms,
> And midnight watches in the chilling dew.
> At this, pale Gallia trembles thro' her coasts . . .[41]

Two decades later, during the American Revolution, the poet Edward Thomas used the Arthurian legend to commemorate Admiral George Rodney's defeat of the French fleet in the Caribbean, a victory which did much to restore a British confidence severely shaken by Cornwallis's surrender at Yorktown a few months earlier. In 'Briddyn Jubilee' (1782), Thomas utilizes an Arthurian metaphor in order to provide Rodney's glorious achievement with an appropriate precedent:

> Like noble Arthur, in the days of yore,
> His name be echo'd from each grateful tongue.[42]

As these examples indicate, the near-constant military conflicts of the eighteenth century produced a need for heroes embodying martial prowess and chivalric virtue, a role for which Arthur was well suited. Accordingly, he began to make frequent appearances in contemporary patriotic statements, particularly in poetry composed to celebrate military triumphs or to boost sagging morale when the tide of battle was running against the British.

Although it occurred at roughly the same time, Robin Hood's emergence as a national hero followed a different trajectory. Instead of being explicitly compared to British military leaders, he became an

---

[41] *The Yale Edition of Horace Walpole's Correspondence*, ed. W. S. Lewis (London and New Haven: Yale UP, 1974), xxxviii. 50–1; Hugh Reid, 'A Probable Addition to the Poetical Works of Joseph Warton', *Review of English Studies*, 38 (1987), 529.

[42] E. Thomas, 'Briddyn Jubilee, 1782. An Ode', *European Magazine*, 2 (1782), 153.

exemplar of the 'free-born Englishman', an ardent defender of the political rights of the people at large. The concept of freedom was an integral part of eighteenth-century British patriotism, for it provided yet another way for Britons to define themselves against their enemies, in particular the French, who were perceived as slaves to a tyrannical and absolutist regime. 'The pride, the glory of Britain, and the direct end of its constitution,' said the Prince of Wales, the future George III, in 1759, 'is political liberty.'[43]

And what hero better embodied freedom than Robin Hood, whose life of liberty in Sherwood Forest had been celebrated for centuries? In the anonymous opera *Robin Hood*, performed at Bartholomew Fair in 1730, the outlaws offer a proud chant which testifies to their devotion to freedom: 'And Liberty. . . shall smile and crown our Arms.' This motif recurs repeatedly in eighteenth-century literary treatments of the legend. At the outset of John O'Keeffe's theatrical comedy *Merry Sherwood or Harlequin Forester* (1795), the Merry Men sing:

> In merry Sherwood, we merry men
> Live here like the birds most free . . .[44]

In the comic opera *Robin Hood or Sherwood Forest* (1782), with music by William Shield and libretto by Lawrence MacNally, the link between Robin Hood, freedom, and contemporary national identity is made more explicit, as Robin and his beloved Clorinda proudly proclaim:

> Strains of liberty we sing
> To our country, queen and king.[45]

The link between Robin Hood and liberty is further demonstrated by the Robin Hood Society, a 'disputing' club of the 1760s. Although its name was derived from the tavern in which it met rather than from an explicit desire to identify with the famous outlaw, the Society shared much with the legend in terms of its political and social attitudes. Each Monday at the Robin Hood and Little John in London's Butcher Row, the members, who were in the main from the middle classes and upper ranks of the lower classes, debated topics of current political interest.

---

[43] John Brooke, *King George III* (Frogmore, St Albans: Granada, 1974), 108.
[44] Stephen Knight, *Robin Hood: A Complete Study of the English Outlaw* (Oxford and Cambridge, Mass.: Blackwell, 1994), 148; John O'Keeffe, *Airs, Duetts, and Chorusses in Merry Sherwood, or Harlequin Forrester*, in Frederick M. Link (ed.), *The Plays of John O'Keeffe* (New York and London: Garland, 1981), iv. 5. [45] Knight, *Robin Hood*, 151.

Their outlook was thoroughly democratic. According to their mani-
festo, published in 1764:

It is a Duty incumbent on every Man in a free State . . . to fathom the Depths
of Government, and to point out and expose the hidden Rocks and dangerous
Shoals, on which Statesman often split. . . . As a Pigmy mounted upon the
Shoulders of a Giant may be able to see farther than the Giant himself, so
People not Conversant with State Affairs, may strike out some Road that . . .
may lead to Glory and Happiness.

Just as many eighteenth-century interpreters of Robin Hood saw his
rebellious actions as a defence of Britain's precious freedom, the
members of the Society saw their own attempts to stir the people to
action as thoroughly patriotic:

In this Land of Liberty, where the Goddess herself reigns with so much Lustre,
and infuses her chearing [sic] Influence into every Breast, it is absolutely
necessary for every one who has the Good of his Country at Heart, to
scrutinize into, and examine the Measures which are from Time to Time
taken by our State Pilots, in . . . steering the Political Vessel.[46]

   The cultural processes which elevated King Arthur and Robin Hood
to the status of British national heroes can thus be traced back to the
eighteenth century, when Arthur began to be compared to the nation's
current and past military leaders and Robin Hood began to be regarded
as an exemplar of freedom. The different trajectories which they followed
into the national pantheon reveal the dichotomy between the two
legends which we explored at the beginning of this chapter. The Arthurian legend was used as a means of inspiring loyalty and unity by
emphasizing military glory; its purpose was thus inherently conservative.
Eighteenth-century British authors employed Robin Hood, on the other
hand, to represent freedom, as the legend continued to possess radical
connotations. This dichotomy was to become even more prominent
during the period of the French Revolution and Revolutionary Wars.

*'Where wilt thou find their like agen?': The Impact of the French Revolution and the
Napoleonic Wars Upon the Legends of King Arthur and Robin Hood*

'The age of chivalry is gone . . . and the glory of Europe is extin-
guished forever', declared Edmund Burke in his *Reflections on the Revolu-*

---

[46] *The History of the Robin Hood Society* (London, 1764), 63–4.

tion in France in 1790. In this famous passage Burke proclaimed his reverence for the past, and in particular the medieval past. Valuing continuity above all else, Burke went on to argue that rights were inherited rather than inherent: 'From the Magna Carta to the Declaration of Right, it had been the uniform policy of our constitution to claim and assert our liberties, as an entailed inheritance derived to us from our forefathers, and to be transmitted to our posterity; as an estate specifically belonging to the people of our kingdom without any reference to any more general or prior right.'[47]

Burke's attitude was typical of the manner in which British conservatives invoked the Middle Ages in this period. From their perspective, the need for an alternative to classical history became even more pronounced after 1789, when Greek and Roman models became closely linked to the French Revolution. In the late eighteenth and early nineteenth centuries the British ruling elite constructed castles, their own versions of the Bastille, because they wanted to show that, unlike in France, they could still stand unmolested.[48] And why else did the innately conservative George III turn to the Gothic style in this period? Previously the king had preferred neoclassical architecture, but in the 1780s he spent £150,000 gothicizing the state apartments at Windsor inside and out. Still not satisfied, he turned to the construction of an entirely new castle at Kew featuring turrets, moats, arrow windows, and a battlemented gatehouse. For George, Kew was a counterblast to the French Revolution. British radicals certainly did not miss the point: they sarcastically nicknamed the new palace 'the Bastille'.[49]

Conservatives thus used the medieval past to demonstrate the continuity and durability of Britain's political and social institutions. They warned that the new order in France was built on the most abstract general principles and the wildest speculative theories, whereas the established order in Britain was the product of practical experience, sound common sense, and, above all, a long historical evolution. The nation had journeyed from a glorious past to a glorious present without the violent upheavals experienced across the Channel. A pamphlet from the 1790s called upon Britons to

---

[47] Edmund Burke, *Reflections on the Revolution in France* (London, 1912), 73; R. J. Smith, *The Gothic Bequest: Medieval Institutions in British Thought, 1688–1863* (Cambridge: Cambridge UP, 1987), 117.

[48] Lynn Hunt, *Politics, Culture, and Class in the French Revolution* (Berkeley: University of California Press, 1984), 28; Girouard, *Return to Camelot*, 49–50.

[49] Girouard, *Return to Camelot*, 25.

> let them see
> How unchanged the British name.
> Let the ruffians know that WE
> ARE IMMUTABLY THE SAME . . .
>
> Shew them that age to age bequeaths
> The British Character complete.[50]

Not only conservatives, however, looked to the medieval past in the years following the French Revolution. Radicals had long advocated the idea of an ancient constitution under which the British people had enjoyed the benefits of true democracy. These claims were based upon the theory of the 'Norman yoke', which asserted that prior to 1066 the inhabitants of Britain lived as free and equal citizens who governed themselves through representative institutions. The Norman Conquest deprived them of this liberty and established the tyranny of an alien king and his landlords, but the people did not forget the rights they had lost and continually fought to recover them, occasionally extorting concessions from their rulers, such as the Magna Charta.[51]

The theme of the Norman yoke was prominent in the political debates of the seventeenth and eighteenth centuries. In 1771, for example, the anonymous author of *An Historical Essay on the English Constitution* argued that the Saxons had enjoyed such democratic institutions as the franchise for all male taxpayers and annual elections, institutions that were destroyed by the Norman Conquest. They had since been partially—but only partially—restored, and the author demanded that the constitution be brought back to its original Saxon state. Many historians, however, have argued that Paineite rationalism killed off this sort of radical argument in the 1790s. To be sure, in *The Rights of Man* (1790) Thomas Paine had emphatically repudiated all searchings in the past for the precedent of a just society. He declared that 'every age and generation must be as free to act for itself, in all cases, as the ages and generations which preceded it. The vanity and presumption of governing beyond the grave, is the most ridiculous and insolent of all tyrannies.' Paine reserved particular contempt for the Middle Ages,

---

[50] Stella Cottrell, 'The Devil on Two Sticks: Franco-phobia in 1803', in Raphael Samuel (ed.), *Patriotism: The Making and Unmaking of British National Identity*, Vol. 1: *History and Politics* (New York and London: Routledge, 1989), 262–3.

[51] Christopher Hill, 'The Norman Yoke', in *Puritanism and Revolution: Studies in Interpretation of the English Revolution of the Seventeenth Century* (London: Secker and Hudson, 1958), 57.

which he termed the 'quixotic age of chivalric nonsense', and declared that the ancient constitution meant 'little or nothing for any of our modern parties'.[52]

Radical medievalism, however, survived the publication of *The Rights of Man*, as many radicals saw no reason to abandon the mythic history which had served them so well for so long. Writers such as Major John Cartwright and Sir Francis Burdett continued to argue in favour of the idea of an ancient Saxon constitution, and their voices did not go unheeded. In 1794 the London Corresponding Society declared that its primary objectives were 'to restore the constitution to its original purity, and the people to their long lost rights'.[53]

The years following the French Revolution thus saw an avid and active competition to appropriate the medieval past, for conservatives and radicals alike recognized the power it could have as a propaganda weapon. The Middle Ages served as a battleground for the clash between competing visions of what the nation had been and what it should be. In this period, medievalism—and in particular the legends of King Arthur and Robin Hood—helped to create a past around which people could unite, but it also demonstrated just how difficult that unity could be to achieve in the present.

In 1809 Sir Walter Scott published *Marmion*, a long poem about the Battle of Flodden (1513) between the English and the Scots. In the introduction he bemoans the current state of Great Britain as it suffers the hardships of a long and seemingly endless war with France. Scott is particularly concerned about British prospects without William Pitt and Charles James Fox, who had both died three years previously. Since then, he claims, no heroes had arisen to take their place and lead the nation to victory:

> But search the land of living men,
> Where wilt thou find their like agen?

To answer this question Scott turns to the past, and in particular to medieval literature, which, he asserts, contains the tales of great men and noble deeds which will inspire Britain to military victory. And the heroes whose deeds Scott sees as particularly worthy of emulation are those of the Arthurian legend. In particular, he cites Lancelot's entry into the Chapel Perilous and Galahad's successful completion of the quest of the Holy Grail as excellent examplars.[54]

Scott's view was typical of the manner in which the Arthurian legend was employed in the late eighteenth and early nineteenth centuries. In the struggle against the forces of Jacobinism and later against Napoleon, many Britons saw themselves as defending the ancient name and character of their nation, a nation built by the great heroes of the past such as King Arthur. In her poem *England and Spain; or, Valour and Patriotism* (1808), Felicia Dorothea Browne urges her countrymen to rescue Europe from the 'iron sceptre' of Napoleonic tyranny. Browne sees Arthur as worthy of inclusion in her roster of British heroes of the past, men whom she stridently encourages the nation's current warriors to emulate:

> Bright in the annals of th' impartial page,
> Britannia's heroes live from age to age! . . .
> From doubtful Arthur, hero of romance,
> King of the circled board, the spear, the lance;
> To those whose recent trophies grace her shield,
> The gallant victors of Vimiera's field;
> Still have her warriors borne th' unfading crown,
> And made the BRITISH FLAG the ensign of renown.[55]

Such reverence for Arthur was not just felt by English authors, however. In this period unity was a prerequisite for survival, and it was necessary for all of Britain's constituent components—including England, Wales, Scotland, and, after 1800, Ireland—to march into battle together. We have already seen how the Scotsman Walter Scott ignored the conflicts of the past and invoked the Arthurian legend in his search for heroes who could lead the modern British nation to victory. The Welsh, too, were quick to invoke Arthur as a means of declaring their patriotism. In his poem 'British Valour; or, St David's Day' (1812), the Revd David Lloyd, vicar of Llanbister, tells of Wales's distinguished military history, beginning with the country's refusal to submit to Roman rule and concluding with 'the famous field of Agincourt | Where Welshmen fought so well'. In between, he writes proudly

---

[54] Sir Walter Scott, *Marmion: A Tale of Flodden Field* (London, 1809), 12–17.

[55] Felicia Dorothea Browne, *England and Spain; or, Valour and Patriotism* (London, 1808), 7.

> Of King Arthur and a train
> Of heroes, bold and strong,
> Who dar'd their Country's rights maintain.

In case anyone missed Lloyd's intention in describing these past victories, he states it explicitly in the concluding verses:

> The Corsican in vain may boast
> The prowess of his hand,
> Threaten descent upon our coast,
> And slavery to our land;
> For all his threats we value not,
> His prowess we defy,
> And cheerly give our life and lot,
> To Higher Destiny.[56]

In 'The Bard of Snowden, To His Countrymen' (1804), Richard Llwyd also features a patriotic recitation of the nation's military history which urges modern Welshmen to emulate their ancestors. Like Lloyd, Llwyd includes a reference to the Arthurian legend in his roster of Welsh heroes:

> By genuine Freedom's holy flame,
> By Dragon-crested Arthur's name;
> By Deva's waves, when Saxons fled,
> By Mona's sons, when Mervyn led . . .
>
> By every patriot-warrior's name,
> By all that fills the rolls of Fame,
> Unfold your banners, rend the air,
> And proudly show the shields you bear!
>
> Sons of Snowdon, yours the MEED,
> Like Britons live, like Britons bleed;
> Your Country, Parents, Children, save,
> *Or fill one great and glorious grave!*[57]

Llwyd's reference to the Saxons demonstrates that invoking the medieval past in order to foster present unity could be problematic. In the Middle Ages, after all, the Welsh and the English had been bitter enemies, and Wales had suffered the ravages of repeated invasions and,

---

[56] David Lloyd, *Characteristics of Men, Manners, and Sentiments; or, The Voyage of Life and Other Poems* (London, 1812), 284–6.

[57] Richard Llwyd, *Poems. Tales, Odes, Sonnets, Translations from the British, &c. &c.* (Chester, 1804), 190–2.

ultimately, conquest. Here, however, the conflicts of previous centuries are glossed over, and the emphasis is on unity, with the Welsh fighting alongside the English as part of a cohesive war effort.

One reason why the Arthurian legend possessed such a potent appeal during the years of the Revolutionary and Napoleonic Wars was the existence of a centuries-old folk belief that Arthur had not died but would one day return in a time of dire need to rally the British nation. This myth retained its power into the early nineteenth century. Reporting on his tour of South Wales, the antiquarian Edward Donovan observed in 1805 that it 'is as firmly accredited at this day, among the lower orders throughout Wales, as in the darkest ages'. When archaeologists began the excavation of Cadbury Castle in the early nineteenth century, an old man who lived nearby anxiously inquired if they had come to remove the king from where he lay sleeping. Others believed, as the poet Louisa Stuart Costello reported in 1815, that Arthur was 'still on earth in the form of a raven, and their superstition is so great that they will not upon any account kill one of those birds'.[58]

At a time when the nation's future was under dire threat from the armies of France, such thoughts were comforting. And in truth, it seemed to many people that King Arthur had indeed returned, in the unlikely guise of a diminutive, hook-nosed Irishman named Arthur Wellesley. In the early nineteenth century the cult of heroism which focused upon the Duke of Wellington included reference to his ostensibly chivalric qualities, and the coincidence of his sharing his Christian name with Britain's great medieval hero was simply too much to resist. In 1814 J. H. Merivale wrote in his poem *Orlando in Roncesvalles*:

> Sleeps Arthur in his isle of Avalon?
> High-favour'd Erin sends him forth once more
> To realize the dream of days far gone.

Nor was Merivale alone in seeing Wellington as Arthur returned. In a poem celebrating the success of the British army in the Peninsular campaign, an anonymous author in the *European Magazine* declared that through Wellington, 'ARTHUR's chivalry returns'. Similarly, in 'St Michael's Mount' (1814), Sir Ambrose Hardinge Giffard gazes south across Mount's Bay towards Spain, where Britain's army is fighting:

[58] Edward Donovan, *Descriptive Excursions through South Wales and Monmouthshire, in the Year 1804, and the Four Preceding Summers* (London, 1805), 116; Neil Fairbairn and Michael Cyprien, *A Traveller's Guide to the Kingdoms of Arthur* (London: Evans Brothers, 1983), 106; Louisa Stuart Costello, *The Maid of the Cyprus Isle, and Other Poems* (London, 1815), 56.

Thy ruby Cross aloft they raise,
Thine ancient star of victory;
They emulate our ARTHUR's days,
And ARTHUR's self again they see.

The association with Wellington represented the culmination of the eighteenth-century tradition of comparing King Arthur to the nation's greatest military leaders. In fact, so close did this association become that, after 1815, Arthur was rarely compared to any other military figure.[59]

The Revolutionary and Napoleonic Wars thus had a major impact upon the Arthurian legend. In this period it was used even more frequently and overtly than it had been previously to encourage Britons on and off the field of battle. It celebrated their victories, or in darker moments assuaged their fears and raised their hopes. Throughout, however, it was used to promote the war effort, not to question the ideology upon which it was based. The Arthurian legend thus remained the vehicle of those who used the medieval past to support a conservative vision of the British nation.

The specific nature of the political and social context of the late eighteenth and early nineteenth centuries thus raised King Arthur to the position of one of Britain's leading national heroes. Given the number of different meanings that 'patriotism' could have during this period, however, a single hero would simply not suffice to represent all the virtues and qualities which Britons saw as essential features of their national character. It is therefore not surprising that Robin Hood

[59] J. H. Merivale, *Orlando in Roncesvalles, A Poem* (London, 1814), 91; 'Vittoria', *European Magazine*, 64 (1813), 146–7; Sir Ambrose Hardinge Giffard, *Verses* (London, 1824), 30. See also Giffard's 'Roncesvalles', in *Verses*, 26–7. Throughout the first half of the nineteenth century Arthur continued to be compared with Wellington. See e.g. M. J. O'Sullivan's 'No Longer the Harp of Old Erin Shall Slumber', in his *A Fasciculus of Lyric Verses* (Cork, 1846), 63–4. As the Duke entered the world of politics, however, these comparisons were frequently made in a satirical sense by his critics. See Leigh Hunt, 'The Dogs', *The Liberal*, 1 (1822), 246–59; Percival Leigh, *Jack the Giant Killer* (London, [1843]), 52–3; William Maginn, 'The Fraserians; or, The Commencement of the Year Thirty-five', *Fraser's Magazine*, 11 (1835), 1–2; 'An Oxonian', 'Lines Written After Reading the Romance of Arthur's Round Table', *Blackwood's Edinburgh Magazine*, 27 (1830), 705; and William and Robert Whistlecraft, *Prospectus and Specimen of an Intended National Work . . . Intended to Comprise the Most Interesting Particulars Relating to King Arthur and his Round Table*, 2nd edn. (London, 1818), 13. As late as the mid-1890s the Revd Prebendary Vernon wrote in *The Sunday at Home*: 'In the old myth, there was the tradition of the future coming of Arthur, again to save his country at her extreme need. (Strange, by the way, that an "Arthur" we did receive, who came . . . in an extreme need of England, and of Europe, as deliverer.)'. 'The Passing of Arthur', *The Sunday at Home* (1896–7), 292.

was depicted in a very different—but equally patriotic—way in this period. As the ideals of liberty and freedom which he had long represented became increasingly associated with radicalism and reform, so did he. This trend became apparent even before the French Revolution. Leonard MacNally's comic opera *Robin Hood; or, Sherwood Forest*, which premiered at the Theatre Royal, Covent Garden, in 1788, reflects the growing political and social turbulence of the time. When the outlaws capture a well-dressed young man named Edwin who is attempting to make his way through the forest, Little John inquires about the nature of his business:

LITTLE JOHN: Who are you, Sir?

EDWIN: A *gentleman*, courteous Sir, who wishes to be considered *your* humble servant.

LITTLE JOHN: Fairly spoken—An humble servant is good, because it is a rarity, most servants assuming more impudence than their masters. Now *Gentleman* is bad; though it is a good title to travel with, or live by: for every fellow, who has neither property or profession, and is too lazy to work, begs or plunders under the character of *Gentleman*.[60]

As this passage reveals, the validity of the old categories of the social hierarchy was beginning to be questioned, and MacNally presents Robin Hood as one of those doing the asking.

It is important to notice, however, that this new form of radicalism was inherently patriotic, for it was intended not to destroy the nation but to improve it. MacNally's Robin Hood remains steadfastly loyal to his country, and willing to fight to defend it, even if he questions certain aspects of its political and social structure. When his beloved Clorinda hears from her uncle at court that 'the French have threatened an invasion', Robin at first refuses to take up arms, declaring that he will not fight for a nation which has banished him on a false accusation and stigmatized him 'with the imputation of a rebellious spirit'. But Clorinda entreats him to reconsider:

Your king has been insulted by an enemy, and will you, my sweet Robin . . . endowed with those noble qualities Courage and Generosity, neglect the duty you owe your country, consuming life and reputation within the sequestered shades of a forest? . . . [W]hen our country is in danger, all offences should be absolved; the remembrance of injuries be forgotten; all parties should unite; every heart pant and every arm act, for her honour and defence.

---

[60] Leonard MacNally, *Robin Hood; or, Sherwood Forest* (Dublin, 1788), 7.

Robin Hood is convinced: 'Oh! thou hast soothed my resentments—conquered them—hath roused my loyalty—thy patriot flame now blazes in my bosom. Yes, Clorinda, I will join my country's arms, and head my merry-men'.[61]

In subsequent decades British radicals frequently invoked the figure of a Robin Hood-like outlaw as a symbol of both their resistance to government repression and their ultimately patriotic objectives. In the radical thinker William Godwin's *Things as They Are; or, The Adventures of Caleb Williams* (1794), the hero's employer attempts to have him imprisoned for a crime he did not commit. He flees into the forest, where he encounters a group of thieves 'full of chearfulness and merriment' who bear a striking resemblance to Robin Hood and his men. Their leader tells him:

Our profession is the profession of justice . . . We undertake to counteract the partiality and iniquity of public institutions. We, who are thieves without a licence, are at open war with another set of men, who are thieves according to law. If any one disapprove our proceedings, at least we have this to say for ourselves, we act not by choice, but as our wise governors force us to act. . . . Time will one day decide whether we or our oppressors be the genuine patriots: for the present we are censured, only because they are the stronger party.

Here, we see many of the components of the traditional British conception of the outlaw hero coming together: the separation drawn between legal and true justice, the notion that honest men turn to banditry only as a last resort, and, above all, the essentially patriotic character of the outlaw's actions. The revolutionary context, however, gave a new and more powerful meaning to such stories. William Wordsworth's verse drama *The Borderers*, written before he rejected radicalism in the late 1790s, traces the activities of a group of brigands along the border between England and Scotland during the reign of Henry III. Much as does Godwin, Wordsworth commends those who seek a private form of justice and argues that it is one's moral duty to resist tyranny:

> 'Tis slavery—all is slavery, we receive
> Laws, and we ask not whence those laws have come.[62]

---

[61] Ibid. 33–4.
[62] William Godwin, *Things as They Are; or, The Adventures of Caleb Williams* (London, 1794), ii. 28; William Wordsworth, *The Borderers*, in *Poems, Chiefly of Early and Late Years* (London, 1842), IV. ii. 190–1.

Given the predilection of British radicals for outlaw heroes, it is hardly surprising that in 1795 the antiquarian Joseph Ritson published a collection of the Robin Hood ballads. Although he had in his younger days been a Jacobite, by then Ritson had become firmly committed to the principles of the French Revolution. On a visit to Paris in 1791 he wrote to a friend, 'I admire the French more than ever. They deserved to be free, and they really are so. You have read their new constitution: can any thing be more admirable? We, who pretend to be free, you know, have no constitution at all.' He returned to Britain convinced that the Revolution would soon spread across the Channel. In 1792, however, William Pitt's government issued its first proclamation against seditious meetings and publications, and Ritson soon found himself under close surveillance. Throughout these years Ritson feared that he would be arrested and imprisoned. Nevertheless, as William Godwin wrote in his obituary in 1803, he 'till his death remained firmly attached to the principles of republicanism'. He adopted the French Revolutionary calendar, and the Revolutionary style of concluding his letters with a hearty 'fellow citizen' or 'fellow democrat'. As late as 1796 he maintained his belief that a revolution was imminent in Britain, writing that 'not a soul seems to have the remotest idea how Mr. Pitt will be able to weather the impending storm. The 30th instant will be a momentous day. Ah, ça ira, ça ira, ça ira, &c'.[63]

Not surprisingly, Ritson issued his collection of Robin Hood ballads with a polemical introduction which used the legend as a vessel for expressing his political ideas. Ritson's Robin Hood was 'a man who, in a barbarous age, and under a complicated tyranny, displayed a spirit of freedom and independence, which has endeared him to the common people, whose cause he maintained, (for all opposition to tyranny is the cause of the people)'. In response to the question of who gave Robin Hood a commission to rob from the rich and give to the poor, Ritson testily replied:

That same power . . . which authorises kings to take it where it can be worst spared, and give it where it is least wanted. Our hero, in this respect, was a knight-errant; and wanted no other commission than that of Justice, whose cause he militated. His power, compared with that of the king of England, was

---

[63] *The Letters of Joseph Ritson*, ed. Joseph Frank (London, 1833), i. 203; *Monthly Magazine*, 16 (1803), 376; Bertrand H. Bronson, *Joseph Ritson Scholar-at-Arms* (Berkeley: University of California Press, 1938), ii. 134.

by no means, either equally usurped, or equally abused: the one reigned over subjects (or slaves) as a master (or tyrant), the other possessed no authority but what was delegated to him by the free suffrage of his adherents, for their general good. . . . In a word, every man who has the power has also the authority to pursue the ends of justice; to regulate the gifts of fortune, by transferring the superfluities of the rich to the necessities of the poor; by relieving the oppressed, and even, when necessary, destroying the oppressor. These are the objects of the social union; and every individual may, and to the utmost of his power should, endeavour to promote them.[64]

The radical content of Ritson's *Robin Hood* was not popular in conservative quarters. The *British Critic* declared that 'it is surely a just matter of most strong complaint, that a careless, or literary, reader cannot look for a Ballad of Robin Hood, or an account of his life, without meeting with what must either shock his feelings, or corrupt his principles'. Clearly, Ritson's *Robin Hood* signalled that radicals were not going to abandon control of the medieval past without a fight. Here was a very different view of the Middle Ages from Burke's, for Ritson emphasized the democratic institutions and vigorous outbreaks of peasant protest which he saw as characteristic of medieval society. He also impressed upon his readers that Robin Hood's actions, which he deemed 'patriotic exertions', were not traitorous.[65] Patriotism, he asserted, meant more than just blindly taking up arms to defend one's country from its external enemies. Sometimes 'true' patriotism meant recognizing that the real 'traitors'—the opponents of liberty and equality—were those who were most eager to wave the flag and beat the war drum, and acting to overcome the oppression and tyranny they promoted. It was this second kind of patriot which, according to Ritson, Robin Hood had been. Ritson's work was extremely influential in transforming Robin Hood into a national hero, albeit of a very different sort from King Arthur. While Arthur served as a potent reminder of Britain's past and, through the link with Wellington, present military success, Robin Hood's presence in radical circles demonstrated that not everything regarding the nation's future would be determined on the battlefield.

The years of and immediately following the French Revolution and the Revolutionary Wars marked an apotheosis for both King Arthur and

---

[64] Joseph Ritson, *Robin Hood: A Collection of Poems, Songs and Ballads Relative to that Celebrated English Outlaw* (London, 1795), vol. i, pp. xi–xii and xl.

[65] *British Critic*, 9 (1797), 17; Ritson, *A Collection*, vol. i, p. ix.

Robin Hood. Sir Walter Scott's satiric poem *The Bridal of Triermain* (1813) represented the first Arthurian literary work by a major British author in almost a century. A number of other literary works followed, including Henry Hart Milman's epic *Samor, Lord of the Bright City* (1818) and John Hookham Frere's long burlesque poem *The Monks and the Giants* (1817–8). By the mid-1820s Arthur was such a prominent figure in contemporary British culture that Richard Warner could proclaim that 'no hero . . . has ever enjoyed so much posthumous fame as the British Arthur. Poets and historians are equally his eulogists. Fancy has strewn her flowers over his tomb, and learning has dedicated many a laborious page to his honour'.[66]

It is possible to date the *annus mirabilis* of Robin Hood with even greater precision, for 1818 gave birth to three important interpretations of the legend which heralded the beginning of an era in which there would be an 'extraordinary degree of lively interest in every circumstance with which the name of Robin Hood is connected'.[67] Once again, Walter Scott led the charge. In 1818 he began writing *Ivanhoe*, the most influential nineteenth-century treatment of the legend. That same year Thomas Love Peacock composed the bulk of his novel *Maid Marian*, although it did not appear until 1822. And finally came John Keats's poem 'Robin Hood: To a Friend', which, although it is not one of his better-known works, must surely rank as one of the most beautiful of all literary treatments of the legend.

That all of these works appeared in a single decade was no coincidence. The apotheosis of King Arthur and Robin Hood was directly linked to the unique political, social, and cultural conditions produced by the French Revolution and the Revolutionary and Napoleonic Wars. This period firmly established them as national heroes—albeit heroes possessing very different meanings—in British culture, a position which they would maintain for the remainder of the nineteenth century and beyond.

---

[66] Richard Warner, *A History of the Abbey of Glaston; and the Town of Glastonbury* (Bath, 1826), 164.
[67] Thomas Hastings, *The British Archer; or, Tracts on Archery* (London, 1831), 22.

CHAPTER TWO

'Sung of throughout the length and breadth of the land': The Popularity and Meaning of the Legends of King Arthur and Robin Hood in the Nineteenth Century

BEFORE UNDERTAKING an analysis of the role that the legends of King Arthur and Robin Hood played in the construction of British national identity in the nineteenth century, two fundamental questions must be answered. First, why use this type of material to address the issue of nationalism? And second, why use these two legends in particular?

The first question is the easier to answer. In recent years scholars have increasingly come to argue that national consciousness comes into being through narratives that erase contradictions, defuse paradoxes and fill in discursive gaps, thereby transforming the often tempestuous creation of a national identity into a logical, linear, seemingly inevitable process.[1] In other words, every nation requires a 'national history' in which the community's evolution and existence is explained and validated; history not only creates nations, but nations also create their own histories.[2] Anthony Smith claims that 'the concept of a nation . . . cannot be sustained without a suitable past. . . . In order to create a convincing representation of the 'nation', a worthy and distinctive past

---

[1] Patrick Joyce, *Democratic Subjects: The Self and the Social in Nineteenth-Century England* (Cambridge: Cambridge UP, 1994) 120; Homi K. Bhabha, 'Introduction: Narrating the Nation', in Bhabha (ed.), *Nation and Narration* (London and New York: Routledge, 1990), 1.

[2] Benedict Anderson, *Imagined Communities: Reflections on the Origins and Spread of Nationalism*, rev. edn. (London and New York: Verso, 1991), 11–12; Ernest Gellner, *Nations and Nationalism* (Ithaca: Cornell UP, 1983), 56; E. J. Hobsbawm, *Nations and Nationalism Since 1780: Programme, Myth, Reality*, 2nd edn. (Cambridge: Cambridge UP, 1992), 73; John R. Gillis, 'Memory and Identity: The History of a Relationship', in Gillis (ed.), *Commemorations: The Politics of National Identity* (Princeton, NJ: Princeton UP, 1994), 4.

must be rediscovered and appropriated. Only then can the nation aspire to a glorious destiny for which its citizens may be expected to make some sacrifices.' According to Smith, this 'suitable past' functions in a variety of ways to support 'the concept of a nation'. By creating the belief that the nation has existed from time immemorial, it acts to 'satisfy the quest for authenticity'. By locating and rooting the community in a historic space, 'the land of the fathers', it provides the nation with a definite geographical location. By pointing to ancestral heroes from whom the nation's present inhabitants are purportedly descended, it suggests a degree of continuity between generations. By reminding the members of a community of its past greatness, it instills them with a sense of inner worth and collective dignity. And finally, by displaying the past as a mirror of the future, it points the community toward a glorious destiny.[3]

An invented history is therefore crucial to the development of nationalism. But how do nations go about creating a past for themselves, and what source materials do they use as its building blocks? As a crucial element of this process, every nation requires national myths, which provide 'the means for members of a community to recognize that, broadly, they share a mindset, they are much in the same thought-world. Through myth, boundaries are established within the community and also with respect to other communities. Those who do not share in the myth are by definition excluded'.[4] This study will examine how two myths in particular, those of King Arthur and Robin Hood, were used to construct a sense of national identity in nineteenth-century Britain. Before turning to that question, however, we must first examine the historical and historiographical context in which this work is situated.

Building the Perfect Union: The Construction of a 'British' Past

In the nineteenth century many nation-states turned to mythical material as they sought to celebrate and clarify their national identity. This trend, however, has been viewed primarily as a feature of nations that either were new or were attempting to redefine themselves in a fundamental way. The American and French revolutionaries, for

---

[3] Anthony Smith, 'The "Golden Age" and National Renewal', in Geoffrey Hosking and George Schöpflin (eds.), *Myths and Nationhood* (New York: Routledge, 1997), 36, 48–52.
[4] George Schöpflin, 'The Functions of Myth and a Taxonomy of Myths', ibid. 20.

example, urged their countrymen to forget all that had come before and build their respective nations anew.[5] As a result, the past became a blank slate that had to be filled in, and for this purpose both nations turned to myth and legend.[6] In the United States a number of stories were created or embellished in order to give the heroes of the American Revolution status as the 'Founding Fathers' of the new nation.[7] And in France the legendary past was repeatedly invoked during the Revolutionary, Napoleonic, and Restoration periods in order to support current political aspirations.[8] Meanwhile in Germany, another emerging nation, patriotic scholars eagerly searched the legendary past for models from which to reshape the present and build the future. After 1815 the rediscovery of German history served not only as a way to assert a distinctive national character in the wake of Napoleonic occupation, but also as a means by which patriots could express their desire for unification in the face of continued political fragmentation.[9]

Britain, however, has traditionally been viewed as an exception to this trend. Neither a new nation like the United States and Germany nor one struggling to redefine itself like France, it was blessed with the early development of a strong central government, a centralized economy, and a relatively high literacy rate—all key factors, according to recent studies, in the creation of a nation-state. Britain, so says the conventional wisdom, stood apart from—and ahead of—the rest of Europe in the growth of its nationhood and nationalism.[10] But perhaps

[5] David Lowenthal, *The Past is a Foreign Country* (Cambridge: Cambridge UP, 1985); Lynn Hunt, *Politics, Culture and Class in the French Revolution* (Berkeley: University of California Press, 1984), 27. For a discussion that compares the American and French Revolutions in this respect, see François Furet, 'The Ancien Régime and the Revolution', in Pierre Nora (ed.), *Realms of Memory: Rethinking the French Past*, Vol. 1: Conflicts and Divisions (New York: Columbia University Press, 1996), 79–106.

[6] Gillis, 'Memory and Identity', 7.

[7] See e.g. Barry Schwartz, *George Washington: The Making of an American Symbol* (New York: Free Press, 1987). See also Lowenthal, *The Past in a Foreign Country*, 117–21.

[8] See Harry Redman, Jr., *The Roland Legend in Nineteenth-Century French Literature* (Lexington, Ky.: University of Kentucky Press, 1991); Barbara G. Keller, *The Middle Ages Reconsidered: Attitudes in France from the Eighteenth Century Through the Romantic Movement*, Studies in the Humanities Literature—Politics—Society, 11 (New York: Peter Lang, 1994).

[9] Peter Paret, *Art as History: Episodes in the Culture and Politics of Nineteenth-Century Germany* (Princeton: Princeton UP, 1988), 147. See also David E. Barclay, 'Medievalism and Nationalism in Nineteenth-century Germany', in Leslie J. Workman (ed.), *Medievalism in Europe*, Studies in Medievalism, 5 (Cambridge: D. S. Brewer, 1993), 5–22.

[10] Hobsbawm, *Nations and Nationalism*, 104; and Stefan Collini, *Public Moralists: Political Thought and Intellectual Life in Britain 1850–1930* (Oxford: Clarendon Press, 1991), 345–6.

we should not be so quick to accept this argument. To use Benedict Anderson's oft-invoked phrase, Britain was and is in many ways an 'imagined community', albeit in a different way from most of its European neighbours. A useful way of looking at nationhood might be to examine efforts to reconcile borders with self-perceptions. In the case of a nation like Germany, the self-perception of nationhood came first, followed only after a protracted and arduous struggle by the establishment of acceptable borders. But for Britain the borders came first, and the struggle occurred over the self-perception. It is a nation created not from romantic dreams of the fatherland, but from the pragmatic goals of its legislators, who amalgamated first Wales, then Scotland, and finally Ireland in a ruthless quest to preserve national security. And because Britain is (and always has been) a multinational construct, a particularly British form of nationalism had to be built up that was capable of both domestic discipline and external mobilization.[11] Britain thus shares certain characteristics with countries such as the former Yugoslavia or the former Soviet Union, nations in which a number of different peoples were forced to live together for purposes of administrative convenience. These places ultimately failed to overcome the tensions created when several different communities were thrust together. But although Britain has experienced some of the same problems, for the most part the vision of a 'United Kingdom' has held together. How has it managed to succeed?

An important part of the answer lies in Britain's success in constructing a 'history' for itself over the course of the nineteenth century, a period in which the selective mobilization of the past acted to overcome the tensions caused in the present by the tempestuous relationship among the nation's constituent communities. As the boundaries of the nation expanded both internally, in terms of citizenship, and externally, in terms of dominion, national unity was maintained and asserted by giving unprecedented attention to the past. In the nineteenth century works of history enjoyed a tremendous popularity. This was, after all, the age of Thomas Babington Macaulay, whose *History of England* (1849–61) was one of the century's best sellers; of the Oxford academics A. E. Freeman, William Stubbs, S. R. Gardiner, and J. A. Froude, who lifted professional historical scholarship to new heights of prestige; and of J. R. Green, whose *Short History of the English People*

---

[11] Tom Nairn, *The Enchanted Glass: Britain and Its Monarchy*, new edn. (London: Picador, 1990), 178.

(1874) represented the first attempt to write social history for a wide audience.[12]

But what sort of history did these texts present? Above all, they were explicitly *national* histories that were concerned with telling the story of the nation's past, with a thinly veiled subtext of explaining and setting the stage for the nation's present accomplishments. This, however, raises another question: with which nation were they primarily concerned? The vast majority of these works were conceived, written, and marketed specifically as histories of *England*. They were written for an English audience in praise of English institutions, and it was English national identity which they helped to define and proclaim. The great nineteenth-century historians believed that everything of value had been born and bred in England. They were content to take English exceptionalism for granted and to assume it to be a positive development; the historian's task was merely to describe and applaud.[13]

Indeed, most nineteenth-century histories were so Anglocentric that they barely acknowledged the existence of the other parts of the British Isles, and they were completely devoid of any awareness that Scotland, Wales, and Ireland had separate identities and separate pasts. The story they told was one of a triumphal English expansion, an inexorable process of domination and absorption with a civilizing mission at its heart. Without England, so went the standard argument, the remainder of the British Isles would have been doomed to a marginal existence as provincial backwaters; with it, they were blessed to be parts—albeit subordinate ones—of the greatest nation on the face of the earth.

This version of the 'British' past became so prevalent that in many ways it lingers into the present. It is important to realize, however, that it is not only in recent years that attempts have been made to write a genuinely *British* history. For much of the eighteenth century true histories of Britain were readily available, and the assumption of the inherent superiority of England was not made so unquestioningly. A recent study by Colin Kidd, for example, shows that prior to 1750 there was a Scottish version of history claiming that the Scots, like the English, had their own 'ancient constitution' from which their present

---

[12] David Cannadine, 'British History as a "New Subject": Politics, Perspectives and Prospects', in Alexander Grant and Keith Stringer (eds.), *Uniting the Kingdom?: The Making of British History* (London and New York: Routledge, 1995), 14.

[13] Edwin Jones, *The English Nation: The Great Myth* (Thrupp, Stroud, Glos.: Sutton, 1998), ch. 7; and Cannadine, 'British History', 16.

liberties derived. According to Kidd, however, in the middle of the eighteenth century Scottish culture underwent a 'fundamental transformation' that had 'devastating effects' on conceptions of Scottishness and Scottish history. Instead of taking pride in their nation's independent political achievements, the Scots came to see themselves as socially and economically inferior, and they saw the only method of remedying these defects as lying in closer integration with their more 'modern' and 'civilized' southern neighbour. Thus, while they retained an 'emotional bond' with their own past, the Scots came to see English history as pointing the way to the future.[14]

These conclusions are reinforced by the work of Murray G. H. Pittock, who argues that, beginning in the 1760s and 1770s, the 'Jacobite' version of Scottish history—a version stressing independence and distinctiveness—was increasingly subsumed into a British view dominated by English concerns. Pittock sees writers like Robert Burns and Sir Walter Scott as participants in a process of romanticizing the distinctively Scottish elements of the past while making it clear that present-day practicalities demanded assimilation into the British state. By the Victorian age many Scottish traditions—such as the kilt and the bagpipes, which in the eighteenth century had often carried treasonous associations—had become so sentimentalized as to be entirely devoid of real political content. Even the royal family could wear tartans without any hint of disloyalty to their Hanoverian ancestors.[15]

A similar scenario occurred regarding Welsh history in the eighteenth and nineteenth centuries. As in the case of Scotland, a distinctively Welsh past had existed prior to the eighteenth century. This past was based on three fundamental concepts: first, that the Welsh were the descendants of the original inhabitants of the British Isles; second, that the Welsh had been the earliest Christians in Britain; and third, that there was a long line of Welsh princes who had descended from tribal leaders. By 1700, however, this version of Welsh history was in decay; many aspects had been entirely discredited, and what remained survived only in the form of peasant folklore. In response to this decline, Prys Morgan argues, a 'nostalgia for a way of life that seemed to have been happier and merrier than the polite and sober present'

[14] Colin Kidd, *Subverting Scotland's Past: Scottish Whig Historians and the Creation of an Anglo-British Identity, 1689–c.1830* (Cambridge: Cambridge UP, 1993), 97, 209. See also Marinell Ash, *The Strange Death of Scottish History* (Edinburgh: Ramsay Head Press, 1980).

[15] Murray G. H. Pittock, *The Invention of Scotland: The Stuart Myth and the Scottish Identity, 1638 to the Present* (London and New York: Routledge, 1991).

developed, and as a result there arose a movement dedicated to recovering 'by a self-conscious process all that had slipped away with barely a thought'.[16] This movement led to the printing of books in Welsh, the founding of religious and secular Welsh societies and associations, and the revival of Welsh cultural traditions such as the eisteddfod.

Much like the new version of Scottish history which emerged in the late eighteenth and early nineteenth centuries, however, the Welsh past became romanticized to the point of distortion. Moreover, the intensity of this Welsh pride in the past hindered the development of a Welsh nationalist movement in the present. In the first place, it encouraged Welsh nationalists to focus on cultural rather than political matters. And secondly, it made things Welsh appear charmingly quaint, which had the effect of associating Wales with the distant past rather than the future. Contemporary Wales came to be seen as backward and archaic, and, as in the case of Scotland, many Welsh people turned to England as the model of a modern society. By the middle of the nineteenth century the Welsh had 'a burning desire to transform themselves . . . to modernise their culture, to get on in the world as their English neighbours had done'.[17] Just as was happening to 'Scottishness' in Scotland, 'Welshness' came to be associated firmly with the past, and the road to the future was thought to lead directly through England and an adoption of English ways and attitudes.

What we see emerging by the middle of the nineteenth century, therefore, is an extremely Anglocentric version of British history. Both Scottish and Welsh history were on the defensive, and survived only in a romanticized form that made them seem irrelevant to the present concerns of the British nation. The constituent parts of Britain were indeed coming to share a common past, but that past was dominated by English history. Combining factual and fictional elements, the process of creating this new past involved the use of mythical material, including, as the rest of this study will establish, the legends of King Arthur and Robin Hood.

---

[16] Prys Morgan, 'From a Death to a View: The Hunt for the Welsh Past in the Romantic Period', in Eric Hobsbawm and Terence Ranger, eds., *The Invention of Tradition*, new edn. (Cambridge: Cambridge UP, 1992), 45–6; Prys Morgan, *The Eighteenth Century Renaissance, A New History of Wales*, ed. Ralph A. Griffiths, Kenneth O. Morgan, and J. Beverley Smith (Llandybïe, Dyfed: Christopher Davies, 1981), 38.

[17] Morgan, *Eighteenth Century Renaissance*, 113, 154.

*'The legend is spread everywhere': The Popularity and Historical Development of
the Legends of King Arthur and Robin Hood*

To return to the second of the two questions posed above: why focus
exclusively on the legends of King Arthur and Robin Hood in the case
of a nation so rich and varied in its mythology as Great Britain? The
primary reason for this choice has to do with their popularity. In the
nineteenth century these two legends were extremely prevalent in
British culture. 'There is no character of British story more familiar
to our knowledge, or interesting to our minds, than the renowned
Arthur', wrote the antiquarian Richard Warner in 1826. Equally
sweeping claims were made regarding the popularity of Robin
Hood, who was said to be 'sung of throughout the length and breadth
of the land'.[18]

This section contains a brief survey of some of the many places in
which King Arthur and Robin Hood appeared in British culture in the
late eighteenth and nineteenth centuries. The following chapters, however, will emphasize their prevalence in one area in particular: literature. The prevalence of King Arthur and Robin Hood in print is
significant because, before the invention of modern forms of electronic
media, printed matter was the most crucial source in the creation of
nationalism. It laid the basis for national consciousness by creating
what Benedict Anderson terms 'unified fields of exchange and communication', in which speakers of the same language became aware of
the thousands, even millions, of people who shared their language-
field, and simultaneously recognized that *only* those thousands or millions did so. These fellow-readers, visible and connected to each other
by print, formed 'the embryo of the nationally imagined community'.[19]

In the British case, technological advancements and social changes
led to the dissemination of print on an unprecedented scale in the
nineteenth century. The most important factor underlying the emergence of a mass reading public was a dramatic growth in the literacy
rate. In 1750 only half of the English population could read, but by
1900 the official illiteracy rate had fallen to below 1 per cent. Seeking to
exploit this burgeoning market, publishers devoted substantial attention and resources to the production and sale of cheap literature, and

---

[18] Richard Warner, *A History of the Abbey of Glaston; and the Town of Glastonbury* (Bath,
1826), 160; William Allingham, *The Ballad Book: A Selection of the Choicest British Ballads*
(London and Cambridge, 1864), p. xxiii.

[19] Gellner, *Nations and Nationalism*, 8; Anderson, *Imagined Communities*, 44.

the commercialization of the publishing industry helped printed matter to supersede older, oral forms of communication.[20]

But of course, it is not just reading and writing but what is read and written that counts.[21] In other words, people could have read or written about any number of subjects in nineteenth-century Britain; why did they so frequently select tales of King Arthur or Robin Hood? They did so because Britons recognized in both figures qualities considered vital to their experience as members of a national community. The remainder of this work will identify those characteristics, and will use them to draw some broader conclusions concerning the nature of British national identity in the nineteenth century.

First, however, we must attempt to assess the cultural prominence and relevance of King Arthur and Robin Hood. In the nineteenth century the legends intruded into the lives of more British people in more ways than ever before.[22] Simply counting their appearances, however, does little to explain *why* they were so prominent, and so the final section of this chapter will explore the meanings which the two legends possessed for their nineteenth-century interpreters.

In 1870 the *Dublin Review* reported that the characters of the Arthurian legend were 'now so well known that gentlemen of the turf have for some time been calling their racehorses after them'. This claim is borne out by a survey of the racing calendar for the previous decade, which features horses named 'King Arthur', 'Guinevere', 'Vivien', and 'Vortigern'. Nineteenth-century racehorses were also named after characters from the legend of Robin Hood. During the 1860s alone there were two 'Robin Hoods', as well as a 'Maid Marian', a 'Will Scarlet', a 'Friar Tuck', and an 'Allen-a-Dale.'[23] And racehorses were

[20] The most recent study of literacy in nineteenth-century England is David Vincent, *Literacy and Popular Culture: England 1750–1914* (Cambridge: Cambridge UP, 1989).

[21] Gellner, *Nations and Nationalism*, 31.

[22] In recent years historians have used varied methods and sources in their efforts to determine the strength and significance of 'hero cults' in different cultures. See Derek Beales, 'Garibaldi in England: The Politics of Italian Enthusiasm', in John A. Davis and Paul Ginsbourg (eds.), *Society and Politics in the Age of the Risorgimento: Essays in Honour of Denis Mack Smith* (Cambridge: Cambridge UP, 1991), 188–9; Peter Karsten, *Patriot Heroes in England and America: Political Symbolism and Changing Values over Three Centuries* (Madison: University of Wisconsin Press, 1978), 6; Ilene V. O'Malley, *The Myth of the Revolution: Hero Cults and the Institutionalization of the Mexican State, 1920–1940* (New York and London: Greenwood, 1986), 147–9; Kathleen Wilson, 'Admiral Vernon and Popular Politics in Mid-Hanoverian Britain', *Past and Present*, 121 (1988), 88.

[23] 'Mr. Tennyson's Arthurian Poems', *Dublin Review*, 70 (1870) 423. For the names of contemporary racehorses, see the 'Racing and Steeple Chase Calendar' in the *Sporting Magazine* for the 1860s.

not the only things built for speed that were named after characters from the two legends. In the mid-1850s Alexander Hall's yard at Aberdeen launched clipper ships called the *Robin Hood* and the *Friar Tuck*, and in 1865 the famous Steele Bros. firm of the Clyde shipyards launched the *Sir Lancelot*, which set a record for the fastest passage from China to London four years later.[24]

Back on land, wealthy Britons attended costume balls dressed as characters from the two legends. In his *Fancy Dresses Described; or, What to Wear at Fancy Balls* (1879), Arden Holt listed several hundred ladies' costumes, including the Arthurian characters Elaine, Enid, and Guinevere, as well as Maid Marian from the legend of Robin Hood, whose costume featured

a brown satin short skirt, bordered with dark fur; a pelisse of green velvet, the skirt gathered to the bodice, with reverse of red satin, and red and brown on the cuffs; the sleeves long, bordered with fur, light brown satin ones beneath; leather band and knife round the waist, with quiver at back; round velvet cap bordered with fur. . . . A horn is carried at the side; boots bound with fur; hair in plaits.

Men, too, donned costumes derived from the two legends. Among the guests at the Grand Fancy Ball at Brecon in March 1827 were a Mr Ross and Mr Powell of the Royal Welch Fusiliers, dressed as Robin Hood and Little John. In July 1897 Lord and Lady Rodney attended the Duchess of Devonshire's famous ball costumed as King Arthur and Queen Guinevere, surrounded by a retinue of Knights of the Round Table.[25]

Inside the Victorian home, those who could afford it indulged in elaborate decorating schemes based upon the two legends. In 1862 the Bradford merchant Walter Dunlop commissioned from William Morris and Company a series of stained-glass windows depicting the Tristram legend for the entrance hall of Harden Grange, his Yorkshire estate.[26]

---

[24] Steele Bros. also built two less famous vessels named the *King Arthur* and the *Guinevere*. See Cyril L. Hume and Malcolm C. Armstrong, *The Cutty Sark and Thermopylae Era of Sail* (Glasgow: Brown, Son & Ferguson, 1987); Basil Lubbock, *The China Clippers*, new edn. (London: Century Publishing, 1984); David R. MacGregor, *The Tea Clippers: An Account of the China Tea Trade and of Some of the British Sailing Ships Engaged in it from 1849 to 1869* (London: Percival, Marshall and Co., 1952).

[25] Arden Holt, *Fancy Dresses Described; or, What to Wear at Fancy Balls*, 4th edn. (London, 1879), 1, 49, 51, 66, and 85; *Carmarthen Journal*, 9 Mar. 1827, 3; Sophia Murphy, *The Duchess of Devonshire's Ball* (London: Sidgwick and Jackson, 1984).

[26] A. Charles Sewter, *The Stained Glass of William Morris and His Circle* (New Haven and London: Yale UP, 1974), ii. 26–7; Herbert E. Wroot, 'Pre-Raphaelite Windows at Bradford', *Studio*, 72 (1917), 69–73.

In 1870, also for Morris and Company, Edward Burne-Jones designed two panels depicting Lancelot and Elaine for Lunefield in Kirby Lonsdale, a house built by the noted architect Alfred Waterhouse. Burne-Jones later installed four panels illustrating the quest for the Holy Grail on a landing in his own North End House at Rottingdean. Morris and Company also used Arthurian motifs in its textiles, including embroideries and tapestries. In 1890 Morris hung a series of six tapestries depicting the quest for the Holy Grail in the dining room of Stanmore Hall, Middlesex, the home of William Knox D'Arcy, an Australian mining engineer who had made a fortune speculating in oil rights.[27] Other design firms also utilized Arthurian motifs in their tapestry designs. In 1879 the Royal Windsor Tapestry Manufactory received a commission from the MP Coleridge Kennard for a tapestry series depicting the court of King Arthur.[28]

Although the legend of Robin Hood was not used as frequently as a decorative motif, it did feature in nineteenth-century interior and exterior designs. In 1842 the Duke of Portland built a lodge in Sherwood Forest near Clipstone. Used as schoolhouse, it featured statues of Richard I, Allen-a-Dale, and Friar Tuck on the north side and Robin Hood, Little John, and Maid Marian on the south. In the 1860s the Earl of Manvers erected a statue of Robin Hood in the courtyard of his newly refurbished house at Thoresby. Inside, the library featured an elaborately carved chimneypiece flanked by near-life-size statues of Robin Hood and Little John.[29]

Of course, the commission of a hand-carved fireplace or hand-woven tapestry was not an inexpensive enterprise. The Holy Grail tapestries made for Stanmore Hall by Morris and Company, for example, cost over £3,500. There were numerous ways, however, in which people of lesser financial resources brought King Arthur or Robin Hood into their homes. Victorian children, for example, played with toy theatres featuring the outlaws of Sherwood or the knights of Camelot. And in the mid-nineteenth century a Staffordshire pottery

---

[27] Oliver Fairclough and Emmeline Leary, *Textiles by William Morris and Co., 1861–1940* (London: Thames and Hudson, 1981), 21–8, 61, 107–8; 'The Arras Tapestries at Stanmore Hall', *Studio*, 15 (1899), 98–104; Linda Parry, 'The Tapestries of Sir Edward Burne-Jones', *Apollo*, 102 (1972), 324–8.

[28] Beryl Platts, 'A Brave Victorian Venture: The Royal Windsor Tapestry Manufactory', *Country Life*, 166 (1979), 2003–6.

[29] January Searle, *Leaves from Sherwood Forest* (London, 1850) 95; *Thoresby Hall* (Hanley: English Life Publications, 1978); Alexander Beattie, *Thoresby Hall: The Home of the Pierrepont Family* (Hanley: Wood, Mitchell & Co., 1964).

figurine depicting Robin Hood and Little John was produced in considerable quantities and sold at a relatively low price.[30]

And some glimpses of the two legends in nineteenth-century Britain cost absolutely nothing. A visitor strolling through almost any town would very likely have encountered the two legends on the signs of local public houses. In his *Tavern Anecdotes and Sayings* (1881), Charles Hindley reported that Robin Hood pubs had 'of late years been very much on the increase'. And King Arthur, too, appeared on pub signboards. In his *A Second Walk through Wales* (1799), Richard Warner reported that in Caerleon a sign displaying 'a military figure, intended to represent King Arthur' read:

> 1200 years and more are pass'd
> Since Arthur ruled here:
> And that to me once more he's come
> Think it not strange or queere.
>
> Though o'er my door, yet take my word,
> To honour you he's able;
> And make you welcome with good Ale,
> And Knights of the Round Table.[31]

Another popular figure on tavern signboards was Merlin, the famed Arthurian enchanter. In the nineteenth century there were several Merlin pubs in London, as well as examples in Pontypridd, Leeds, Edinburgh, Chalfont St Giles, and Andover.[32]

Indeed, apart from Arthur himself, Merlin was the most famous character from the legend. A newspaper entitled the *Monmouthshire Merlin* was founded at Newport in 1829; in an early issue a contributor offered an explanation and apology for the choice of names:

---

[30] Peter Baldwin, *Toy Theatres of the World* (London: Zwemmer, 1992); Nicola Johnson, 'Penny Plain, Tuppence Coloured', in Raphael Samuel (ed.), *Patriotism: The Making and Unmaking of British National Identity*, Vol. 3: *National Fictions* (London and New York: Routledge, 1989), 252–61; George Speaight, *Juvenile Drama: The History of the English Toy Theatre* (London: MacDonald & Co., 1946); P. D. Gordon Pugh, *Staffordshire Portrait Figures and Allied Subjects of the Victorian Era* (Woodbridge, Suffolk: Antique Collectors Club, 1970), 521–2.

[31] Charles Hindley, *Tavern Anecdotes and Sayings*, new edn. (London, 1881), 303; Richard Warner, *A Second Walk through Wales* (Bath, 1799), 22.

[32] The most famous Merlin pub was the Merlin's Cave, which opened in the mid-1730s on Rosomon Street in Clerkenwell. A new Merlin's Cave still stands on Margaret Street, just to the north of the old site. Gillian Bebbington, *Street Names of London* (London: B. T. Batsford, 1972), 218–9; Margaret McDerby, *The Borough of Finsbury Official Guide*, 3rd edn. (London: Pyramid Press, 1963), 31.

Merlin is the appellation of one celebrated in old annals for his supposed skill in the black art. . . . Lest any witty and ingenious person should hereafter be inclined to declare that the *Monmouthshire Merlin* is 'no conjurer', we anticipate that piece of jocoseness, and voluntarily abjure on its behalf all prescience and science of every description, save that, and that only, which it may become an honest man to be acquainted with.[33]

One of the most intriguing of Merlin's manifestations were the efforts of the eccentric inventor John Joseph Merlin to capitalize on the notoriety of his famous namesake. In the early 1780s he opened a mechanical exhibition in London. Among the objects on display were two mini-ature brass models of 'Merlin's Necromantic Cave', a full-sized version of which he intended to build on a site near Paddington. In order to advertise the scheme, he commissioned a medal and printed admission tickets, and in 1802 he had his carriage painted with 'various emble-matical figures of . . . the ancient British Magician'.[34]

Unfortunately, John Joseph Merlin proved a better engineer than businessman, and he failed to raise the funds necessary to construct his 'Necromantic Cave'. Those Britons who wished to visit the home of the great Arthurian wizard, however, had several other options from which to choose. In her guide to the scenery of North Wales, published in 1845, Louisa Stuart Costello cited Welsh traditions that 'Merlin's famous grotto' was to be found close to Mount Snowdon, where 'the voice of the mighty master may . . . be frequently heard . . . amongst the hollow rocks, reverberating along the mountains in thunder'. Others, however, located the cave further south, near Carmarthen. In his *Descriptive Excursions through South Wales and Monmouthshire* (1805), Edward Donovan told how

there is a lofty eminence within sight of [Carmarthen] . . . that caught our observation as we retraced our journey back towards Aberguilly. . . . The cluster of trees upon this eminence, was pointed out to us by a shepherd's boy, under the title of Merlin's grove, and a cavity he mentioned on one side, of course by that of Merlin's cave. Subsequent enquiry has confirmed the truth of the boy's assertion.[35]

---

[33] Christopher Dean, *A Study of Merlin in English Literature from the Middle Ages to the Present Day* (Lewiston, NY: Edward Mellen Press, 1992), 94; 'Merlin Redivivus: A Dramatic Scene', *Monmouthshire Merlin*, 23 May 1829, 4.

[34] *John Joseph Merlin: The Ingenious Mechanick* (London: Greater London Council, 1985), 26–7; 'Merlin's Cave', *Chimney Corner Companion*, 10 (1827), 223–4; 'The Life of Mr John Joseph Merlin', *The Wonderful and Scientific Museum*, 1 (1803), 274–9.

[35] Louisa Stuart Costello, *The Falls, Lakes and Mountains of North Wales* (London, 1845), 123; Edward Donovan, *Descriptive Excursions through South Wales and Monmouthshire, in the Year 1804, and the Four Preceding Summers* (London, 1805), ii. 206–7.

And Merlin's cave was only one of a plethora of Arthurian locales to attract the attention of nineteenth-century travellers. Having little basis in verifiable history, these sites were often the result of over-zealous local enthusiasm for the legend or the greed of enterprising entrepreneurs, but their decidedly spurious nature did not prevent tourists from flocking to places such as Tintagel and Glastonbury, where they could stay in the 'King Arthur Hotel' or drink in the 'King Arthur Tavern'. 'The indiscriminate use of Arthur's name often shows an extravagance of imagination and a reckless disregard of what is appropriate', complained the historian Algernon Herbert. 'The legend is spread everywhere, but there are no verities.'[36]

A fascinating example of the process by which the legend became attached to a place which had no previous Arthurian associations is provided by Alderley Edge, a steep wooded ridge in North Cheshire. In 1805 an anonymous traveller wrote a letter to the *Manchester Mail* in which he reported that, while on a recent trip through Monks-heath, about two miles from Alderley Edge, he observed a sign on a local public house depicting a pair of large iron gates, thrown wide open to reveal a deep cavern 'in which several military horses [were] asleep, with men, arms, &c'. Near the mouth of the cavern stood an enchanter dressed in medieval costume and carrying a magic wand. Before him knelt a man in modern dress, behind whom a gray horse started back in terror.

His curiosity piqued, the traveller made some enquiries as to the origin of the sign. The local curate explained that it 'bore some allusion to a popular tradition, which has long been current in that neighbourhood'. According to the tradition, about eighty years previously a man had journeyed from Mobberley to Macclesfield to sell a fine white horse at Barnby Fair. As he passed over Alderley Edge, he met an old man who offered to buy the horse. Finding the offer insufficient, the man refused and continued on to the Fair, but there he found no takers. On the return journey he again encountered the old man, who asked if he was now ready to accept the price offered in the morning. He consented, and the stranger led him to a pair of iron gates, which flew open to reveal a deep cavern containing an immense number of horses and soldiers, all fast asleep. The enchanter led him inside to a large treasure chest, out of which he paid for the horse. After returning to the surface, the man hastened to tell the local

---

[36] Algernon Herbert, *Britannia after the Romans* (London, 1836), 90–1.

populace what had occurred, but a long search for the gates proved fruitless. Nevertheless, the townspeople remained 'fully convinced . . . that the place was enchanted'.[37]

In this, its earliest nineteenth-century form, the legend had no Arthurian associations. But in 1838 Elizabeth Gaskell sent a letter to a friend asking: 'If you were on Alderley Edge . . . could I not point out to you the very entrance to the cave where King Arthur and his knights lie sleeping in their golden armour till the day when England's peril shall summon them to her rescue?' The following year James Roscoe presented a more extensive version of 'The Iron Gate—A Legend of Alderley' in *Blackwood's Edinburgh Magazine*. Roscoe's poem tells of a miller who one day goes to market on his prized gray horse. On the way a monk suddenly appears in front of him and demands to buy the horse. The miller consents, and is led through an iron gate to a cavern in which 'twice ten thousand men' lie sleeping. The monk tells him:

> These are King Arthur's chivalry,
> The noblest in the land! . . .
> By Merlin's power they here are laid,
> But will go forth anew.[38]

After paying for the horse, the monk leads the miller out of the cave. When he turns to look back, both monk and cave have disappeared without a trace, never to be seen again. This story is virtually identical to the one told in the *Manchester Mail* in 1805. In the intervening decades, however, there had been one important embellishment: the identification of the sleeping knights with the Arthurian legend.

A similar pattern can be detected in the growth of place-names and local traditions associated with Robin Hood. In 1847 the *Edinburgh Review* declared that 'there is scarcely a county in England, or any class of ancient remains, which, in some place or other, does not claim a kind of relationship to this celebrated hero'. Although a handful of these associations date back hundreds of years, most date from no earlier than the nineteenth century. As in the case of King Arthur, the primary explanation for the growth of Robin Hood place-names

---

[37] 'The Cheshire Enchanter', *Manchester Mail*, 28 May 1805, 3.
[38] *The Letters of Mrs. Gaskell*, ed. J. A. V. Chapple and Arthur Pollard (Manchester: Manchester UP, 1966), 32; James Roscoe, 'The Iron Gate—A Legend of Alderley', *Blackwood's Edinburgh Magazine*, 5 (1839), 273. For later versions of this tale, see *Alderley Edge and Its Neighbourhood* (Macclesfield, [1843]), 20, 27; *Alderley Edge: A Guide to All Its Points of Interest* (Manchester, 1863), 12–14; Egerton Leigh, *Ballads and Legends of Cheshire* (London, 1867), 106–11 and 284–90; William Axon, *Cheshire Gleanings* (Manchester, 1884), 56–8.

was a desire for financial gain linked to the rapid expansion of the tourism industry. For example, in an effort to attract visitors, the local citizenry of Ripon, Yorkshire, organized a civic festival in August 1886. To celebrate Ripon's history, the organizers looked to the 'characters, with whose names the city will always be associated'. One such character was Robin Hood, who according to tradition had fought a quarterstaff battle with Friar Tuck at nearby Fountains Abbey. This famous encounter was commemorated in a short play by Augustine Dawtrey of Nottingham, who won a prize of ten guineas for his effort 'Ye Merrie Geste of Robyn Hode and ye Curtal Fryer'. Local volunteers played the leading roles, although not very adeptly if the *Yorkshireman*'s review is to be trusted:

The Friar . . . occasionally forgot his role, and returned to the business of fooling. . . . Robin Hood lost his wig in the affray; the music went hideously wrong all through the play; the bugle was sounded when Robin Hood did not blow, and Robin blew in vain for the music which did not come; the foresters came bouncing into the arena before the bugle called them, and the spectators had to wait an unconscionable period before the appearance of the monks.[39]

Undismayed by these difficulties, however, the audience was reported to have responded enthusiastically.

A final area of British culture in which the popularity of the legends of King Arthur and Robin Hood needs to be assessed is in the visual arts. Here, the Arthurian legend was clearly dominant. In the first half of the nineteenth century there were no more than a handful of Arthurian works per decade, but after 1860 the subject exploded in popularity, as Table 2.1 illustrates. In contrast, Robin Hood provided the subject for only two nineteenth-century paintings, an oil by Daniel Maclise in 1839 and a watercolor by Richard Dadd in 1859. This dearth of artworks related to the outlaw legend was primarily due to its close association with popular culture, which made it seem an inappropriate subject in the eyes of many painters. There was no shortage of visual representations of Robin Hood in the late eighteenth and early nineteenth centuries, however, as he was depicted in a wide variety of illustrations for books, chapbooks, ballads, and other printed texts.

---

[39] *Edinburgh Review*, *86* (1847), 123; J. C. Holt, *Robin Hood*, rev. edn. (London: Thames and Hudson, 1989), 179; W. Harrison, *Ripon Millenary: A Record of the Festival* (Ripon, 1892), 197.

TABLE 2.1. *Arthurian artworks exhibited at the Royal Academy, Royal Society of the British Artisits, and Royal Scottish Academy, 1800–1899*

Decade	Number of paintings	Decade	Number of paintings
1800–9	0	1850–9	4
1810–9	1	1860–9	63
1820–9	1	1870–9	32
1830–9	1	1880–9	35
1840–9	1	1890–9	31

Source: Christine Poulson, 'Arthurian Legend in Fine and Applied Art of the Nineteenth and Early Twentieth Centuries: A Catalogue of Artists', *Arthurian Literature*, IX, ed. Richard Barber (Cambridge: D. Brewer, 1989), 81–142.

This survey provides some sense of the popularity of King Arthur and Robin Hood in the late eighteenth and nineteenth centuries. The vast majority of British people in this period would not have been surprised to encounter one or both of the legends as they went about their daily business. What sort of images, though, did King Arthur and Robin Hood bring to mind when they were seen on a racing form or pub sign or hanging on the wall at an art exhibition? In other words, what did they mean to contemporary Britons?

'The protection of the community': The Arthurian Legend in the Nineteenth Century

In 1820 an anonymous political tract entitled *The Round Table* was published in London. Stressing the need for a strong leader who could contain the 'discordant and repulsive' impulses of 'the extreme elements of society', the author argued that the British monarchy represented 'a physical and moral force' which served to 'protect the possessions of opulence, the fruits of industry, and the personal safety of all'. Next he praised the nobility: 'a proud, a high-minded and an honourable Body, invested with power and pledged by personal interests to protect public liberty'. He concluded by criticizing the 'convulsionary Muse of Jacobinism', which sought to abolish the monarchy and aristocracy. Instead, he argued that ruler and ruled should ideally enjoy a symbiotic relationship in which each fulfilled certain obligations to the other: 'The duty of the Subject was obedience; that of the

Sovereign to administer justice, and to provide for the protection of the community'.[40]

By arguing that the primary role of the king and the nobility was to 'protect' the realm and its inhabitants, the author defined patriotism as an expression of loyalty to a father-figure, a recognition of a familial bond transmuted to the realm of the nation-state. In the first half of the nineteenth century dramatic economic and social change reinvigorated notions that society could best be managed by men of authority, property, and rank fulfilling their obligations towards a community bound to them by ties of deference and dependence.[41] The severe economic crisis of the late 1830s and 1840s, in particular, cast doubt on the idea that continued adherence to a laissez-faire approach could solve the problems of rural pauperism and urban poverty. In some quarters a more promising answer seemed to be an increased attention to duty by men of wealth and status.[42]

In their search for a historical precedent upon which to base their arguments, many conservatives looked to the Middle Ages, an era in which they believed that the upper orders had been more benevolent and the lower more deferential, with society more harmonious as a result.[43] And what better medieval model than King Arthur's Camelot, a community led by a noble elite dedicated to protecting the weak from the strong? It was no coincidence that the author of the tract cited above titled his work *The Round Table*, for his invocation of an Arthurian image reminded his audience of the benefits of a strong monarchy and aristocracy.

Other conservative authors attempted to use the legend for similar purposes. In *England: An Historical Poem* (1834), John Walker Ord offers a vigorous polemic against the passage of parliamentary reform in 1832. In the preface, Ord announces that he was motivated to compose the work by the 'terrible state of insubordination and dissatisfaction' into

---

[40] *The Round Table. The Order and Solemnities of Crowning the King: and the Dignities of His Peerage with Remarks in Vindication of Both* (London, 1820), 3–6, 25, 95, 105.

[41] J. H. Grainger, *Patriotisms: Britain 1900–1939* (London: Routledge, 1986), 3; David Roberts, *Paternalism in Early Victorian England* (London: Croom Helm, 1979), 8. Boyd Hilton has criticized many aspects of Roberts's work, but even he admits that 'traces of an older paternalist tradition survived and periodically flourished' in the first half of the nineteenth century. Boyd Hilton, *The Age of Atonement: The Influence of Evangelism on Social and Economic Thought, 1785–1865* (Oxford: Clarendon Press, 1988), p. viii.

[42] Roberts, *Paternalism*, 63.

[43] Debra N. Mancoff, 'In Praise of Patriarchy: Paternalism and Chivalry in the Decorations in the House of Lords', *Nineteenth-Century Contexts*, 16 (1992), 50.

which Britain had 'fallen by a long continuance of seditious and
revolutionary measures, on the part of ministers bred in the school
of French and anti-national politics'. Contrasting the 'old heroic
times' with the present, he celebrates Arthur and his followers as
emblems of the kind of heroic chivalry and patriotism which has all
but disappeared from modern Britain. In Arthur's day, he asserts,
valiant knights 'kept the wolves and bears behind their forest screen'.
But now:

> The rascal rebel lingers in our halls;
> The soot-brow'd traitor tramps each pleasant way;
> They seek for other flowers upon the walls,
> Than clothe the abbey seams, with gold and purple palls.
>
> Like vipers, they are twined in the grass,
> And hiss at every royal thing of state;
> The mountain wells are poison'd where they pass—
> The air is rank with death: they lie in wait
> Among our palaces, and yell with hate . . .[44]

Similarly, in his poem 'La Belle Tryamour' (1823), John Moultrie
also attempts, albeit in a more lighthearted manner, to use the
Arthurian legend to remind his readers of the advantages of strong,
conservative rule. Describing himself as an 'anti-Gallican', Moultrie,
who later became parson of Rugby School and a close friend of
Thomas Arnold, espouses his faith in time-honored beliefs and
practices:

> And I acknowledge that I've still preferr'd
> The old worn paths—for I can safely trust 'em;
> To love one's country, and to keep one's word,
> Are good old maxims, nor will time e'er rust 'em—
> Our modern creeds are wiser, I dare say,
> But sometimes lead us deucedly astray.

Such dyed-in-the-wool conservatism is borne out by Moultrie's political opinions, which are concerned with the dangers of mob rule.
After Arthur sinks into an illness from which his doctors declare he will
not recover

> all sorts of fears,
> In every loyal breast, of course were rife,
> And mobs were all together by the ears,

---

[44] John Walker Ord, *England: An Historical Poem* (London, 1834), vol. i., p. vii and ii. 91–3.

> Ready to settle, with club, fist, or knife
> Who was to tax them . . .[45]

Ord and Moultrie did not, however, attempt to link their arguments to a specific political programme. It was not until the 1840s that such an effort was made by the Young England movement, a small group of earnest young Tories who sought to remind the ruling elite of their traditional obligations. Their leader, Lord John Manners, summarized their blatantly paternalist creed in his poem *England's Trust* (1841). In heroic couplets rife with chivalric sentiment, he calls for a return to the Middle Ages, when

> Each knew his place—king, peasant, peer or priest,
> The greatest owed connexion with the least . . .

True to these words, Manners and his followers attacked those commercial interests who supposedly put profit ahead of humanity, the ambitious and avaricious men who were ruining the nation by exploiting rather than protecting their workers. And the Young Englanders saw in the legend of King Arthur a model for their vision of a new England untainted by such corruption. In 1843 the Young Englander and Tory MP Alexander James Beresford Hope pleaded for Arthur's return in his poem 'A Vision of Babylon':

> O for an hour Arthur to awaken
> High feelings chivalrous, and turn men's minds
> From pelf and politics' engrossing strife,
> To quiet contemplation of old times,—
> And marvelling admiration of the prowess,
> That animated in the days of faith
> Earth's boldest champions to a righteous fight!

Without the proper spirit of high-minded generosity on the part of its ruling elite, Beresford Hope argues, Britain's economic and imperial might means little.[46]

Invocations of the Arthurian legend for political purposes were not limited to members of the Tory party, however, for Whigs too found the Arthurian legend appealing. In 1831 Edward George Earle Lytton Bulwer (known after 1843 as Edward Bulwer Lytton, and after 1866 as

---

[45] John Moultrie, *Poems* (London, 1837), 263.
[46] Mark Girouard, *The Return to Camelot: Chivalry and the English Gentleman* (New Haven and London: Yale UP, 1982), 83; Alexander James Beresford Hope, *Poems* (London, 1843), 15–8.

Baron Lytton of Knebworth) entered the House of Commons, where he quickly joined Lord Durham's radical circle and became an ardent spokesmen for political reform. Bulwer Lytton was no democrat, however. He supported an extension of the franchise because he saw it as a means by which the lower orders could remind their superiors of their fundamental duties. Only such a profound jolt, he believed, could deliver the shock necessary to rouse the ruling elite from its complacency.

This point of view is displayed in Bulwer Lytton's poem 'The Rats and the Mice; A Fable, of the Days of King Arthur', published in the year of his arrival in parliament. Taking advantage of the fact that the Duke of Wellington, the current prime minister, shared his Christian name with the legendary king, he used an Arthurian setting to ridicule Wellington's stalwart opposition to even the most minor of reforms. In his thinly veiled satire of the contemporary political scene, the Rats (the aristocracy) and Mice (the people) join forces in the struggle against the cats (the French during the Napoleonic Wars). Once the cats are defeated, however, their unity is jeopardized by the arrogance of the Rats, who have grown over-fond of the luxuries and comforts which the hard-working Mice provide for them. At first the Mice do not protest against these inequities, but as population growth produces food shortages, hunger leads to discontent. The Mice go to the Senate, where they are appalled to see huge stockpiles of cheese. The Rats, however, are unmoved, and accuse the Mice of being 'base Levellers' who would bring down the government with their petty grievances. Infuriated by the refusal of the Mice to listen to reason, an old Rat, 'in many a war well known', stands up and indignantly replies:

> O idle theorists or rebellious rogues!
> Dupes—dreamers—drivellers—dunces—demagogues—
> Think you the Rats to humbug, and enlist 'em
> Against the glories of the present system.
> What raised this happy nation to its height?
> What brought such phalanxed heroes to the fight?
> What—when our valour won returning ease—
> Heaped all our treasuries with such loads of cheese?
> What made us grow so famous and so fat?
> What fired the nations with the name of Rat?
> What favoured virtue? What subjected vice?
> What—but our mode of representing Mice?

Bulwer Lytton clearly intended this diatribe as a parody of the November 1830 speech in which Wellington avowed his staunch opposition to reform. Cowed, the Mice beat a hasty retreat, protesting meekly as they depart that

> Your reasoning may for Rats indeed suffice;
> But O, great Sir! you quite forget the Mice![47]

Here, Bulwer Lytton is not expressing his support for radicalism. Instead, he attempts to use the threat of revolution to convince the elite that something must be done to ameliorate the condition of the population at large. The upper classes, he asserts, must rediscover their sense of responsibility towards their inferiors, for status brings not only privileges but obligations. This opinion emerged even more prominently later in Bulwer Lytton's career, after he broke with the Whigs in the mid-1840s over the repeal of the Corn Laws. Published in 1849, Bulwer Lytton's epic poem *King Arthur* depicts the famished paupers of the 'Hungry 40s' cowering over their 'fireless hearths . . . all labour-bow'd, with wither'd look'. What is the cause of this misery and degradation? According to Bulwer Lytton, laissez-faire economic practices and the unrestricted operation of the free market are to blame:

> This is the state that the sages most approve;
> This is Man civilized!—the perfect sway
> Of Merchant Kings;—the ripeness of the Art
> Which cheapens men—the Elysium of the Mart.

As in the early 1830s, however, the solution to popular distress lies not in revolution. Bulwer Lytton composed *King Arthur* in the tumultuous years leading up to 1848, when governments across Europe were threatened by disgruntled populations. In particular, he saw Louis Philippe of France as an especially acute example of the danger courted by a ruler who ignored his duties to his people. In *King Arthur* the French leader is represented by the wily despot Ludovick, King of the Vandals, who uses his 'conjurer's skill' to avoid fulfilling the promises he makes. But as Bulwer Lytton hastens to point out, his removal brings no improvement in the lives of the French people, for the attempt of 'King Mob' to install democratic rule only increases the chaos:

---

[47] Edward Bulwer Lytton, *The Siamese Twins. A Satirical Tale of the Times. With Other Poems* (London, 1831), 379–84.

> Poor Vandals, do the towers, when foes assail,
> So idly soar above the level wall?
> Harmonious Order needs its music-scale;
> The Equal were the discord of the All.
> Let the wave undulate, the mountain rise;
> Nor ask from Law what Nature's self denies.[48]

Instead, Bulwer Lytton argues in favor of a strong leader who will listen to and care for his people, a leader much like his King Arthur.

In his novel *The Misfortunes of Elphin* (1834), Thomas Love Peacock also turns to the Arthurian legend to supply a model of benevolent aristocratic leadership. Like 'The Rats and the Mice', *The Misfortunes of Elphin* emerged from the crisis over parliamentary reform. Peacock, too, recognized the dangers posed by the uncompromising inflexibility of the Tory hardliners, and he intended his novel, set in sixth-century Wales, to serve as a warning to the ruling elite. The first four chapters focus upon a devastating flood which inundates the kingdom of Gwaelod, a clear reference to the consequences of a too-staunch opposition to change. The drunkard Seithenyn, the Lord High Commissioner of the embankment that is supposed to protect the kingdom, is a blatant parody of a reactionary nobleman blinded by tradition. 'Decay is one thing,' he declares,

and danger is another. Every thing that is old must decay. That the embankment is old, I am free to confess; that it is somewhat rotten in parts, I will not altogether deny; that it is any worse for that, I do must sturdily gainsay. . . . Our ancestors were wiser than we: they built it in their wisdom; and, if we should be so rash as to try to mend it, we should only mar it. . . . There is nothing so dangerous as innovation.

The rulers who come to power in the generation after the flood— clearly intended by Peacock to represent Britain's current government— learn nothing from the failures of their predecessors. The thuggish Maelgon and the ruthless Melvas are weak men who only seem strong, and the dynasty which they head serves as an allegorical representation of monarchical government by brute force. In their world, might *is* right; the 'powerful' take all they can 'from their subjects and neighbours' and stamp out any sign of 'disaffection'.[49]

---

[48] Edward Bulwer Lytton, *King Arthur* (London, 1848), ii. 17–8, 169, 173.

[49] Marilyn Butler, *Peacock Displayed: A Satirist in His Context* (London, Boston and Henley: Routledge, 1979), 155–82; Thomas Love Peacock, *The Misfortunes of Elphin* (London, 1829), 23, 80–1.

Despite the serious flaws of these rulers, however, Peacock, like Bulwer Lytton, does not advocate revolutionary change. The embankment, symbolizing the existing British constitution, is a positive institution, the preserver of the 'life and human happiness' of Gwaelod. And for his archetype of leadership he looks, like Bulwer Lytton, to King Arthur, who appears at the end of the novel to dispense justice and restore order. A bastion of civilization amid the 'wild solitudes' of untamed rural Wales, Arthur's court functions as the source of all political authority.[50] Thus, Bulwer Lytton and Peacock both choose King Arthur as their model of an ideal ruler, and their attitudes cluster around certain shared assumptions, for both deplore the corrosive effect of modern life and propose a return to a society based on mutual obligations and loyalties between the classes.

In the early 1850s a group of middle-class professionals and clergymen took up the defence of the working man and woman. Led by J. M. Ludlow, F. D. Maurice, Charles Kingsley, Thomas Hughes, and E. V. Neale, this group came to identify itself under the rubric of 'Christian Socialism', although its ideas could not be considered 'socialist' by any conventional definition of the term. Instead, the Christian Socialists saw the solution to the nation's ills as lying in the education and moral regeneration of the working classes, which was to be carried out through a series of co-operative enterprises that would restore traditional feelings of brotherhood and social harmony.[51]

The Christian Socialists had no intention of fundamentally altering the structure of society. On the contrary, they wanted to reinforce what Maurice called the 'primary, eternal' bonds of mutual dependence between ranks. 'If the rich help and defend the poor, and the poor respect and love the rich, and are ready to serve them as far as they can, that parish is a happy one', Charles Kingsley declared in a sermon of 1849. For a model of this system in action, the Christian Socialists turned to the Middle Ages, which they saw, in Kingsley's words, as the home of 'the patriarchal and feudal spirit in which master and servant enjoyed a natural interdependence'. Within this medievalist paradigm, the Christian Socialists saw themselves as crusading knights searching

[50] Peacock, *Misfortune of Elphin*, 14, 103.

[51] See Peter d'A. Jones, *The Christian Socialist Revival, 1877–1914: Religion, Class and Social Conscience in Late-Victorian England* (Princeton: Princeton UP, 1968); Edward Norman, *The Victorian Christian Socialists* (Cambridge: Cambridge UP, 1987); Charles E. Raven, *Christian Socialism, 1848–1854* (London, 1920).

the countryside for wrongs to right. Kingsley referred to himself in 1849 as a 'knight-errant of God', and complained that materialism and commercialism were destroying all that was 'time-honoured, refined, and chivalric in English society'.[52]

And what better source for models of chivalry than the Arthurian legend? To be sure, the Christian Socialists compared themselves explicitly to Arthurian heroes only occasionally, such as when Thomas Hughes described E. V. Neale as a 'Knight of the Round Table'.[53] The legend's influence upon Christian Socialism, however, was pronounced, as is evidenced by the movement's efforts to create a facility in which the working classes could enjoy the benefits of higher education. Founded in 1854, the London Working Men's College ostensibly sought to provide its students with a basic curriculum in an egalitarian atmosphere. Its real intention, however, was to convince educated gentlemen to fulfill their duty to those less fortunate than themselves.

One such person who responded to this summons was Frederick Furnivall, a young barrister who went on to become a noted scholar of medieval literature. During his legal studies Furnivall met the socialist John Malcolm Ludlow, who became his mentor. As a means of combining his devout religious beliefs with his political views, Furnivall turned to Christian Socialism. He threw himself enthusiastically into the activities of the Working Men's College, conducting students on botanical and geological excursions, leading long hikes, and organizing rowing parties, cricket matches, and picnics.[54]

His most important contribution, however, was the teaching of moral values through English literature, and he turned to the Arthurian legend as an ideal vehicle through which to impart his lessons. The story of the quest for the Holy Grail, for example, taught that

not by arms of human strength or worldly make can these glorious gifts be won, but by entire chastity and purity of spirit, soul, and flesh. Surely, a lesson needed by the so-called Christian Chivalry of the twelfth century, rejoicing in its feats of arms, its bravery and pomp, but stained by violence and sin; surely, a lesson needed by the so-called Christian England now, with its pride of birth and place, its money-worship, and the many foul spots on its social life.[55]

---

[52] Norman, *Victorian Christian Socialists*, 17 and 53.

[53] Girouard, *Return to Camelot*, 133.

[54] See William Benzie, *Dr. F. J. Furnivall: Victorian Scholar Adventurer* (Norman, Okla.: Pilgrim, 1983).

[55] Frederick Furnivall (ed.), *La Queste del Saint Graal* (London, 1864), p. iv.

For Furnivall, the Arthurian legend thus functioned as a didactic tool which he used in his efforts to 'improve' the moral conduct of the working classes. He recognized that the legend offered a vision of society whose upper ranks recognized and fulfilled their duties to their inferiors.

Although the Christian Socialists had dispersed by the mid-1850s, their beliefs exerted a powerful influence for the remainder of the nineteenth century. The chivalrous ideal of service they had fostered contributed to the founding of a bevy of missions, clubs, institutes, halls, and societies in impoverished urban areas. Such activities were the product of a strong belief in the idea that the fortunate must do what they could to aid the unfortunate, even if it meant giving up the comforts of a wealthy person's life and the rewards of a more conventional career. These reformers came to embrace a high-minded commitment to leadership with which they sought to reconcile the conflicting interests of the different classes of contemporary society for the good of the whole.[56]

Like the Christian Socialists, these men and women did not advocate democracy. When they invoked the idea of 'community' they envisioned it as based upon hierarchy rather than equality. For them, the term meant a set of vertical relations bound together by obligations and responsibilities that were mutual yet governed by an authority that emanated from the top down. But if their motives were somewhat open to question, their degree of commitment was not. They felt that simple charitable endeavour was inadequate as a remedy for the problems of modern society, for it only served to encourage the wrong sort of dependence. Instead, they saw it as necessary for the reformers to go and live amongst the poor, in order to provide them with exemplars of moral leadership. This belief led to the creation of 'settlements' in some of Britain's most notorious urban neighborhoods. In 1884 the first settlement, Toynbee Hall, was founded in the East End of London, and numerous others followed soon thereafter.[57]

These ardent young reformers saw their actions as explicitly chivalrous and often as explicitly Arthurian. In J. Lockhart Haigh's juvenile novel *Sir Galahad of the Slums* (1907), a young clergyman named Vernon

---

[56] Standish Meacham, *Toynbee Hall and Social Reform 1880–1914: The Search for Community* (New Haven and London: Yale UP, 1987), 2.

[57] Ibid. 3; and K. S. Inglis, *Churches and the Working Classes in Victorian England* (London: Routledge, 1963), ch. 4.

Carruthers is compared to the famous Knight of the Round Table. In the opening scene Carruthers declares that he has decided to take up 'the preaching of His Gospel among the poor as my life-task'.[58] Sent into Liverpool's 'gloomiest and most difficult' area, he at first is disappointed by the lack of response to his efforts, but soon his 'idealism and devotion' win him converts. Only these sorts of efforts, Haigh declares in the conclusion, can hope to make an impact upon the social problems engendered by urban poverty. He thus intended *Sir Galahad of the Slums* to function as a didactic encouragement to young men with university educations to go among the poor and devote themselves to their moral and spiritual improvement.

It was not only zealous young Protestants, however, who saw themselves as modern-day Galahads going out to tilt at the evils created by the squalid conditions of late Victorian slums. In October 1884 a young Roman Catholic botanist named James Britten was walking in London when he noticed that many bookshops specialized in vulgar and venomous attacks on his faith. In response, he established the Catholic Truth Society (CTS), which had four main objectives: 'to spread among Catholics small devotional works'; 'to assist the uneducated poor to a better knowledge of their religion'; 'to spread among Protestants information regarding Catholic faith and practice'; and 'to promote the circulation of good and cheap Catholic literature'.[59] By 1890 the CTS enjoyed the blessing of the Vatican and the co-operation of a large body of priests and laymen.

An integral part of the CTS's mission involved the distribution of information about Catholicism in impoverished urban areas. This required the active participation of lay volunteers, and much of the CTS's propaganda work was directed towards the recruitment of young men for this purpose. And, as in the case of similar Protestant efforts, the legend of Sir Galahad was drafted into service. Amy Mary Grange's *A Modern Galahad*, published by the CTS in 1895, tells the story of Edmund Franklyn, a young Oxford graduate who contemplates an ecclesiastical career in the Church of England. He goes to his local vicar, the symbolically named Arthur Pollack, who recognizes that Edmund is 'just the sort of neophyte for whom his heart yearned . . . [a] Galahad seeking the Sangreal'.[60]

---

[58] J. L. Haigh, *Sir Galahad of the Slums* (London, [1907]), 5.

[59] C. Collingwood, *The Catholic Truth Society* (London: Catholic Truth Society, [1955]), 2.

[60] A. M. Grange, *A Modern Galahad* (London, 1895), 5, 104.

Edmund begins by assisting Pollack in his efforts to help the poor, but he is eager for true 'slum-work' and succeeds in obtaining a post in the 'particularly close, dirty, fusty, smoky, and morally disreputable' London neighborhood of 'Snagwell'. He finds his work extremely rewarding, but soon grows tired of the constant arguments over doctrine among the Anglican clergy. He visits a Catholic religious house, where the calm 'unity and certainty' convinces him to convert. Edmund begins to study for the priesthood, and the novel culminates in his ordination, the 'crowning event' of his life.[61]

Although they represent different denominations, both *Sir Galahad of the Slums* and *A Modern Galahad* invoke the image of an Arthurian knight to encourage young, well-educated men to participate in efforts to assist the urban poor. By elevating their heroes to the status of chivalric crusaders who have a moral and religious duty to help their inferiors, however, these works create awkward barriers between helper and helped and make true social equality impossible. The 'community' they envision has little to do with bridging the gaps between ranks and everything to do with preserving them.

The traditional conservatism and orientation towards the elite which had been displayed by the Arthurian legend from its inception, therefore, continued into the nineteenth century. Now it is time to turn and examine the legend of Robin Hood, in order to trace its evolution in the same period. We have previously seen how two versions of the legend had developed, one featuring a dangerous rebel who wished to overturn the conventional social and political establishment, and the other a much less subversive figure who was more displaced nobleman than true outlaw. In the nineteenth century both versions of Robin Hood survived, and indeed flourished. On the one hand, he was drafted into the standard, conservative version of the past which historians now refer to as the 'Whig interpretation of history', a version which glorified traditional English institutions. On the other, however, Robin Hood retained at least some of his more radical characteristics, and at least on occasion appeared in a subversive guise.

---

[61] Grange 100, 262.

'That senseless spirit of opposition to authority': The Legend of Robin Hood in the Nineteenth Century

A main component of the so-called 'Whig interpretation' of history as it emerged in the nineteenth century was a belief in the superiority of English political institutions. This superiority had been confirmed at certain key moments in the past, when brave heroes had arisen to defend those vaunted institutions. One such moment had occurred in the mid-thirteenth century, when a group of nobles led by Simon de Montfort, Earl of Leicester, revolted against King Henry III. In earlier historical accounts de Montfort had been vilified as a rebel who had challenged the legitimate authority of the British monarchy, but in the early nineteenth century he was reinterpreted as an heroic defender of English liberties who led a valiant—if fruitless—struggle against royal oppression and thereby helped to preserve the power of Parliament, the proud body which ensured the superiority of the British system of governance. In 1840 the historian J. O. Halliwell wrote: 'His was not a contest for the equalization of property, made by one who had nothing to lose, in the hope of being bettered by a revolution; nor was it that senseless spirit of opposition to authority, merely because it is authority, which sometimes arises after a long continued peace; but it was a contest for freedom, for justice, and for natural and reasonable rights'. In *The Barons' War* (1844), William Henry Blaauw took an even more ardently Whiggish approach to de Montfort, declaring that under his guidance 'English freedom rose to so vigorous a manhood, and acquired so confirmed a development, as to enable the spirit of their principles long to survive the downfall of their promoters, and to this day we are enjoying the full maturity of their effects'.[62]

Although the link may not be obvious to a twentieth-century audience, the apotheosis of Simon de Montfort in the nineteenth century had a profound effect upon the legend of Robin Hood. As early as the mid-fifteenth century, the Scottish chronicler Walter Bower had suggested that Robin Hood was one of the dissidents who had joined de Montfort's rebellion. This notion, however, was largely forgotten for almost three centuries, until it was revived in the early Victorian era. In March 1840 a lengthy article appeared in the

---

[62] J. O. Halliwell (ed.), *The Chronicle of William de Rishamger, of the Barons' Wars. The Miracles of Simon de Montfort* (London, 1840), p. xl; William Henry Blaauw, *The Barons' War Including the Battles of Lewes and Evesham* (Lewes, 1844), 3.

Westminster Review tracing de Montfort's career and lamenting his defeat. According to the author, who identified himself only by the initials 'G. F.', the spirit of resistance was not entirely annihilated, for one of de Montfort's followers, a 'Robert Hood', had 'drawn too strong a bow, in too good and old a cause, to be one of the first to lay it down'. He and the handful of survivors who gathered around him 'preferred the unconquered outlaw's life, beset with perils and hardships, and bereft of domestic endearments as it was, to the acceptance of the paltry dole of mercy held out to them by the mean and faithless tyrant'. In this guerrilla fashion Robin Hood continued the fight, thereby claiming a share of de Montfort's reputation as a heroic leader of 'the national cause' and gaining everlasting fame:

> It surely cannot lessen our interest in the fate and fame of the noble-spirited outlaw, to have discovered that he fought in the ranks and shared the proscription of the man to whose comprehensive sagacity and whose expansive heart we are indebted for the birth of that legislative institution, through the progressive modifications of which alone we can hope to enjoy the fortune, yet unexampled among the nations, of eventually emerging from the last stage of feudalism without passing through the horrors and miseries of a social convulsion.[63]

During the 1840s the idea that Robin Hood had been one of de Montfort's followers came to be widely accepted as a likely explanation for the sentence of outlawry which had been passed upon him. According to the Nottinghamshire poet Spencer Hall, 'that his powers were devoted to the side of his country's rights in that memorable movement, which cost its leader his life, while it laid the foundation of a more extensive representation of the people in the legislative assembly ... there cannot be the slightest doubt'.[64] In November 1841 a Sherwood Forest Festival was held in Edwinstowe, Nottinghamshire, as an extension of the activities of the local Mechanics' Institute. The festival was intended to honour 'those worthies who have contributed by their works to the renown' of the region'. Following the dinner on the first evening, one 'Francis Fisher, Esq.' proposed a toast to 'the

---

[63] Stephen Knight, *Robin Hood: A Complete Study of the English Outlaw* (Oxford and Cambridge, Mass.: Blackwell, 1994), 36; *Westminster Review,* 33 (1839–40), 439, 441–2, 443, 490–1.

[64] Spencer T. Hall, *The Forester's Offering* (London, 1841), 33–4. For later exponents of this theory, see *The Life and Exploits of Robin Hood: and Robin Hood's Garland* (Halifax, 1862), 35; William Wood, *Tales and Traditions of the High Peak (Derbyshire)* (London and Derby, [1862]), 148; William Andrews (ed.), *The Derbyshire Gatherer of Archaeological, Historical, Biographical Facts, Folklore, Etc.* (Buxton, 1880), 6.

eternal renown of Robin Hood', and observed that 'whatever might be the character of those tales which fabulists and romancers in modern times chose to found on the great hero's name, history proved him to have been one of those noble patriots who rose with the Barons under Simon de Montfort in defence of that deathless germ of English liberty, Magna Charta'. This theory was so pervasive that even the radical Tory novelist G. P. R. James accepted it, suggesting that the 'Whig interpretation' of history was endorsed not only by Whigs. In *Forest Days* (1843), James depicts Robin Hood as 'an English yeoman, of a very superior mind . . . outlawed, in all probability, for his adherence to the popular party of the day, and taking a share in the important struggle between the weak and tyrannical, though accomplished, Henry III, and that great and extraordinary leader, Simon de Montfort, Earl of Leicester'.[65]

Here, then, we have Robin Hood defending traditional English institutions. This is not the only guise in which he appeared in the nineteenth century, however, for he also frequently donned a more radical costume. In one early-nineteenth-century outburst of Luddite activity in Nottinghamshire, for example, a public notice signed by 'General Lund's [*sic*] Office, Sherwood Forest' was posted, suggesting that the leaders of the uprising identified with Robin Hood.[66] It was rare, however, for the legend to be tied into radical politics so explicitly. The Chartists, for example, never made reference to his legend. Instead, Robin Hood functioned as a vehicle for the expression of a less focused sort of popular radicalism which incorporated much rhetoric about the rights and liberties of the people without attempting in any substantive way to define what those rights and liberties were.

The outlaw hero who functioned as a heroic embodiment of freedom and independence was a popular motif in early nineteenth-century popular literature. The outlaw represented a way in which conventional social and political hierarchies could be inverted so that the low would be high and the high low, a theme which, judging from the frequency of its appearance, possessed a strong appeal.[67] In ballads

[65] Spencer T. Hall, *Rambles in the Country* (London, 1842), 147, 153; G. P. R. James, *Forest Days: A Romance of Old Times* (London, 1843), vol. i, p. vi.

[66] I am grateful to Mr Adrian Henstock, Principal Archivist, Nottinghamshire Archives and Southwell Diocesan Record Office, for this information.

[67] Peter Linebaugh, *The London Hanged: Crime and Civil Society in the Eighteenth Century* (London and New York: Penguin, 1991), 189; Patrick Joyce, *Visions of the People: Industrial England and the Question of Class 1848–1914* (Cambridge: Cambridge UP, 1991), 254.

and chapbooks it was most commonly displayed in scenes in which the reigning monarch goes among the people in disguise and unrecognized. In *The Celebrated History of the Renowned Robin Hood, the Merry Outlaw of Sherwood Forest*, a chapbook printed in Glasgow in 1830, King Richard I disguises himself as a monk and goes to Sherwood Forest in search of the famous outlaw. He is captured by the Merry Men, but when he declares that he is travelling on the king's business, Robin Hood immediately releases him, exclaiming 'God save him! and confound all his enemies!' He invites Richard to dinner, during which the king asks: 'Now, my brave fellow, if I were to procure your pardon and that of your men, would you turn faithful and useful subjects?' This being Robin Hood's 'first wish', he unhesitatingly agrees. At this moment Richard throws off his monk's cloak and reveals himself. The outlaws kneel reverently before him, and the king duly pardons them for their 'past offences'.[68] This scene contains all the classic elements of social inversion. At the outset, the king moves freely among his people and communes with them as their equal. In the process he learns of their true loyalty and love for him, and so, when the normal order is re-established with the king safely back on his throne, he is able to reward them and right their wrongs.

In many nineteenth-century popular ballads and chapbooks this reversal of high and low was often expressed as a more specific inversion of rich and poor. The poor, whose honest toil is presented as the root of a properly functioning society, are treated as the moral superiors of the idle rich. Once again this motif resonates with the traditional themes of the legend of Robin Hood, in which the notion of 'robbing from the rich to give to the poor' plays a central role. Robin Hood's programme of wealth redistribution is treated as an act of moral heroism and an effort to correct unjust socio-economic imbalances. Robin Hood is the friend of the destitute, who pray 'for his prosperity and long life, because if he met any of them, he would not only refrain from injuring or robbing them, but gave them money; nay, wheresoever he heard any were sick or in want, he was sure to send his succour and assistance to relieve them in their necessitous circumstances'. His enemies are their enemies: 'He never loved to rob any

---

[68] *The Celebrated History of the Renowned Robin Hood, the Merry Outlaw of Sherwood Forest* (Glasgow, [1830]), 20–1.

body but people that were very rich, and that had not the spirit to make good use of their riches'.[69]

In the nineteenth century the popular ballads and chapbooks featuring the legend of Robin Hood thus emphasized populist values which appealed to working people. At the legend's core were basic aspirations virtually identical to their own—justice, equality, and above all, independence. Not surprisingly, then, it is possible to detect its presence in some of the efforts working people made to realize these aspirations.

On 3 November 1841 a 'Sherwood Gathering' was held at Edwinstowe, a small village in Nottinghamshire, to celebrate the success of the local Mechanics' Institute. A proud group of nearly a hundred 'farmers, artisans, woodmen, and agricultural labourers' gathered in the Birkland and Bilagh Lodge Room, where they sat down to a hearty meal. Afterwards, Christopher Thomson, the Institute's founder, declared that 'thanks to the spread of information, the sun of intellectuality no longer shines upon the College and Boarding-school alone, but throws her refulgent rays upon the sequestered village, the peering hamlet, and, indeed, into every nook and cranny of our island'.[70] Thomson made it clear that these improvements were due to the efforts made by working people on their own behalf, and not by initiatives on the part of the upper classes. Virtually every sentence of this speech met with enthusiastic cheers and shouts of 'Hear, hear!' from the audience.

Hovering over Thompson's words was the spirit of Robin Hood. After Thompson sat down, the chairman proposed a toast to 'the eternal renown of Robin Hood . . . a brave, kind, warm-hearted man, and a constant friend to the poor and distressed'. The group then sang a song composed by the local poet Spencer T. Hall especially for the occasion:

> Methinks I see him standing now in dignity and pride,
> With Little John, his faithful friend and servant, by his side,

---

[69] Joyce, *Visions*, 368–9; *The Extraordinary Life and Adventures of Robin Hood, Captain of the Robbers of Sherwood Forest* (London, [1810?]), 8; *The History of Robin Hood* (London, [1816]), 10.

[70] Ian Inkster, 'Introduction: The Context of Steam Intellect in Britain (to 1851)', in Inkster (ed.), *The Steam Intellect Societies, Nottingham Studies in the History of Adult Education* (Nottingham: Department of Adult Education, University of Nottingham, 1985), 9; Hall, *Rambles*, 149–50.

> Contriving how some slave to free, some tyrant how to chide,
> Like a fine old English Patriot, the glory of all time![71]

Clearly, Hall believed that the legend embodied the same values of freedom and independence which the Mechanics' Institute was attempting to instill in local working people.

This connection was made even more explicitly in the second 'Sherwood Gathering', which took place in July 1842. This time the festivities were held in a tent erected 'within sight of the majestic oaks of old Sherwood'; inside, it was decorated with boughs of oak, birch, ivy, and other greenery in an attempt to create a forest-like atmosphere. The attendees drank a toast to the 'memory and eternal renown of Robin Hood', and a poem by Elizabeth Sheridan Carey explicitly compared the working people present at the gathering to the famous outlaws of old:

> Not e'vn the 'gath'ring' in the blithe greenwood,
> Of him—that prince of archers—Robin Hood
> And his brave knot of Sherwood-men
> (Whose peers these glades shall never greet again!) . . .
> Not these were more inspiring sights to see
> Than Edwinstowe, of late beheld in thee![72]

The Edwinstowe Mechanics' Institute thus represents one instance in which the legend of Robin Hood was linked to the efforts of working people to gain some degree of independence. Were there other, similar instances? In order to answer this question we must turn to another form of working-class self-help in the nineteenth-century, the friendly society. Friendly societies were mutual benefit clubs which provided working people with a modest amount of health and life insurance in return for a small annual contribution. One of the most widespread social institutions in Victorian Britain, they boasted over 4 million members by 1891.[73]

There were two types of friendly society: small, local, independent clubs and affiliated orders, which were comprised of a national organization with local branches. One of the largest affiliated orders was the Ancient Order of Foresters, which had over half a million members

---

[71] Hall, *Rambles*, 153.

[72] Christopher Thomson, *The Autobiography of an Artisan* (London, 1847), 360, 367.

[73] The classic studies of the history of friendly societies are P. H. J. H. Gosden, *The Friendly Societies in England, 1815–1875* (Manchester: Manchester UP, 1961), and his *Self-Help: Voluntary Associations in the Nineteenth Century* (London: B. T. Batsford, 1973).

in the early 1880s.[74] Given its name, which was derived from a
shadowy, quasi-Jacobite eighteenth-century secret society called the
Royal Foresters, it is not surprising that the organization made considerable use of Robin Hood in its initiation rituals and public cere-
monies. His portrait featured prominently on the club's emblems, and
characters from the legend made regular appearances on the
'tableaux' which the Foresters used in their processions.[75] Why was
the legend so attractive to them? The Foresters turned to the legend
because it represented ideals of community and the independence of
working people, ideals which the friendly societies attempted to
embody. According to the *General Laws for the Government of the Ancient
Order of Foresters* (1846): 'a good Forester is a man, who jealous of his
rights as a citizen, maintains them in a temperate, manly, and decorous
manner; at the same time he knows his duties too, performs them well,
and pays a ready and willing obedience to his country's laws; neither
cringing or servile on one hand, nor wild and factious on the other'.[76]

The emphasis which this and other statements from the official
publications of the Foresters place upon duty and decorum has led
some historians to argue that the friendly societies were complicit in
the attempts made by the Victorian middle classes to impose their
values upon the working population.[77] They claim that friendly societies accepted middle-class notions of 'respectability' and encouraged
their members to embrace principles such as thrift, prudence, and
moral probity. Despite their superficial commitment to bourgeois
values, however, the friendly societies by no means abandoned their
quest for genuine independence of a sort very different from the 'self-
help' variety advocated by the middle classes. A recent study shows
how they resisted the 'coercive power' of the middle-class discourse of
respectability by offering alternative definitions and appropriating

---

[74] For the history of the Ancient Order of Foresters, see Walter G. Cooper, *The Ancient
Order of Foresters Friendly Society 150 Years: 1834–1984* (Southampton: Executive Council of
the Ancient Order of Foresters Friendly Society, 1984).

[75] I owe this information to Dr Martin Gorsky. Dr Gorsky is the only historian to have
considered the significance of the Foresters' use of the legend of Robin Hood.

[76] *General Laws for the Government of the Ancient Order of Foresters* (Manchester, 1846), 6.

[77] See e.g. Geoffrey Best, *Mid-Victorian Britain, 851–1870*, new edn. (Glasgow: Collins,
1982), 282–4. In recent years, however, historians have acknowledged that Victorian
notions of respectability were more a source of contention than consensus, as they
changed drastically according to the context in which they were used. See Geoffrey
Crossick, 'The Labour Aristocracy and Its Values: A Study of Mid-Victorian Kentish
London', *Victorian Studies*, 19 (1976), 306–20; Neville Kirk, *The Growth of Working-Class
Reformism in Mid-Victorian Britain* (Urbana, Ill.: University of Illinois Press, 1985), 220–2.

some of its key concepts for their own, class-specific ends.[78] It was this spirit of independence which the Foresters recognized in the legend of Robin Hood.

In both the case of the Edwinstowe Mechanics' Institute and the Ancient Order of Foresters, the legend of Robin Hood thus functioned as a symbolic representation of the desire of working people for independence. The traditional themes of the legend were easily adapted for this purpose. A plebeian hero who robbed from the rich and gave to the poor, Robin Hood served as an ideal model for those who wished to see the nation's social and economic imbalances adjusted along more equitable lines, while his forest commonwealth provided a political model through which this adjustment could be carried out. Instead of deference and obedience, life in the greenwood offered democratic choice and the opportunity for ordinary men and women to govern themselves.

[78] Trygve R. Tholfsen, *Working-Class Radicalism in Mid-Victorian England* (London: Croom Helm, 1976), 288; Simon Cordery, 'Friendly Societies and the Discourse of Respectability in Britain, 1825–1875', *Journal of British Studies*, 34 (1995), 41.

CHAPTER THREE

'The love of our own language': The Legends of King Arthur and Robin Hood and the Rise of English Studies

LANGUAGE IS often mentioned as a key element in definitions of nationhood, for it would seem to be essential in distinguishing one group from another. Ignorance of another's speech constitutes the most obvious bar to communication, and thus serves as the simplest determinant of divisions between disparate peoples. But do linguistic barriers truly function to separate nations? Languages consist of a complex of local variants or dialects, some of which may be utterly incomprehensible to speakers from outside each other's regions. Until very recently there were no truly 'national' languages which extended across these dialectal boundaries, for it was not until the emergence of general primary education that this became possible. But the establishment of such an educational system presupposes the existence of a sufficiently large political entity to institute and maintain it, and the only entity of such magnitude is the modern nation-state. In the vast majority of cases, the 'national language' is thus far younger than the nation itself.[1]

We should not, however, entirely discount the contribution of language to the construction of national identity because that contribution occurs after the nation is in existence rather than before. To be sure, what Eric Hobsbawm has termed 'the mystical identification of nationality with a sort of platonic idea of the language' may be an 'ideological construction', but this does not entirely preclude its significance.[2] For there may still be a strong cultural identification with a particular language, even if the language in question is an arbitrary selection. Once a language is accepted as 'standard', it acquires a fixity

---

[1] Ernest Gellner, *Nations and Nationalism* (Ithaca, NY: Cornell UP, 1983), 35–7; E. J. Hobsbawm, *Nations and Nationalism Since 1780: Programme, Myth, Reality*, 2nd edn. (Cambridge: Cambridge UP, 1992) 54.   [2] Hobsbawm, *Nations and Nationalism*, 57.

and sense of longevity which make it appear far more 'eternal' than it truly is, and it thereby becomes well-positioned to serve as a totem of national identity.

Indeed, in virtually all nineteenth-century European nationalist movements, what Benedict Anderson has labelled 'national print-languages' were of central importance. According to Anderson, the comparative study of languages made possible a new patriotic pride in vernaculars which had previously been regarded as far inferior to Greek and Latin. The emergence of philology as an important academic discipline allowed a 'motley plebeian crowd of vernacular rivals' to share an equal ontological footing with their classical brethren, for now they, too, were worthy of study and admiration. These scholarly efforts were reinforced by a simultaneous growth in literacy and developments in the spheres of industry, commerce, and communications which created powerful new forces promoting linguistic unification, all of which allowed these new vernacular 'languages-of-state' to assume even greater status.[3]

At this point it became desirable and even necessary for the communities which had elevated a particular vernacular to the status of a 'national language' to create and cultivate myths and genealogies concerning that language's origin and development. It was thus through artifice that language and nationality came to be linked. One way in which this linkage was forged was through the establishment of a national literature. The elevation of certain texts to canonical status— texts which were selected not only on the basis of their literary merit, but also because of their ostensible contribution to the development of the national culture—was a crucial element in the sanction of a particular language as the 'official' vernacular of a nation.

'Heroic and patriotic example': Medieval Literary Texts and the Rise of English Studies in the Nineteenth Century

Any attempt to trace the valorization of English as a literary language must begin at the dawn of English nationalism in the sixteenth century. In this period the commitment to the idea of the nation was expressed with great vigour in secular literature, as a whole new class of authors

---

[3] See Benedict Anderson, *Imagined Communities: Reflections on the Origin and Spread of Nationalism*, rev. edn. (New York and London: Verso, 1991), ch. 5.

and scholars arose whose main preoccupation was to write about England in English. More specifically, they celebrated their nation's literary past by praising the 'old masters' such as Chaucer, and they celebrated their nation's literary present by proclaiming the virtues of Thomas More, Philip Sidney, and Edmund Spenser.[4]

Accompanying the rise of this Anglocentric literary nationalism was an attempt to elevate the English language above all others. English, according to numerous Tudor commentators, was inherently superior to its continental counterparts, which had previously been regarded as the standards of linguistic excellence. The elevation of English not only required the diminution of continental European languages, however, but also the destruction, or at least attempted destruction, of the other languages of the British Isles. Celtic languages were brutally suppressed by Tudor and early Stuart governments, who saw linguistic uniformity as a necessary corollary to their efforts to impose their authority upon the peripheral regions of the British Isles. The Act of Union with Wales (1536), for example, decreed that all government and legal business would henceforth be conducted in English, which led inevitably to the decline of Welsh, at least among those desiring social and occupational advancement. The following year, the 'Act for the English Order, Habit, and Language' was passed for Ireland; it demanded that all Irish people, 'to the utmost of their power, cunning, and knowledge, shall use and speake commonly the English Tongue and Language'. Similar legislation was enacted in Scotland, though not until the early seventeenth century. There, the chief aim of the Act for the Settling of Parochial Schools (1616) was 'that the vulgar Inglishe toung be universallie plantit, and the Irishe language, whilk is one of the cheif and principall causes of the continewance of barbaritie and incivilities amongis the inhabitantis of the Ilis and Heylandis, may be abolisheit and removeit'.[5]

The elevation of the English language and its literature continued over the next two centuries. As rising cultural nationalism further diminished uncritical acceptance of the dominance of the classics,

---

[4] See Richard Helgerson, *Forms of Nationhood: The Elizabethan Writing of England* (Chicago and London: University of Chicago Press, 1992); Andrew Hadfield, *Literature, Politics and National Identity: Reformation to Renaissance* (Cambridge: Cambridge UP, 1994).

[5] Liah Greenfeld, *Nationalism: Five Roads to Modernity* (Cambridge, Mass.: Harvard UP, 1992), 69; Victor Edward Durkacz, *The Decline of the Celtic Languages: A Study of Linguistic and Cultural Conflict in Scotland, Wales and Ireland from the Reformation to the Twentieth Century* (Edinburgh: John Donald, 1983), 1–5.

native achievements came to be regarded as the equal of or even superior to their ancient predecessors. In order for the nation's cultural achievements to be recognized, the English needed to acknowledge the limits of the Greeks and Romans, for classical culture was 'an inadequate model for a modern nation seeking its own civilization'. In its place was required the 'creation of a modern [English] canon that, national pride insisted, was the equal of any nation's past and the qualitative victor over any nation's future'. The most obvious beneficiary of this turn towards native literature was Shakespeare, whose reputation rose to new heights in the era of the Seven Years War, an important period in promoting resistance to the domination of foreign influences over English culture.[6] Other authors inducted into the new English literary pantheon included Chaucer, Spenser, and Milton. Nor was English accomplishment limited to the past, as contemporary writers such as Dryden and Pope were compared to—and even elevated above—their Greek and Roman counterparts. And if these authors were highly regarded, then so was the language in which they wrote. English, numerous eighteenth-century commentators asserted, was at least the equal, if not the superior, of classical tongues. According to Henry Felton in his *Dissertation on Reading the Classics* (1713): 'Our English of all Modern Languages that have been cultivated, is upon Experience and Comparison justly thought most capable of all the Beauty, Strength, and Significancy of Greek and Latin'.[7]

In the eighteenth century, however, praise of English did not always have as its flip-side denigration of Celtic languages and literatures as it had in the sixteenth. On the contrary, the second half of the century saw a growing Celtomania which generated considerable acclaim for the cultural achievements of the peripheral regions of the British Isles. This Celtomania was the product of several overlapping factors, including the broadening of antiquarian research to include non-classical civilizations and the ending of the Jacobite threat at Culloden in 1745. Most significantly, however, it stemmed from a general European phenomenon, the rise of 'primitivism'. Appearing first in the writings of Jean-Jacques Rousseau, the celebration of autochthonous cultures which were perceived as free from the over-sophisticated artificiality of the modern world gradually broadened into a flood of

---

[6] Howard D. Weinbrot, *Britannia's Issue: The Rise of British Literature from Dryden to Ossian* (Cambridge: Cambridge UP, 1993), 3–6; Michael Dobson, *The Making of the National Poet: Shakespeare, Adaptation and Authorship, 1660–1769* (Cambridge: Cambridge UP, 1992).

[7] Weinbrot, *Britannia's Issue*, 75.

interest and enthusiasm for the innocent, uncorrupted, and uncivilized. In this context, the ancient Celtic inhabitants of the British Isles became a subject worthy of consideration and even admiration.[8] What had previously been a source of embarrassment was now a source of patriotic pride, as contemporary Britons boasted of—rather than apologized for—the primitive simplicity of their ancestors.

Celtomania had a profound impact on the status of Celtic culture in Britain. In the late eighteenth and early nineteenth centuries the Celts were widely regarded as having imparted a healthy dose of energy to British culture, and England was seen as having profited from the alliance of its national literature with its Celtic counterparts. In their *Prospectus and Specimen of an Intended National Work . . . Intended to Comprise the Most Interesting Particulars Relating to King Arthur and the Round Table* (1818), William and Robert Whistlecraft contrasted what they saw as the robust simplicity of Celtic culture to the stiffness and over-sophistication of the classics:

> The Muses serv'd those Heathens well enough—
> Bold Briton take a Tankard or a bottle,
> And when the bottle's out, a pinch of snuff,
> And so proceed in spite of Aristotle—
> Those rules of his are dry, dogmatic stuff,
> All life and fire they suffocate and throttle—
> And therefore I adopt the mode I mention,
> Trusting to native judgment and invention.

And this burst of Celtomania included a reassessment of Celtic languages, which were no longer condemned as the tongues of a barbaric people but rather given pride of place as having made a major contribution to the development of English. In *The Philosophy of Words* (1769), Rowland Jones proclaimed that 'we can afford to abolish three fourths of our vocables; retaining only those of our own original CELTIC growth, which far exceed those of the Greeks and Romans, as its natural and original expressions'.[9]

This new regard for Celtic culture parallels the more general rise described previously of a truly *British* nationalism in the eighteenth

[8] Samuel Smiles, *The Image of Antiquity: Ancient Britain and the Romantic Imagination* (New Haven: Yale UP, 1994), 16.

[9] William and Robert Whistlecraft, *Prospectus and Specimen of an Intended National Work . . . Intended to Comprise the Most Interesting Particulars Relating to King Arthur and the Round Table*, 2nd edn. (London, 1818), 26; Weinbrot, *Britannia's Issue*, 481.

century. As Britain was being forged into a nation, the literary and linguistic accomplishments of all parts of the realm came to be recognized. The nineteenth century, however, saw this new emphasis upon British literary achievement discarded in favour of a retreat towards English culture. This process represented another example of the shift toward a specifically *English* nationalism and away from the British variety which prevailed earlier. And if this shift is to be understood fully, it must be considered in the light of the emergence of the study of English as a major academic discipline. Before 1800, when the term 'English' was used in relation to education it signified only one among a motley group of modern languages perceived as far inferior to their classical counterparts.[10] From grammar school to university, students focused upon the close scrutiny of Greek and Latin texts, pursuing an extremely circumscribed curriculum with no place for the study of the vernacular.[11]

Ironically, much of the impetus for the development of English studies came from the European continent, and in particular from Germany, where in the final decades of the eighteenth century philologists such as Friedrich von Schlegel and Franz Bopp began using vernacular languages to trace the origins of civilizations. Inspired by these efforts, English scholars also came to recognize the importance of the study of their native tongue for tracing the roots of their nation and its culture. Accordingly, academic attitudes towards the study of English began to change. In 1828 the Revd Thomas Dale's appointment as Professor of English Language and Literature at University College, London, marked the first creation of a professorship dedicated to the study of English, and many provincial universities established similar posts in subsequent decades.[12] At Oxford and Cambridge, the 'ancients' who wished to preserve the traditional system of instruction in the classics managed to prevail until the end of the nineteenth century, but eventually even those stalwarts were forced to give way. In 1890 English was separated from other languages in the new Cambridge

---

[10] Brian Doyle, 'The Invention of English', in Robert Colls and Philip Dodd (eds.), *Englishness: Politics and Culture 1880–1920* (London, Sydney and Dover, NH: Croom Helm, 1986), 92. Doyle has developed these arguments more fully in his *English and Englishness* (London and New York: Routledge, 1989), 17–40.

[11] See D. J. Palmer, *The Rise of English Studies: An Account of the Study of English Language and Literature From Its Origins to the Making of the Oxford English School* (London, New York and Toronto: Oxford UP, 1965), ch. 1.

[12] See Franklin E. Court, 'The Social and Historical Significance of the First English Literature Professorship in England', *PMLA* 103 (1988), 796–807; Palmer, *Rise of English Studies*, 56–64.

Tripos regulations, and four years later Oxford established the English School. By the end of the nineteenth century the majority of educators had come to see English as a key component of the modern curriculum.

The rise of English studies was, as Stefan Collini has argued, part of a 'wider process of national self-definition'.[13] Throughout Europe in the nineteenth century nation-builders turned to vernacular languages and literatures, and the activities of lexicographers, grammarians, and philologists were central to the shaping of contemporary nationalisms. And England was far from immune to this trend. Projects such as the creation of what was to become the *Oxford English Dictionary* in many ways derived from the same nationalistic impulses as did similar efforts on the European continent.

Given this general context, it is not surprising that the study of the English language became heavily invested with patriotic sentiment. In particular, the language was praised for its continuity, which was thought to parallel the continuity of English political and legal institutions. In his children's story *When Lion Heart was King* (1908), Escott Lynn declared that 'it cannot be too often asserted that this manly, forceful English which we speak to-day comes down to us directly from the days of Alfred the Great'.[14] This sense in turn produced a demand for texts from the nation's glorious literary past so that this continuity could be demonstrated. Accordingly, medieval English literature began to receive an unprecedented degree of attention. The nineteenth century saw the discovery, rediscovery, and dissemination of numerous previously obscure manuscripts, which were unearthed from the dusty libraries where they had languished, virtually ignored, for centuries. Inevitably, this development affected the fortunes of the legends of King Arthur and Robin Hood, for a considerable proportion of the deluge of medieval texts that issued from contemporary presses contained tales of their adventures and exploits.

The growing appreciation of medieval literature was reflected in the increasingly professional way in which it was prepared for publication. Previously the editors of medieval manuscripts had almost all been amateurs, but by the mid-nineteenth century specialists had largely taken over the field. Sir Frederic Madden, for example, dedicated his

---

[13] Stefan Collini, *Public Moralists: Political Thought and Intellectual Life in Britain 1850–1930* (Oxford: Clarendon, 1991), 347.

[14] Escott Lynn, *When Lion Heart Was King: A Tale of Robin Hood and Merry Sherwood* (London, 1908), 5–6.

life to the discovery and publication of Arthurian texts. His greatest achievements, an anthology of medieval literature related to the Gawain legend published in 1839 and an edition of Layamon's *Brut* published in 1847, resulted from decades of intense labour. In contrast to the fragmentary and error-riddled 'Selections', 'Specimens', and 'Remains' produced by the previous generation of medieval literary scholars, Madden offered complete, impeccable manuscript transcriptions with extensive commentaries, notes, and glossaries.[15]

The legend of Robin Hood, too, benefited from the professionalization of medieval literary studies, beginning with the publication of Joseph Ritson's *Robin Hood* in 1795. Forever ferreting out new information, Ritson displayed impressive diligence. His efforts were remarkably successful: only five texts have subsequently been added to the thirty-three he gathered. But Ritson was too concerned with using the outlaw legend to put forth his own radical political opinions to establish a new academic standard for the study of early Robin Hood literature. That task was left to later editors such as John Matthew Gutch, whose *A Lytell Geste of Robin Hode with other Ancient and Modern Ballads* (1847) attempted to correct the errors of its predecessors while offering a comprehensive and accurate version of the texts. Gutch's important and influential collection served to familiarize many nineteenth-century Englishmen and women with the original Robin Hood ballads.[16]

Increased professionalization of editorship did not mean, however, that the audience for medieval literature was limited to specialists. To be sure, in the first half of the nineteenth century medieval literature was published almost exclusively by learned societies comprised of wealthy book-collecting enthusiasts. These learned societies did not attempt—or desire—to supply books to the general public. The approach of the Roxburghe Club, founded in 1812, was typical. Each member was responsible for furnishing reprints of 'some rare old tract, or composition' to the rest of the club, a policy which resulted in editions of less than fifty copies.[17]

---

[15] See Gretchen P. Ackerman, 'Sir Frederic Madden and Arthurian Scholarship', in Valerie M. Lagorio and Mildred Leake Day (eds.), *King Arthur Through the Ages* (New York: Garland, 1990), ii. 27–38.

[16] Joseph Ritson, *Robin Hood: A Collection of Poems, Songs and Ballads Relative to that Celebrated English Outlaw* (London, 1795); John Matthew Gutch, *A Lytell Geste of Robin Hode with other Ancient and Modern Ballads and Songs Relating to this Celebrated Yeoman* (London, 1847).

[17] See Clive Bigham, *The Roxburghe Club: Its History and Its Members 1812–1927* (Oxford: Oxford UP, 1928).

By the mid-nineteenth century, however, there was a trend towards making medieval literature available to a wider audience. There were various ways by which editors attempted to accomplish this. Price was obviously an important consideration; by the 1850s Ritson's *Robin Hood* could be purchased for a mere shilling. In addition, illustrators could be hired to provide visual representations of a text's more exciting events, or the editor could append helpful aids such as glossaries and explanatory notes to assist readers who were unfamiliar with the narrative.

Sometimes, however, even these expedients were insufficient. For many readers, medieval texts were simply too long and repetitive, and so publishers issued a variety of abridgments and adaptations, omitting redundancies and emphasizing the parts of the narrative most likely to awaken interest. A perfect example of this strategy was *The Life and Exploits of Robin Hood* (1862), a ballad collection which, according to the editor, was 'not intended for the critic or the antiquary, but for that large proportion of the reading public who have no leisure, and but little inclination, for recondite discussions'. Accordingly, the ballads were not printed in their 'original form, full of quaint phrases and obsolete words', but rather were 'clothed in modern language'. In addition, a glossary was provided 'for the benefit of those readers who have little, if any, acquaintance with the older dialects of our language'.[18]

Even the formerly exclusive learned societies got into the act, as a new generation of printing clubs began to issue medieval works in far larger numbers than had their predecessors. The Camden Society, founded in 1838, was the largest of these clubs, issuing editions which frequently exceeded a thousand copies.[19] More specifically concerned with the publication of Arthurian texts was the Early English Text Society (EETS), founded in 1864 by Dr Frederick J. Furnivall, one of the most tenacious, industrious, and enthusiastic Victorian scholars of medieval literature, whose Christian Socialist activities were described in the previous chapter. Although the EETS was established primarily to provide linguistic evidence from reliably edited early English material in order to assist in the preparation of what ultimately became

---

[18] *The Life and Exploits of Robin Hood; and Robin Hood's Garland* (Halifax, 1862), pp. x, 33.
[19] Two of its publications contained Arthurian material: John Robson's *Three Early English Metrical Romances* (1842), which included 'The Awntyrs of Arthure at the Tarne Wathelynne' and 'The Avowynge of King Arther, Sir Gawan, Sir Kaye, and Sir Bawdewyn of Bretan', and J. O. Halliwell's *The Thornton Romances* (1844), which featured 'Perceval'.

the *Oxford English Dictionary*, Furnivall felt that its 'chief object' of the EETS was the printing 'in accessible form of all the English Romances relating to Arthur and his Knights'. Although its original twenty-two subscribers featured some of the most prominent members of the Victorian intelligentsia, including Alfred, Lord Tennyson and John Ruskin, its objectives were from the outset thoroughly democratic, and its membership fee of only £1 per year made participation possible for the middle classes. By 1865 the EETS had over 250 subscribers, and thousands more enjoyed the cheaply priced texts it produced. That same year the *Gentleman's Magazine* congratulated Furnivall for his efforts, declaring that 'we hail the appearance of these publications . . . with pleasure and much approval, arising . . . from the fact that such Texts are made more generally available to the public'.[20]

By the middle of the nineteenth century medieval literature was clearly being read by more than just scholars and eccentric enthusiasts for the days of chivalry. The publication history of the romance *Sir Gawain and the Green Knight* provides an excellent case in point. Madden's edition of 1839, though undeniably accomplished in scholarly terms, appeared in a large, expensive format, and was printed in extremely limited quantities for exclusive circulation among the members of the Bannatyne Club. In 1864 Richard Morris edited *Sir Gawain and the Green Knight* for the EETS; the resulting volume, while far less elaborate than Madden's, cost only ten shillings and was issued in far larger numbers. Morris also appended sidenotes 'to enable the reader to follow with some degree of ease the author's pleasant narrative of Sir Gawayne's adventures'. He preserved the original Middle English, but included a summary in modern English as well as an extensive glossary.[21] Even more catholic in its appeal, however, was Jessie Weston's 1898 edition of *Sir Gawain*. Weston dispensed entirely with the original Middle English in favor of a prose translation into modern English. 'It is the real difficulty and obscurity of the language,' she avowed, 'which in

---

[20] William Benzie, *Dr. F. J. Furnivall: Victorian Scholar Adventurer* (Norman, Okla.: Pilgrim, 1983); F. J. Furnivall, preface to *Le Morte Darthur* (London and Cambridge, 1864), p. xxv; *Gentleman's Magazine*, ns 18 (1865), 227-8.

[21] Richard Morris (ed.), *Sir Gawayne and the Green Knight: An Alliterative Romance-Poem* (London, 1864), p. v. Morris's efforts to render the poem more accessible were at least partially successful. On 30 July 1866 Furnivall wrote to William Carew Hazlitt, encouraging him to join the EETS in order to secure one of the editions, which were dwindling rapidly: 'All the Gawains are sure to be gone, and if you don't join us soon, you'll not be able to buy a copy'. British Library, Add MS 38899, fos. 69-70.

spite of careful and scholarly editing will always place the poem in its
original form outside the range of any but professed students of
medieval literature, which has encouraged me to make an attempt
to render it more accessible to the general public, by giving it a form
that shall be easily intelligible'.[22]

From what source flowed this new concern to democratize medieval
literature? Doubtless the influence of the profit motive should not be
underestimated; nineteenth-century editors and publishers were certainly eager to capitalize upon the contemporary predilection for all
things medieval. They were also responding to demands from the
professional sector of English society, for by the 1870s nearly all exam-
inations for the civil service, armed forces, and professions included
English as a subject, and many editions of medieval texts were specifically intended for prospective test-takers. In addition, however, many
editors and publishers felt that a broad audience should experience the
moral and intellectual benefits of reading early English literature. 'It is
literature', proclaimed Thomas Dale in the 1830s, 'which prepares us
best of all for the examination of those moral truths which are not only
the worthiest exercise of our reason, but most concern our future
destiny'.[23]

These 'moral truths' were believed to be vested in the legends of
King Arthur and Robin Hood, both of which were utilized to impart
lessons intended to improve the conduct of their readers. 'The growing popularity of the Arthur story is surely a wholesome sign of the
times . . .,' wrote J. T. Knowles in his adaptation of Malory's *Morte
d'Arthur*, published in 1862. 'Whatever else it may mean, it is pleasant
to think of it as meaning an increasing protest . . . against the low
and selfish side of a too commercial life. Unselfish chivalrous devotion,—the constant and courageous sense of duty and of God,—a high
disdain of all things churlish—are the vital essence of the tales'. The
moral value of the legend of Robin Hood was a more contentious issue.
He was, after all, a thief and an outlaw. Nevertheless, most commentators agreed that Robin Hood had been a man of high moral standards, despite his unlawful behavior. The serial novelist Pierce Egan
proclaimed:

---

[22] Stanley Edgar Hyman, 'Jessie Weston and the Forest of Broceliande', *Centennial
Review,* 9 (1965), 509–21; Jessie L. Weston, *Sir Gawain and the Green Knight: A Middle-English
Arthurian Romance Retold in Modern Prose* (London, 1898), pp. vi and xi–xii.

[23] Palmer, *Rise of English Studies,* 21.

His character, traced through every rhyme, ballad, song, tradition, proverb, or tale, in which he figures, is that of a man noble in spirit, unequalled in courage and daring, active and powerful, prudent, patient, just in his awards, generous and kind-hearted in his dispensations, of charity unbounded, and so full of every estimable quality, that he was not only devotedly beloved by his followers—no instance of any one proving unfaithful or treacherous appearing in any ballad or tradition extant—but he was revered by the people at large . . . as the true and faithful friend who stood between them, starvation, injury, and oppression.[24]

Advocates of the study of English literature for the purpose of moral improvement often related their efforts to the rejuvenation of national life and culture. Robert Chevenix Trench, the prominent mid-Victorian philologist, wrote in his influential work *English Past and Present* (1855):

The love of our own language, what is it in fact but the love of our country expressing itself in one particular direction? If the great acts of that nation to which we belong are precious to us, if we feel ourselves made greater by their greatness, summoned to a nobler life by the nobleness of Englishmen who have already lived and died . . . what can more clearly point out their native land and ours as having fulfilled a glorious past, as being destined for a glorious future, than that they should have acquired for themselves and for those who came after them a clear, a strong, an harmonious, a noble language?

Trench and numerous other contemporary commentators claimed that the humanizing influence of English literature was required to lead the general populace away from the divisive consequences of class conflict and restore national unity. Literary study would create an all-encompassing national identity, in which, as the Christian Socialist F. D. Maurice asserted, 'class may be united to class, not by necessity only, but by generous duties and common sympathies'. Many mid-Victorians felt that the spiritual and physical conditions of the industrial revolution had impoverished the cultural lives of the British people by cutting them off from the traditions of the past, and that therefore a new means of connection with the national cultural heritage was needed. The study of English literature was seen by many as a panacea that could bring, as Matthew Arnold described it, 'a true

[24] J. T. Knowles, *The Story of King Arthur and his Knights of the Round Table* (London, 1862), pp. viii–ix; Pierce Egan, *Robin Hood and Little John; or, The Merry Men of Sherwood Forest*, 2nd edn. (London, 1850), p. viii.

bond of unity' to a society that seemed to be in imminent danger of 'falling into anarchy'.[25]

This nationalist strand of English literary studies became even more prominent in the final decades of the nineteenth century. The period after 1880 was marked by a growing concern for 'national efficiency' brought about by increased challenges to Britain's global economic, commercial, and military hegemony. In order to serve national interests at home and abroad, the nation's leaders attempted to establish more effective programmes for educating and governing the mass of the population. The movement to advance the academic status of English must be considered in this context, as educators searched for new and better ways of building and disseminating a national sense of ancestry, tradition, and citizenship. In 1894 Lord Playfair told the London Society for the Extension of University Teaching that 'the main purpose [of reading English literature] is not to educate the masses, but to permeate them with the desire for intellectual improvement. . . . Every man who acquires a taste for learning and is imbued with the desire to acquire more of it, becomes more valuable as a citizen, because he is more intelligent and perceptive'.[26] In the final decades of the nineteenth century a close alliance with nationalist politics thus shaped the study of English literature, as its great works were called upon to assist in the crucial educational work that would make the achievement of national goals possible.[27]

The heroes of national legend were thought to be particularly well suited to this purpose. John Churton Collins, who had led the fight to establish the Oxford English School, declared in *The Study of English Literature* (1891) that '[the people] need . . . to be impressed sentimentally by having the presentation in legend and history of heroic and patriotic example brought vividly before them'. He was not alone in voicing this sentiment. According to W. Carew Hazlitt in *Tales and Legends of National Origin* (1892): 'The exploits and sentiments handed down to us in these fictions ought . . . to acquire in our eyes an

---

[25] Hans Aarsleff, *The Study of Language in England, 1780–1860*, new edn. (London: Athlone, 1983), 245–6; Franklin E. Court, *Institutionalizing English Literature: The Culture and Politics of Literary Study, 1750–1900* (Stanford: Stanford UP, 1992), 40–1; Chris Baldick, *The Social Mission of English Criticism 1848–1932* (Oxford: Clarendon Press, 1983), 63; Palmer, *Rise of English Studies*, 39–40; Robert Holton, '"A True Bond of Unity": Popular Education and the Foundation of the Discipline of English Literature in England', *Dalhousie Review*, 66 (1986–7), 35.

[26] Doyle, 'The Invention of English', 90–1; and Baldick, *Social Mission*, 64.

[27] Doyle, 'The Invention of English', 98.

augmented charm and worth, when we . . . are enabled to add them to the material for tracing the development of our country and our race'.[28] And no legendary heroes were more appropriate for 'tracing the development of our country and our race' than King Arthur and Robin Hood. In her *Legendary Tales of the Ancient Britons* (1864), Louisa L. J. Menzies declared that 'the nervous vigour and manly simplicity of the [tales of Arthur] must strike even a casual reader; to us they seem . . . to be strangely in harmony with the national character of the little Island which . . . stands forth as a Champion of freedom, a Queen among the nations'. The legend of Robin Hood was similarly thought to remind its readers of the glories of the nation which had produced it. In his children's story *In Lincoln Green* (1897), Edward Gilliat, assistant master at Harrow, declared that Robin Hood was 'the great name which no Englishman ever mentioned without feelings of love and reverence and admiration'.[29]

The breezily confident tone of these declarations of the essential 'Englishness' of King Arthur and Robin Hood, however, belies the difficulties which they encountered in their assimilation into the national canon. In the case of the legend of Robin Hood, the ballad genre in which the legend was first recorded was regarded with contempt by many scholars until the second half of the nineteenth century. Prior to that period editors had refused to countenance the publication of ballads unless they were 'improved' in order to make them conform to contemporary literary tastes. In the later decades of the nineteenth century, however, ballads came to be linked to the notion of 'merrie England', a pseudo-historical concept which offered a solution to what was perceived by many as the nation's primary problem—the detrimental effects of urbanization. In this way they were elevated to a position of high status in the nationalist literary canon.

The Arthurian legend faced a different sort of struggle for acceptance into the English literary canon. In its case, the English claim of ownership faced challenges from a number of other nations, first the French in the late eighteenth century and then the Welsh in the nineteenth. It was not until after 1850, when Sir Thomas Malory's *Morte d'Arthur* became the major textual source for the legend, that the

[28] Baldick, *Social Mission*, 64; W. Carew Hazlitt (ed.), *Tales and Legends of National Origin or Widely Current in England from Early Times* (London, 1892), p. vi.

[29] Louisa L. J. Menzies, *Legendary Tales of the Ancient Britons, Rehearsed from the Early Chronicle* (London, 1864), pp. iv–v; Edward Gilliat, *In Lincoln Green: A Merrie Tale of Robin Hood* (London, 1897), 135.

English could feel content, at least in their own minds, that the legend belonged to them alone.

'Truly national songs': The Robin Hood Ballads and the Construction of English National Identity

Of the forty or so extant Robin Hood ballads, only five—'Robin Hood and the Monk', 'A Little Gest of Robyn Hode', 'Robin Hood and the Potter', 'Robin Hoode his Death', and 'Robin Hood and Guy of Gisborne'—can be identified as genuinely medieval, most likely dating from the late thirteenth or early fourteenth century. The remainder are creations of the sixteenth and seventeenth centuries, when balladry was gradually relegated to the possession of the 'folk'—a term used in a pejorative sense to mean those who were incapable of enjoying entertainment or assimilating information through more sophisticated channels.

At first glance, the eighteenth century seems an unlikely era to have engendered a sudden burst of interest in the ballad, for the wit, urbanity, elegance, and artifice of the contemporary literary style were seemingly antithetical to the rough simplicity of traditional balladry. Nevertheless, the first faint stirrings of a new enthusiasm for the genre can be identified in the endeavours of collectors such as Robert Harley, Earl of Oxford, who amassed several hundred black-letter broadsides in the first decades of the century. Such projects, however, were the work of amateur antiquarians whose efforts were strictly private. A wider public first became aware of the growing appreciation for traditional balladry in 1711, when Joseph Addison gave serious consideration to three of its best-known examples, 'Chevy Chase', 'The Hunting of the Cheviot', and 'The Babes in the Wood', in *The Spectator*. Beneath Addison's somewhat patronizing and apologetic tone lurked a clear affection for these works, which he praised for their 'extreme natural' sentiment and 'majestic simplicity'.[30] Initially, critics scorned Addison's opinions and continued to castigate ballads for their lack of conscious artistry, roughness of verse, and blatant disregard for rationality. Addison's tentative interest was vindicated, however, by the appearance of *A Collection of Old Ballads* (1723–5), the

---

[30] Evelyn Kendrick Wells, *The Ballad Tree: A Study of British and American Ballads, Their Folklore, Verse, and Music* (London: Methuen, 1950), 225–6.

first major ballad anthology. The successive prefaces of its three volumes reveal a steady decline in the degree of contempt displayed towards the genre, as the editor—most likely Ambrose Phillips— gradually lost his fear of ridicule for bringing such material before the world. In addition, the lengthy headnotes appended to each ballad, which recapitulated the story, offered praise or criticism, and occasionally provided bits of antiquarian lore, mark this as the first attempt at collecting balladry in a scholarly manner.

The influence of *Old Ballads* promoted a new-found regard for the genre, and eminent figures such as David Hume and Edmund Burke began to praise ballads. This increased sense of appreciation was to be found not only among the scholarly elite, but among a more popular audience as well. In an imitation of the consciously antiquarian approach of *Old Ballads*, the purveyors of lowbrow street literature began to adopt marketing methods which emphasized the historic interest of their wares. In the 1790s, for example, the Whitechapel printer Larken How issued an entire series of Robin Hood ballads in an archaic broadside style, complete with illustrations copied from seventeenth-century woodblocks.[31]

These commercial developments must be viewed in the light of the vigorous cultural nationalism which emerged over the course of the eighteenth century. The years between 1740 and 1789 comprised what Gerald Newman describes as 'a period of extraordinary and unprecedented activity in the collection, study, and promotion of everything pertaining to the national cultural heritage'. Much of this activity focused upon the careful preservation and close study of earlier 'literary remains', in particular those works thought to be genuine expressions of the voice of the English people in previous centuries. This emphasis is present in earlier collections of popular poetry such as Allan Ramsay's *Evergreen* (1724), the preface to which argues in favour of literature neither 'pilfered' nor trimmed with 'foreign embroidery' nor 'spoiled in transportation from abroad'.[32] It did not move to the forefront of editorial concerns, however, until Thomas Percy published his *Reliques of Ancient English Poetry* in 1765. The *Reliques* contained no less than twenty-four Robin Hood ballads, including the first printed text

[31] Dianne Dugaw, 'The Popular Marketing of "Old Ballads": The Ballad Revival and Eighteenth-Century Antiquarianism Reconsidered', *Eighteenth-Century Studies*, 21 (1987), 72, 89.
[32] Gerald Newman, *The Rise of English Nationalism: A Cultural History* (New York: St. Martin's, 1987), 111–2, 114.

of a truly medieval example, 'Robin Hood and Guy of Gisborne'. Before the end of the nineteenth century Percy's work had gone into more than twenty-five editions, providing several generations of authors with a source upon which to base their own interpretations of the outlaw hero.

Percy himself, however, had little inkling that his work would attain such lofty heights, for in the 1760s a collection of popular poetry was still likely to attract considerable ridicule from critics sceptical of its literary merit. In the introduction to the *Reliques* he adopted an apologetic tone:

In a polished age, like the present, I am sensible that many of the reliques of antiquity will require great allowances to be made for them. . . . [A]s most of them are of great simplicity, and seem to have been meerly [*sic*] written for the people, [I] was long in doubt, whether in the present state of improved literature, they could be deemed worthy of the attention of the public.

So why did he undertake a venture which was so unlikely to meet with a favorable reception? In order to comprehend Percy's motives, it is necessary to dissect his editorial methods. He included no foreign compositions in the *Reliques*, confining his efforts, as he wrote to the Welsh antiquary Evan Evans in December 1764, 'merely to the Minstrels, and Romantic Songs of our own nation'.[33] This was no accident, for Percy took a consciously nationalist approach in his study of English popular poetry. Having previously edited or translated works of ancient Chinese and Spanish literature, he now turned to the early cultural products of his own native tongue in order to show the progress of both the language and its speakers. 'Such specimens of ancient poetry have been selected', he wrote in the preface to the first volume, 'as either shew the gradation of our language, exhibit the progress of popular opinions, display the peculiar manners and customs of former ages, or throw light on our earlier classical poets'. When popular poetry was considered in this context all need to apologize for its deficiencies disappeared, and accordingly Percy became more aggressive in his defence of the texts, declaring that 'the Editor hopes he need not be ashamed of having bestowed some of his idle hours on the ancient literature of our own country, or in

[33] Thomas Percy, *Reliques of Ancient English Poetry: Consisting of Old Heroic Ballads, Songs and other Pieces of our Earlier Poets* (London, 1765), vol. i, p. ix–x; The Correspondence of Thomas Percy and Evan Evans, ed. Aneirin Lewis (Baton Rouge: Louisiana State UP, 1957), 103.

rescuing from oblivion some pieces . . . which tend to place in a striking light, their taste, genius, sentiments, or manners'.[34]

But Percy's patriotic pride in the early cultural productions of English poetry was not so pronounced as to permit him to publish them in their original, unadulterated form. Instead, he aggressively intervened to render the ballads more acceptable to an eighteenth-century audience. His actions included not only relatively minor alterations of syntax and the glossing of archaic words and phrases, but also radical revisions in order to make the texts more amenable to contemporary tastes. His decision to handle the material in this manner has frequently been criticized, but without his 'improvements' the *Reliques* almost certainly would not have attained the same level of popularity among a British public which emphatically preferred pseudo-medieval imitations such as James Macpherson's *Ossian* poems to original works still considered to be ill-formed compositions of wild fancy and rude metre. Although Percy provided some discussion of the history of popular English literature for the serious student, his work was primarily addressed to non-specialist readers who had little interest in acquiring first-hand knowledge of medieval texts. He recognized that success with this sort of audience depended upon his ability to mediate between a past that was still something of an embarrassment and the present need to identify in that selfsame past the roots of a superior national culture. The *Reliques* thus won over a wide audience not with scholarly accuracy, but by presenting a congenial portrait of the nation's history which appealed to the preconceptions and prejudices of his audience.[35]

The success of Percy's work spawned a number of imitators. In 1777 Thomas Evans published a collection entitled *Old Ballads, Historical and Narrative*, which contained more than twenty Robin Hood ballads. Like Percy, Evans apologized for the shortcomings of the literary fragments he had accumulated. 'A polished age will make allowances', he wrote, 'for the rude productions of their ancestors.' But, also like Percy, he recognized that these shortcomings were easily overcome by the inherent nationalist interest which these centuries-old examples of

---

[34] Percy, *Reliques*, vol. i, pp. ix and xiv.

[35] Joseph P. Donatelli, 'Old Barons in New Robes: Percy's Use of the Metrical Romances in the *Reliques of Ancient English Poetry*', in Patrick J. Gallacher and Helen Damico (eds.), *Hermeneutics and Medieval Culture* (Albany: State University of New York Press, 1989), 228; id., 'The Medieval Fictions of Thomas Warton and Thomas Percy', *University of Toronto Quarterly*, 60 (1990), 435–51.

popular poetry possessed. 'The Ballad may be considered as the native species of poetry of this country . . .', he asserted. '[I]n them the character of the nation displays itself in striking colours'.[36] Evans, too, made textual alterations to ensure that his collection fulfilled the expectations of an audience who wished to identify in it the origins of their national culture. And he, too, saw his efforts rewarded by commercial success. Despite its hefty three-volume bulk, *Old Ballads* had gone into three editions by 1810.

The work of editors like Percy and Evans made possible a patriotic appreciation of ballad literature, and of the Robin Hood ballads in particular. They created a context in which these ballads came to be thought of as relevant to the evolution of the nation's culture. What they did not do, however, was make it possible for these texts to be appreciated on their own terms, with no editorial interventions to render them more suitable to modern tastes. The first editor to provide a collection of the Robin Hood ballads in their original, unadulterated state was Joseph Ritson, whose *Robin Hood: A Collection of Poems, Songs, and Ballads Relative to that Celebrated English Outlaw* (1795) served as the first truly scholarly anthology. Ritson's political predilections, and the effect which they had upon his interpretation of Robin Hood, have been discussed previously. Of greater relevance here are his editorial skills, which were considerable, if somewhat idiosyncratic. An inveterate believer in adhering strictly to his manuscript sources, Ritson saw any attempt to alter the original as sacrilege:

To correct the obvious errors of an illiterate transcribeër, to supply irremediable defects, and to make sense of nonsense, are certainly essential dutys of an editour of ancient poetry; provideëd he act with integrity and publicity, but secretly to suppress the original text, and insert his own fabrications for the sake of provideing more refine'd entertainment for readers of taste and genius, is no proof of either judgement, candour, or integrity.[37]

By providing subsequent authors with an accurate source-book, Ritson gave them the opportunity to re-create Robin Hood in their own imagination. He also permitted countless readers to enjoy the ballads in their original state, unsullied by the hands of over-zealous editors bent on eradicating their ostensible defects. His collection was

---

[36] Thomas Evans, *Old Ballads, Historical and Narrative, with Some of Modern Date* (London, 1777), vol. i, preface.

[37] This citation preserves Ritson's unique spelling style. Joseph Ritson, *A Select Collection of English Songs* (London, 1783), vol. i, p. x (note).

reprinted dozens of times over the course of the nineteenth century, making it accessible to a large and socially diverse audience. Nearly a century after *Robin Hood* was first published, Cornelius Brown declared in his *Lives of Nottinghamshire Worthies* (1882) that 'through Ritson . . . the surviving ballads are well known'.[38]

In the short term, however, most contemporary critics continued to regard ballads as an inferior literary genre. The *British Critic* preferred Percy's methods, complaining that the ballads as Ritson printed them 'contain wretched corruptions' and were 'absolutely *unreadable*':

> In truth, we wanted something like an elegant or classical edition of these popular songs, the delight of our childhood, and the amusement of the great mass of the people: and nothing could have been more acceptable than such a collection of them, as, by collating the old copies, and by ingenious conjectural emendations where necessary, would have left them in such a state that they could be read with pleasure, and admitted on the shelves of an elegant library; something like what hath been done . . . in the *Reliques of Ancient Poetry*.[39]

To be sure, the opposition of many critics to Ritson's radical politics clearly prejudiced their opinions of his scholarly work. Also identifiable, however, was a lingering bias against balladry, which they saw as fit only for the entertainment of children, and not the edification of adults or the attention of scholars.

By the end of the eighteenth century the ballad had thus succeeded, thanks to the efforts of Percy, Ritson, and numerous other dedicated editors, in gaining a degree of prestige in scholarly circles and attracting a certain amount of interest from the British reading public. Ballads were gradually coming to be seen as key texts in efforts to trace the nation's cultural and linguistic roots to their medieval origins, for in them could be identified the specifically *English* qualities which would later flower so brilliantly. On the other hand, this growing interest did not yet translate into an unmitigated appreciation of the ballad in its original form. The vast majority of editors continued to alter their texts in order to render them more suitable to contemporary tastes, and the handful who did not, such as Ritson, were subjected to harsh judgements from critics incensed at the idea of such 'inferior' cultural productions being brought before the public eye.

These vestiges of hostility to popular balladry dissipated rapidly in

---

[38] Cornelius Brown, *Lives of Nottinghamshire Worthies and of Celebrated and Remarkable Men of the County from the Norman Conquest to AD 1882* (London and Nottingham, 1882), 15.

[39] *British Critic*, 9 (1797), 19–21.

the nineteenth century, however. In this period, the role of the ballad as the wellspring of English literature easily eclipsed any remaining doubts regarding quality. 'Just as we can trace our individuality in our Saxon ancestors, so may we see the promise of our later and more polished and glorious literature in the vigorous and stirring ballads composed by the singers of past ages', wrote George Barnett Smith in his *Illustrated British Ballads, Old and New* (1881). In such a context, there was no longer any need to make allowances for the deficiencies of the genre. In sharp contrast to the eighteenth century, any editor who dared tamper with the original texts met with a strong negative reaction. In his *The Ballad Book: A Selection of the Choicest British Ballads* (1864), which included four Robin Hood ballads, William Allingham delivered an obvious slap at Percy and other editors with a penchant for 'improving' their material:

These narrative songs . . . came in a later day into the baskets of literary collectors, were transferred into the editorial laboratories, there sifted, mixed, shaken, clarified, improved (or the contrary), no one can ever tell how much, and sent at last into the World of Books in a properly solemn shape, their triviality duly weighted with a load of antiquarianism, and garnished with fit apologies for the presentation of such 'barbarous productions' to 'a polished age like the present', and assurances that those high literary personages, the 'ingenious' Mr. This and the 'elegant' Mr. That, whose own poems are so justly, &c. (read now, forgotten), have given some countenance to the venture.[40]

The trickle of ballad collections which had been issuing from print-ing presses in the eighteenth century became a torrent in the nine-teenth, as publishers scrambled to slake the contemporary thirst, particularly for ballads related to the legend of Robin Hood. 'The name of Robin Hood has been so closely interwoven with the history of English romance', wrote the noted antiquary and founder of *Notes and Queries* William John Thoms in 1828, 'that a collection of our ancient fictions, which should not include some popular account of this renowned outlaw. . . would possess little claim to be considered either judicious or complete'. Robin Hood's presence was considered crucial to any ballad collection not just because of his enduring popularity, but also because, without him, no such collection could be truly 'national'. This was acknowledged by John Matthew Gutch, the editor of the most

[40] George Barnett Smith, *Illustrated British Ballads, Old and New* (London, Paris and New York, 1881), 3; William Allingham, *The Ballad Book: A Selection of the Choicest British Ballads* (London and Cambridge, 1864), p. x.

comprehensive mid-nineteenth-century selection of the Robin Hood ballads: '[A]s truly national songs, illustrative of the manners and exploits of popular characters of by-gone days, there is no doubt, that those on Robin Hood have exerted considerable influence over a large portion of the community. . . and they retain to the present day a strong hold upon the public mind and memory'.[41]

In the mid-Victorian period, popular literary forms such as the ballad came more than ever to be regarded as integral to efforts to trace the nation's cultural roots. Editors excluded from their collections not only ballads composed by foreign authors, as Percy had done, but those on 'foreign subjects' and even those in which 'the scene is laid in foreign countries'.[42] This increased patriotic intensity was due largely to the influence of the romantic nationalism of the late eighteenth and early nineteenth centuries, which emphasized the role of tradition, myth, and legend in national development. These ideas had originated in Germany in the work of Johann Gottfried Herder, who argued that it was not only desirable but absolutely essential to build a nation upon native cultural foundations. Herder claimed that each nation began as an independent cultural entity which gradually evolved into a distinct national unit whose organic structure was reflected in what he called 'national character'.[43] For a nation to build upon a cultural foundation other than its own meant the breaking of the continuity of past and present and a disruption of its essential organic unity, resulting in the suffocation of native cultural forms and, ultimately, the death of the nation itself. Herder thus believed that each nation must establish its own language, art, literature, religion, customs, and laws—all of which he saw as expressions of the national character—in order to preserve its strength and unity. He insisted that the German people must redis-cover their own culture; he begged them not to abandon their native traditions, but rather to cherish the ways of life inherited from their forefathers. In order to do this, he advocated a return to the Middle Ages, before German culture had been corrupted by foreign influ-ences. Through the study and imitation of medieval cultural forms, the

[41] William John Thoms, *A Collection of Early Prose Romances* (London, 1828), vol ii, p. i; Gutch, *A Lytle Geste*, pp. xx–xxi.

[42] R. Brimley Johnson, *Popular British Ballads* (London, 1894), vol. i, p. xxxiii; Revd J. D. Parry, *The Legendary Cabinet: A Collection of British National Ballads, Ancient and Modern* (London, 1829), p. vi.

[43] Wolf Koepke, 'Johann Gottfried Herder's Concept of "Nation"', in *Transactions of the Seventh International Congress on the Enlightenment III*, Studies on Voltaire and the Eighteenth Century, 265 (Oxford: Voltaire Foundation, 1989), 1656–9.

German people could build a healthy, durable national culture on native foundations.

But how to bridge this centuries-wide gap between past and present? For Herder, there was only one way: through folk poetry, 'the archives of a nationality', from which one could learn 'the mode of thought of a nationality and its language of feeling'.[44] In these songs could be discovered the German language in its most pristine state, before it had become so encumbered with foreign words and expressions that it was scarcely recognizable. Herder's efforts on this front, and in particular the publication of his *Volkslieder* in 1778–9, helped to overcome the opposition of sceptics who continued to regard the songs of the common people with scorn. It also inspired numerous imitators. In the late eighteenth and early nineteenth centuries the collection oral and written folk material was avidly pursued in Germany, culminating in the famous *Kinder und Hausmärchen* published by Jacob and Wilhelm Grimm in 1812–15.

Herder's idea that each nation must develop its own culture was eagerly accepted by a variety of European ethnic groups. His influence in England, however, has generally been perceived as minimal. Early scholars of English folklore, it is often argued, did not display such overtly nationalist concerns, but concentrated instead upon purely antiquarian objectives.[45] But, undeniably, many of the same cultural conditions which precipitated Herder's support for the link between folklore and nationalism were also present in contemporary England. As we have seen, England too experienced a strong reaction to the long-standing domination of foreign culture in this period, a reaction which resulted in the revival of many native cultural forms, including medieval popular poetry. Indeed, the stimulation for many of Herder's ideas came from his reading of some of the early documents of the English folklore revival, including Percy's *Reliques*. It is misleading, therefore, to see the renewal of scholarly and popular interest in the folk poetry of the Middle Ages in England as a distinct cultural and political phenomenon from the similar revivalist movements occurring elsewhere in Europe, where their nationalist significance has long been recognized.

---

[44] William A. Wilson, 'Herder, Folklore and Romantic Nationalism', *Journal of Popular Culture*, 6 (1973), 826.

[45] Wilson, for example, refers to the 'antiquarian emphasis' of early British folklore studies, which he claims focused upon 'survivals and . . . the historical reconstruction of the past or of past forms of present lore'. Ibid. 819.

This hypothesis is confirmed by an examination of the discourse surrounding the publication of popular ballads in England in the nineteenth century. In the 1840s Gutch declared:

The Songs of every Nation must always be the most familiar as well as the most pleasing part of its poetry. They are uniformly the first fruits of fancy and feeling of rude societies; and even in the most civilized times are the chief and favourite poetry of the great body of the people. Their influence, therefore, upon the character of a country has been universally felt and acknowledged.

Like Herder, English ballad collectors emphasized the role of folk poetry as the foundation of the nation's culture. 'There can be no doubt that the ballads of an infant nation are a great factor in the formation of the national character, and help to mould the minds of its future citizens', wrote Edward Walford in the preface to his edition of Percy's *Reliques* in 1880. And also like Herder, these collectors asserted that folk poetry must be cherished in order to ensure that the national culture retained its strength and purity. According to Edward Arber in the preface to his *An English Garner* (1877):

Few of us adequately realize the immense Literature which has descended to us from our ancestors. Generation after generation has passed away; each of which has produced (in the order of its own thought, and with the tuition of its inherited or acquired experience) many a wise, bright or beautiful thing: which having served its own brief day, has straightaway passed away into utter forgetfulness, there to remain till Doomsday; unless some effort like the present, shall restore it to the knowledge and enjoyment of English-speaking peoples.[46]

In such statements, the Robin Hood ballads were frequently singled out as the most 'national' of this style of uniquely uncorrupted native poetry. In the *Penny Magazine* in 1838 Allan Cunningham declared that 'there is more of the national character in them than in all the songs of classic bards or the theories of ingenious philosophers', by which he meant that they were written in 'a true and hearty English taste and spirit'. Similarly, a commentator in *Notes and Queries* in the 1880s referred to the 'thorough English characteristic' which was 'stamped upon every verse of the Robin Hood ballads'. In more effusive prose, F. Mary Wilson proclaimed in the *Temple Bar* in 1892 that 'some [Robin

[46] Gutch, *A Lytle Geste*, p. xvii; Edward Walford, 'Preface', in Thomas Percy, *Reliques of Ancient English Poetry: Consisting of Old Heroic Ballads, Songs and Other Pieces of our Earlier Poets*, ed. Edward Walford (London, 1880), 18; Edward Arber, *An English Garner, Ingatherings from our History and Literature* (London, 1877–96), vol. i, preface.

Hood ballads] are good, many are bad, others only tedious . . . but taken altogether they form a corn-sheaf of national legends relating to a national hero. . . . English they are and real and vivid'.[47]

The ballad revival in England continued to have nationalistic implications into the final decades of the nineteenth century. More specifically, in this period it came to be associated with an emerging vision of English national identity which was based upon pastoral ideals. A ruralist strain in English culture was not, of course, entirely new; Raymond Williams has traced it to the late Middle Ages, when it appeared in William Langland's *Piers Plowman* and other contemporary works of literature. But the particular connection between the rural landscape and national identity which developed in the late nineteenth century was the product of social conditions specific to that period. In the years after 1870 many upper- and middle-class Victorians came increasingly to fear the consequences of the steady migration of the nation's population into urban areas, where the social order seemed in imminent danger of breaking down as a result of massive overcrowding, poor health, prolonged unemployment, and endemic poverty. In the cities, contemporary commentators warned, the separation of classes had led to the collapse of traditional social relationships and methods of social control.[48]

How, then, to combat these negative consequences of urbanization and thereby rescue the nation from impending doom? A potential solution that received considerable support in the late nineteenth century focused upon the basic premiss that Englishmen and women had to be convinced—or even compelled if necessary—to return to the land. In this period, 'country life' came to represent order, stability, and naturalness, values which its urban counterpart seemed to be rapidly annihilating. As a corollary to this idealization of the rural, the historical came to be highly valued as well. By the end of the nineteenth century the recent past had come to be defined as inherently un-English, dominated as it was by a set of values unnatural to the English people. Accordingly, the past came more and more to serve as a source of alternative values, as disenchantment with the consequences of

---

[47] Allan Cunningham, 'The Old English Ballads', *Penny Magazine*, 7 (1838), 170; E. Stredder, 'Who Was Robin Hood?', *Notes and Queries*, 7: 3 (1887), 282; F. Mary Wilson, 'England's Ballad-hero', *Temple Bar*, 95 (1892), 407-8.

[48] Raymond Williams, *The Country and the City* (London: Paladin, 1973), ch. 1; Gareth Stedman Jones, *Outcast London: A Study in the Relationship between the Classes in Victorian Society* (Oxford: Clarendon, 1971), 251.

'progress' increased. England, it was widely argued, was an *old* nation, with a precious historical heritage in imminent danger of being obliterated.[49]

This combination of rural and historical values found its most explicit expression in the construction of 'Merrie England', a cultural ideal which located the remedy for the evils of modern life in a golden age found sometime in the late-medieval or Tudor era. Then, it was argued, English society had been from top to bottom wholesome, prosperous, and healthy. Relying upon a set of ideas and images constructed in the present and transferred to the past, the concept of 'Merrie England' was emphatically not based upon historical fact, but its inherent falsity did nothing to decrease its power. In a world in which community was thought to have disappeared and connections between individuals to have broken down, people of many different ideological persuasions looked back longingly to an agrarian past when institutions such as the manor or the village bound men together in relationships strengthened by mutual interests and affections. Robert Blatchford's *Merrie England* (1894), a socialist polemic which described agriculture as the basis of a healthy national life and strongly criticized the rise of the factory system, sold over a million copies in its first years of publication.

In the context of such near-universal acceptance of the superiority of the rural past over the industrial present, the cultural traditions which seemed most appealing were sanctioned by their longevity and their association with country life. 'As society grows more and more artificial and prosaic in its day by day routine . . .', wrote W. Carew Hazlitt in 1892, 'we may . . . expect to see a more widely diffused sympathy with stories and traditions which owe much of their charm to their strong contrast with existing conditions and possibilities'. The Robin Hood ballads suited this agenda perfectly. Featuring images of uninhibited merriment, boisterous action, rude hospitality, and healthful masculinity, they provided a vision of 'Merrie England' at its most vigorous and hearty. The literary critic William Winter wrote in 1892:

It is not the England of the mine and the workshop that [Robin Hood] represents. . . . [I]t is the England of the feudal times—of grey castle towers, and armoured knights, and fat priests, and wandering minstrels, and crusades

---

[49] Alan Howkins, 'The Discovery of Rural England', in Colls and Dodd (eds.), *Englishness*, 67–9; Martin J. Wiener, *English Culture and the Decline of the Industrial Spirit, 1850–1980* (Cambridge: Cambridge UP, 1981), 45.

and tournaments; England in rush-strewn bowers and under green boughs. . . .
To enter into that realm is to leave the barren world of prose; to feel again the
cool, sweet winds of summer upon the brow of youth; to catch, in fitful
glimpses, the shimmer of the Lincoln green in the sunlit, golden glades of
the forest, and to hear the merry note of the huntsman commingled, far away,
with horns of Elfland faintly blowing.[50]

As middle-class observers fretted about the puny stature of urban
children and the effects of lives spent almost entirely indoors, the
ballads displayed Robin Hood's 'great muscular arms' and Maid
Marian's healthy 'sun-tan'. As thousands of unemployed English men
and women starved in the slums of contemporary cities, the ballads
offered a vision of a time in which 'the game with which the forest
abounded afforded an ample supply of food fit for a royal table'. As the
social order seemed in imminent danger of breaking down under the
pressures of modern industrial life, the ballads overflowed with rowdy
camaraderie, boisterous good cheer, and 'a feeling of unity and
brotherhood'. In short, the ballads offered a vision of the nation which
seemed to contrast sharply with late-Victorian England. In them,
modern readers could 'discern the life of the greenwood, the deer
leaping through the shadows, the venison hung in the branches of
the Larder Oak, the merry men loving their life and their dinner
and true to one another, the arrows that whizzed'.[51]

Neither the idea of 'Merrie England' nor its link to the Robin Hood
ballads was new to the late nineteenth century. Historians have identified the presence of similar notions in the 1830s and 1840s, another
period of industrial crisis and urban upheaval.[52] It was not until the
final decades of the century, however, that this concept came to be
regarded as a specifically nationalist vision which could rescue England
from its present difficulties. In this period, the idealization of rural life
and of the cultural forms associated with it, such as the Robin Hood
ballads, served not just as a comforting form of escapism for

---

[50] Hazlitt, *Tales and Legends*, p. v; Stephen Knight, *Robin Hood: A Complete Study of the
English Outlaw* (Oxford and Cambridge, Mass.: Blackwell, 1994), 205 6; William Winter,
Shadows of the Stage (Edinburgh, 1892), 272.

[51] Wilson, 'England's Ballad-hero', 407 8; Brown, *Lives of Nottinghamshire Worthies*, 10.

[52] See Joanna Banham, '"Past and Present": Images of the Middle Ages in the Early
Nineteenth Century', in Joanna Banham and Jennifer Harris (eds.), *William Morris and the
Middle Ages* (Manchester and Dover, NH: Manchester UP, 1984), 121 46; Peter Mandler,
'"In the Olden Time": Romantic History and English National Identity, 1820 50', in
Laurence Brockliss and David Eastwood (eds.), *A Union of Multiple Identities: The British
Isles, c.1750 c.1850* (Manchester and New York: Manchester UP, 1996), 78 92.

disgruntled city-dwellers. More significantly, it also functioned as a means of redefining English national identity. In 1905 the folk-dance teacher Mary Neale declared that the revival of such popular traditions was 'part of a great national revival, a going back from the town to the country, a reaction against all that is demoralising in city life. It is a reawakening of that part of our national consciousness which makes for wholeness, saneness, and healthy merriment'.[53]

The long struggle of the Robin Hood ballads for acceptance as an important element in English literary culture thus ended in the final decades of the nineteenth century, when they achieved a lofty position as crucial documents in the construction of English cultural national-ism, and more specifically in the emergence of 'Merrie England' as the historical blueprint for that construction. No longer subject to the 'improvements' of editors embarrassed by their inferiority, ballads were instead celebrated as expressions of the 'national genius' in its pure and uncorrupted state. It is important to realize, however, that this 'national genius' was an exclusively *English* one. Those who elevated the Robin Hood ballads made no attempt to incorporate the other parts of the British Isles into the nation and national culture which they so vigorously celebrated. An examination of medieval Arthurian texts in nineteenth-century Britain will reveal that this Anglocentric point of view was repeated there as well.

'The epic of the English mind': The Incorporation of Thomas Malory into the English Literary Canon

'The origin of the cycle of romances, which have for their subject the adventures of King Arthur and his knights . . . appears to be involved in impenetrable mystery', declared the noted literary antiquary Thomas Wright in 1858.[54] Indeed, to this day it remains unclear precisely which country gave birth to Arthurian literature. In spite of this, or perhaps because of it, a number of nations have attempted to claim the legend as their own. This situation made the incorporation of the Arthurian legend into the English literary canon problematic, for it was also claimed by the French and the Welsh. Until these challenges

---

[53] Howkins, 'Discovery', 72.

[54] *La Mort d'Arthure. The History of King Arthur and of the Knights of the Round Table*, ed. Thomas Wright (London, 1858), p. v.

were met and refuted, there could be no English national pride in Arthurian literature. In other words, an English author had to be found who could be identified as the creator of the legend in an original form. It was not until the mid-nineteenth century, when Sir Thomas Malory's *Le Morte d'Arthur* came to be regarded as the greatest Arthurian work ever written, that this was accomplished.

In the first half of the eighteenth century the scant regard given to the Arthurian legend by British scholars, who believed that classical texts were the only works of antiquity worthy of consideration, meant that the British were by and large content to let other nations claim Arthur. They thus barely protested when French scholars argued that all Arthurian romances in other languages were mere translations of French antecedents. After 1750, however, there was an increasingly strong sense in England that the French 'cultural yoke' ought to be cast off and supplanted by a more explicitly national cultural identity. In this context, it was extremely unlikely that English literary scholars would continue to permit French claims to Arthur to go unchallenged. 'I am sure [the French] and all other nations must have borrowed [the tales] about King Arthur and his Knights originally from British histories or Romances', declared Evan Evans, an expert on early Welsh literature, in a letter to Bishop Thomas Percy in 1764. Percy later utilized this correspondence in his *Reliques of Ancient English Poetry.* '''Tis most likely', he wrote in the introduction to the third volume, 'that all the old stories concerning King Arthur are originally of British growth, and that what the French and other southern nations have of this kind were at first exported from this island'.[55]

By the late eighteenth and early nineteenth centuries, only the most ardent British Francophiles continued to support the idea that the Arthurian legend was of French origin. Instead, the majority of scholars argued that the legend was a product of the British Isles. The literary antiquary Gregory Lewis Way, for example, declared that 'the French Trouveurs borrowed many of their subjects from the Bards of Britain'. More specifically, the most common story of the legend's origin claimed that it had been created by Welsh bards at the Norman court, where it was bequeathed to French minstrels who carried it across the English Channel. In the introduction to his *Specimens of Early*

---

[55] Newman, *Rise of English Nationalism*, 109–14; *Correspondence of Thomas Percy and Evan Evans*, 70; Percy *Reliques*, iii. 314.

English Metrical Romances (1805), George Ellis denied that the legend was a product of French soil and instead asserted that 'the courts of our Norman sovereigns, rather than those of the kings of France, produced the birth of romance literature'. To provide support for this hypothesis, Ellis disparaged the 'glaringly absurd' belief that Celtic culture had been entirely eradicated by the Saxons, instead favouring the idea that the two cultures had blended. Having thus survived the Saxon onslaught, the Welsh bards had in the period after 1066 travelled to the court of William the Conqueror, where they 'had every opportunity of comparing the traditional fables of their ancestors, and of imparting them to the French minstrels with whom they associated'.[56] It was in this manner that the tales of King Arthur and his knights were passed from British into French hands.

In a climate favourable to the idea of Celtic influence upon British culture, Ellis's argument fitted right in. As the nineteenth century wore on, however, the idea that the Arthurian legend had been of Celtic origin became more problematic due to a change in the English perception of Celtic culture. In the late 1860s Matthew Arnold delivered a series of lectures at Oxford in which he aimed to establish the contribution of Celtic authors to English literature. On the surface Arnold was complimentary towards the Celts, whose 'lively' nature he contrasted favourably with the 'impassive dullness' of the English. He saw the 'Celtic muse' as being characterized by delicacy and spirituality, qualities which could, if cultivated sufficiently, rescue Britain from the philistinism of the Victorian age. His view at first glance thus appears to parallel earlier notions that Celtic writers had infused English literature with a pure, uncorrupted vitality. At a time when anti-Irish prejudice was rife in Britain, Arnold must be given credit for seeing value in Celtic culture, and he was criticized in some quarters for seeming excessively favourable to it. *The Times*, for example, denounced his 'irresponsibility' for agreeing to attend the Chester Eisteddfod of 1866, which was described as 'a foolish interference with the natural progress of civilisation and prosperity'.[57]

There is, however, another dimension to Arnold's argument, and this is where a change can be identified from the view that had prevailed earlier in the century. Arnold claimed that the Celts paid a

---

[56] Gregory Lewis Way, *Fabliaux or Tales, Abridged from French Manuscripts of the XIIth and XIIIth Centuries by M. Le Grand* (London, 1796), 236; George Ellis, *Specimens of Early English Metrical Romance* (London, 1805), i. 38, 117–8.   [57] Durkacz, *Decline*, 201–2.

high price for their vitality, for they suffered grievously from a lack of 'steadiness, patience, sanity'. Thus, while he admitted that Celtic contributions deserved a place in British culture, that place was clearly subordinate to that of English authors. In his view, the cultural life of Scotland, Wales, and Ireland could have no existence outside of a satellite relationship with England. Arnold was, in short, a cultural imperialist who had little regard for Celtic literature apart from its potential contribution to English culture. He foresaw a Britain in which 'all the inhabitants of these islands' would be fused 'into one homogeneous, English-speaking whole', and in which 'the breaking down of barriers between us, the swallowing up of several provincial nationalities, is a consummation to which the natural course of things irresistibly tends; it is a necessity of what is called modern civilisation'. Arnold's arguments were diffused widely throughout late-nineteenth-century British culture. From the English perspective, the colonization and subordination of Celtic literature came to be seen as inevitable and natural, as the superior culture asserted its dominance over its inferior.[58]

In a climate in which the idea of an independent and accomplished Celtic culture was increasingly disparaged, the identification of the Arthurian legend as being of Celtic origin met with less and less favour. The seeds of change sprouted as early as the 1840s. In 1842 the literary scholar John Robson agreed with Ellis that the Welsh had preserved 'traditions, perhaps poems, relating to their struggles with the Saxons'. He argued, however, that these tales had not been directly bequeathed to the Normans by the Welsh bards. Instead, Robson asserted that the Saxons had 'availed themselves of these sources' and passed them on to the Normans: 'That after the Conquest, the Normans reaped a plentiful harvest from the labours of their Saxon predecessors, is more likely than that they should have troubled themselves with the scarcely accessible and difficult ground of ancient British traditions'.[59]

In Robson's account, the Saxons are elevated to the position of cultural interpreters of the 'difficult' Celtic traditions. From there it was only one more small step to removing the Celts from the equation altogether, and in the case of the Arthurian legend this scenario had

---

[58] Ibid. 202; Philip Dodd, 'Englishness and the National Culture', in Robert Colls and Philip Dodd (eds.), *Englishness: Politics and Culture 1880–1920* (London, Sydney and Dover, NH: Croom Helm, 1986), 11–12.

[59] John Robson, *Three Early English Metrical Romances* (London, 1842), pp. xii–xiv.

occurred by the end of the nineteenth century. In 1897 the literary critic George Saintsbury took up the key question of determining the legend's country of origin in his *The Flourishing of Romance and the Rise of Allegory*. Saintsbury explained that there were three theories: one, that the legend was Welsh; two, that it was French; and three, that it was English. Regarding the first, he admitted that 'there were references to Arthur' in 'old Welsh literature', but he dismissed their significance because 'they were very meagre and . . . had little if anything to do with the received Arthurian story'.[60] Saintsbury next tackled the French claim, for which the best supporting evidence was that 'without exception, all of the oldest texts in which the complete romantic story of Arthur appears are in the French language'. He pointed out, however, that this fact alone failed to reveal the nationality of the writers, because French was widely spoken among the European elite who would have served as the primary audience for the tales. That left the English claim, to which Saintsbury gave his wholehearted support. 'If, as I think may fairly be done', he declared, 'the glory of the Legend be chiefly claimed for none of these, but for English or Anglo-Norman, it can be done in no spirit of national *pleonexia*, but on a sober consideration of all the facts of the case'. How did Saintsbury justify giving England credit for the Arthurian legend? He argued that the legend was English because it was English authors who had succeeded in combining the disparate elements of the legend taken from various national traditions into a coherent whole that was far more than the sum of its parts. 'Classical rhetoric, French gallantry, Saxon religiosity and intense realisation of the other world, Oriental extravagance to some extent, the "Celtic vague"—all these things are there', he wrote. 'But they are all co-ordinated, dominated, fashioned anew by some thing which is none of them, but which is the English genius'.[61]

In order completely to overturn both French and Celtic claims to the Arthurian legend, however, Saintsbury and other scholars who asserted that it was of English origin would have to trace it to a specifically English source, a source which displayed this 'English genius' for combining various literary elements in order to create a brilliant original work. This search would not be easy, for the vast majority of the twenty-three extant medieval Arthurian romances written in

---

[60] George Saintsbury, *The Flourishing of Romance and the Rise of Allegory* (Edinburgh and London, 1897), 135.   [61] Ibid. 137-8, 146-7.

English seemed extremely pedestrian and derivative when compared to their continental counterparts. 'It must be admitted', wrote the eminent Arthurian scholar Jessie Weston in 1897, 'that it strikes an English student disagreeably to find that, in taking up the study of a subject so essentially national in spirit, the English books which can be relied upon for information are so few in number, and . . . of so little value in comparison with the foreign literature'.[62]

In 1895 the literary critic S. Humphreys Gurteen attempted to deal with this problem. Agreeing with Saintsbury, Gurteen emphatically declared that the Arthurian legend was 'national property,' but he admitted that this did not necessarily mean that the English had been responsible for the earliest tales of Arthur. Instead, he readily acknowledged that the legend's roots could be traced 'to the dim twilight of British literature . . . when the daring deeds and heroic valour of the Welsh gave rise to the first faint beginnings of Welsh song'. How, then, could the Arthurian legend be English 'property'? Because it had taken an English author, Sir Thomas Malory, to create a true Arthurian masterpiece, in the form of his *Le Morte d'Arthur* in the late fifteenth century. Malory, according to Gurteen, had revived 'the good old Saxon' tongue which had been 'outcast', 'insulted', and 'oppressed' during the centuries after the Norman Conquest. 'Romance after romance appeared', Gurteen asserted, 'and the language was French', but all the while the Saxon language was acquiring the 'power . . . which was destined ere long to overthrow its oppressor'. At last, 'the crisis arrived', and Malory's work appeared in Middle English, which gave it 'a subtle, magnetic charm that is irresistible': 'Even the conspicuous absence of artificial finish only tends to heighten the effect upon the mind, and to one who is accustomed to the close drawing-room atmosphere of the modern fashionable novel to turn to Malory, is to exchange the crowded city for the free air, the green fields, and the utter listlessness of an ideal landscape'.[63] Gurteen thus grants to Malory the role in English literary history formerly allotted to the Celts: the imparting of a healthy dose of fresh air and strength to what had formerly been cramped, feeble, and corrupted.

[62] Jessie L. Weston, *The Legend of Sir Gawain: Studies upon Its Original Scope and Significance* (London, 1897), 3.

[63] S. Humphreys Gurteen, *The Arthurian Epic: A Comparative Study of the Cambrian, Breton, and Anglo-Norman Versions of the Story and Tennyson's Idylls of the King* (New York and London, 1895), 11, 56, 82–5.

And Gurteen was far from the only Victorian commentator to elevate Malory to such lofty heights.[64] 'No man need go farther than that book for the Great King's history', declared B. Montgomerie Ranking in 1871. Some critics even compared Malory to Homer and Virgil. According to the ninth edition of the *Encylopaedia Britannica* (1879), *Le Morte d'Arthur* was 'truly *the* epic of the English mind as the *Iliad* is the epic of the Greek mind'. And indeed, it was regarded as being a specifically *English* cultural product. *Le Morte*, according to William Minto in his *Characteristics of the English Poets* (1874), featured 'simple old English', dominated by monosyllabic words and uncontaminated by foreign phrases. *Blackwood's* concurred, declaring that *Le Morte*'s 'terse, idiomatic language' was 'the purest English extant'.[65] Some literary scholars extended this argument even further, claiming that Malory wrote not only in an English but in an explicitly 'Saxon' style, untainted by 'Norman' influences, even though *Le Morte d'Arthur* had been composed over four centuries after the Norman Conquest. George Marsh, the author of the popular philological study *The Origin and History of the English Language* (1862), praised Malory's 'Saxon English', and the Oxford Professor of English, Walter Raleigh, described Malory as 'a master in the telling use of Saxon speech'.[66]

Such declarations of Malory's inherent 'Englishness' helped to establish *Le Morte d'Arthur* as the major source for English interpreters of the Arthurian legend. Alfred, Lord Tennyson owned no less than four different editions, which he utilized heavily in the writing of the *Idylls of the King*. Matthew Arnold used Malory as a key source for his poem 'Tristram and Iseult' (1852), as did William Morris for the four Arthurian poems he included in *The Defence of Guenevere and Other Poems* (1858)

---

[64] The most comprehensive survey of Malory criticism in the nineteenth century is Marilyn Jackson Parrins, 'A Survey of Malory Criticism and Related Arthurian Scholarship in the Nineteenth Century', unpublished Ph.D. dissertation, University of Michigan, 1982.

[65] B. Montgomerie Ranking, *La Mort D'Arthur. The Old Prose Stories Whence the 'Idylls of the King' Have Been Taken by Alfred Tennyson* (London, 1871), 9–10; 'Malory', *Encyclopaedia Britannica*, 9th edn. (Edinburgh, 1879), x. 173; William Minto, *Characteristics of the English Poets from Chaucer to Shirley* (Edinburgh and London, 1874), 106; 'King Arthur and His Round Table', *Blackwood's Edinburgh Magazine*, 88 (1860), 318.

[66] George Marsh, *The Origin and History of the English Language and of the Early Literature It Embodies* (London, 1862), 490; Walter Raleigh, *The English Novel; Being a Short Sketch of Its History from the Earliest Times to the Appearance of Waverley* (London, 1894), 15.

and Algernon Charles Swinburne for *Tristram of Lyonesse* (1882) and *The Tale of Balen* (1896).[67]

Malory's lofty status in the late nineteenth century is all the more remarkable in light of the fact that prior to 1800 his work had been little known and rarely appreciated. After the edition published by William Stansby in 1634, *Le Morte d'Arthur* was not printed in Britain for almost two centuries. In 1816, however, two different editions of the *Morte* appeared, one edited by Alexander Chalmers and the other by Joseph Haslewood.[68] Both, however, were based upon the error-filled Stansby edition of 1634 and thus were of little use to serious scholars of medieval romance. Somewhat better for this purpose was the edition prepared by Robert Southey, which Longman published the following year and which was reprinted 'with scrupulous exactness' from the first edition of *Le Morte d'Arthur*, rather than from the corrupt Stansby text. But although the Southey edition would remain the most authoritative text for over half a century, it was not impeccable. Southey's copy of the original edition was missing eleven leaves, and he had been forced to fill the gap by cobbling together a number of other sources, with mixed results. In addition, the 250 standard-size copies each cost a princely £8 8s., thus making this edition inaccessible to all but the wealthiest lovers of medieval literature.[69]

The next editor to tackle Malory was Thomas Wright in 1858. Wright was an astonishingly energetic and prolific—if not always accurate—handler of medieval texts who produced works for the Shakespeare Society, the Caxton Society, and the Roxburghe Club. His *Morte* was undeniably popular, for it appeared in five editions before the end of the nineteenth century, but Wright, like Chalmers

---

[67] Yuri Fuwa, 'Malory's *Morte Darthur* in Tennyson's Library', in Workman (ed.), *Medievalism in England*, 161–9; Mary Byrd Davis, 'A Source for Arnold's Tale of Merlin and Vivian', *English Language Notes, 14* (1976), 120–3; David Staines, 'Morris's Treatment of His Medieval Sources in *The Defence of Guenevere and Other Poems*', *Studies in Philology, 70* (1973), 439–64; David Staines, 'Swinburne's Arthurian World: Swinburne's Arthurian Poetry and Its Medieval Sources', *Studia Neophilologica, 50* (1978), 53–70.

[68] *The History of the Renowned Prince Arthur, King of Britain*, ed. Alexander Chalmers (London, 1816); *La Mort d'Arthur*, ed. Joseph Haslewood (London, 1816). For a detailed survey of early-nineteenth-century editions of Malory, see Barry Gaines, 'The Editions of Malory in the Early Nineteenth Century', *Papers of the Bibliographical Society of America, 68* (1974), 1–28.

[69] Robert Southey, *The Byrth, Life and Acts of King Arthur* (London, 1817), p. xxviii. In addition, 50 more copies were printed on large paper, each costing £12 12s. For the full publication history of the Southey edition, see Barry Gaines, *Sir Thomas Malory: An Anecdotal Bibliography of Editions, 1485–1985* (New York: AMS, 1990), 16–19.

and Haslewood, reprinted the Stansby edition rather than the original, thus duplicating its numerous errors. Also flawed was Sir Edward Strachey's edition of 1868. Strachey, who had consulted both extant copies of the original text, offered a reprint 'with the spelling modernised, and those few words which are unintelligibly obsolete replaced by others which . . . are still in use, yet with all the old forms retained which do not interfere with this requirement of being readable'. Unfortunately, part of this modernization process demanded the exclusion of 'what is offensive to modern manners', resulting in over 400 omissions from the original text.[70]

Nineteenth-century Britons thus still lacked an entirely accurate edition of *Le Morte d'Arthur*. Ironically, it was not an English but a German scholar who took on the formidable task of providing one. In 1887 Heinrich Oskar Sommer received a six-month leave of absence from the Royal Prussian Ministry of Public Instruction so that he could prepare a reprint of Malory's original text. Sommer was a diligent scholar who was determined to ensure accuracy by transcribing and proof-reading every line himself, and his monumental edition, which appeared in three volumes between 1889 and 1891, set the scholarly standard for over three-quarters of a century. The Sommer edition made serious scholarly analysis of *Le Morte d'Arthur* possible for the first time. More significantly, it marked the culmination of the process of Malory's incorporation into the English literary canon that had begun over seventy years before.

As a foreigner, Sommer had little interest in promoting Malory as a source of patriotic sentiment. His diligent scholarship, however, overcame many of the lingering difficulties which had precluded Malory's inclusion in the English canon. For centuries, the mysterious 'Sir Thomas Malory, Knt.' who had composed *Le Morte d'Arthur* had been thought to be a Welshman, a situation which was problematic for those who wished to minimize the contribution of the Celts to contemporary British culture.[71] Sommer, however, declared emphatically that Malory

---

[70] *Morte Darthur*, ed. Edward Strachey (London, 1868), pp. xvii–xvii; Yuri Fuwa, 'The Globe Edition of Malory as a Bowdlerized Text in the Victorian Age', *Studies in English Literature* (Japan), English Language No. (1984), 6. The nineteenth-century debate over the morality of *Le Morte Darthur* will be discussed at greater length below.

[71] That Malory was Welsh had been proposed as early as 1548, when John Bale, Bishop of Ossory and noted antiquary, declared in a biographical dictionary of famous British authors that Malory was 'Britannus natione' and that he had been born in 'Mailoria in finibus Cambriae, Devæ flumini vicina'. Despite the fact that it was extremely unlikely that a fifteenth-century Welshman would have composed a long romance

had been English. 'There is no reason to suppose', he wrote in the *Academy*, 'that Malory was a Welshman'. Subsequent scholarship reinforced his arguments, and by the mid-1890s it was all but definitively established that Malory had been of English birth.[72]

A second difficulty facing Malory was the charge that he lacked originality. After all, a work could hardly be accepted as a proud product of the national culture if it was regarded as, in the words of one early-nineteenth-century critic, 'a mere compilation' of works by authors from other nations. Sommer's precise identification of *Le Morte*'s sources, however, allowed scholars to make detailed comparisons of the text and its antecedents and in the process to achieve a greater appreciation of Malory's accomplishment. According to Sommer, Malory was 'no mere translator'. Instead, 'he evidently endeavoured—and with no little measure of success—to weld into an harmonious whole the immense mass of French romance. After a comparison with his sources, his work gives the impression that he did not servilely copy his originals, but . . . that he impressed upon the whole the stamp of his own individuality'. After the publication of Sommer's edition, virtually every critic praised Malory for his originality. In the *Temple Bar* in 1896 Frederick Dixon wrote:

He took the volumes in existence . . . as a weaver takes his skeins, and, using his pen as his shuttle, wove out of them the history of his 'Round Table', as Matilda and her maidens pictured the story of the Conquest in the tapestry of Bayeaux. Not that he was a mere literary carpenter, for, if like Shakespeare

---

in English, the notion that Malory had been Welsh survived until well into the nineteenth century. See Robert Watt, *Bibliotheca Britannica; or A General Index to British and Foreign Literature* (Edinburgh and London, 1824), ii. 638; George Burnett, *Specimens of English Prose-Writers, from the Earliest Times to the Close of the Seventeenth Century* (London, 1807), i. 247–59. For Leland and Bale, see Marilyn Jackson Parins (ed.), *Malory: The Critical Heritage* (London and New York: Routledge, 1988), 52–5.

[72] H. Oskar Sommer, 'The Sources of Malory's "Le Morte Darthur"', *Academy*, 37 (1890), 11. In 1897 A. T. Martin announced in the *Athenaeum* that he had discovered the will of a Thomas Malory of Papworth St Agnes in Huntingdonshire. See A. T. Martin, 'The Identity of the Author of the "Morte d'Arthur," with Notes on the Will of Thomas Malory and the Genealogy of the Malory Family', *Archaeologia*, 56 (1898), 165–82; 'Sir Thomas Malory,' *Athenaeum*, 2 (1897), 353–4; '"Mailoria" and Sir Thomas Malory', *Athenaeum*, 2 (1898), 98; 'Society of Antiquaries—June 16', *Athenaeum*, 2 (1898), 827. Also in 1897 the distinguished American scholar George Lyman Kittredge of Harvard University proposed that the real Thomas Malory had been a man from Newbold Revel in Warwickshire. See G. L. Kittredge, 'Who Was Sir Thomas Malory?', *Studies and Notes in Philology and Literature*, 5 (1897), 97–106; T. W. Williams, 'Sir Thomas Malory', *Athenaeum*, 2 (1896), 64–5, 98.

he made use of the materials ready to his hand, like Shakespeare he imbued them with an individuality entirely his own.[73]

Sommer thus not only provided English readers with an authoritative text of *Le Morte d'Arthur*, he also provided them with scholarship which helped to remove many of the problems which had for centuries inhibited its incorporation into the English literary canon. But one final problem had to be solved before this incorporation would be complete. The morality of *Le Morte d'Arthur* had long been questioned, and a work of literature could not be considered truly 'national' in the second half of the nineteenth century if its moral values did not comply with the broader 'improving' aims of contemporary mass education. Malory's work would thus have to be made to conform to Victorian attitudes and educational objectives.

In the eyes of many contemporary scholars, editors, and publishers of medieval literature, the only method by which this could be accomplished was to expunge the morally dubious elements from the text. From the 1860s onwards *Le Morte d'Arthur* thus became the object of a zealous expurgating impulse. In 1862 James T. Knowles brought out a popular abridgment of Malory whose preface justified the excision of parts of the text on the grounds that they were not 'fitted for boys'. In order to remedy this defect, Knowles 'suppressed and modified where changed manners and morals have made it absolutely necessary to do so for the preservation of a lofty original ideal'. In particular, he eliminated any specific details of Guinevere's adulterous relationship with Lancelot. He also implied that Arthur's birth was legitimate rather than the result of an adulterous affair, and he eliminated all reference to Mordred as Arthur's illegitimate son, begotten with his half-sister. Thus, despite his claim that he had done 'little but abridge and simplify' Malory's original text, in truth his changes were quite extensive and significantly altered the story.[74]

Other editors of abridged versions of *Le Morte d'Arthur* took a similar approach. In 1868 the Revd Edward Conybeare blamed Malory's 'occasional coarseness' for his current unpopularity. Conybeare hoped to obviate this by 'taking liberties with the text': 'The coarse passages

---

[73] Ellis, *Specimens*, i. 308; Sommer, 'Sources', 11; Frederick Dixon, 'The Round Table', *Temple Bar*, *109* (1896), 210.

[74] Knowles, *Story of King Arthur*, pp. ii–iii; Marilyn Jackson Parins, 'Malory's Expurgators', in Mary Flowers Braswell and John Bugge (eds.), *The Arthurian Tradition: Essays in Convergence* (Tuscaloosa and London: University of Alabama Press, 1988), 148–9.

have been cut out, [and] the book generally much abbreviated'. He, too, omitted the details of Arthur's illegitimate birth, and he mentioned the love between Lancelot and Guinevere only in extremely circumspect language. Going one step further, Henry Frith's abridgement of 1884 eliminated the adulterous relationship altogether. Frith declared in the introduction:

It has been found necessary to expunge and . . . to alter the relationship of the characters as given in the old romance. The necessity for these modifications, in preparing the volume for the young, will be apparent to every adult student of the 'Morte d'Arthur'. . . . We have . . . endeavoured to preserve the consistency of the narrative while purging it of any questionable matter, and 'toning down' motives and conduct, which if painted in their true colours would offend.[75]

This expurgating impulse affected not only the numerous abridgements and adaptations of Malory that were published in the second half of the nineteenth century, however, but also supposedly complete editions of the text. Despite his solemnly stated intention of publishing a text which was as close to Malory's original as possible, Edward Strachey omitted 'such phrases or passages as are not in accordance with modern manners' in his Globe edition of 1868. This resulted in the removal of hundreds of words and phrases, especially those which had sexual connotations (such as 'bed', night', and 'lie by'); blasphemous expressions (such as 'so God me help' and 'a mercy Jesus'); and vulgarities (such as 'belly', 'gut', 'buttock', and 'bawdy'). He permitted only the vaguest suggestion that Mordred was the product of Arthur's incest, and even the most implicit reference to physical contact between the sexes was avoided. In Malory's original text, for example, Merlin declares to Uther Pendragon, Arthur's father, that 'the first night that ye shall lie by Igraine ye shall get a child on her', but Strachey's text reads, 'after ye shall win Igraine ye shall have a child by her'.[76]

For the most part, reviewers supported these decisions to alter Malory's work in the interest of elevating its morality. In 1868 the *Athenaeum* proclaimed that Strachey 'has given evidence of sound

[75] Edward Conybeare, *La Morte D'Arthur: The History of King Arthur, Compiled by Sir Thomas Malory* (London, 1868), pp. iv–v; Henry Frith, *King Arthur and his Knights of the Round Table* (London, 1884), p. iv.

[76] Strachey, *Morte D'Arthur*, p. xviii; Fuwa, 'The Globe Edition', 6; Parins, 'Malory's Expurgators', 153.

judgment. By the few omissions which he has made, in order to exclude some things that are offensive, the book has gained rather than lost'. Similarly, *Notes and Queries* observed that Strachey had 'judiciously revised' *Le Morte d'Arthur* 'as to suit it to our times'. With the assistance of numerous Victorian expurgators, Malory's work became a text worthy for use as a guide to proper moral conduct. In the *English Illustrated Magazine* in the late 1880s Frederick Ryland pointed to a plethora of virtues which could be emulated by *Le Morte d'Arthur*'s readers:

Among the more conspicuous . . . are courage, love of justice and hatred of injustice, loyalty, fidelity to promises and to the unspoken obligations implied by friendship and brotherhood, self-control, and disregard of mere bodily ease. Clemency is held in the highest estimation. . . . While the motive for action is often love of fame, the best knights are notable for their humility; and lofty self-respect is combined with almost child-like simplicity. Gentleness, generosity, and courtesy, among lesser excellencies which go to make up the character of a gentleman, are there; and with them sincere reverence for God and man, the absence of which lies at the root of half our modern failures and follies. The influence of a definitely Christian feeling is seen not only in the high place given to the virtues of mercy for the fallen and tenderness for the weak, but in the supreme importance attached to purity. The almost superstitious exaltation of bodily chastity is due to a vivid realisation of the beatitude which promises to the pure the vision of God. With this lofty ideal before them, the shortcomings of the knights are often lamentable; but it would hardly be correct to say that we have greatly improved in our practice, while in its reverence for purity the *Morte d'Arthur* is distinctly in advance of much of the popular fiction of today.

There were thus valuable moral lessons to be gleaned from a reading of a bowdlerized version of Malory. As B. Montgomerie Ranking declared in 1871, 'no man need go farther for an example of goodly life'.[77]

The transformation of *Le Morte d'Arthur* into a guide to moral conduct served as a key step in the long process of its assimilation into the English literary canon, and of the English assumption of ownership of the Arthurian legend. In the 1890s the noted editor of medieval texts William Wells Newell declared that 'for Arthurian story English readers are disposed to entertain that affection which is engendered by a sense of proprietorship'. Without *Le Morte d'Arthur*, however, such a

[77] *Athenaeum*, 1 (1868), 695; *Notes and Queries*, 4: 1 (1868), 428; F. Ryland, 'The Morte D'Arthur', *English Illustrated Magazine*, 6 (1888 9), 92; Ranking, *La Mort D'Arthur*, 10.

sense of possession would not have been possible. In the introduction to yet another edition in 1897, Israel Gollancz wrote that it had 'done more than any other work to nationalise the ancient story of Arthur and his Knights'.[78]

The dominance of Malory, however, does not mean that all other British medieval Arthurian texts were entirely ignored in the nineteenth century. On the contrary, additional examples were unearthed and republished as well. In 1849, for example, Lady Charlotte Guest published a collection of Welsh tales which she called *The Mabinogion*, several of which featured King Arthur. As they were undeniably several centuries older than *Le Morte d'Arthur*, these tales would seem to have lent credence to Welsh claims to the legend. 'It appears . . . that a large portion of the stocks of medieval Romance proceeded from Wales', Guest wrote in the introduction.[79]

A closer examination of her arguments, however, reveals that beneath the pro-Celtic surface were a number of tensions about the relationship between Welsh and English culture. First and most obviously, Guest chose to publish *The Mabinogion* in an English translation, with the original Welsh tacked onto the end and thus reduced to what was very much a secondary position. In the second edition of 1877 she eliminated the Welsh text altogether and removed all Welsh quotations from the notes, thereby making it even easier to ignore the Welsh origins of the tales. (It was not until 1880 that an all-Welsh edition of *The Mabinogion* was published in England.)[80] Furthermore, Guest went out of her way to proclaim her pro-Welsh sentiments in a nonthreatening, non-nationalist manner. She expressed her glorification of Welsh cultural achievement in extremely romanticized terms and made no attempt to connect it to current political aspirations for Welsh independence. In this sense, *The Mabinogion* belongs to that mode of nineteenth-century Welsh cultural nationalism which tried to create a mythical and romantic national past, a past that could serve as a source of pride but at the same time made Wales appear archaic and quaint.[81]

---

[78] William Wells Newell (ed.), *King Arthur and the Table Round, Tales Chiefly after the Old French of Crestien of Troyes* (London, [1897]), p. iii; Israel Gollancz (ed.), *Le Morte Darthur by Sir Thomas Malory* (London, [1897]), i. 316.

[79] Lady Charlotte Guest, *The Mabinogion, from the Welsh of the Llyfr Coch O Hergest and Other Ancient Welsh Manuscripts, with an English Translation and Notes* (London, 1838–49), vol. i, p. xvi.   [80] *Y Mabinogion Cymreig* (Liverpool, 1880).

[81] See Prys Morgan, 'From a Death to a View: The Hunt for the Welsh Past in the Romantic Era', in Eric Hobsbawm and Terence Ranger (eds.), *The Invention of Tradition* (Cambridge: Cambridge UP, 1983), 43–100.

It was not, in other words, a text which was intended to overturn English claims to the Arthurian legend, or to resist the dominance of Malory's *Morte d'Arthur*.

There were others besides Guest who refused to relinquish the field without a fight, however, and the theory that the Arthurian legend was of Welsh origin continued to be professed into the late nineteenth century. In 1891, for example, John Rhys reiterated the old argument that the legend had been created by the Welsh and then modified by the Normans. Rhys also claimed that the Celtic influence on English literature far outweighed the Saxon:

The Celtic strain in English literature has since the Middle Ages been greatly reinforced from time to time by the genius of such men as Shakespeare and Spenser, Tennyson and Swinburne. Whatever, then, may be said of the pedigree of the English people, the pedigree of English literature is well established. Teutonic it cannot be to any great extent, whereas we have seen how largely it must be Celtic. Any attempt, therefore, to throw light on the genesis and history of the Arthurian legend may be expected to appeal not only to those who have an interest in Celtic, but also to some whose interest clings chiefly to the English language and the grand literature which is the reflection of her fairest features.

Rhys was himself Welsh, however, and his argument in many ways stems from the same patriotic motives as do the Anglocentric claims of the English critics cited above. In certain respects, some of the premises of Celtic cultural nationalism in this period ratified rather than challenged the claims of Arnold and his supporters. As Arnold sought to reduce Celtic culture to the status of a minor contributor to its superior English counterpart, the best alternative for Celtic cultural nationalists seemed to be vigorous and vehement assertions of independence from English influences. What this meant, however, was that Arnold's racialist belief that each nation possessed its own essential characteristics was often accepted without protest. The search for a 'pure' cultural identity which was unsullied by, and inherently superior to, English culture led many nationalists towards a search for non-existent Celtic 'essences'. To be sure, this helped to preserve Celtic cultural institutions, but it also increased the sense of separateness between Celtic and English cultures.[82] From an English perspective, this meant that when Welsh commentators such as Rhys pressed their

---

[82] John Rhys, *Studies in the Arthurian Legend* (Oxford, 1891), 390; Dodd, 'Englishness', 13–4.

claims regarding Arthur's Celtic origins, they could be dismissed as expressing a nationalist sentiment which was at best hopelessly biased and at worst the thin end of a wedge that could destroy cultural 'unity' (i.e., the dominance of English culture) in the British Isles.

It is also important to realize that, by the end of the nineteenth century, *only* Welsh scholars were arguing in favor of the Celtic origins of the Arthurian legend, while English critics claimed the legend for their own nation. This marked a significant change from the late eighteenth and early nineteenth centuries, when English commentators had been willing to see the legend as a *British* cultural product and the distinction as to whether it was Welsh or English was not so crucial. The fact that these English commentators were no longer willing to share Arthur with their Welsh brethren reveals much about the increasingly Anglocentric nature of English cultural nationalism in the late nineteenth century, and about the trajectory of nationalist sentiment within the British Isles in general.

The evolution of the respective relationships of the Robin Hood ballads and Malory's *Morte d'Arthur* to English culture over the course of the nineteenth century demonstrates the importance of the construction of an English literary tradition for contemporary nationalism. The emergence of English as an autonomous academic discipline simultaneously reflected and contributed to growing pride in the language and its literature, a pride which manifested itself in a surge of interest in the publication of medieval texts. And the legends of King Arthur and Robin Hood both benefited from this trend. The Robin Hood ballads came to occupy an exalted position as expressions of the 'national genius' in its infant state, while Sir Thomas Malory came to be regarded as a master of English prose worthy of comparison to the nation's greatest authors, which meant that the Arthurian legend could now be claimed as a specifically English cultural product. Both, in different ways, were celebrated as proud products of the national literary tradition, and both, in different ways, contributed to the growth of a specifically *English*—as opposed to British—cultural nationalism in this period.

CHAPTER FOUR

'Our fathers were of Saxon race': Robin Hood, King Arthur, and the Rise of Anglo-Saxon Racialism

IN ITS conventional usage, the term 'ethnicity' refers to the common origin and descent of a particular group of people who share certain fundamental characteristics due to their kinship. Taken literally, this definition is by and large irrelevant to an examination of nationalism, for the populations of nation-states are almost invariably too hetero-geneous to claim any sort of common biological heritage. Nevertheless, the invocation of 'blood' has obvious advantages in bonding together members of a group by excluding outsiders. Although it rarely exists as a component of nationalism in a strictly biological sense, the influence of ethnicity must therefore be taken into account, for 'blood' ties are often invented in order to permit a nation to create an identity for itself.[1]

Nineteenth-century Britain provides a striking case in point. In this period an elaborate racial hierarchy was erected which placed the Anglo-Saxon peoples at the top, a crude biological determinism seem-ingly confirmed by Britain's pre-eminent political, economic, and military position. The construction of British national identity upon this new racial basis would not prove so simple, however. The emphasis upon racial exclusivity fractured the 'Britishness' which had been built up over the course of the eighteenth century and replaced it with a far less ethnically inclusive 'Saxon-ness'. This change would ultimately prove problematic for a nation whose population was far too diverse to claim any sort of common genetic origin.

This chapter will examine the creation of this new racialist identity

---

[1] E. J. Hobsbawm, *Nations and Nationalism since 1780*: Programme, Myth, Reality, 2nd edn. (Cambridge: Cambridge UP, 1992) 63; George Schöpflin, 'The Functions of Myth and a Taxonomy of Myths', in Geoffrey Hoskings and George Schöpflin (eds.), *Myths and Nationhood* (New York: Routledge, 1997), 24.

and how it influenced attempts to pinpoint the historical identities of King Arthur and Robin Hood. The term 'scientific racism' is often used to describe nineteenth-century views of race, but the discussion was far from confined to the realm of science. Instead, racial theory penetrated British culture at many levels, pervading not just the natural sciences, but also anthropology, archaeology, classics, geography, geology, folklore studies, history, languages, law, literature, and theology. As the future prime minister Benjamin Disraeli put it in 1847: 'All is race; there is no other truth'.[2] Regarding the legends of King Arthur and Robin Hood in particular, the effort to uncover their basis in historical reality—or lack thereof—became intimately involved with the production of Anglo-Saxon racialist mythology. In order for King Arthur and Robin Hood to function as true national heroes, they had to be assimilated with the prevailing ideas regarding race and national identity.

'No taint of Norman blood': Robin Hood as Saxon Hero in Nineteenth-Century Britain

'Who was Robin Hood?' asked W. F. Prideaux in *Notes and Queries* in 1886.[3] This question aroused an intense debate in nineteenth-century Britain. On the one hand, there were those who believed that Robin Hood was an entirely fictional creation. In the late 1840s the *Edinburgh Review* asked: 'What do contemporary English chroniclers say about him? Not a word. What evidence does any contemporary author afford concerning him? None at all. What proof is there, in short, that he ever existed, or did any one of the feats attributed to him?' At the very end of the nineteenth century Sir Sidney Lee afforded Robin Hood the paradoxical and perhaps unique distinction of an entry in the *Dictionary of National Biography* arguing that he never existed. The preponderance of Victorian commentators, however, argued in favour of Robin Hood's historical reality. 'We cannot but here enter a protest against

---

[2] Robert J. C. Young, *Colonial Desire: Hybridity in Theory, Culture and Race* (London and New York: Routledge, 1995), 93.

[3] W. F. Prideaux, 'Who Was Robin Hood?', *Notes and Queries*, 7: 2 (1886), 421. For recent attempts to answer the question of Robin Hood's reality, see John Bellamy, *Robin Hood: An Historical Enquiry* (Bloomington: Indiana UP, 1985); P. Valentine Harris, *The Truth about Robin Hood*, new edn. (Mansfield: Linneys, 1971); J. R. Madicott, 'The Birth and Setting of the Ballads of Robin Hood', *English Historical Review*, 93 (1978), 276–99.

the sceptical spirit of the present day, which has led many to doubt the very existence of Robin Hood, and to treat the long-cherished traditions of him as no better than myths', wrote the Revd J. Stacye in his history of Sherwood Forest in 1875. Others concurred; the prominent literary antiquarians John W. Hales and Frederick J. Furnivall declared in 1867 that 'we are not inclined to deny the existence of Robin Hood'.[4]

This debate represented more than a mere squabble among antiquaries. A denial of the reality of a national hero like Robin Hood was also a challenge to the nation's history and thus, in a sense, to the nation itself. Joseph Hunter, an assistant keeper at the Public Record Office, had strong words for those 'unpatriotic' scholars who refuted Robin Hood's reality:

Trusting to the plain sense of my countrymen, I dismiss these theorists to that limbo of vanity, there to live with all those who would make all remote history fable, who would make us believe that everything which is good in England is a mere copy of something originated in countries eastward to our own, and who would deny to the English nation in past ages all skill and all advancement in literature or in the arts of sculpture and architecture.

In the early 1850s Hunter identified a plausible candidate for the 'real' Robin Hood, a fourteenth-century man whose biography dovetailed with many of the legend's details. Arguing that the ballad entitled the *Little Gest of Robin Hood* was 'entitled to no small consideration as an historical document', Hunter focused upon a scene in which a 'King Edward' makes a progress through Lancashire.[5] He discovered that Edward II had indeed made such a progress in November 1323, when he spent a fortnight at Nottingham. The *Gest* goes on to describe how Edward encounters the outlaws, pardons them for their crimes, and brings Robin Hood into his service. Here, Hunter again found evidence linking the fictional tale to known history. Between March and November of 1324 a 'Robyn Hood' was paid three pence per day as one of the king's valets. His disappearance from the records there-

[4] *Edinburgh Review*, 86 (1847), 134–6; Sir Sidney Lee, 'Robin Hood', in *Dictionary of National Biography* (London, 1891) xxvii. 258–9; Revd J. Stacye, 'The Ancient History of Sherwood Forest', in Robert White, *Nottinghamshire. Worksop, 'The Dukery,' and Sherwood Forest* (Worksop, 1875), 184; John W. Hales and Frederick J. Furnivall, *Bishop Percy's Folio Manuscript. Ballads and Romances* (London, 1867), i. 5.

[5] Joseph Hunter, 'The Great Hero of the Ancient Minstrelsy of England, "Robin Hood"', in his *Critical and Historical Tracts*, No. IV (London, 1852) 3; British Library, Add MS 24480, fo. 304.

after, according to Hunter, coincided with the *Gest*'s claim that he had quickly tired of courtly life and returned to the forest. 'There is surely a remarkable coincidence between the ballad and the record', he wrote, 'hardly to be accounted for by the chance occurrence of two persons of the same name'.[6]

Despite its archival authority, however, Hunter's argument never really seized the imagination of the Victorian public, and no work of nineteenth-century fiction was based upon it. The view of Robin Hood as a servant to the king working for a daily wage did not conform to contemporary notions of what constituted a national hero. Instead, it was a very different vision of the historical Robin Hood which won the day, a vision which identified him as a heroic Saxon freedom fighter struggling against Norman oppression. In distinct contrast to Hunter's, this hypothesis was supported by no real evidence, but none the less it became widely popular because it appealed to the patriotism of contemporary Britons, many of whom saw their Saxon heritage as the source of their nation's finest qualities.

The earliest references to Robin Hood as a specifically Saxon figure date from the second half of the eighteenth century. In his influential *Reliques of Ancient English Poetry* (1765), Thomas Percy declared that 'the severity of those tyrannical forest-laws, that were introduced by our Norman kings, and the great temptation of breaking them by such as lived near the royal forests . . . must constantly have occasioned great numbers of outlaws', among whom he included Robin Hood. Joseph Ritson, the editor of the most important eighteenth-century collection of Robin Hood ballads, also linked the legend to Saxon resistance to the Norman conquest.[7]

In this period, however, ideas regarding the superiority of the Saxons emphasized the unique nature of their institutions rather than the innate supremacy of their blood. In particular, the concept of a distinct, superior Saxon 'race' rested on two historical myths. First, there was the religious myth of a pure Saxon church, which dated from the 1530s when it was used to justify Henry VIII's break with Rome. According to this myth, the Henrician Reformation had returned the English church to the purer practices of the period before the

---

[6] Hunter, 'Great Hero', 36–7.
[7] Thomas Percy, *Reliques of Ancient English Poetry: Consisting of Old Heroic Ballads, Songs and other Pieces of our Earlier Poets* (London, 1765), i. 74; Joseph Ritson, *Robin Hood: A Collection of Poems, Songs, and Ballads Relative to that Celebrated English Outlaw* (London, 1795), i. vi.

Norman Conquest and cleansed it of the abuses introduced over the centuries by corrupt Roman Catholicism. The second myth of Saxon superiority had to do with political institutions. In the seventeenth century parliamentarians such as Sir Edward Coke turned to Saxon precedents to supply a historical rationale for their opposition to increases in royal power. In Saxon times, Coke and others claimed, the denizens of England had been protected by good laws, and representative institutions had flourished. In the period following the Glorious Revolution these ideas evolved into the 'Whig' view of the past, which centred upon the notion that a golden age of good government had existed in England before it had been destroyed by the Norman Conquest. The Conquest had been followed by a long struggle for the restoration of political rights, which had begun with the Magna Carta and culminated in the recent triumph over Stuart usurpations. As a result of these victories, this myth claimed, England was a nation with a unique continuity and superiority of legal and political institutions, institutions which could be traced directly to the Saxons.[8]

But although both of these myths argued that Saxon institutions were superior, neither attempted to attribute that superiority to racial causes. It was not until the early nineteenth century that the seeds of a new, racially based Saxon-ism were sown. Of central importance to this development was the Romantic movement. In Germany the idea that each nation possessed its own *Volksgeist*, or special national spirit, became a focal point of Romantic thought. At the same time, burgeoning German nationalism came to emphasize the continuity, uniqueness, and superiority of German culture and the German people. Thinkers such as Johann Gottlieb Fichte and Friedrich Schleiermacher exalted the German state and the people who inhabited it, in the process helping to demolish the Enlightenment vision of the unity of mankind. Elsewhere in Europe these ideas were incorporated into arguments depicting the Germanic peoples as a constantly expanding force in western history. These arguments helped to spread the idea of the noble, free simplicity of the tribes of the ancient German forests, from whom had supposedly descended the modern Germans, Anglo-Saxons, and Scandinavians.[9]

The influence of these new racial ideas was soon felt in Britain.

---

[8] Reginald Horsman, *Race and Manifest Destiny: The Origins of American Racial Anglo-Saxonism* (Cambridge, Mass. and London: Harvard UP, 1981), ch. 1.

[9] Ibid. 26–7, 30.

Sharon Turner's *History of the Anglo-Saxons* (1799–1805), the first complete treatment of Saxon history, depicted the Saxons as a strong and freedom-loving people. The most important text in the early development of Saxon racialism in Britain, however, was Sir Walter's Scott's *Ivanhoe* (1820), which focuses upon a still-pervasive conflict between the Saxons and the Normans a century after William the Conqueror had landed on English shores. In the first chapter Scott writes that 'four generations had not sufficed to blend the hostile blood of the Normans and Anglo-Saxons, or to unite, by common language and mutual interests, two hostile races'.[10] Significantly, Robin Hood plays a key role in this conflict, functioning as a symbol of patriotic Saxon resistance to Norman oppression.

In proclaiming the existence of innate, immutable differences between the Saxons and the Normans, Scott was contradicting the most respected contemporary historical scholarship. He believed, however, that ethnic distinctions were inevitable and natural, and could be identified throughout history. 'The degree of national diversity between different countries', he declared in his *Letters of Malachi Malagrowther* (1826), 'is but an instance of that general variety which nature seems to have adopted as a principle through all her work'. His Saxons are Saxons and his Normans are Normans not because of the unique nature of their political and social institutions, which he all but ignores in *Ivanhoe*, but because of an inherent biological distinction between them. Although Scott stops short of analysing British society through a theory of race, his work contains implications of racial exclusivity.[11]

Scott's influence upon subsequent treatments of the legend of Robin Hood can scarcely be exaggerated. His view received its first scholarly treatment at the hands of a young Frenchman named Augustin Thierry, who in the early 1820s was a prominent liberal journalist in Paris. Like Scott, whom he greatly admired, Thierry saw the past as an important weapon in the present political struggle. He also shared the belief that the peoples of Europe could be divided into different racial 'types' distinguishable by blood, law, language, and ideas.[12] In 1825

---

[10]   Sir Walter Scott, *Ivanhoe*, ed. A. N. Wilson (London and New York: Penguin, 1984), 8.

[11]   *The Prose Works of Sir Walter Scott*, Vol. 21: *Letters of Malachi Malagrowther on the Currency* (Edinburgh, 1830–6), 373; Clare A. Simmons, *Reversing the Conquest: History and Myth in Nineteenth-Century Literature* (New Brunswick, NJ, and London: Rutgers UP, 1990), 87.

[12]   Lionel Gossman, 'Augustin Thierry and Liberal Historiography', in his *Between History and Literature* (Cambridge, Mass., and London: Harvard UP, 1990), 83; Ivan Hannaford, *Race: The History of an Idea in the West* (Baltimore and London: Johns Hopkins UP, 1996), 240–1.

Thierry published his first—and most popular—work of historical scholarship, his *History of the Conquest of England by the Normans.* Celebrating their heroic resistance to the Normans, he set out to show how the Saxons were not entirely annihilated by the Conquest, but rather continued to struggle for liberty, a struggle which ultimately permitted the English to enjoy greater freedom than any other European people. His preface reveals the influence of Scott:

A great people are not so quickly subjugated as would seem to be intimated by the official acts of those who govern by right of force. . . . Patriotic regret still lies deep in the breasts of men, long after all hope for the old cause of the country has expired. This feeling, when it has no longer the power to create armies, still creates bands of partizans, political brigands in the forests or on the mountains; and causes such of them as die on the gibbet, to be venerated as martyrs.

For Thierry, as for Scott, the most famous and important of these 'political brigands' was Robin Hood, whom he described as the 'hero of the . . . Anglo-Saxon race'.[13]

Thierry was chiefly responsible for giving scholarly credence to Scott's fictional depiction of Robin Hood. Joseph Hunter reported in the early 1850s that the *History of the Conquest* had 'attained a wide popularity in England', and by 1856 it had appeared in three English editions. The *Westminster Review* had high praise for Thierry, declaring that he had 'made the nearest approximation that any modern writer has yet done, to a just view of Robin Hood's historical character and popularity'.[14]

With assistance from the scholarly reinforcement provided by Thierry, Scott's vision of Robin Hood as a Saxon hero struggling against Norman oppression came to dominate nineteenth-century views of the legend. In the early 1840s the poet Spencer Hall declared:

I do not believe a tithe of the trash that is told in relation to Robin Hood, some of it too silly for the most childish mind. . . . But pare away all we can, there is still enough of pith to prove that at a given time the title was paramountly borne by and recognized in one magnificent hero, as much the idol of the common people as he was the terror of tyrants and extortioners . . . and especially the friend of all who resented the Norman encroachment.

[13] Augustin Thierry, *History of the Conquest of England by the Normans: with its Causes from the Earliest Period, and its Consequences to the Present Time* (London, 1825), vol. i, pp. xiv–xv and vol. iii, pp. 237–8.

[14] Hunter, 'Great Hero', 2; *Westminster Review,* 33 (1839–40), 426.

Indeed, contemporary authors were so enamoured of this vision of Robin Hood that they were willing to ignore theories—such as Hunter's—that were supported by far more evidence. In October 1860 the opera *Robin Hood*, with lyrics by John Oxenford and words by G. A. Macfarren, premiered at Her Majesty's Theatre. Focusing upon the conflict between Saxon and Norman, the opera had clearly been inspired by Scott. 'Despite the hypothesis of the Rev. J. Hunter,' the programme declared, 'the celebrated outlaw Robin Hood is supposed, as in *Ivanhoe*, to flourish in the reign of Richard Coeur de Lion, and to be particularly serviceable as a friend . . . of the oppressed Saxons during the regency of Prince John'. This was reinforced by the opera's content. According to one song:

> Englishmen by birth are free;
> Though their limbs you chain,
> Glowing thoughts of liberty
> In their hearts remain.
> Normans, do whate'er you can,
> Ne'er you'll crush the Englishman!
>
> Our fathers were of Saxon race,
> With Hengist here they came;
> And when they found this resting-place,
> They lit a sacred flame.
> It did not blaze from altar or from pyre;
> But burning in the English heart is still that deathless
>   fire!
>
> The deathless flame of liberty
> We prize, a treasure dear;
> Though hidden for a while it be,
> At length 'twill re-appear.
> In vain our proud oppressors seek
> The Saxon race to quell;
> Their bonds of iron are but weak,
> While freedom in the soul can dwell.[15]

Despite the lack of historical evidence to support it, nineteenth-century British authors were willing to go to considerable lengths to

[15] Cornelius Brown, *Lives of Nottinghamshire Worthies and of Celebrated and Remarkable Men of the County from the Norman Conquest to AD 1882* (London and Nottingham, 1882), 12; programme for *Robin Hood*, Her Majesty's Theatre, Microfiche No. 19, Theatre Museum, Covent Garden, London; John Oxenford, *Robin Hood: An Opera in Three Acts* (London, 1860), 17.

promote this view of Robin Hood. Virtually every major fictional text written after 1820 features the conflict between Saxon and Norman as a prominent motif. In Pierce Egan's *Robin Hood and Little John* (1840), for example, the outlaw proclaims, 'I love my country and my countrymen, and hate the Norman race, for they are usurpers here, and oppressors with their usurpation'. Egan focuses upon certain traits which he regards as inherent racial characteristics. 'It is a Norman's nature', declares Little John, 'to deal in deceit and trickery'. The Saxons, in sharp contrast, are 'free, gentle, and simple'.[16] In post-*Ivanhoe* literary treatments of the legend of Robin Hood racial distinctions are also manifested in physical form. In his novel *Forest Days* (1843), G. P. R. James describes the Merry Men as 'strong and tall, with the Anglo-Saxon blood shining out in the complexion'. Similarly, in her children's story *The Boy Foresters* (1868) Anne Bowman describes Robin as 'tall and well-formed, with a bright and cheerful Saxon face'.[17] According to these authors and numerous others, Robin Hood's size, strength, and dexterity were all directly attributable to his Saxon blood, and this physical prowess would ultimately allow him, and his race, to triumph over their enemies.

The frequency with which these racialist ideas appeared in treatments of the legend of Robin Hood reflects the context in which they written. By the mid-nineteenth century Saxonism had grown into a national myth, for it seemed obvious to many Britons that the growing power of their nation stemmed from an inherent racial advantage. This belief was ostensibly confirmed by contemporary scientific study, which reified the concept of race and endowed it with explanatory powers far beyond its initial taxonomic purpose. With each passing year, more and more scientists argued that the successes or failures of individuals, peoples, and nations were directly attributable to race. Races were no longer thought of as the superficial and changeable products of climate and environment, as scientists had formerly claimed, but as stable and essential entities which caused or prevented the flowering of particular civilizations.[18]

---

[16] Pierce Egan, *Robin Hood and Little John or the Merry Men of Sherwood Forest*, 2nd edn. (London, 1850), 126, 194, 198.

[17] G. P. R. James, *Forest Days: A Romance of Old Times* (London, 1843), i. 107; Anne Bowman, *The Boy Foresters. A Tale of the Days of Robin Hood* (London, [1868]), 236.

[18] Elazar Barkan, *The Retreat of Scientific Racism: Changing Concepts of Race in Britain and the United States between the World Wars* (Cambridge: Cambridge UP, 1992), 14; Nancy Leys Stepan, *The Idea of Race in Science: Great Britain 1800 1960* (Hamden, Comm.: Archon, 1982), 4.

In Britain, these claims were used to support the notion that the Saxon 'race' was superior to all others. Here, a pivotal figure was the Edinburgh anatomist Robert Knox. Knox had begun his professional life as an academic whose anatomy courses attracted hundreds of students, but his reputation had been sullied by his association with the notorious murderers Burke and Hare, from whom he had accepted cadavers for use in medical dissections. Embittered and angry, Knox had embarked upon a new career as a lecturer. At first his ideas on race generated little interest, but by the early 1850s he was regarded as the pre-eminent British authority on the subject. In 1850 he published his arguments in a work entitled *Races of Men: A Fragment*. Although much of it is incoherent and inconsistent, it is worth examining because it summarizes the contemporary state of British racialist thought. Knox claimed that human history was not the product of accident, environment, or circumstance, but of biology and nature. He asserted that human embryos were arrested at different points in their development, thus forming the different races and making some superior to others. As an example Knox turned to the Saxons, the dominant race in the world, who supposedly had the most highly developed embryos.

The precise details of how and why the Saxons' triumph had occurred were probably less important to Knox's readers than his emphasis on race as the determining factor in human history. By the middle of the nineteenth century the hierarchy of races was believed to correspond to, and indeed to be the cause of, human accomplishment. This burgeoning racialism exerted a profound influence upon treatments of the legend of Robin Hood. Indeed, its influence was so profound that it even manifested itself in the opinions of those who did not believe that the legend had any basis in historical reality. In the mid-nineteenth century some scholars argued that Robin Hood had been invented by the Saxons as a sylvan quasi-deity. In 1846 Thomas Wright, a prominent Victorian antiquary, declared that Robin Hood could be placed 'with tolerable certainty among the personages of the early mythology of the Teutonic people'. Seventeen years later Edwin Goadby asserted in *Sharpe's London Magazine* that Robin Hood had been a great hero of northern European mythology, and even went so far as to say that he was an incarnation of 'the god Woden himself'. Such an origin, Goadby declared, gave to 'our national hero an antiquity and nobility which links . . . our earlier life to the races from which we have descended, and completes all other proofs. . . . The ballads of Robin

Hood are still true to the life of the Teuton race and the heart of its whole mythology'.[19]

The fact that even those scholars who argued against Robin Hood's historical reality endorsed the idea that he had been of Saxon origin indicates just how central this concept had become to the legend. In the mid-nineteenth century, however, few authors completely adhered to a strict dichotomy between Norman and Saxon which depicted the former as entirely inferior and the latter as entirely superior. In *Ivanhoe*, for example, Sir Walter Scott points to the social and cultural improvements brought about by the Norman Conquest and criticizes the Saxons for their simplicity and lack of refinement. He argues that the best hope for the nation's future lies in the assimilation of the two peoples. In the final scene, the marriage of Ivanhoe and Rowena, which is attended by both Normans and Saxons, represents 'a pledge of future peace betwixt two races which, since that period, have been so completely mingled, that the distinction has become wholly invisible'.[20]

Other contemporary literary treatments of Robin Hood also look towards the ultimate assimilation of the Saxons and the Normans. Bowman's *The Boy Foresters*, which tells the story of three orphans who are taken in by Robin Hood, is on the surface a conventional tale of racial animosity. 'The Saxon thanes still hated the Norman nobles who had dispossessed them of many of their lands', Bowman writes, 'and the Normans, in their turn, despised and trampled on the old possessors of the soil'. But, in truth, the view of racial relations which Bowman adopts is far more complex. The children are the product of an 'interracial' marriage, twelfth-century style: their father was a Norman and their mother was a Saxon. These heterogeneous origins are a source of pride rather than embarrassment. Hubert, the eldest, tells his sister Rica that 'we . . . who are both Norman and Saxon, must look with love and charity on the people of both races'.[21] By taking the best attributes from both the Norman and Saxon races, Scott and Bowman argue that nineteenth-century Britons had reaped the benefits of the infusion of new blood into the old stock, a stock which otherwise might have gone into an irreversible decline.

In the final decades of the nineteenth century, however, racial

---

[19] Thomas Wright, *Essays on the Literature, Superstitions, and History of England in the Middle Ages* (London, 1864), i. 164–5, 200, 211; Edwin Goadby, 'Who Was Robin Hood?', *Sharpe's London Magazine*, 23 (1863), 311–2.   [20] Scott, *Ivanhoe*, 515.
[21] Bowman, *Boy Forester*, 2, 132–3.

distinctions came to be much more sharply delineated. There were several factors behind this intensification of racial attitudes. First, there was the impact of Charles Darwin's *The Origin of Species* (1859). Darwin's identification of natural selection as the primary mechanism of evolution seemingly lent scientific validity to claims that some peoples were destined to rule over others due to their innate biological superiority. Later, when Darwin extended his arguments to human beings in *The Descent of Man* (1871), he argued in favour of an evolutionary continuity between animals and man. This left him, however, with a dilemma: how to explain the seemingly vast difference between highly civilized Europeans and primitive apes? Here, Darwin turned to contemporary anthropological scholarship and used the so-called 'lower races' to fill the gap. He argued that the mental and moral capacities of many 'savages' were scarcely greater than those of animals. To explain the existence of these 'savages', Darwin utilized the principle of natural selection, which he claimed operated to elevate the most fit races on the scale of civilization. Although he recognized that progress was not invariable, he believed that natural selection had brought certain races, and above all white Europeans, to the highest point of moral and intellectual life.[22] The 'lower races' were those that had evolved least far up the evolutionary ladder.

Although Darwin himself was no blatant racist, many of the scientists who pursued the implications of his work found it all too easy to interpret it as endorsing a hierarchy of human races. He provided a new language with which to express old prejudices, and his arguments were subsequently used to promote efforts to improve the 'biological health' of the British population. If evolution and natural selection were the key principles of natural existence, the 'social Darwinists' argued, then they were applicable to social life, which meant that less successful individuals were in that condition because of some innate deficiency in their physical and intellectual capacity. This inevitably led to the conclusion that biologically superior persons must be encouraged to breed, while the inferior must be discouraged or even forcibly prevented. In *Hereditary Genius* (1869), Darwin's cousin Francis Galton proposed that humankind could be improved by selective breeding, in the process doing quickly what natural selection accomplished gradually. Galton's arguments, which eventually came to be referred to by the term 'eugenics', were initially not well received due

---

[22] Stepan, *The Idea of Race*, 47–59.

to the threat they represented to established marriage and childbearing practices. By the end of the nineteenth century, however, they were meeting with a more favourable reception.

Another factor which influenced racial attitudes in Britain in the latter part of the nineteenth century was imperialism, which reinforced notions of racial superiority. There were two imperial events in particular which contributed to the hardening of racial attitudes: the Indian 'Mutiny' of 1857 and the Jamaican Insurrection of 1865. The Indian population, it had long been assumed, would gradually become more 'civilized' through contact with the British, but the Mutiny caused a reassessment of this idea. Perhaps the differences between the two peoples, many Britons concluded, were in fact the product of innate biological differences and therefore immutable. Eight years later the British empire received another shock to the system. At Morant Bay, Jamaica, in October of 1865 a series of sporadic outbreaks against British rule resulted in the deaths of eighteen men (half of them white) and the injury of thirty-five others. The governor, Edward Eyre, responded by executing 439 persons, flogging 600 more, and burning a thousand homes. A government inquiry for the most part exonerated Eyre, but the episode led to a storm of public controversy. Clearly, the incident had conjured up the ghosts of the Indian Mutiny by calling into question Britain's ability to 'civilize' those under its imperial charge. And once again, racial differences were cited as the key factor. According to *The Times*: 'It seemed to be proved in Jamaica that the Negro could become fit for self-government. . . . Alas for the grand triumphs of humanity, and the improvement of races, and the removal of primeval curses, and the expenditure of twenty millions sterling, Jamaica herself gainsays the fact and belies herself'.[23]

There is also the impact of the American Civil War on British racialism to consider. How could slavery exist in the United States, a country whose constitution proclaimed that 'all men are created equal'? To answer this thorny question, pro-slavery American arguments divided whites from non-whites, with the latter group being classified as a lower species that did not possess all the characteristics of civilized human beings. This point of view made its way to Britain primarily through the efforts of Henry Hotze, officially a commercial representative of the southern states in London from 1861 to 1865, but

---

[23] Ronald Hyam, *Britain's Imperial Century, 1815–1914: A Study of Empire and Expansion*, 2nd edn. (Lanham, Md.: Barnes and Noble, 1993), 153.

unofficially a secret agent with a brief to persuade the British government to recognize the Confederacy. He never succeeded, but he did manage to convince many Britons that Confederate views of race had some merit. His main forum was the newspaper *The Index*, which he founded in 1862. In it, he wrote of the dangers of miscegenation: 'Amalgamation must, we should think, revolt the feelings of every member of the superior race'.[24]

A final factor which contributed to the increased virulence of racial attitudes in Britain in the second half of the nineteenth century is the impact of immigration. In this period an increasing influx of immigrants made their way to British shores, where they sought greater economic opportunity and freedom from religious or ethnic persecution. What they often found on their arrival, however, was considerable xenophobic opposition to the entry of foreigners. Amidst rising concern that Britain had passed its zenith, fears grew that the nation was burdened with an over-large population drawing upon diminishing resources. In such a climate newcomers were hardly likely to be welcomed with open arms, and the idea of racial assimilation became far less attractive.[25]

The hardening of racial attitudes was reflected in treatments of the legend of Robin Hood, which in the final decades of the nineteenth century came to employ far more strident language to describe the 'racial' conflict between Saxon and Norman. In 1869 George Emmett's *Robin Hood and the Outlaws of Sherwood Forest* emphasizes 'the undying enmity between the Norman and the Saxon race'. Nowhere are the inherent differences between Norman and Saxon more clearly expressed than in this song performed by Friar Tuck:

> Findest thou aught foul or bad,
> Be assured 'tis Norman.
> Rogues, liars, cheats, and knaves are they,
> To see such churls makes one quite sad.
> Then to my toast, let none say nay—
> Confusion to the Norman.

---

[24] Young, *Colonial Desire*, 138.

[25] For the impact of increased immigration upon nineteenth-century British society, see the essays in Colin Holmes (ed.), *Immigrants and Minorities in British Society* (London: George Allen and Unwin, 1978); Panikos Panayi, *Immigration, Ethnicity and Racism in Britain, 1815–1945* (Manchester: Manchester UP, 1984); James B. Walvin, *Passage to Britain: Immigration in British History and Politics* (Harmondsworth and New York: Penguin, 1984).

> Findest thou aught fair or just,
> Rest quite sure 'tis Saxon.
> Good men, and true, and loyal too,
> Base Normans they can never trust.
> In wine quite old and goblets new,
> Drink honour to the Saxon.

By the final decades of the nineteenth century virtually every literary treatment of Robin Hood argued in favour of Saxon blood uncontaminated by its 'inferior' Norman counterpart. In his children's story *Edwin the Boy Outlaw* (1887), J. Frederick Hodgetts describes Robin Hood as a 'thorough Englishman' with 'no taint of Norman blood' in his veins. Hodgetts takes a disdainful view of arguments claiming that the two races had eventually united and that it was the blood of both which flowed through modern Britons:

The general theory of amalgamation of jarring nations and their fusion into one has been accepted as the truth, in spite of the facts related in the chronicles, sagas, and lays of our race, and I have endeavoured . . . to show that Normans and English did not mix, but that the few Normans that were left were either blotted out and lost in the surging wave of English that rolled over and swamped them or became approximately English.[26]

Such claims were found not only in late-nineteenth-century fiction, however, but also among scholars and antiquarians. We have previously noted the existence of a tradition claiming that Robin Hood had been of noble birth, an idea which dates to the sixteenth century. In the 1740s the Lincolnshire antiquary William Stukeley embellished this claim by concocting a pedigree which identified him as one Robert fitz Ooth, Earl of Huntington. In the nineteenth century, however, many historians and antiquaries recognized that Robin Hood's aristocratic birth had been a spurious addition to the legend. 'No reliance whatever can be placed on this view of the question', declared the Scottish historian and scientist Robert Chambers in 1864. More lay behind these attacks upon Robin Hood's nobility than a simple desire for greater historical accuracy, for what really motivated them was a desire to assign a more appealing racial identity to a national hero. In Stukeley's genealogy, Robin's grandfather was one Ralph Fitzooth, a Norman lord who had come to England with William Rufus. In the

---

[26] George Emmett, *Robin Hood and the Outlaws of Sherwood Forest* (London, 1869), 126, 293; J. Frederick Hodgetts, *Edwin the Boy Outlaw, or The Dawn of Freedom in England* (London, 1887), 8–9.

eighteenth century this aspect of Robin Hood's ancestry was of relatively little significance other than to establish his noble pedigree. But 150 years later such a lineage had become problematic, as the Normans were now vilified as the oppressors of the heroic Saxons to whom the modern English traced their ancestry. In this context it was impossible to continue boasting of the Norman origins of a national hero such as Robin Hood. Instead, he was reinvented in a form more in line with contemporary racialist ideals. In 1887 one E. Stredder proclaimed his belief in Robin Hood as a Saxon hero in *Notes and Queries*: 'For a myth, for a creation of the popular imagination, would Englishmen have risked imprisonment and exile? But . . . if he were the leader of the refugees, the lingering remnant of the outlawed Saxons, who had learned from their ancestors to live free or die . . . then we can understand the why and how his name was graven so deeply on the English heart'.[27] In order to reinforce his argument, Stredder concocted a pedigree for Robin Hood just as outlandish as Stukeley's had been. He argued that Robin was a descendant of Waltheof, a great Saxon leader captured by the Normans at Hastings who had escaped to lead the continuing opposition to the Conquest. There was no more evidence for this version of Robin Hood's origins than there had been for Stukeley's, but that mattered little. It was far more important to have him fit conceptions of what a national hero should be than to uncover the truth.

Literary and linguistic research also contributed to the incorporation of the legend of Robin Hood into contemporary racialist doctrine. Over the course of the nineteenth century efforts to determine the origins of the Indo-European language group had come to possess strong racial overtones. Most philologists erroneously assumed that affinity of language meant affinity of race, and this assumption led to an intense search for the homeland of the Indo-European people, who were widely believed to be the ancestors of the modern western Europeans. In turn, this search generated the theory that in the far distant past a particularly gifted people had spilled out of the region between the Indus and Ganges rivers and pressed westward, bringing with them civilization, glory, and heroic principles.

Although most of the work was done by German scholars, the basis

---

[27] Stuart Pigott, *William Stukeley: An Eighteenth-Century Antiquary*, rev. edn. (New York: Thames and Hudson, 1985); Robert Chambers, *The Book of Days: A Miscellany of Popular Antiquities* (London and Edinburgh, 1864), ii. 609; E. Stredder, 'Who Was Robin Hood?', *Notes and Queries*, 7: 3 (1887) 324.

for these arguments was provided by the British philologist Sir William Jones. In the late eighteenth century Jones served as a judge in India, where he founded the Asiatic Society. In 1786 he published a seminal paper in which he claimed that Sanscrit, Greek, and Latin had all come from the same source, an argument which quickly became entangled with the notion of an Asiatic origin for the Indo-European people. In order for this argument to be incorporated into burgeoning Saxonist racialism, however, it had to be grafted onto the belief in the superiority of the primitive Germans. This step was duly taken by Friedrich von Schlegel, who argued that the Germanic people had originally come from the steppes of central Asia to save the western world from Roman decadence. To describe his purported ancestors, Schlegel used the term 'Aryan', which had originally been employed by Herodotus to denote the ancient Persians. Schlegel's ideas made their way to Britain primarily through the efforts of Friedrich Max Müller, Sanscritist at Oxford University. Max Müller did not hesitate to associate race with language and took for granted the existence of a once-great Aryan nation. 'It is hardly possible to look at the evidence hitherto collected', he wrote, 'without feeling that these words are the fragments of a real language, once spoken by a united race at a time which the historian has till lately hardly ventured to realize'.[28] Max Müller's circle included such luminaries as the historian James Anthony Froude, the novelist Charles Kingsley, and the philosopher Thomas Carlyle, all of whom supported at least some aspects of his theories.

Given the fact that in Britain Aryanism and Anglo-Saxonism were so closely linked, it is not surprising that as the legend of Robin Hood came to be more and more closely associated with the latter, it was also influenced by the former. In the *Academy* in 1883 the noted philologist Isaac Taylor introduced a new theory explaining the legend's origin. 'Is [Robin Hood] not', Taylor asked, '. . . a faint western echo of the solar heroes of Aryan mythology?' A few issues later, this suggestion was eagerly taken up by Henry Bradley, who emphatically declared that:

It must . . . be admitted that a considerable portion of this story is ultimately derived from the great Aryan sun-myth. . . . When, however, Hood had come to be regarded as a merely human personage, and genuine historical incidents had been blended in his story, his career . . . naturally became a theme for

---

[28] Thomas W. Thompson, *James Anthony Froude on Nation and Empire: A Study in Victorian Racialism* (New York and London: Garland, 1987), 16.

romantic fiction. As invention always tends to run in accustomed channels, the story of Hood . . . was enriched with incidents which belonged originally to the Aryan solar myth.[29]

Like other nineteenth-century racialist arguments, Aryanism was never about simply exalting one race; it was also about denigrating others. At the century's end it came to be about denigrating one people in particular: the Jews. The argument that western Europeans were from a different racial origin than the Jews proved to be by far the most pervasive aspect of Aryanism, lingering on until well into the twentieth century and rearing its ugliest head in Nazi Germany. Although Britain never experienced such virulent anti-Semitism, it was far from immune to the general growth of hostility towards the Jews in late-nineteenth-century Europe.

This increased intolerance is demonstrated by the representation of Jewish characters in literary treatments of the legend of Robin Hood. While anti-Semitism had long existed in British society, in the first half of the nineteenth century Jews were regarded with a grudging tolerance, at least relative to the hostility they encountered in other European nations. This fairly liberal attitude is reflected in *Ivanhoe*.[30] To be sure, Isaac, the Jewish moneylender of York, is extremely avaricious, but he is also loyal to his friends and passionately devoted to his daughter Rebecca, as well as brave, resilient, and determined. Rebecca, for her part, is a beautiful, enchanting, and noble heroine.[31]

Scott's portraits of Jewish virtue spawned a number of imitations in the numerous adaptations of *Ivanhoe* which appeared on the contemporary stage. The prologue to George Soane's *The Hebrew*, performed at the Theatre Royal Drury Lane in 1820, contains a strong statement in favor of tolerance towards Jews:

> No longer scoff'd, in peaceful compact blend
> Christian and Jew, by turns each other's friend.

---

[29] Isaac Taylor, 'Robin Hood', *Academy*, 24 (13 Oct. 1883), 250; Henry Bradley, 'Robin Hood', *Academy*, 24 (8 Dec 1883), 384.

[30] Abba Rubin, *The Jew in English Literature 1660–1830* (Westport, Conn.: Greenwood, 1984), 123. See also Harold Fisch, *The Dual Image: The Figure of the Jew in English and American Literature* (New York: Ktav, 1991), 59–62.

[31] Stephen Knight, *Robin Hood: A Complete Study of the English Outlaw* (Oxford and Cambridge, Mass.: Blackwell, 1994) 177. See also Esther L. Panitz, *The Alien in Their Midst: Images of Jews in English Literature* (London and Toronto: Associated UP, 1981), 96–100.

Similarly, the Brough brothers' *The Last Edition of Ivanhoe* (1850) concludes with a declaration from Ivanhoe himself for 'old grudges [to] cease—each prejudice unbend'. A chorus is sung to the tune of *Rule Britannia* espousing the advantages to be gained from a spirit of tolerance and harmony:

> But Britain first with ev'ry land,
> In friendship just to see remain,
> In friendship, friendship, just to see remain
> And just to start her—to start her as we stand,
> Our places keep to sing this strain.
> Rule Britannia, Britannia thus behaves,
> Britons send ill feelings ever—ever to their graves!

In a final 'grand allegorical tableau' groups representing all the peoples of the world parade across the stage. The Jews are included, as Rebecca looks forward to a day when

> Heigho! pr'aps England will some day or other
> Think e'en an Israelite a man and brother.[32]

In the latter part of the nineteenth century, however, such open-mindedness was supplanted by increasing anti-Semitism. On the one hand, this intolerance was directed at poor Jews. Beginning in the 1880s, a steady flow of Jewish immigrants from eastern Europe arrived in Britain. Although they totalled fewer than 80,000, these new arrivals met with a hostility out of all proportion to demographic reality. Histrionic articles in the press proclaiming the dangers of the 'foreign flood' led to a series of official reports and ultimately to the Aliens Act of 1905, which imposed restrictions on further immigration. To justify such initiatives, some argued that Jews were undercutting wages and engaging in unfair trading practices, while others claimed that they were unhealthy, unsanitary, and prone to engage in criminal activity. In truth, however, what lay at the heart of this antipathy was a deep-rooted anti-Semitism.[33]

---

[32] George Soame, *The Hebrew. A Drama* (London, 1820), 7; Brough Brothers, *The Last Edition of Ivanhoe* (London, [1850]), 20, 43.

[33] For changing perceptions of Jewish immigrants in Victorian society, see Anne and Roger Cowen (eds.), *Victorian Jews Through British Eyes* (Oxford and New York: Oxford UP, 1986); David Feldman, *Englishmen and Jews: Social Relations and Political Culture, 1840–1914* (New Haven and London: Yale UP, 1994); Israel Finestein, *Jewish Society in Victorian England: Collected Essays* (London and Portland, Oreg.: Vallentine Mitchell, 1993); Bernard Gainer, *The Alien Invasion: The Origins of the Aliens Act of 1905* (London: Heinemann, 1972);

At the same time, there also developed an increased antipathy towards wealthy Jews, many of whose families had been in Britain for centuries. In the late nineteenth and early twentieth centuries theories of Jewish conspiracies to take over the British establishment were rife. Several prominent liberals attempted to blame Jewish interests for Britain's involvement in the Boer War; the well-known journalist J. A. Hobson declared that the economic resources of the Transvaal had fallen 'into the hands of a small group of international financiers, chiefly. . . Jewish in race'. Meanwhile, anti-Semitism also grew on the extreme right, where the relative decline of Britain's economic and military power was blamed on the Jews. In 1901 the journalist Arnold White wrote in his *Efficiency and Empire*: 'It is growing rule by foreign Jews that is being set up. The best forms of our national life are already in jeopardy'.[34]

These blatantly anti-Semitic sentiments made their presence felt in contemporary treatments of the legend of Robin Hood.[35] In J. E. Muddock's *Maid Marian and Robin Hood* (1892), Maid Marian flees from her father, who is attempting to force her to marry against her will, and seeks refuge with 'a rich Jew in Leeds'. Unlike in *Ivanhoe*, however, his daughter is no gentle Rebecca. On the contrary, she is jealous of Marian's beauty and cruel to her, locking her in a dungeon until she agrees to renounce the Christian faith and convert to Judaism. Equally anti-Semitic is Edward Gilliat's novel *Wolf's Head: A Story of the Prince of Outlaws* (1899), which repeatedly shows Jews to be greedy and therefore appropriate targets for the outlaws' depredations. When Robin Hood hears that a wealthy merchant is riding through Sherwood Forest carrying 1,500 gold marks, he tells his men that 'he is a stingy, grasping Jew [and] we must make an example of him'.[36] By the end of the nineteenth century the relatively tolerant attitude found

J. A. Garrard, *The English and Immigration: A Comparative Study of the Jewish Influx 1880–1910* (London: Institute of Race Relations, 1971); Lloyd Gartner, *The Jewish Immigrant in England 1870–1914*, 2nd edn. (London: Simon Publications, 1973); Colin Holmes, *Anti-Semitism in British Society, 1876–1939* (New York: Holmes and Meier, 1979); Vivian D. Lipman, *A History of the Jews in Britain Since 1858* (Leicester: Leicester UP, 1990).

[34] Panayi, *Immigration*, 117, 155.

[35] For the late-nineteenth-century literary perception of Jewish characters, see Bryan Cheyette, *Constructions of 'the Jew' in English Literature and Society: Racial Representations, 1875–1945* (Cambridge and New York: Cambridge UP, 1993).

[36] J. E. Muddock, *Maid Marian and Robin Hood: A Romance of Old Sherwood Forest* (London, 1892), 299; Edward Gilliat, *Wolf's Head: A Story of the Prince of Outlaws* (London, 1899), 251.

in *Ivanhoe* and its adaptations had thus been replaced by an ugly, unmitigated anti-Semitism.

In creating an image of a Robin Hood whose essential components included untainted Saxon blood, late-nineteenth-century authors reinforced contemporary arguments proclaiming that racial purity must be maintained if Britain's predominant position in the world were to continue. The heterogeneity of nineteenth-century Britain, however, made this simplistic Saxon racialism difficult to sustain. Until the very end of the century an intense debate continued to rage over the place of other bloodlines in the nation's lineage, a debate in which the legend of another medieval hero—King Arthur—came to play a prominent role.

'Not so fit for worship as a demigod': King Arthur as Celtic Hero

'The question naturally arises—Was there ever a real King Arthur?' asked the *English Illustrated Magazine* in the late 1880s. On the one hand, doubters abounded in nineteenth-century Britain. The literary critic Walter Irving brusquely dismissed the legend as 'a mass of incredulities', and declared that: 'To ask reasonable beings, living in the nineteenth century, to be delighted and instructed by a mass of falsehoods, impossibilities, and absurdities compared with which the story of Jack the Giant Killer is sober truth, is a demand which we cannot comprehend'. Like Robin Hood, however, Arthur had more defenders than deniers of his reality. Jessie Weston, a leading late-nineteenth-century Arthurian scholar, proclaimed that 'we may . . . believe that [Arthur] really lived', while the literary critic S. Humphreys Gurteen complained that 'to disbelieve in the historic existence of such a personage as Arthur simply shows an unhealthy skepticism'.[37]

Those who argued in favor of Arthur's historical existence relied upon two ancient Welsh chronicles, the *Historia Brittonum* (*c*.800) and the *Annales Cambriae* (*c*.960), both of which refer to Arthur as the victor of the Battle of Badon Hill, an encounter between the Celts and

[37] F. Ryland, 'The Morte D'Arthur', *English Illustrated Magazine*, 6 (1888–9), 89; Walter Irving, *Tennyson* (Edinburgh and London, 1873), 6, 8–9; Jessie L. Weston, *The Legend of Sir Gawaine: Studies upon Its Original Scope and Significance* (London, 1897), 3; S. Humphreys Gurteen, *The Arthurian Epic: A Comparative Study of the Cambrian, Breton, and Anglo-Norman Versions of the Story and Tennyson's Idylls of the King* (New York and London, 1895), 97.

Saxons which took place about AD 520. Because they had been provided with a probable—or at least potential—date for Arthur's existence, nineteenth-century authors enjoyed less freedom to mould his legend than did their counterparts who wrote about Robin Hood. The absence of clear references to Robin Hood in medieval records made it possible to assign him to virtually any period between the eleventh and fourteenth centuries, which greatly assisted efforts to transform him into a hero who conformed to contemporary nationalist ideals, particularly regarding his racial origins. Those authors who treated the Arthurian legend, however, had no such liberty, for historical accuracy required them to depict him as an early-sixth-century participant in a battle against the Saxons. John Herman Merivale's *A Chronicle of the Kings of England* (1828) tells the story from the first arrival of the Saxons on British shores:

> Still, as the danger thicken'd, the more to meet it rose
> The spirit which, in nobled minds, with opposition grows:
> Then lived renownéd Arthur, who, as old stories tell,
> Was begotten of a dragon, with aid of Merlin's spell . . . .
> A valiant native prince, who his country's cause upheld,
> And Cerdic, with his ravagers, at Badon's mount repell'd.

Similarly, Arthur fights against 'the Saxon arms' in Thomas Hogg's *The Fabulous History of the Ancient Kingdom of Cornwall* (1827) and 'the Saxon horde' in Alexander James Beresford Hope's 'A Dream' (1843).[38]

This scenario gave rise to a problem, however. Such references to Arthur were often highly critical of the Saxons, focusing in particular upon their barbarity and bellicosity. In 1802, for example, Joseph Ritson referred to the Saxons as 'treacherous strangers', 'an ignorant and illiterate people', and 'a spiritless and cowardly race'.[39] In the context of the Arthurian legend, this harsh treatment made perfect sense, for the enemies of a national hero like Arthur were necessarily enemies of the nation. But, of course, these so-called 'barbarians' were the selfsame Saxons whose blood was a source of great pride to many Britons. How, then, was the Arthurian legend to be reconciled with contemporary racialist thinking?

In order to understand how this reconciliation took place, it is

---

[38] John Herman Merivale, *Poems Original and Translated* (London, 1828), 304–5; Thomas Hogg, *The Fabulous History of the Ancient Kingdom of Cornwall* (London, 1827), 203; Alexander James Beresford Hope, *Poems* (London, 1843), 76.

[39] Joseph Ritson, *Ancient English Metrical Romances* (London, 1802), p. lxxxii.

important to notice that, for much of the nineteenth century, there were other possible racial ideals which existed alongside the Anglo-Saxonist model. To be sure, there was the growing pride of the Victorians in their Saxon origins, but it was also widely accepted that the Saxons were not the only race that had made a positive contribution to the nation's bloodline. As we have seen, the Normans were not regarded in an entirely negative sense before the final decades of the nineteenth century. And during this same period, the Celts, the race of the historical King Arthur, occupied a similarly ambivalent position.[40]

In his fragmentary 'Morte d'Arthur', written sometime between 1810 and 1820, the clergyman Reginald Heber, later the first Anglican Bishop of Calcutta, all but regrets the day the Saxons first set foot on British shores:

> When I rehearse each gorgeous festival,
> And knightly pomp of Arthur's elder day,
> And muse upon these Celtic glories all,
> Which, save some remnant of the minstrel's lay,
> Are melted in oblivious stream away,
> (So deadly bit the Saxon's blade and sore)
> Perforce I rue such perilous decay,
> And, reckless of my race, almost deplore
> That ever northern keel deflower'd the Logrian shore.[41]

Heber's verse shows that, at least in the first decades of the nineteenth century, the Saxons did not occupy an undisputed position at the top of the British racial hierarchy. On the contrary, here they are criticized as ruthless, bloodthirsty warmongers who came from a foreign land to demolish Britain's 'Celtic glories'.

This passage is typical of contemporary literary treatments of the Arthurian legend, many of which allot to the Celts a significant contribution to the nation's history. J. F. Pennie's drama *The Dragon King* (1832), for example, celebrates the Celts for their Christian religious beliefs and superior laws. 'Let us . . . hear no more of the . . . shallow cant which ignorantly pretends to cast the disgrace of savage barbarity on the ancient Britons . . .', Pennie writes in the preface, 'and proclaim them to have been a noble and a mighty people'. Other authors

---

[40] Roy Foster, 'Paddy and Mr. Punch', in his *Paddy and Mr. Punch: Connexions in Irish and English History* (London: Penguin, 1993), 193.

[41] Reginald Heber, *The Poetical Works of Reginald Heber*, new edn. (London, 1854), 177.

concurred, arguing in favour of racial unity rather than the superiority of one people over the other. In the verse drama *The Fairy of the
Lake* (1801), by the erstwhile radical leader John Thelwall, the Saxon
queen Rowenna pleads for peace between the warring Celts and
Saxons:

> But, in our hearts,
> The touch humane of cordial sympathy
> Is now more vital than revengeful wrath
> And national aversions; which too long
> Have thin'd our rival tribes. Therefore we arm
> Our tongues with gentle courtesies, not hands
> With weapons of destruction; and invite
> To equal brotherhood your warrior Knights—
> Yourself, to equal empire.[42]

The Revd Henry Hart Milman presents a similar vision in *Samor, Lord
of the Bright City*, an Arthurian epic poem published in 1817. In the
conclusion, the Saxon leader Argatyr predicts that the animosity
between Saxon and Celt will ultimately give way to a peace that will
benefit the British nation:

> I tell thee, Briton, that thy sons and mine
> Shall be two meeting and conflicting tides,
> Whose fierce relentless enmity shall lash
> This land into a whirlpool deep and wide,
> To swallow in its vast insatiate gulph
> Her peace and smooth felicity, till flow
> Their waters reconcil'd in one broad bed,
> Briton and Anglian one in race and name.[43]

Authors of Arthurian literature continued to offer similar interpretations of the historical conflict between Saxon and Celt until well into
the nineteenth century. In the preface to his epic poem *King Arthur*
(1849), Edward Bulwer Lytton emphasizes the future unity of the two
races. After winning a great victory over the Saxons on the battlefield,
Arthur accepts their leader Harold's offer of peace, and the two

---

[42] Roger Simpson, *Camelot Regained: The Arthurian Revival and Tennyson*, Arthurian
Studies, 21 (Cambridge and Wolfeboro, NH: D. S. Brewer, 1990) 40; J. F. Pennie, *Britain's
Historical Drama; A Series of National Tragedies* (London, 1832), p. xiii; John Thelwall, *Poems,
Chiefly Written in Retirement*, 2nd ed. (Hereford, 1801) 79.

[43] H. H. Milman, *Samor, Lord of the Bright City. An Heroic Poem*, 2nd edn. (London, 1818),
355–6.

peoples agree to live in harmony in the future. As the two kings clasp hands, Merlin prophecies the eventual unity of the Celts and Saxons:

> Still the old brother-bond in these new homes,
> After long woes, shall bind your kindred races;
> Here, the same God shall find the sacred domes;
> And the same land-marks bound your resting-places,
> What time, o'er realms to Zeus and Thor unknown,
> Both Celt and Saxon rear their common throne.[44]

   Pennie, Thelwall, Milman, and Bulwer Lytton thus all utilize the Arthurian legend to promote unity between the Celts and the Saxons. But although they each emphasize the Celtic role in Britain's history, none of the four was himself a Celt. How, then, did Celtic authors of Arthurian works interpret the historical conflict between Saxon and Celt? The answer to this question is complex. On the one hand, a strong current of nationalism runs through many early-nineteenth-century treatments of the legend by Welsh authors, who frequently represent Arthur's struggle against the Saxons as a precursor to the long history of Welsh resistance to English rule. In his poem *Llewelyn ap Iorwerth* (1818), for example, W. E. Meredith claims that Llewellyn ap Gruffydd, the leader of a thirteenth-century rebellion against English rule, told his troops that 'the blood of Arthur's knights still revels in your veins' before a battle against Henry III.[45]

   But despite this prominent strain of nationalism, such celebrations of the nation's heroic past and Arthur's contribution to it rarely extended to demands for the restoration of Welsh sovereignty in the present. Instead, Welsh authors for the most part emphasized the advantages of the Union. We have already seen how this emphasis upon co-operation was evident during the Revolutionary and Napoleonic Wars, when many Welsh authors turned to the Arthurian legend as a means of declaring their patriotism. Long after the war had ended, however, similar pronouncements invoking Arthur as a symbol of Wales's adherence to the Union continued to appear. In August 1832 the 13-year-old Princess Victoria, heiress presumptive to the British throne, visited the annual Eisteddfod held at Beaumaris.[46] There, local poets

---

[44] Edward Bulwer Lytton, *King Arthur* (London, 1849), i. 299.

[45] W. E. Meredith, *Llewelyn ap Iorwerth. A Poem, in Five Cantos* (London, 1818), 3, 15. For a similarly themed poem, see 'Welsh War Song', *Carmarthen Journal*, 9 Mar. 1827, 4.

[46] See Stanley Weintraub, *Victoria: An Intimate Biography* (New York: E. P. Dutton, 1987), 77–9; Elizabeth Longford, *Victoria R. I.* (London: Weidenfeld and Nicolson, 1964), 41–2.

competed to proclaim their loyalty to the young princess and the nation she was soon to rule, and several employed the Arthurian legend in order to express their allegiance. George Haslehurst begins his 'Song' with an account of Arthur's great battles, taking care not to mention him in an explicitly anti-Saxon context, before turning to Welsh participation alongside the English in the more recent war against the French:

> Is there a dastard boor
> For his country would not stand?—
> Nor blench at the sound of the cannon's roar,—
> Or fight for his father-land?

Haslehurst, however, was outdone by Henry Davies, whose 'Ode' showers Victoria with effusive praise and emphasizes the happiness which her visit has brought to Wales. As the culmination of his panegyric, he refers to her as a descendent of Arthur:

> When Wallia from her deepest dell,
> To Snowdon's sun-lit peak,
> Echoes exulting to the swell
> Of joy and triumph, that bespeak,
> The smile to Cambria long unknown,
> The presence of the princely heir to British Arthur's
> crown.[47]

For their part, English authors responded to such invocations of Arthur's immortal spirit and its continuing connection with Welsh patriotism with cautious approval, supporting the inclinations towards unity without encouraging any hints of separatism which they might conceal. Like the poem by Meredith cited above, Joseph Cottle's *The Fall of Cambria* (1811) describes Llewellyn ap Griffith's rebellion. But whereas the Welsh author has Llewellyn invoke Arthur's immortal spirit to inspire the Welsh forces, Cottle emphasizes that Arthur is dead, never to return to conquer Wales's oppressors. Prior to facing Llewellyn's troops in battle, Edward III visits a prophetess in an effort to foresee the outcome. She tells him to go back to England or face defeat, for this is the long-predicted day of Arthur's return from the dead, when he will exact revenge upon the enemies of his country:

---

[47] George Haslehurst, *Penmaen-Mawr, and Day-Break: Poems* (London, 1849), 77–80; Henry Davies, 'Ode', *Cambrian Quarterly Magazine*, 4 (1832), 544–5.

Arthur still doth being share,
Tho' none his warrior form may see . . .
The noon is at hand,
When from Cambria's land
To destruction, his sword shall proud Edward's
pursue.

Edward, however, refuses to heed the prophecy and scornfully proclaims that 'Arthur is dead! 'Neath Glastonbury's pile'. He goes on to
crush Llewellyn on the field of battle. Immediately afterwards, a
footnote relates, he goes to Glastonbury Abbey, the purported site of
Arthur's grave, and has the tomb opened 'in the presence of several
Cambrians' in order to show them the remains contained therein.
Arthur, Cottle asserts, is truly dead, and the Welsh would be wise to
cease looking to him for their future redemption. Instead, Cottle looks
to a future of co-operation and harmony for the English and Welsh
peoples, presumably based upon the continued domination of the
former over the latter. 'One of the morals to be deduced from this
poem,' he writes:

I always designed to arise from a cause, like the Cambrian . . . terminating in
defeat. A sceptical spectator of human events, in that period, might have
observed, 'We have witnessed the overthrow of an ancient empire, and the
subjugation of a brave and virtuous people, where is the evidence of an
equitable and Supreme Governor?' Yet if such a reasoner could have pierced
into futurity, he would have acquiesced in the occurrences which he deplored,
from a perception of the ulterior advantages which were to result to both
nations.[48]

But even though English and Welsh authors may in some ways
have viewed the historical relationship between the Saxon and Celtic
peoples from different perspectives, it is crucial to recognize that they
shared an emphasis upon their assimilation as beneficial to the British
nation as a whole. In the first half of the nineteenth century a balanced
interpretation prevailed which allowed for the positive contribution of
both peoples to the nation's history.

Slowly but inexorably, however, the dual role of the Saxons and
Celts in British history came to be seen as an unequal partnership, as
the Saxon contribution to the nation was increasingly emphasized over
the Celtic. This was due primarily to the hardening of racial attitudes

[48] Joseph Cottle, *The Fall of Cambria*, 2nd edn. (London, 1811), pp. xxvii and 237–40.

discussed previously. Before the mid-nineteenth century even the most outspoken critics of the Celts rarely attributed their inferiority to inherent racial defects, but rather argued that their shortcomings would be overcome through the beneficial influence of long-term exposure to English civilization. But as the nineteenth century wore on, the ostensibly more primitive nature of Celtic culture and society came to be ascribed to immutable biological factors which condemned the Celts to permanent degradation. In his *Races of Men* (1850), Robert Knox described the 'Celtic race' as 'the source of all evil', and declared that it must be forced to leave the country, 'by fair means, if possible; still they must leave. England's safety requires it. I speak not of the justice of the cause; nations must ever act as Machiavelli advised: look to yourself'.[49]

By this time, the climate was much less amenable to the idea of the British as a 'mixed race'. In the second half of the nineteenth century there emerged an increasing preoccupation with and hostility towards racial hybridity, as it came to be widely believed that different races belonged to different species and that any attempt to combine them would lead to their degradation and ultimately their destruction. The most influential work on the subject was Count Arthur Gobineau's *Essay on the Inequality of Races* (1853–5). In formulating a theory to explain the decline and fall of civilizations, Gobineau fixed upon race as the key factor. He argued that the world was divided into three races—white, yellow, and black—which no longer existed in 'pure' form. Instead, each modern nation represented a fusion of races which had occurred when one had conquered another. Over time, the blood of the conquerors mixed with that of the indigenous inhabitants until the two peoples became one. Gobineau claimed that ultimately, however, this process would lead to the destruction of the superior race: 'From the very day when the conquest is accomplished and the fusion begins, there appears a noticeable change in the quality of the blood of the masters'. This 'adulteration', as Gobineau put it, was a 'poison' or a 'plague' that would ultimately spell the death of the nation, as its people became progressively more degenerate. For Gobineau, therefore, miscegenation equaled destruction in terms of its impact on civilization.[50]

In the late 1850s the discussion shifted towards a theory of immutable racial 'types'. In the revised edition of *The Races of Men*,

[49] Horsman, *Race and Manifest Destiny*, 73.   [50] Young, *Colonial Destiny*, 99–104.

published in 1862, Robert Knox asserted that 'from the earliest historic times, mankind were already divided into a certain number of races, perfectly distinct'. And any intermingling of these racial types, Knox claimed, would lead to the 'degradation of humanity' and would be 'rejected by nature'. Others agreed. The evolutionist Herbert Spencer maintained that hybridization between widely distinct races would be disastrous, and as proof pointed to the inhabitants of Mexico, who were the product of two completely different races, the Spanish and the Indians: 'Modern Mexico, and the South American Republics, with their perpetual revolutions, show us the result'.[51]

In such a climate, the belief that the presence of different racial elements in the blood of the modern Briton was beneficial to the nation's health became much more difficult to maintain. And with regard to the Celtic peoples in particular, the arguments against miscegenation were fuelled by the mass migrations of the impoverished Irish into England and Scotland instigated by the Potato Famine of the mid-1840s.[52] Numbering in the hundreds of thousands, these new arrivals encountered strong opposition from the host society in their efforts to gain acceptance. Contemporary periodicals depicted the 'Paddy' as intemperate, improvident, violent, unhygenic, mendacious, and undependable, deficiencies which were attributed to the inferiority of the Celtic race.[53] In the second half of the nineteenth century, physical anthropologists subjected the Celts to anthropometrical measurements and found them wanting, thus transforming what had formerly been largely a religious prejudice into a racial one. John Beddoe claimed that he had found a similarity between the Celtic racial type in Ireland and Cro-Magnon man, and he linked both to an

---

[51] Young, 15; Stepan, *Idea of Race*, 105.

[52] For Irish immigration into nineteenth-century England and Scotland, see David Fitzpatrick, '"A peculiar tramping people": the Irish in Britain, 1801–70', in W. E. Vaughan (ed.), *A New History of Ireland*, Vol. V: *Ireland under the Union*, (Oxford: Oxford UP, 1989), 623–57; Lynn Hollen Lees, *Exiles of Erin: Irish Migrants in Victorian London* (Manchester: Manchester UP, 1979); Roger Swift, 'The Outcast Irish in the British Victorian City: Problems and Perspectives', *Irish Historical Studies*, 25 (1986–7), 264–76; the essays in Roger Swift and Sheridan Gilley (eds.), *The Irish in Britain, 1815–1939* (London: Pinter, 1989); the essays in Swift and Gilley (eds.), *The Irish in the Victorian City* (London: Croom Helm, 1985).

[53] See, in addition to the essay by R. F. Foster cited above, L. P. Curtis, Jr., *Anglo-Saxons and Celts: A Study of Anti-Irish Prejudice in Victorian England* (Bridgeport, Conn.: Conference on British Studies, 1968), and his *Apes and Angels: The Irishman in Victorian Caricature* (Washington, DC: Smithsonian Institution Press, 1971). Curtis's work has been criticized by Sheridan Gilley in his 'English Attitudes to the Irish in England, 1789–1900', in Holmes (ed.), *Immigrants and Minorities*, 81–110.

'Africanoid' race. Intermingling with the Celts was therefore responsible for what he termed the 'nigrascence' of the British population. Such views penetrated into mainstream British culture, and in the popular press it came to be commonplace for the Irish to be portrayed as simian creatures.

This situation presented a problem for authors who wished to promote King Arthur as a national hero, for the best historical evidence suggested that he was a member of a race widely perceived as inferior. Signs of these difficulties are clearly present in Charles H. Pearson's historical study *The Early and Middle Ages of England* (1861). According to Pearson: 'No doubt, there were some real noblenesses in Arthur's character, which have given him a life beyond the grave, as the type of the knightly ideal which the imaginative Keltic race has exalted through all time, above the more statesman-like virtues that secure life and property or success in national enterprizes'.[54] Here, Pearson praises the Celts for their 'imaginative' qualities, but he also blames these selfsame qualities for their lack of 'statesman-like virtues', mysterious attributes which presumably the Saxon peoples possessed in abundance and which were directly responsible for their great 'success in national enterprizes'.

The existence of ostensibly genuine references to Arthur in medieval sources, however, meant that his historical identity, unlike that of Robin Hood, could not be completely reinvented to conform to contemporary racialist ideals. How was it, then, that as one commentator wrote in 1895, 'a native British king became the hero of the English national epic'?[55] In the second half of the nineteenth century British authors developed a simple strategy for dealing with Arthur's problematic historical identity as a Celtic warrior king: they ignored it. By virtually divorcing him from history altogether, they were able to reinvent him in a more congenial form. This did not mean that they argued that Arthur had never existed. Rather, they claimed that the Arthur of history and the Arthur of fiction were two entirely different characters, and that it was the latter who was the true exemplar of what a national hero should be.

Nineteenth-century historians readily acknowledged that there were essentially two Arthurs, the Arthur of fact and the Arthur of fancy. 'It is . . . necessary in writing of Arthur', declared T. W. Shore

---

[54] Charles H. Pearson, *The Early and Middle Ages of England* (London, 1861), 58.
[55] Gurteen, *Arthurian Epic*, 41.

to bear in mind the two-fold character in which he appears in English literature; first and very largely, as a hero whose career and adventures were the
invention of the romancers of the Middle Ages . . . and secondly as a real
British king or chieftain, who lived in the early part of the 6th century, during
the period of the struggle between the British people and the invading Saxons.

Britons were thus accustomed to separating the 'Arthur of romance'
from the 'Arthur of sober history', and the majority preferred the
former to the latter. In the preface to *The Story of Arthur and Guinevere*
(1879), 'G. R. E.' briefly sketched the scanty details known about
Arthur's historical career before concluding with a dismissive 'that is
nearly all that is known of the Arthur of History'. He was far more
enthusiastic, however, about 'the Arthur of Legend', of whose 'greatness there can be no doubt': 'Thousands of readers who know little of
the fierce struggles in western Britain thirteen hundred years ago are
familiar with the brave king Arthur who established the order of the
Knights of the Round Table, who were vowed to defend the poor
against the weak, to be truthful, pure, and courteous, whose valour was
the wonder of medieval Christendom'.[56]

Once Arthur had been divorced from history, a number of options
were open to authors who wished to transform him into a figure more
compatible with contemporary racialist arguments. One possibility was
to alter the identity of Arthur's foes so that they were no longer Saxons.
In his poem 'The Sword of Kingship' (1868), Thomas Westwood
transforms the enemies of the Britons into Viking marauders:

> the sea grew black with barks
> Of Vikings, that like kestrels round the coast
> Hovered, and froze the people's hearts with fear.
> At dead of night the hills broke out a-blaze
> With beacon-fires—wild Norsemen scoured the plains,
> And drove the herds—and wives, that sat at home,
> Wept wearily for those that came no more.[57]

This sort of strategy, however, left unresolved the problem of
Arthur's own historical identity as a member of the ill-regarded Celtic

---

[56] T. W. Shore, *King Arthur and the Round Table at Winchester* (Hampshire, 1900), 187–8;
Jonathan Hughes, 'Celliwig', *Notes and Queries*, 8: 7 (1895), 90; *The Story of Arthur and
Guinevere, and the Fate of Sir Lancelot of the Lake. As Told in Antique Legends and Ballads, and in
Modern Poetry* (London, [1879]), 17–8.

[57] Thomas Westwood, *The Quest of the Sancgreall, The Sword of Kingship, and Other Poems*
(London, 1868), 90.

race. It was insufficient for Arthur not to be an enemy of the Saxons; he would have to become a Saxon himself.

From the mid-nineteenth century onwards, the historical—that is, Celtic—Arthur was gradually supplanted by a figure better suited to the prevailing racialist climate. In a review of Bulwer Lytton's *King Arthur, Sharpe's London Journal* declared that, even if Arthur was of 'Celtic origin', he was also of 'Saxon character'. In contrast, the other characters of the legend, while 'brave and loyal, pious, and enterprising, with no lack of steadfastness and energy upon occasions', were fatally flawed by their bloodline. 'They are all . . . more or less mercurial and light-minded', the reviewer wrote, 'in accordance with their Celtic origin'. Thus, although 'they may be more amusing and agreeable companions than the most noble King Arthur', they 'are not so fit for love and reverence,—not so fit for worship as a demigod; at least in English eyes'.[58] The ludicrous nature of this argument—that Arthur had been a Saxon king of Celtic knights—did not occur to this writer, nor, presumably, to most of his readers. Its conformity with contemporary racialist arguments rendered it far preferable to a historically accurate account.

By far the most influential promoter of King Arthur's 'Saxon' origins was Alfred, Lord Tennyson, whose *Idylls of the King* had a profound impact upon the development of the Arthurian legend. When they appeared in 1859, the first four *Idylls* sold over 10,000 copies in their first weeks of publication, and future instalments received an equally enthusiastic reception. Contemporary critics noted the difficulty of transforming a Celtic legend into an English national epic. 'Strange to say, it does not seem to have occurred to him . . . that it was Celtic and not Saxon', wrote the Revd James A. Campbell in 1896. In fact, however, Tennyson was well aware of Arthur's Celtic origins. He utilized Welsh sources such as the *Mabinogion* in the composition of the *Idylls*, and he made several trips to Wales in order to explore the purported sites of the legend's major events. But his Anglocentric patriotism would not permit him to present Arthur as a Celt. In a letter of 1861, the socialite Caroline Fox described a conversational encounter with Tennyson at a dinner party: 'The Welsh claim Arthur as their own, but Tennyson gives all his votes to us'.[59]

[58] *Sharpe's London Journal*, 9 (1849), 374.

[59] James A. Campbell, *Tennyson's Idylls of the King, Epic and Allegory* (Dublin, 1896), 12; *The Letters of Alfred Tennyson*, ed. Cecil Y. Lang and Edgar F. Shannon, Jr. (Cambridge, Mass.: Belknap Press, 1987), ii. 267.

In order to bring about this reorientation of Arthur's historical identity, Tennyson deliberately presents the chronological aspects of the legend in as vague a manner as possible. In *The Coming of Arthur*, the first of the poems, Tennyson makes no attempt to establish with any precision the names of the warring forces; Arthur is not referred to as a Celt, nor are his enemies specifically described as Saxons, but rather as the 'heathen host' (l. 8).[60] Neither this poem nor any of the *Idylls* is set in a place and time which can be linked to any real geographical location or historical era. By thus removing Arthur from the realm of history, Tennyson is able to imply that he was a Saxon rather than a Celt. When King Leodogran wants to ascertain that Arthur is the true son of Uther Pendragon before permitting him to marry his daughter Guinevere, he asks Arthur's sister Bellicent, Queen of Orkney, to verify the circumstances of her brother's birth. While probably not of great comfort to a father anxious to secure a good match for his daughter, the answer he receives would have undoubtedly been popular with many mid-nineteenth-century Britons:

> What know I?
> For dark my mother was in eyes and hair,
> And dark in hair and eyes am I; and dark
> Was Gorlois, yea and dark was Uther too,
> Wellnigh to blackness; but this king is fair
> Beyond the race of Britons and of men.
>
> (ll. 325–30)

Fair skin and hair are, of course, physical attributes traditionally associated with the Saxon race. Thus, while he cannot entirely over-turn Arthur's Celtic identity, Tennyson does, through obscurity and implication, hint that Arthur had been a Saxon. In the first half of the nineteenth century most British authors had attempted to present the Arthurian legend in a manner generally consistent with prevailing scholarly opinion, which held that he had been a sixth-century Celt. The *Idylls of the King*, however, marks a new departure for literary treatments of the legend. Although he makes no explicit effort to challenge Arthur's historical identity, Tennyson also refuses to acknowledge it.

Contemporary critics noted the ahistorical nature of the *Idylls*. In 1870, the *Dublin Review* observed that 'to surround the wigwams of the

---

[60] *Idylls of the King*, ed. J. M. Gray (New Haven and London: Yale UP, 1983). Subsequent citations to this work are given in the text.

only possible Camelot with accessories borrowed from feudal ages and chivalric associations, is nearly, if not quite, as absurd as if the body of Elaine were to be described as borne to its rest by special train on the Astolat and Camelot Junction Railway'. This reviewer was hardly complaining about such anachronism, however. Although he suggested that Tennyson could have 'tried to come as nearly as possible to reality in his delineation of the character, with the aid of various correct historical and archaeological details', such a strategy would have 'produced a figure as stiff and ungraceful' as the representations of saints which adorned many medieval churches. It was far better 'to adopt the Arthur of romance . . . perfected by the poet's own conceptions of what best befitted the kingly and knightly character, and adorned by the poet's picturesque imagination'.[61]

In 1878 Henry Elsdale adopted a virtually identical line in his critique of the *Idylls*. 'We . . . find innumerable historical anachronisms in the details of the poems', he wrote. 'Instead of the mental sphere and horizon, the habits and modes of thought, the mind and spirit of the sixth or even of the twelfth century, we find those of the eighteenth or nineteenth'. But like the *Dublin Review*, Elsdale saw Tennyson's removal of the legend from its historical context as a virtue rather than a flaw. 'We are not justified in laying too much stress upon the question of historical inaccuracy. . .', he declared. 'Mr. Tennyson has, no doubt, better consulted the taste of the large majority of his nineteenth century readers by taking the . . . line which he has actually taken, in engrafting nineteenth century notions upon the original stock supplied him by the legends'.[62] And some of these 'nineteenth century notions' were undeniably of a racialist nature. For most contemporary Britons, the ideal Arthur was a Saxon Arthur, and that was precisely what Tennyson gave them.

When combined with the influence of contemporary racialist theory, Tennyson's powerful voice was sufficient to inspire subsequent authors to follow suit. In the second half of the nineteenth century Arthur was transformed from a Celt to a Saxon, and from an ancient British chieftain to—as one children's book described him—the 'King of all England'. And as part of Arthur's transformation from a Celtic to a Saxon king, he was assimilated into the same Aryan racialist beliefs as

---

[61] 'Mr. Tennyson's Arthurian Poems', *Dublin Review*, 70 (1870), 419.
[62] Henry Elsdale, *Studies in the Idylls: An Essay on Mr. Tennyson's 'Idylls of the King'* (London, 1878), 127-33.

was the legend of Robin Hood. In a lecture delivered to the Bombay branch of the Royal Asiatic Society in 1868, Edward Tyrrell Leith claimed that the Arthurian legend was 'originally an archaic Aryan myth . . . carried westwards into Britain with the wave of Celtic migration'. More significantly, in his influential *The Mythology of the Aryan Nations* (1870), George W. Cox argued that 'the epic poems of the Aryan nations are simply different versions of one and the same story'. Into this framework Cox fitted the Arthurian legend, which he claimed was 'useless for all historical purposes', but 'valuable to the comparative mythologist', because once it had been 'stripped . . . of its adventitious matter, [it] assumes a form common to the traditions and folk-lore of all the Teutonic or even all the Aryan nations'. Cox's arguments were accepted at least in some measure by many Arthurian scholars; in the 1890s no less an authority than Jessie Weston, one of the leading contemporary scholars of Arthurian literature, suggested that the legend contained 'some survivals of Aryan folk-lore, shared alike by all nations of the same stock'.[63]

Perhaps the most unusual association between the Arthurian legend and Aryanism occurred in John S. Stuart Glennie's play *King Arthur: or, The Drama of the Revolution* (1870). The play was intended as one of a trilogy which would depict 'the conflict of those great Human Forces which are unrevealed in the scientific study of Man's History, and more particularly of our Present Historical Period', which, according to Glennie, was 'defined by the European, or rather indeed, Aryan . . . revolutionary movement'. To those who doubted the existence of such a 'revolutionary movement', Glennie declared that it 'has long been seen by student and thinkers' that it 'will change, not only the religious Creeds, but the social Institutions of the Aryan nations'. He further claimed that

it is a movement originating, not only in profound intellectual and social causes, but in a new Enthusiasm of Humanity, a new Passion of Fraternal Sentiment. And, as thus originating, the Revolution, in its moral aspect, appears as the working in men's minds of a New Ideal to which the progress of the intellectual and social movements gives ever-increasing clearness and effectiveness.

[63] *Six Ballads about King Arthur* (London, 1881), 9; Edward Tyrrell Leith, *On the Legend of Tristan: Its Origin in Myth and Its Development in Romance* (Bombay, 1868), 35; George W. Cox, *The Mythology of the Aryan Nations* (London, 1870), 309; Jessie L. Weston, *The Story of Tristan and Iseult: Rendered into English from the German of Gottfried von Strassburg* (London, 1899), vol. i, p. xi.

Glennie believed that this 'New Ideal' would be brought about by the racial unity of the Aryan nations: 'The Future in this New Ideal is that of the Race rather than of the Individual'.[64] As eccentric as Glennie's ideas undoubtedly were, they echoed other, more sober arguments regarding the link between the Arthurian legend and Aryan racial theory, arguments which in turn played a crucial role in divorcing Arthur from his Celtic roots and realigning him with nineteenth-century Anglo-Saxonism.

The crowning achievement of Arthur's transformation into an English king was J. Comyns Carr's play *King Arthur*, which premiered at Henry Irving's Lyceum Theatre on 12 January 1895. Best known as the director of the Grosvenor Gallery, Carr had been recruited by Irving to compose a drama that would serve as the basis for a lavish production employing the leading talents of the contemporary British stage. The result closely resembled *The Idylls of the King*, for Carr made no attempt to provide his play with a realistic historical setting, and Edward Burne-Jones's dark and mist-shrouded sets reinforced the dreamlike atmosphere of the production. 'There is no question of historical accuracy here', wrote Clement Scott in his review. By disengaging Arthur from history, Carr did not have to allude to Arthur's Celtic origins. Instead, he was able to present him as an English hero. Indeed, Carr's Anglocentric patriotism was so pronounced that Burne-Jones was revolted at the first rehearsal by the 'jingo bits about the sea and England'. The play opens with a prologue in which Merlin brings the young Arthur to the shore of 'the magic Mere', where he informs him that he is the son of Uther Pendragon, 'England's chosen lord'. Arthur accepts his birthright eagerly, and vows to lead England towards the brilliant future for which the Spirits prophecy it is destined:

> I see that throng of England's unborn sons,
> Whose glory is her glory: prisoned souls
> With faces pressed against the bars of Time,
> Waiting their destined hour. Give me my sword,
> That I may loose Time's bonds, and set them free.

Carr continues to associate Arthur with a specifically English patriotism throughout the play. In the final scene Arthur is killed in battle, but Merlin tells Guinevere not to lament, for he can never truly die:

---

[64] John S. Stuart Glennie, *King Arthur: or, The Drama of the Revolution* (London, 1870), pp. vi–viii, xi.

> . . . he doth but pass who cannot die,
> The King that was, the King that yet shall be;
> Whose spirit, borne along from age to age,
> Is England's to the end.

The chorus's patriotic chant, 'England's sword is in the sea', reinforces the nationalistic content of the play.[65]

The reaction of the theatregoing public to *King Arthur* was extremely positive, suggesting that Carr's vision of the legend conformed to their own. The play ran for a hundred nights in London, toured America and Canada successfully in 1895–6, and it might well have been revived had not a warehouse fire destroyed its scenery in 1898. This reception indicates that, by the end of the nineteenth century, it had become not only plausible but expedient to present Arthur as an English hero. The majority of the theatregoing public clearly wanted not the historical, Celtic King Arthur but one which conformed to contemporary racialist beliefs.

To be sure, there were some scholars who objected to such a blatantly ahistorical treatment of the legend. Their complaints, however, were quickly quashed by the force of Anglo-Saxonist opinion. 'Have we any right to look on King Arthur as a national hero?' Jessie Weston asked in 1899. 'It has been objected that since Arthur was a British chieftain we are entirely wrong in treating him as an English hero. This is surely a pedantic accuracy which over-shoots its own mark; we might as reasonably contend that the French have no right to glory in the *Matière de France*, since Charlemagne was certainly no Frenchman!'[66] The Anglo-Saxonists had laid claim to the Arthurian legend, and it was accordingly transformed from a British to an English national epic.

In the first half of the nineteenth century racial unity was often offered as the primary explanation for Britain's success. The British, it was conventionally argued, reigned supreme because they had assimilated the best qualities of a number of distinguished ancestors into a single bloodline. This perspective is reflected in contemporary literary treatments of the legends of Robin Hood and King Arthur, which

---

[65] Clement Scott, *From 'The Bells' to 'King Arthur.' A Critical Record of the First-night Productions at the Lyceum Theatre* (London, 1896), 376; Jennifer R. Goodman, 'The Last of Avalon: Henry Irving's *King Arthur* of 1895', *Harvard Library Bulletin*, 32 (1984), 242; J. Comyns Carr, *King Arthur* (London, 1895), 2–7, 66.

[66] Jessie L. Weston, *Popular Studies in Mythology, Romance and Folklore* (London, 1899), 3.

emphasized the amalgamation of different peoples. In the second half of the century, however, new developments in racialist theory produced a more exclusively Anglo-Saxonist point of view. In this context, Robin Hood and King Arthur were reconfigured into Saxon heroes to fit these new racial ideals.

CHAPTER FIVE

'I have made his glory mine': Women and the Nation in the Legends of King Arthur and Robin Hood

In J. F. Pennie's verse drama *The Dragon King: A Tragedy* (1832), King Arthur's realm is besieged by the Saxons. As Arthur's Britons face a desperate struggle for national survival, a more private crisis unfolds behind the scenes. Mouric Medrawd, a knight of the Round Table, begs Arthur's queen 'Gwenyfar' to flee with him. Initially, Gwenyfar resists his entreaties, protesting that her departure would have serious consequences for the British nation:

> And shall I leave my husband? that brave prince,
> The pillar of the Cymry, on which leans,
> Its sole support, the empire of the Britons!

Mouric continues to plead his case, however, regaling her with grisly tales of what will happen after the 'detested pagans' crush Arthur and his knights. Finally, Gwenyfar relents, and her betrayal does indeed have near-catastrophic consequences for the British nation, for Arthur is devastated when he learns of her departure. Only his loyal lieutenant Meridoc's success in convincing him to set aside his private woes for the good of his country prevents national disaster:

> Let not despair
> O'ercome the great deliverer of his country—
> She claims thy thoughts, thy energies, thy powers,
> Before all private wrong.[1]

Published almost seventy years later, *Little Red Robin* (1900), a burlesque by Vivian Matthews and Alick Manley, also focuses on the nature of a woman's duty to her husband and her nation during wartime, but

---

[1] J. F. Pennie, *The Dragon King: A Tragedy*, in *Britain's Historical Drama; A Series of National Tragedies* (London, 1832), 432, 448–51.

presents that duty in a very different light. When King Richard the
Lion-hearted comes to Sherwood Forest in search of soldiers for the
Crusades, Robin Hood and his Merry Men enthusiastically volunteer:

> Down with the yardstick and up with the bow,
> We'll follow our leader where'er he may go;
> To fight for the King as all true Britons should,
> And we'll all go a-roving with bold Robin Hood!

Eager to join them is Robin Hood's beloved Maid Marian, who
declares that she will gladly fight for her country. The King, Robin
Hood, and the Merry Men welcome her with open arms, and make no
objection to the idea of a woman doing battle alongside them. As the
scene closes, Maid Marian leads her male companions in a patriotic
chorus:

> For our swords they swing and our spurs they ring,
> As we ride in the train of our Soldier King;
> Whether by land, or whether by sea,
> Or who is the foeman, what care we?
> 'Here's to the hearts that are brave and true!'
> We sing in a rousing chorus;
> 'Here's to the Red and the White and the Blue
> Of the flag that's waving o'er us!'[2]

The contrast between these two episodes reveals much about the
complex position of women in nineteenth-century British society, and
the relationship of that position to contemporary national identity. On
the one hand, the predominant social mores encouraged women to
stay at home, where they would support male efforts to protect the
nation from its enemies. A refusal to remain confined to the domestic
realm and obey patriarchal standards of 'proper' feminine conduct
threatened the foundations not only of their own families, but of the
entire British nation. Nevertheless, women stepped outside domestic
confines with increasing frequency as the nineteenth century wore on,
and took on more active roles in national affairs. Once in the public
sphere, they met with widely varying responses. On the one hand, they
were frequently accused of destroying the nation's moral fabric, but on
the other, a growing minority of people, male and female alike, saw
their efforts as a chance to redefine the nation along new, more broadly

---

[2] Vivian Matthews and Alick Manley, *Little Red Robin; or, the Dey and the Knight. Original
Burlesque Extravaganza* (London, [1900]), 10 and 15.

based lines. The following chapter will examine the relationship between nineteenth-century British womanhood and national identity through the legends of King Arthur and Robin Hood, and more specifically through their female characters, who represent a variety of contemporary feminine archetypes.

First, however, it is necessary to examine some important questions regarding the status of women in this period that have been raised in recent scholarship. In the last two decades historians of nineteenth-century British women have negotiated between the doctrine of 'separate spheres', which suggests that there was a strict divide between the male and female domains in the nineteenth century, and a less rigid approach which emphasizes the increasingly frequent forays which woman made into traditionally male-dominated areas. The first view, to be sure, has much validity. For much of the nineteenth century women were subjected to a variety of legal restraints which ensured that their public role was limited. Reform came only very slowly, and was still far from complete by the century's end.[3]

These legal restraints were paralleled by social attitudes which reinforced sexual inequality. The social code dictated that a woman's proper place was in the home, where she was responsible for maintaining the household, whereas the man moved in the public world outside its walls, supporting his family and performing the duties which citizenship necessitated. Under threat of sanction—ranging from ridicule to violent retribution—if they violated these accepted gender boundaries, nineteenth-century women rarely ventured into the public world, and it was generally assumed that a woman engaged in business was without a private income or a husband to support her.[4]

Thus, the articulation of sexual difference in the form of a binary opposition between 'manly' men and 'womanly' women was a characteristic feature of Victorian thought. In recent years, however, some scholars have attempted to refine the 'separate spheres' paradigm and to suggest that the gender divide was not always strict. Certainly, substantial numbers of women were elected to local office from the 1860s onwards, and the efforts of 'advanced' women from the educated classes in the final decades of the nineteenth century achieved at least some success in legitimizing female employment and promoting the

---

[3] See Mary Lyndon Shanley, *Feminism, Marriage and the Law in Victorian England, 1850–1895* (London: I. B. Tauris, 1989).

[4] Leonore Davidoff and Catherine Hall, *Family Fortunes: Men and Women of the English Middle Class, 1780–1850* (London: Hutchinson, 1987).

suffrage movement.[5] When these points are taken into account, what emerges is a complex picture of women in nineteenth-century society. On the one hand, tradition and the law combined to establish the boundaries of the female sphere, boundaries which were transgressed only at the risk of social stigma and sanction. But on the other, an increasing number of women took that risk and entered the public sphere, where they worked in paid employment, pursued voluntary philanthropic work, and played a significant role in local government.

This chapter will not attempt to resolve the debate over the validity of 'separate spheres'. Instead, it will explore the complexities of contemporary womanhood by examining the treatment of the female characters in the legends of King Arthur and Robin Hood. In particular, it will examine those complexities as they related to the role of women as members of the British nation in an era in which they did not enjoy full rights of citizenship. Were women to stay at home, where they would serve as the nation's moral guardians? Or were they to venture out into the public arena, where they would function as equal citizens alongside their husbands and fathers? These questions were crucial in determining the relationship which women had with their nation in nineteenth-century Britain.

'Shun that lovely snare': The Arthurian Legend and Gender Roles in the Nineteenth Century

'The ladies of the [Arthurian legend] do not so generally shine as the men', declared Henry Frith in the introduction to his adaptation of Thomas Malory's *Morte Darthur* in 1884. Indeed, the depiction of women in nineteenth-century Arthurian literature is rarely positive. Contemporary authors generally view them as threats to Arthur's realm who at best distract the knights of the Round Table from the path of virtue and duty and at worst actively plot the downfall of

---

[5] See Patricia Hollis, *Ladies Elect: Women in English Local Government 1865–1914* (Oxford: Clarendon Press, 1987); Pat Jalland, *Women, Marriage and Politics 1860–1914* (Oxford: Oxford UP, 1986); Jane Lewis, *Women in England 1870–1950: Sexual Divisions and Social Change* (Sussex: Wheatsheaf, 1984); David Rubinstein, *Before the Suffragettes: Women's Emancipation in the 1890s* (Brighton: Harvester Press, 1986); Martha Vicinus, *Independent Women: Work and Community for Single Women 1850–1920* (London: Virago, 1985); Judith R. Walkowitz, *Prostitution and Victorian Society: Women, Class and the State* (Cambridge: Cambridge UP, 1980); Judith R. Walkowitz, *City of Dreadful Delight: Narratives of Sexual Danger in Late Victorian London* (London: Virago, 1992).

Camelot. In both cases, it is their specifically 'female' powers which are at issue, for they use their beauty and sexual allure to achieve their destructive and often overtly malevolent objectives. In his poem *The Bridal of Triermain* (1813), Sir Walter Scott describes the problems which feminine enticements could cause for Arthur and his followers. Riding out in search of a 'vent'rous quest', Arthur comes to a castle inhabited by 'a band of damsels fair' who take him to their queen, Guendolen, with whom Arthur falls deeply in love. Here, Scott interposes an authorial warning which emphasizes the threat this infatuation poses to Arthur's kingdom:

> A sage, who had that look espied,
> Where kindling passion strove with pride,
> Had whisper'd, 'Prince, beware!
> From the chafed tyger rend the prey,
> Rush on the lion when at bay,
> Bar the fell dragon's blighted way,
> But shun that lovely snare!'

Scott's dire prophecy soon proves true. Guendolen, who intends 'to sink in slothful sin and shame | The Champions of the Christian name', convinces Arthur to spend the night. Soon, he has entirely abandoned his realm, and Britain's enemies use the opportunity to attack:

> The Saxon stern, the pagan Dane,
> Maraud on Britain's shores again.
> Arthur, of Christendom the flower,
> Lies loitering in a lady's bower;
> The horn, that foemen wont to fear,
> Sounds but to wake the Cumbrian deer,
> And Caliburn, the British pride,
> Hangs useless by a lover's side.[6]

Three months elapse before Arthur can rouse himself to leave his life of idle comfort and return to his realm. He arrives in the nick of time to save his kingdom from destruction, a narrow escape from the perils of what Scott clearly views as a too-intense enjoyment of the pleasures of female company.

The theme of women as a distraction from more important national tasks recurs in numerous nineteenth-century literary treatments of the

---

[6] Henry Frith, *King Arthur and his Knights of the Round Table* (London, 1884), p. v; Sir Walter Scott, *The Bridal of Triermain* (Edinburgh, 1813), 29, 44–5, 53–5, 57.

Arthurian legend. In Edward Bulwer Lytton's epic poem *King Arthur* (1849), Arthur falls in love with the queen of the Etrurians and forgets his mission to rescue Britain from the Saxon threat. He lingers in happy romantic bliss for months until one day a raven arrives bearing a message from Merlin:

> Weak Loiterer from thy toil,
> The Saxon's march is on thy father's soil.

Stung by this reminder of his delinquency, Arthur immediately recalls his duty:

> Thine be my people—thine this bleeding soil;
> Queen of my realm, its groaning murmurs hear!
> Then ask thyself, what manhood's choice should be;
> False to my country, were I worthy thee?[7]

Both Scott and Bulwer Lytton thus assert that men belong in the public world, where they must act to defend the nation. The female, domestic world has its charms, to be sure, but men must partake of them only in moderation. These authors support the model of a binary opposition between the sexes, a model which was socially realized in the idea of separate spheres for men and women. To transgress the boundaries between these spheres is to court disaster. Excessive male enjoyment of feminine domesticity, Scott and Bulwer Lytton imply, leads to weakness, loss of masculinity, and impotence, on both an individual and national level. A nation filled with men who dally too long at home will find, like Arthur in *The Bridal of Triermain*, that its sword 'hangs useless' by its side.

In the second half of the nineteenth century literary treatments of the Arthurian legend continued to accuse women of distracting men from their public duties, but the nature of these distractions began to take on a new, more explicitly sexual form. This change was related to a broader shift in attitudes towards sexual activity, which in this period shed its primary association with reproduction within the family and came to be associated with non-reproductive activities both inside and outside marriage. This change gave rise to considerable anxiety, as Victorian observers struggled to define new sexual norms, a struggle which generated considerable debate over which sexual activities were

---

[7] Edward Bulwer Lytton, *King Arthur* (London, 1849), i. 184, 190.

to be defined as 'dangerous'. This debate focused almost exclusively upon female sexuality. The overwhelming majority of educated Victorian opinion argued that efforts at curbing excessive or deviant sexual behaviour must be aimed at women because, unlike men, they were not dominated by 'irrepressible' physical urges.[8] Accordingly, a double standard came to be established in which male sexual activity was condoned as a sign of 'masculinity', while its female counterpart was condemned as an indication of deviant behaviour.

Contemporary Arthurian literature reflects these concerns about the dangers of unbridled female sexuality. In Thomas Westwood's 'The Quest of the Sancgreall' (1868), the ladies of Arthur's court attempt to dissuade their husbands from fulfilling their vow to go upon the quest for the Holy Grail. The night before the knights are due to depart:

> In each silken bower,
> By queen (ah! evil heart!) and courtly dame,
> And damsel, in her seventeen summers' sheen,
> Soft spells were woven, and subtle cantrips planned,
> To snare men's souls.

Those knights who successfully resist their wives' entreaties to stay behind later face other challenges from women eager to distract them from their objectives. Sir Galheron encounters a fairy queen who begs him to 'tarry' and enjoy 'love and rest in greenwood shade', but he breaks 'the elfin spell' and proceeds upon the quest. Sir Lancelot is not so fortunate. A 'white-limbed maiden' with 'ivory breasts half-veiled' leads him to the 'happy isles', where dozens of her companions lie in wait:

> Passive, the knight went wheresoe'er they would.
> They led him through the boskage of the shore,
> And through the winding vales and odorous woods,
> Till faint their frolic grew, and faint the chime
> Of laughter and of song. They led him on
> To festal bowers—to strange forbidden rites—
> To joys accursed. Ah me! Sir Lancelot,
> King Arthur's foremost knight! Sir Lancelot,
> The crown of Christendom! Sir Lancelot,
> The Knight of Christ! gone, gone, for ever gone![9]

---

[8] See Walkowitz, *City of Dreadful Delight*, 6; Elaine Showalter, *Sexual Anarchy: Gender and Culture at the Fin de Siècle* (London: Bloomsbury, 1991).

[9] Thomas Westwood, *The Quest of the Sancgreall, The Sword of Kingship, and Other Poems* (London, 1868), 10, 39, 50.

Here, Lancelot's abandonment of a properly 'masculine'—that is, active—role leads to disaster, for it ensures that he will fail to achieve the quest for the Grail. Westwood clearly views the maidens as deviants when he refers to their 'strange forbidden rites' and 'joys accursed'. Like Scott and Bulwer Lytton, he sees the public, sexual woman as a threat to masculine enterprise, as well as in a more general and ominous sense to the nation at large.

Much of this anxiety derived from changes in the status of patriarchy in mid-Victorian Britain, as the traditional conception of masculinity based upon aggressive, bellicose characteristics and physical prowess gave way to a more domesticated model which demanded that males display formerly 'feminine' qualities such as fidelity, modesty, purity, self-restraint, stability, and tenderness. The Arthurian legend was a useful vehicle for displaying these changes and exploring their consequences, for its central theme focuses upon Arthur's efforts to transform a warrior society based upon bloodthirsty conquest into a realm based upon a gentler, less combative code of conduct. It is thus not surprising that nineteenth-century authors often utilized the legend to explore definitions of a new kind of masculinity capable of functioning in an increasingly domestic sphere.[10]

Their efforts, however, were fraught with confusion and worry. Nineteenth-century Arthurian literature persistently reflects concerns that a domesticated man was ultimately an emasculated one. In *The Story of Queen Guinevere and Sir Lancelot of the Lake* (1865), Charles Bruce describes the corrosive effect which the coming of peace has upon Camelot, for it 'unmans' the knights by confining them to the domestic sphere, where women reign supreme:

> Yet, save the warfare that love wages,
> Fight now no more their thought engages;
> For in the hero's thought
> Love holds its camp and court,
> And men, whose arms could death-blows deal
> On giants, woman's chains must feel.
> For in the storm of battle tossed,
> Men's heart ne'er yet its freedom lost;
> But peaceful charms have oft undone
> The conquest strength hath dearly won;

---

[10] Margaret Linley, 'Sexuality and Nationality in Tennyson's *Idylls of the King*', *Victorian Poetry*, 30 (1992), 367–9.

> When peace asserts its sacred ban,
> Then woman lords it over man.

In his poem 'Arthur's Knighting' (1875), Sebastian Evans also brings this concern to the fore. Evans laments the disappearance of the heroic, masculine world of Arthur's youth and contrasts it with its Victorian successor, in which

> Men no more durst speak the manly word,
> But waste their wit in woman jest and jeer;
> And courtly things that strut and wear a sword
> Whisper to high-born dame, and crouch and leer
> And sneer a double meaning to the tale
> No loyal knight could tell nor maiden hear.
> Even in council, clad in useless mail,
> They give and chatter, each in fooling phrase
> Girding at other till their lips are pale
> With such small wrath as in emasculate days
> May vent itself in slander and be safe.

Evans asserts that in these 'emasculate days' men have acquired what would have been regarded in Arthur's day as feminine characteristics. 'Honour is dead', he complains, because 'now no blood is spilt | To prove its value'. According to Evans, the destruction of traditional forms of masculinity will lead to national decay: 'The whole realm is smitten at the core | With the restless boding of supremer ills'.[11]

Inevitably, such overriding anxiety had a major impact upon depictions of the Arthurian legend's female characters. Concerned for their own apparently weakening power, men began to fear and denigrate female strength, which seemed to threaten what they saw as their ever more tenuous position. Throughout the nineteenth century Arthurian literature was explicitly concerned with the degree to which women acted as guardians or destroyers of the moral and socio-political fabric of the British nation. And more often than not, they functioned in the latter role. Contemporary treatments of the legend frequently focused upon the decline of a community from an ideal state to one of utter collapse, and the key agent of this collapse was often uncontrolled and uncontrollable female sexuality.[12] In particular, the treatment of the

[11] Charles Bruce, *The Story of Queen Guinevere and Sir Lancelot of the Lake* (London, 1865), 2; Sebastian Evans, *In the Studio: A Decade of Poems* (London, 1875), 166–7, 176–7.
[12] Elliot L. Gilbert, 'The Female King: Tennyson's Arthurian Apocalypse', *PMLA* 98 (1983), 864.

characters of Elaine, Vivien, and, most obviously, Guinevere reveals much about the anxieties and tensions in nineteenth-century Britain regarding the relationship of women to their nation.

'She that saw him': Elaine

In the nineteenth century it was widely believed that domestic peace and harmony translated directly into national security and prosperity. In this context, the home functioned as a microcosm of the British state. 'The Home', wrote Samuel Smiles in his famous *Self-Help* (1859), 'is the crystal of society—the very nucleus of national character; and from that source, be it pure or tainted, issue the habits, principles and maxims, which govern public as well as private life'. And it was a woman's duty to ensure that her family's home remained 'pure' and not 'tainted' so that it could function as the source of national stability.[13] A woman who refused to fulfill this duty thus represented a threat to the nation, for she had the potential to destroy society at its very core.

In the context of Arthurian literature, authors focused upon female domesticity through the character of Elaine, 'the lily maid of Astolat'. Despite her relatively minor role in Malory's *Morte d'Arthur* as a young maiden who dies pining for Lancelot's love, Elaine was an extremely popular figure in nineteenth-century Britain. In her guise as 'the Lady of Shalott' she featured in numerous paintings and book illustrations. There were also characters modelled upon her in several Victorian novels, including Charles Dickens's *Little Dorrit*, George Eliot's *Middlemarch*, and Thomas Hardy's *Jude the Obscure*.[14]

Elaine's popularity was directly attributable to the fact that, at least on the surface, she represented the archetype of the Victorian female: beautiful, passive, and safely sequestered. Louisa Stuart Costello's poem 'The Funeral Boat' (1829) tells of a beautiful damsel dying from too strong a love for Sir Launcelot, who has abandoned her. On her deathbed she instructs her maidens to place her corpse in a

---

[13] Lynda Nead, *Myths of Sexuality: Representations of Women in Victorian Britain* (Oxford and New York: Basil Blackwell, 1988), 33; Carol T. Christ, 'Victorian Masculinity and the Angel in the House', in Martha Vicinus (ed.), *A Widening Sphere* (Bloomington, Ind.: Indiana UP, 1977), 146–62.

[14] *Ladies of Shalott: A Victorian Masterpiece and Its Contexts* (Providence, RI: Brown University Department of Art, 1985); Jennifer Gribble, *The Lady of Shalott in the Victorian Novel* (London and Basingstoke: Macmillan, 1983).

'gilded bark | And launch it in the rolling tide' (ll. 7–8). The bark lands on a riverbank near King Arthur's court. When Launcelot recognizes the damsel's face he is filled with remorse, and he vows to forswear Arthur's court for one year as an act of penitence. 'The Funeral Boat' thus presents Elaine as a passive victim for whom only death can bring the empowerment necessary to punish Launcelot.[15]

Four years later Letitia Elizabeth Landon published another poetic version of the Elaine story, 'A Legend of Tintagel Castle'. In the first scene Lancelot is riding through the forest when he sees the reflection of a maiden's face in a stream. Entranced by her beauty, he accompanies her to a cave, where she 'trusts her whole being to him'. When he hears 'the sound of the trumpet', however, he is lured 'again to the war' and abandons her, going back to the male, public world. The scene then shifts to Arthur's court several months later, where a small vessel suddenly appears bearing a funeral bier on its deck. When the wind lifts the pall to reveal the dead maiden, Lancelot is overwhelmed by guilt and weeps as he kneels by her corpse.[16]

As one of the first professional female authors, Landon transgressed contemporary notions of conventional gender roles as she attempted to enter what was regarded as a male occupation, and she frequently encountered strong criticism from male colleagues threatened by the idea of a woman earning her living by writing. For that reason, Landon was extremely conscious of the need to present herself in a conventionally 'feminine' manner.[17] Accordingly, her poetry, including 'A Legend of Tintagel Castle', rarely challenges established gender roles. As in 'The Funeral Boat', her Elaine can only express her dissatisfaction by sacrificing her life.[18]

---

[15] Roger Simpson, 'Costello's "The Funeral Boat": An Analogue of Tennyson's "The Lady of Shalott"', *Tennyson Research Bulletin*, 4 (1984), 131.

[16] *Poetical Works of Letitia Elizabeth Landon 'L.E.L.': A Facsimile Reproduction of the* 1873 Edition, ed. F. J. Sypher (Delmar, NY: Scholars Facsimiles and Reprints, 1990), 494–5.

[17] Glennis Stephenson, 'Letitia Landon and the Victorian Improvisatrice: The Construction of L.E.L.', *Victorian Poetry*, 30 (1992), 3.

[18] It was a sacrifice which Landon herself was forced to make only five years later. Her determination to forge a career as a professional author clearly disturbed many male critics. By the end of the 1830s rumours of her improper sexual conduct were circulating, including stories of bawdy propositions and illegitimate children. In 1838 she married the disreputable George MacClean, Governor of the Ivory Coast, in an effort to escape from the scandals plaguing her in London. Three months later that escape became final: her corpse was discovered in Cape Coast Castle. It remains unclear whether she committed suicide or was murdered, but whichever was the case, Landon paid the ultimate price for her transgressions of the boundary between the male and female worlds.

In the poems by Costello and Landon Elaine thus functions as a symbol of female confinement. When Alfred Tennyson decided to tackle the story in 'The Lady of Shalott' (1833), he, too, focused upon this theme. The poem tells of a young woman mysteriously imprisoned in a tower on a lonely island. A curse forces her to gaze at the world outside exclusively through a mirror. One day she catches a glimpse of Sir Lancelot, with whom she immediately falls deeply in love. She runs to the window in order to see him in the flesh, thereby causing the mirror to crack and ensuring her doom. She descends from the tower and climbs into a boat, in which she dies on the way to Camelot.

In its narrative structure Tennyson's poem differs little from the earlier treatments by Costello and Landon. 'The Lady of Shalott', however, displays even greater anxiety over Elaine's decision to leave her private space and move into the public world, for it represents a threat not only to herself, but also to society at large. Upon sighting her corpse, Arthur's knights 'cross'd themselves for fear', suggesting that her escape from the tower somehow endangers Camelot. How could a young and innocent maiden threaten Arthur's powerful realm? The danger lies in her attempt to subvert conventional gender boundaries by refusing to remain confined to the private, female sphere. For Tennyson, her attempt to escape is a source of anxiety, for it challenges the patriarchal norms which governed nineteenth-century Britain. Only her death, tragic but timely, prevents disaster.

One of the most significant ways in which 'The Lady of Shalott' manifests this anxiety is by means of what one women's historian has termed 'the discourse of the gaze'. In the nineteenth century the act of looking was typically identified with a masculine subject, while women functioned as silent and passive objects. For a woman to appropriate the gaze was an act of self-empowerment, a crossing of the gender divide from 'feminine' to 'masculine'. This is precisely what the Lady does in Tennyson's poem. At first she is forced to mediate her gaze through a mirror, averting her eyes from the world in a conventionally 'feminine' fashion. But in the third section of the poem the gap is bridged, when she crosses to the window to admire Lancelot:

> She saw the water-lily bloom,
> She saw the helmet and the plume,
> She looked down to Camelot.
> (ll. 111–13)

In these lines the Lady becomes the desiring subject rather than the desired object. In this way, at least, she accomplishes her crossing from the 'female' to the 'male' sphere.[19]

Almost three decades later, Tennyson returned to the Elaine story in the first instalment of the *Idylls of the King*, published in 1859. That the first four *Idylls*—'Geraint and Enid', 'Merlin and Vivien', 'Guinevere', and 'Lancelot and Elaine'—all focus upon female characters is no coincidence. Tennyson wrote these poems during the long parliamentary debates over the Matrimonial Causes Act, better known as the 'Divorce Act'. As the first major piece of British legislation to focus attention on the legal position of married women, the bill came under intense scrutiny from the time of its introduction, culminating in marathon sessions in the House of Commons in the summer of 1857. The rhetoric of the debate reveals that male legislators were unwilling to countenance any changes which might disturb established gender relations. As a result, the Act did not substantially alter the sexual double standard, and husbands and wives continued to be treated very differently under the law.

Given this context, it is not surprising that anxieties about gender roles were the dominant concern of the 1859 group of *Idylls*. In 'Lancelot and Elaine', Tennyson introduces his heroine as 'Elaine the fair, Elaine the lovable' (l.1), a description which conforms to Victorian notions of female beauty and passivity.[20] But he can only have used the term 'lovable' in an ironic sense, for the remainder of the poem focuses upon her failure to be loved by Lancelot, and her unrequited love for him. Elaine is thus no passive recipient of male adoration. Quite the contrary—it is she who is the active subject, she who adores.

The reversal of the traditional gender roles of active male and passive female continues throughout the poem. As in 'The Lady of Shalott', in 'Lancelot and Elaine' the act of looking is usurped by a female viewer, for Elaine's voyeuristic gaze upon Lancelot is a recurring theme of the poem. Tennyson introduces this motif in the opening scene, in which Elaine stares at Lancelot's shield as she hopes desperately for his return. Each day she climbs to the top of

---

[19] Walkowitz, *City of Dreadful Delight*, 16; Carl Plasa, '"Cracked from Side to Side": Sexual Politics in "The Lady of Shalott"', *Victorian Poetry*, 30 (1992), 258.

[20] All citations from the *Idylls of the King* are taken from Alfred Lord Tennyson, *Idylls of the King*, ed. J. M. Gray (New Haven and London: Yale UP, 1983).

> That eastern tower, and entering barr'd her door,
> Stript off the case, and read the naked shield.
>
> (ll. 15–16)

Here Elaine sees rather than is seen, and who she sees is Lancelot, symbolized by his shield, 'stript' and 'naked'. Men were accustomed to gazing at paintings of female nudes in the nineteenth century, but here Elaine reverses the relationship, thereby transforming it into something more subversive.

Indeed, Elaine's 'view' of Lancelot is at the heart of Tennyson's poem. From the time of Lancelot's arrival at Astolat, she gazes upon him. As she listens to him tell of his knightly exploits, she 'lifted her eyes, and read his lineaments' (l. 243). Later, lying in her bed, she pictures him before her:

> As when a painter, poring on a face,
> Divinely thro' all hindrance finds the man
> Behind it, and so paints him that his face,
> The shape and colour of a mind and life,
> Lives for his children, ever at its best
> And fullest . . .
>
> (ll. 330–5)

Not until the next day as he is preparing to leave does Lancelot return her gaze:

> He look'd, and more amazed
> Than if seven men had set upon him, saw
> The maiden standing in the dewy light.
> He had not dream'd she was so beautiful.
>
> (ll. 348–51)

But although he agrees to wear her sleeve upon his helmet as a token of his affection, Lancelot does not attempt to transform their relationship to the traditional one of male observer and female observed. Instead, he is soon distracted by Guinevere, and Elaine does not encounter him again until he is wounded in a joust and she goes to Camelot to tend his wounds.

Here, once again, contemporary events intruded upon Tennyson's poetic narrative. In the 1850s any reference to nursing inevitably recalled the heroic but still controversial activities of Florence Nightingale during the Crimean War. Nightingale's aggressive interpretation of the duties of a nurse, and more generally of women as a whole, aroused much contemporary debate. Some saw her actions as a threat to conventional gender roles, and these anxieties were heightened by the image of a woman assuming authority over a helpless and dependent male patient.[21] These fears are displayed in Tennyson's poem. Elaine's first look at the wounded Lancelot explicitly contrasts his former and current physical states, emphasizing his present weakness:

> His battle-writhen arms and mighty hands
> Lay naked on the wolfskin, and a dream
> Of dragging down his enemy made them move.
> Then she that saw him lying unsleek, unshorn,
> Gaunt as it were the skeleton of himself.
>
> (ll. 807–11)

Tennyson recognizes the dangers which this situation poses. It is from his sickbed that Lancelot reveals to Elaine that he does not love her, thus draining her position of physical supremacy of its potential power. Her pride gone, she begs him to let her 'serve' him or 'follow' him 'thro' the world' (l. 934), but her words fall upon deaf ears. She is permitted one final glance as the recuperated Lancelot rides away, as she 'unclasping flung the casement back, and look'd | Down on his helm' (ll. 974–5). This time he feels her gaze upon him, but he refuses to acknowledge it, thus depriving it of its power:

> Lancelot knew that she was looking at him.
> And yet he glanced not up . . .
> But sadly rode away.
>
> (ll. 978–80)

'Lancelot and Elaine' thus concludes with the restoration of the conventional gender relations that have been challenged throughout much of the rest of the poem.

The chronological evolution of the four poems examined above demonstrates that, as the 'Woman Question' came to assume an ever-larger place in Victorian culture, gender relations became the focus of a steadily increasing anxiety. Even treatments of a superficially conventional female character like Elaine display the tensions which increasingly surrounded the patriarchal values of Victorian society. In

---

[21] Mary Poovey, *Uneven Developments: The Ideological Work of Gender in Mid-Victorian England, Women in Culture and Society* (Chicago and London: University of Chicago Press, 1988), 171.

order to see these concerns more overtly displayed, however, it is necessary to turn to another female character from the Arthurian legend: Vivien, the evil sorceress who contributes to the downfall of Arthur's realm. In her we see an even clearer image of the increasing threat which the public, aggressive woman was assumed to represent to the Victorian patriarchy.

'A woman's wile': Vivien

In Victorian culture the figure of the harlot, or 'fallen woman', came to be seen as the negation of feminine respectability. By the mid-nineteenth century she had become the object of near-obsessive concern from religious leaders and moral reformers, as well as the focus of attention in a bevy of works of literature and the visual arts.[22] This is borne out in contemporary Arthurian literature, which prominently features the legend's manipulative, deceitful, and malevolent female characters. In particular authors focused upon Vivien, the beautiful but wicked temptress who uses her sexual allure to convince Merlin to reveal the magic spell with which she subsequently confines him to eternal imprisonment. Vivien's actions pose a potent threat, for without the sagacity and clairvoyant abilities of his great wizard, Arthur's realm has little hope of survival.

One of the most popular narrative strands of the legend in the nineteenth century, the story of Merlin and Vivien was retold over and over again in Arthurian literature. And over and over again, authors emphasized Merlin's utter helplessness in the face of Vivien's sexual power. In 1838 R. Williams Buchanan contributed his poem 'Merlin's Tomb' to the *Glasgow University Album*. Buchanan begins his tale with Merlin and 'Viviane' lying 'in dalliance fond and fain' in their 'forest bower'. He has taught her all his knowledge, with the exception of one 'necromantic spell':

> 'But there's one thing I cannot do;
> I pray thee teach it me;'
> (And round his neck her arms she threw,
> And kissed him coaxingly.)

[22] See Susan P. Casteras, *The Substance or the Shadow: Images of Victorian Womanhood* (New Haven: Yale Center for British Art, 1982), 36–8.

Viviane thus uses her feminine charms to persuade Merlin to tell her the spell that she will ultimately use to imprison him for all eternity. Merlin is deeply suspicious of her intentions, but unable to resist her entreaties:

> Sir Merlin frowned—Sir Merlin sighed;
> But as entranced he lay
> On that fair breast, his purpose died,
> He could not say her nay.

Later, after the two lovers have taken 'their disport free', Merlin lies dozing with his head in Viviane's lap. She seizes the opportunity to use the spell against him, encircling him with a magic ring from which he can never leave without her permission. Merlin is enraged but utterly helpless; Viviane only laughs and mocks him for his naivety:

> Sir Merlin frown'd—Sir Merlin sigh'd;
> —Fair Viviane laughed the while—
> 'Such fortune still must fool betide,
> Will trust a woman's wile!'[23]

Written over fifty years later but almost identical in its treatment of Merlin and Vivien is R. Macleod Fullarton's *Merlin: A Dramatic Poem* (1890). In Fullarton's version, Merlin is bewitched from his first glimpse of the 'lissome shape' of the 16-year-old Vivien. He takes her to his forest lair, where she is at first innocent and eager to learn, but soon she begins to make demands, including 'a charm to keep you ever at my side, | And make you love me'. At this point she reveals in an internal monologue that she intends to use her beauty to persuade Merlin to teach her 'all I would know', so that she may seize control of Arthur's realm. 'Vivien shall be King!' she confidently exults, thereby usurping a male role in blatant fashion.[24] First, however, she must eliminate Merlin, the main obstacle to her plans. She convinces him to make a tomb for the two of them, so that they will never be parted, even in death. He realizes her intentions, but is powerless to resist. When the tomb is complete, she asks him to lie in it. He wearily assents, and she closes the lid over him, eternally sealing him within.

'Merlin's Tomb' and *Merlin: A Dramatic Poem* were only two of the

---

[23] R. Williams Buchanan, 'Merlin's Tomb', *The Glasgow University Album for 1838* (Glasgow, 1838), 1–8.

[24] R. Macleod Fullarton, *Merlin: A Dramatic Poem* (Edinburgh and London, 1890), 28, 42, 50.

plethora of versions of the story of Merlin and Vivien in nineteenth-century British literature. In order to understand why this story came to be the object of such intense interest, it is necessary to examine contemporary attitudes towards public morality and its role in national achievement. The Victorians believed that their country's international position depended upon a domestic base, a base whose stability was in turn a product of the moral purity of their society. As we have seen, women were supposed to serve as the guardians of this purity. Thus, when women failed in their duty and turned to vice, they endangered not only their own morality but, far more significantly, the security of the nation as a whole. In this context, Vivien served as a frightening representative of the consequences of female immorality. Using her sexual allure to entice men to their doom, she destroys Arthurian society from within. Her efforts to empower herself by employing her sexual wiles against Merlin display the social and moral chaos that can ensue from deviation from established standards of female sexual conduct.

To Victorian authors and their readers, Vivien's role in Arthur's downfall closely resembled the role which they feared the prostitute was coming to occupy in their own society. Vivien's relationship with Merlin is based upon an exchange of sexual favours for a material reward: the powerful charm which enables her to entrap him. The comparison of Vivien to a Victorian prostitute is developed in Tennyson's 'Merlin and Vivien', which, like 'Lancelot and Elaine', was included in the first instalment of the *Idylls of the King* in 1859.[25] At first Tennyson confines himself to metaphor. As Merlin tries to convince himself not to tell her the charm, he mutters:

> for fine plots may fail,
> Tho' harlots paint their talk as well as face
> With colours of the heart that are not theirs.
> I will not let her know . . .
>
> (ll. 818–21)

In the final lines, however, Tennyson uses the term more directly as he describes Vivien's exultation at having obtained the charm at last:

---

[25] See Rebecca Umland, 'The Snake in the Woodpile: Tennyson's Vivien as Victorian Prostitute', in Martin B. Shichtman and James P. Carley (eds), *Culture and the King: The Social Implications of the Arthurian Legend* (Albany: State University of New York Press, 1994), 274–87.

> Then crying 'I have made his glory mine,'
> And shrieking out 'O fool!' the harlot leapt
> Adown the forest, and the thicket closed
> Behind her.
>
> (ll. 969–72)

Many mid-Victorian commentators recognized—and loathed—Vivien for what she was. Algernon Charles Swinburne, who was certainly no prude, complained that she was 'such a sordid creature as plucks men passing by the sleeve' and criticized the poem for 'describing the erotic fluctuations and vacillations of a dotard under the moral and physical manipulation of a prostitute'. Even Tennyson's friends were disconcerted. In 1856 he sent an early draft of the poem to James Spedding, who commented that 'the effect of the poem is much injured by the predominance of harlotry'. Why was Spedding so appalled by 'Merlin and Vivien'? As the most visible and therefore most threatening manifestation of the ostensible moral degeneration of the British people, the prostitute came to function as a repository for fears of national decay and decline.[26] Invoking images of pollution and violation, numerous commentators conveyed a sense of horror at the social destruction for which prostitution was allegedly responsible.

How, more precisely, did Tennyson see the prostitute as capable of corrupting—and ultimately destroying—the British nation? In his view, her potency derived from her position as an aggressive, 'unnatural' female who challenged conventional gender roles. More specifically, her sexual deviancy rendered her 'masculine' by shifting her identity from pursued to pursuer. Vivien arrives at Camelot at a time when it is particularly vulnerable due to the lack of activity for Arthur's knights: 'And no quest came, but all was joust and play' (l. 143). They are thus confined to the domestic sphere, forced to turn to tournaments and other forms of mock combat to preserve their martial prowess. These games permit the expression of their more aggressively masculine traits, much as the athletic competitions of public schools functioned in mid- and late Victorian Britain.[27] The release which they provide, however, cannot be sustained indefinitely. True manliness, Tennyson implies throughout the *Idylls*, cannot exist in an exclusively domestic context.

---

[26] Ibid. 280; James Eli Adams, 'Harlots and Base Interpreters: Scandal and Slander in *Idylls of the King*', *Victorian Poetry*, 30 (1992), 421; Walkowitz, *Prostitution in Victorian Society*, 32.

[27] Linley, 'Sexuality and Nationality', 369.

In her first days at Arthur's court, however, Vivien scarcely appears to represent a threat. On the contrary, she seems entirely harmless, the epitome of the Victorian feminine ideal. In order to gain entrance to Camelot she prostrates herself before Guinevere, begging for 'shelter for mine innocency' (l. 82). Beneath the surface, however, Vivien is an insidious invader who will contribute to the destruction of Arthur's realm. Like a prostitute enticing a potential client, she plays the role of huntress rather than the conventionally feminine part of hunted. As she watches Guinevere and Lancelot ride away on a hawking expedition, she expresses her intentions to bring down Arthur, declaring that 'royaller game is mine' (l. 106). In the following stanza, Tennyson's description of a falcon who 'pounced her quarry and slew it' (l. 133) foreshadows Vivien's ultimately successful pursuit of Merlin.

Her usurpation of the male role of aggressor becomes clearer as the narrative develops. Hate and a strong desire for revenge, both per-ceived by the Victorians as typically male traits, motivate her actions. Extremely ambitious, she thirsts for fame and power, again qualities conventionally associated with masculine behavior. In the poem's final lines, her gleefully malevolent cry 'I have made his glory mine' (l. 969) completes her reversal of Victorian gender conventions. Vivien's triumph reflects the deep-rooted anxiety underlying mid-Victorian conceptions of masculinity and patriarchy. Merlin, shut forever in a hollow oak tree, symbolizes male impotence in both a political and sexual sense.[28] His disempowerment prefigures—and contributes to—that of Arthur and Camelot, which will also be caused by a woman who refuses to conform to predominant standards of proper female conduct.

'A name of scorn': Guinevere

The previous discussions of the treatment of Elaine and Vivien show how intensely nineteenth-century Arthurian literature focused upon gender relations, and specifically upon the willingness or unwillingness of women to play conventional social and sexual roles. In the vast majority of treatments of these characters, female attempts to trans-gress established gender boundaries met with a reactionary response.

[28] Linda M. Shires, 'Patriarchy, Dead Men and Tennyson's *Idylls of the King*', *Victorian Poetry*, 30 (1992), 416–7.

Elaine's refusal to remain safely confined to her proper sphere endangers Camelot by threatening the patriarchal ideals upon which it is based, while Vivien represents a malevolent force who 'unsexes' herself with her aggressive efforts to destroy Arthur's realm.

The treatment of Elaine and Vivien in nineteenth-century literature suggests that the ideology of separate spheres, in which women preserved the nation's domestic virtue while men tended to its public concerns, held sway. Any attempt by these female characters to cross into the public, masculine world occasioned a swift rebuff: Elaine is punished with death for her transgression, while Vivien is branded a harlot. But what of the treatment of the Arthurian legend's most important female character, Queen Guinevere? Was she, too, expected to remain confined to her 'proper' sphere and censured if she did not?

Certainly, the majority of Victorian authors castigated Guinevere as the sinful queen who was directly responsible for the downfall of Arthur's realm. As George Newcomen wrote in the *New Ireland Review* in 1899, Guinevere 'brought to pass . . . the end of the illustrious order'.[29] Such opinions were in keeping with nineteenth-century attitudes towards female adultery. Since, as we have seen, women were supposed to function as the guardians of the nation's moral virtue, the female participant in an adulterous relationship was customarily held to be at fault. For men, sexual lapses were regarded as regrettable but inevitable due to their strong, 'natural' physical urges.

The existence of this double standard is confirmed by Victorian treatments of Guinevere. In his poem 'Queen Guenevere' (1855), Owen Meredith shows Lancelot being lured to the Queen by 'a strange desire that drew me like a hand'. Lancelot's desire is thus represented as an external force against which he is powerless. The active, and therefore blameworthy, instigator of the affair is clearly Guinevere. This passage is representative of the prevailing attitude in which male infidelity received a relatively limited sanction, while female transgressions were severely criticized. By betraying her marital vows, Guinevere undermines the entire system of patriarchal dominance upon which Camelot is based. Indeed, of all the legend's female characters she was subjected to the most scathing attacks, attacks which were often extended to condemnations of the inconstancy of the female

---

[29] George Newcomen, 'The Lovers of Launcelot (A Critical Study of Sir Thomas Malory's Epic)', *New Ireland Review*, 11 (1899), 45.

sex as a whole. In the drama *Launcelot of the Lake* (1843), Guinevere's conduct prompts Christopher Riethmüller to write:

> There is no faith in woman!
> None! She may be as pure as virgin snow,
> Or crystal dew, that gems the morning-flowers—
> Bright as the sun-beams—beauteous as the stars—
> But never trust her faith![30]

In the 1850s, as Alfred Tennyson was completing his poem 'Guinevere' for the *Idylls of the King*, concern about female adultery reached a peak as Parliament debated the Divorce Bill. As was noted previously, legislators were extremely reluctant to countenance any significant changes in the existing laws regarding marriage. It is therefore not surprising that the Bill as enacted in 1857 continued to enforce a double standard in which even a single act of female adultery was considered sufficient grounds for divorce, but male adultery had to be accompanied by 'aggravating circumstances', such as bigamy, cruelty, desertion, rape, or incest. This provision gave rise to a vigorous public debate over such blatantly inequitable treatment. The vast majority of those who wished to see an extension of the rights of married women, however, were concerned only for those wives who had been victimized by the adultery of their husbands. Women who were themselves the perpetrators of adultery, on the other hand, received almost no sympathy.

Tennyson's 'Guinevere' reflects this attitude. In the poem, Arthur's long speech condemning his queen seems laughably censorious to twentieth-century readers. 'Thou hast spoilt the purpose of my life' (l. 450), Arthur tells Guinevere as she grovels at his feet 'with her face against the floor' (l. 412). He castigates her not because she has ruined their marriage, but because she has destroyed his realm:

> Bear with me for the last time while I show,
> Ev'n for thy sake, the sin which thou hast sinn'd.
> For when the Roman left us, and their law
> Relax'd its hold upon us, and the ways
> Were fill'd with rapine, here and there a deed
> Of prowess done redress'd a random wrong.
> But I was first of all the kings who drew

---

[30] Owen Meredith, *Clytemnestra, The Earl's Return, The Artist, and Other Poems* (London, 1855), 296; Christopher Riethmüller, *Launcelot of the Lake, A Tragedy, in Five Acts* (London, 1843), 19.

> The knighthood-errant of this realm and all
> The realms together under me, their Head,
> In that fair Order of my Table Round,
> A glorious company, the flower of men,
> To serve as model for the mighty world,
> And be the fair beginning of a time.
>
> (ll. 451–63)

It is this 'glorious company', Arthur informs Guinevere, that her sin has annihilated. He can forgive her for the personal anguish she has caused him, but the idyllic society which he sought to establish can never recover from the blow she has dealt it. Her actions result in national collapse as Arthur's realm is rent asunder by the tensions she has brought to bear upon it. By the poem's conclusion Guinevere has come to acknowledge her guilt. 'Mine will ever be a name of scorn', she tells the nuns who inhabit the abbey to which she has fled.

Tennyson's 'Guinevere' thus appears to be a straightforward account of the consequences which female adultery could have for the nation. She fails to fulfill the designated role of the married woman by upholding national virtue. Instead, she challenges patriarchal values by indulging her sexual desire with Lancelot, whose complicity is mitigated due to the irresistible nature of the temptation she presents. Arthur's speech thus represents a conviction that traditional gender roles must be upheld for the good of the nation.

But how could those traditional gender roles be maintained in a nation which was currently ruled not by a man, but by a woman? The anomaly of having a female monarch in Britain between 1837 and 1901 intensified the debate over where precisely a woman's proper place was, and there was clearly a great deal of discomfort at the notion of female rule. Fears of 'petticoat government' were rife, and numerous ostensibly comic images, both textual and visual, showed male politicians and members of the royal family being symbolically humiliated and infantilized by a domineering queen. Victoria herself acknowledged her anomalous position, commenting in 1852 that 'we women, if we are to be good women, feminine and amiable and domestic, are not fitted to reign'.[31]

That Tennyson was aware of the tensions created by a female

---

[31] Adrienne Munich, *Queen Victoria's Secrets* (New York: Columbia UP, 1996), ch. 7; Elizabeth K. Helsinger, Robin Lauterbach Sheets and William Veeder, *The Woman Question: Society and Literature in Britain and America, 1837–1883*, Vol. I: *Defining Voices, 1837–1883* (New York and London: Garland, 1983), 66.

monarch is made clear in his 'Dedication' to the *Idylls*, written in response to Prince Albert's death in 1861. At first glance, the poem endorses patriarchal values by hailing the Prince Consort as the embodiment of the traditionally masculine figure of the 'ideal knight' (l. 6). In truth, however, he represents few conventionally 'knightly' qualities. Instead, Tennyson praises him for attributes which, in the Victorian imagination, were considered 'feminine': modesty, purity, self-restraint, and tenderness. He also celebrates his domestic status as head of his family, the 'noble Father' of Britain's 'Kings to be' (l. 33). This sort of depiction of Albert demonstrates that Tennyson was well aware of the reversal of traditional gender roles caused by the occupation of the British throne by a woman. Albert, he acknowledges, comes by his sovereignty only through his marriage to a female ruler. As Albert himself once remarked, 'the difficulty in filling my place with the proper dignity is, that I am only the husband, and not the master of the house'.[32]

In 'Guinevere' Tennyson duplicates this subversion of the patriarchal hierarchy. The poem contains no episodes of active knighthood; instead, Arthur's expressions of masculinity are confined to the verbal realm, as he impotently attempts to reassert his dominance over his marriage and his kingdom. Here it is Guinevere who is the active figure. She flees to the convent at Almesbury, forcing Arthur to chase her. Her choice of refuge further demonstrates that, even as she pleads for forgiveness, she has not entirely submitted to patriarchal authority. In the nineteenth century a profound distrust existed towards women's religious orders in Britain. In addition to the centuries-old suspicion of anything smacking of popery, there were also widespread concerns that convents led to the disruption of family ties by removing women from their proper roles as mothers and helpmates to men. Guinevere's decision to seek refuge in a convent thus extends her crime rather than serving as a gesture of repentance.[33]

But if Tennyson acknowledges Guinevere's defiance of patriarchal values, he certainly does not condone it. As we have seen, the conventional Victorian response to fears of overly active female behaviour was to attempt to confine women to a passive domesticity. When Guinevere abandons her husband in favour of Lancelot, however, she makes it impossible for the façade of female domesticity to be maintained, and

---

[32] Linley, 'Sexuality and Nationality', 367–8; Munich, *Queen Victoria's Secrets*, 62.
[33] Linley, 'Sexuality and Nationality', 371.

condemnation is swift. Tennyson paints her as a corrupting female influence over a male fellowship which would otherwise have remained pure. A sorrowful Arthur tells her how sad it will be

> To sit once more within his lonely hall,
> And miss the wonted number of my knights,
> And miss to hear high talk of noble deeds
> As in the golden days before thy sin.

(ll. 494–7)

At the end of the *Idylls* Tennyson establishes a very different model of queenship. In 1873 he produced a poem entitled 'To the Queen', which was intended to serve as a companion piece to the 'Dedication' to Prince Albert and as a conclusion to the *Idylls*. But although it is ostensibly a statement in praise of Queen Victoria's qualities as a political leader, the poem fails to depict her in this capacity. Instead, she appears in the more conventional female roles of mother and wife. 'To the Queen' opens with a recollection of the thanksgiving ceremony held in honour of the Prince of Wales's recovery from typhoid fever in February 1872. It then proceeds to a fervent plea to maintain 'our ocean-empire' (l. 29) from which Victoria is virtually absent, except as a symbolic presence with no active role to play. She does not reappear until halfway through the poem, when Tennyson refers to 'thy living love' (l. 34) for the dead Albert. Tennyson then concludes with an anxiety-filled warning about 'the tempest in the distance' (l. 47) which threatens to destroy all that is 'high and holy' (l. 66). Victoria is not referred to in the final twenty lines of 'To the Queen', thus suggesting that whatever the future of the nation will be, Tennyson does not see her as having a hand in guiding Britain towards it.[34]

This view was in keeping with conventional contemporary depictions of Victoria, which highlighted her traditionally 'feminine' attributes, despite her status as ruler of the nation. Rather than being acknowledged as the vital, aggressive, and often disruptive political force that she was, an image was constructed which showed her as a typical nineteenth-century wife and mother. Although Victoria continued to intervene in politics until the very end of her reign, her subjects preferred to see her as, at various stages, a virginal adolescent, a devoted wife, a loving mother, a grieving widow, and a benevolent matriarch. Indeed, the vast majority of contemporary images of

---

[34] *The Poems of Tennyson*, ed. Christopher Ricks (London: Longmans, 1969), 1755–6.

Victoria depict her as a woman first and a ruler second. Even Victoria's long, and to some eyes overindulgent, widowhood was as much a source of admiration as it was of criticism, for it proved to many that she put private concerns above public, as a proper Victorian housewife should.[35] Moreover, her near-constant invocations of the dead Albert allowed her to maintain the image of the devoted, domesticated wife. Without a husband Victoria would have seemed a far more threatening figure, for in Victorian society an unmarried woman was a 'redundant' woman whose presence was not only superfluous but dangerous. It was this sensibility that caused Tennyson to emphasize Victoria's role as 'wife', even though her husband had been dead for ten years at the time 'To the Queen' was written. Tennyson thus begins the *Idylls* by raising questions about traditional gender roles in the 'Dedication', but concludes by reaffirming those roles in 'To the Queen'. And in between, in 'Guinevere', he indicates the problems that can occur when a woman refuses to fulfill her domestic duties.

Some of Tennyson's critics, however, were not so fully convinced that Guinevere was to blame for the downfall of Camelot. His friend and fellow poet George Meredith, for example, had little patience with Guinevere's grovelling. In his review, he declared that Arthur sounded like a 'crowned curate' whose answer to his wife's pleas should have been, 'Get up!' Meredith's reaction suggests that Victorian culture allowed for a more varied response to Guinevere's adulterous actions. Indeed, some authors were quite sympathetic to her plight. In *The Story of Queen Guinevere and Sir Lancelot of the Lake*, Charles Bruce describes how:

> A weary old man she had wed—
> A green graft on a tree long dead.
> Her gentle heart was reconciled
> To love him, as she were his child;
> But all that fans love's bridal fires,
> And swells the waves of youth's desires—
> That weds the manly to the fair—
> Makes youth with youth a comely pair—
> Long since in Arthur died away:
> His heart was cold, his head was gray;

---

[35] Richard Williams, *The Contentious Crown: Public Discussion of the British Monarchy in the Reign of Queen Victoria* (Aldershot: Ashgate, 1997), 205–9.

> But she was in life's glowing spring,
> And long'd for love, a passioned thing;
> All love's sweet fancies teemed in her,
> And Lancelot was young and fair.[36]

Tacit sympathy, however, did not necessarily translate into outright support. The only Victorian author who truly attempted to vindicate Guinevere was William Morris, whose poem 'The Defence of Guenevere' (1857) argues that more important social and moral issues override any questions about her transgression of arbitrary sexual codes. Like Tennyson, Morris took up the story of Guinevere during the debate over the Divorce Bill in the mid-1850s. But unlike Tennyson, who used the story to uphold conventional gender roles, Morris used it to demonstrate his support for a single, rather than double, standard of romantic and marital obligation. Thus, in sharp contrast to Tennyson, Morris endorses Guenevere's claim to freedom from censorious male judgement, and supports her assertion that she has acted rightly, even heroically, in a restrictive and oppressive context. More than any other Victorian author, he gives her the opportunity to explain the circumstances of her behaviour:

> Though still she stood right up, and never shrunk,
> But spoke on bravely, glorious lady fair!

Married at an early age, for political rather than romantic reasons, to a man of 'great name and little love', she preserves beneath the façade of wifely loyalty a strong, faithful attachment to her true love, the man she would have married had she been permitted to make the choice. She refuses to bow down before her interrogators and beg for their mercy:

> God wot I ought to say, I have done ill,
> And pray you all forgiveness heartily!
> Because you must be such right great lords—still . . .

At the poem's conclusion, her rescue by Lancelot only confirms the psychological freedom that she already has won from within.[37] Of all

---

[36] Robert Bernard Martin, *Tennyson: The Unquiet Heart* (Oxford: Clarendon Press, 1980), 424; Bruce, *Story of Queen Guinevere*, 6.

[37] Florence Boos, 'Justice and Vindication in "The Defence of Guenevere"', in Valerie M. Lagorio and Mildred Leake Day (eds), *King Arthur Through the Ages* (New York: Garland, 1990), ii. 89 and 92; William Morris, *The Defence of Guenevere and Other Poems* (London, 1858), 2, 4.

Victorian authors who treated the Guinevere story, only Morris claims that she is essentially guiltless.

But even though Morris attempts to validate Guenevere's actions, the poem's underlying assumptions limit its value as an assertion of female autonomy. Instead of granting her true freedom of choice and expression, Morris deliberately exaggerates her physical helplessness in order to emphasize her repression. He defines her exclusively through her relationships with men, for her destiny will be controlled by either Arthur or Lancelot: she will be punished by the former or rescued by the latter. The best she can hope for is to be able to choose between them, rather than forging any sort of independent identity for herself. In Morris's conception, Guenevere's contribution to the nation can be made only through her husband. On her own, she has no role to play.

Even one of the strongest vindicators of Guinevere's right of self-determination thus fails to press his arguments to the fullest. Although Morris questions the social codes which other treatments of Guinevere uphold, he ultimately does not attempt to overturn them. In the end, 'The Defence of Guenevere' confirms rather than challenges conventional notions of properly 'feminine' behavior. Morris, too, confines her to the private, domestic sphere, and subjects her to the control of her male husband and lover.

The treatment of the female characters of the Arthurian legend by Victorian authors thus suggests that the notion of separate spheres held sway in British society. Elaine, Vivien, and Guinevere were all expected to remain confined to the domestic sphere, where they were entrusted with the duty of guarding the nation's moral virtue. If they failed in this duty, condemnation and punishment were swift. Beneath the surface of these separate and hierarchical gender roles, however, lay important—and often competing—subcultures which, although they were not as powerful or autonomous as the dominant culture, prevented patriarchal values from exerting an unchallenged influence over the position of women in contemporary British society.

These hidden subcultures emerged more openly in literary treatments of the legend of Robin Hood, as they came to be embodied by the legend's main female character, Maid Marian. In distinct contrast to the female characters of the Arthurian legend, Marian was an active, assertive, even aggressive heroine who played an equal role in the management of Robin Hood's forest commonwealth with the Merry Men. And her 'unfeminine' behaviour was not censured by Victorian authors. Instead, for much of the nineteenth century she was treated not only with tolerance but even with approbation. It was not until the century's final decades that opinion began to shift, and Marian became a focal point for criticism of the 'New Woman' who was posing a significant challenge to established gender roles.

'If this be indeed a lady': Maid Marian

In this introduction to his *A Collection of Early Prose Romances* (1828), William John Thoms declared: 'Every hero, whether of history or fable, must have some "ladye of his love" to inspire him with courage in the hour of danger, and be at all times the goddess of his idolatry, accordingly tradition has asserted that Robin Hood, was accompanied in his retreat by a female of whom he was enamoured, and whose real or adopted name was Marian'.[38] Maid Marian, however, was no typical romantic heroine. Instead, Victorian authors portrayed her as a woman who refused to be governed by notions of 'appropriate' feminine conduct. Adept with both bow and sword, in some accounts she even bests Robin Hood himself in hand-to-hand combat. She also takes a leading role in the government of Robin Hood's forest commonwealth, debating issues and offering her opinion on an equal basis with the Merry Men.

From her earliest appearances Maid Marian has embodied a bold, unabashed sexuality that was a far cry from the Victorian model of feminine decorum. In the fifteenth and sixteenth centuries she was first introduced to the legend in the context of the May Games, ostensibly a religious holiday in association with the feast of Saints Philip and James, but in practice a day which saw all veneration for the saints submerged in a welter of secular activities. Rather than a solemn religious ceremony, the May Games more closely resembled an ancient fertility festival permeated with an atmosphere of erotic licence.[39] Given this context, it is no surprise that from the beginning Maid Marian and Robin Hood enjoyed an unabashedly physical relationship. Lewd and swaggering, their conduct befits the bawdy, raucous spirit of the May Games.

[38] William John Thoms, *A Collection of Early Prose Romances* (London, 1828), p. xi.
[39] Francois Laroque, *Shakespeare's Festive World: Elizabethan Seasonal Entertainment and the Professional Stage*, trans. Janet Lloyd (Cambridge and New York: Cambridge UP, 1991), 7.

It was this image of a decidedly ungenteel heroine which English popular culture bequeathed to nineteenth-century interpreters of the legend of Robin Hood. Rather than attempting to subdue Marian's sexual exuberance and free-spiritedness, however, contemporary authors emphasized and even embellished it. In his novel *Maid Marian*, published in 1822, Thomas Love Peacock depicts her as a thoroughly sensual and sensuous figure, and her sexual vitality translates into a broader power of body and spirit which renders her virtually invincible to her male adversaries. For Peacock, everything about Maid Marian represents vigour and activity. She possesses an unquenchable energy which displays itself not only physically in her prowess with a bow, but psychologically as well in her refusal to submit to any attempts to curb her indomitable will. When her father, the Baron Fitzwater, forbids her to go hunting, she, here referred to by her given name 'Matilda', reveals her determination to do as she pleases:

'Well, father', added Matilda, 'I must go to the woods'.
'Must you?' said the baron; 'I say you must not'.
'But I am going', said Matilda.
'But I will have up the drawbridge', said the baron.
'But I will swim the moat', said Matilda.
'But I will secure the gates', said the baron.
'But I will leap from the battlement', said Matilda.
'But I will lock you in an upper chamber', said the baron.
'But I will shred the tapestry', said Matilda, 'and let myself down'.
'But I will lock you in a turret', said the baron, 'where you shall only see light through a loophole'.
'But through that loophole', said Matilda, 'will I take my flight, like a young eagle from its acry; and, father, while I go out freely, I will return willingly: but if once I slip out through a loop-hole—'[40]

In physical combat she proves a match even for the king himself. When Richard I, disguised as an ordinary knight, encounters 'a fine young outlaw' leaning against a tree in Sherwood Forest, the outlaw insists that the knight pay a visit to 'his' master. the knight refuses, and the two become embroiled in a fierce fight, in which 'the knight had in an uncommon degree both strength and skill: the forester had less strength but not less skill than the knight, and showed such a mastery of his weapon as reduced the latter to great admiration'. Suddenly Friar

---

[40] Bryan Burns, *The Novels of Thomas Love Peacock* (London and Sydney: Croom Helm, 1985), 129–31; Thomas Love Peacock, *Maid Marian* (London, 1822), 56–7.

Tuck appears and demands to know why the knight has assailed 'our lady queen'. Astonished to discover the sex of his opponent, Richard declares that 'if this be indeed a lady, man never yet held me so long'.[41]

Peacock's portrayal of Marian is in keeping with his broader views on the position of women in British society. Like his friend Percy Shelley, Peacock criticized the pervasive contemporary valuation of women as passive sex objects rather than active, thinking beings. After reading Mary Wollstonecraft's *Vindication of the Rights of Woman*, he came to believe that female intelligence should be defended against its customary depreciation. According to one modern critic, Peacock's work is 'deeply penetrated' by a 'feminist consciousness'. Indeed, almost without exception, the female characters in his novels are intelligent, independent creatures. These views are easily identifiable in *Maid Marian*. Refusing to be constrained by male authority, Marian transcends conventional gender barriers and fully represents Peacock's vision of the options that would be open to women if they could free themselves from society's demand for submissiveness and domesticity.[42]

There were, however, limits to Peacock's liberalism on the subject of women's rights, and references to him as a 'feminist' should not be confused with the modern meaning of the term. In many ways Peacock's Marian is little more than 'a nature-loving emancipated girl', rather than a true feminist heroine. Indeed, Peacock assures his readers that, underneath her unconventional exterior, Marian is 'not like a virago or a hoyden, or one that would crack a serving-man's head for spilling gravy on her ruff, but with such womanly grace and temperate self-command, as if those manly exercises belonged to her only, and were become for her sake feminine'.[43]

Peacock's characterization of Marian as an active, assertive heroine who nonetheless retains her fundamentally 'feminine' attributes dominated Victorian literature. In Pierce Egan's extremely popular novel *Robin Hood and Little John* (1840), she oscillates between Victorian conceptions of 'feminine' and 'masculine' conduct. In an early scene she faints when confronted by one of the Sheriff's men and is forced to await rescue by Little John. Later, however, when a Norman knight attempts to force himself upon her, she steals his dagger from his belt

[41] Peacock, *Maid Marion*, 241.

[42] Nathaniel Brown, 'The "Brightest Colours of Intellectual Beauty"': Feminism in Peacock's Novels', *Keats–Shelley Review*, 2 (1987), 95; Burns, *Novels of . . . Peacock*, 130.

[43] Marilyn Butler, *Peacock Displayed: A Satirist in His Context* (London: Routledge, 1979), 152; Peacock, *Maid Marion*, 17.

and holds him off until Robin Hood arrives. In his novel *Maid Marian, the Forest Queen* (1849), J. H. Stocqueller displays a similar ambivalence when he describes Marian's physical appearance:

Although the green tunic, the russet boot and the close fitting hose—the broad felt hat, and the black hackle plucked from an eagle's wing—the bugle, the staff, and the couteau de chasse, or hunting knife, would have denoted a man, and he a lawless forest ranger; the face, the delicate limbs, the rich ringlets which covered the hand on which the small head reclined, left no doubt that the recumbent form was that of one of the opposite sex.[44]

In the first half of the nineteenth century British authors thus granted Maid Marian a limited degree of liberation from the constraints placed upon feminine behaviour. At the same time, however, they were careful to indicate that, beneath the surface, she retained her essential feminine qualities.

This characterization of Marian was in keeping with her function as an exemplar of female participation in the sport at which she excelled: archery. In the late eighteenth and nineteenth centuries archery clubs sprang up all over Britain which welcomed the membership of upper- and middle-class ladies. In 1828 Pierce Egan declared that 'archery is equally open to the fair sex, and has for these last thirty years, been the favourite recreation of a great part of the female nobility, the only field diversion they can enjoy without incurring the censure of being thought masculine'. As Egan suggests, archery was acceptable for female participants because it demanded neither excessive strength nor the donning of 'unwomanly' clothing. Indeed, female archers emphasized the innately feminine nature of their chosen pursuit. In 1829 the *Young Lady's Book . . . of Elegant Recreations, Exercises and Pursuits* observed that 'the attitude of an accomplished female archer. . . at the moment of bending the bow, is particularly graceful; all the actions and positions tend at once to produce a proper degree of strength in the limbs, and to impart a general elegance to the deportment'. Men were by and large convinced by these arguments. In his guide from the 1850s, Horace A. Ford, an archery champion, wrote:

To you . . . fair Marians, and to you who, though not as yet enrolled in that band, may still, it is hoped, some day be so, let me observe that Archery is a boon indeed. Your sex have few out-door exercises at all—none, with the

---

[44] Pierce Egan, *Robin Hood and Little John or the Merry Men of Sherwood Forest*, 2nd edn. (London, 1850), 34, 227; J. H. Stocqueller, *Maid Marian, the Forest Queen* (London, [1849]), 2.

exception, perhaps, of riding (which is accessible but to few), that at all brings the muscles generally into healthy action. You cannot say that mere walking or shop-lounging does this; still less that the heated atmosphere of a ball-room allows of it. But Archery does. How many consumptions, contracted chests, and the like, think you, might have been spared, had its practice been more universal amongst you? It is an exercise admirably suited to meet your requirements—general and equal, without being violent—calling the faculties, both of mind and body, into gentle and healthy play, yet oppressing none—brings roses to your cheeks, and occupation to your mind—withal most elegant and graceful . . . . Need I say more to recommend this pastime to you? I think not;—every consideration should induce you to adopt it.

Maid Marian's link with female participation in archery thus demonstrates that her physical vigour did not necessarily pose a challenge to accepted gender distinctions. Although sportswomen opened a new social space in which they could express themselves in the nineteenth century, that expression was not always progressive, as it often acted to confirm rather than overturn the constraints placed upon female behaviour.[45]

As the nineteenth century wore on, however, Maid Marian came to be associated with more conventionally 'masculine' modes of behaviour. In his juvenile novel *The Life and Adventures of Robin Hood* (1865), John B. Marsh points to her archery prowess by having her save Robin Hood and Will Scarlett from a savage attack by 'a magnificent buck':

Marian raised her bow, and, as with bent head and increased speed the deer came on, an arrow pierced its side. The beautiful creature gave a sudden bound, and then fell dead to the ground.

'That was well shot!' exclaimed Robin, with much warmth.

. . . 'Bravo!' shouted Will from his place of safety, as he saw his enemy fall to the ground. 'Well done, Marian! a woman's arrow has saved two lives'.

Similarly, in the serial novel *Little John and Will Scarlett* (1865) she again rescues Robin Hood from life-threatening peril when he slips and falls during a skirmish with his Norman enemies. Just as the Earl of

[45] Kathleen E. McCrone, *Sport and the Physical Emancipation of English Women 1870–1914* (London: Routledge, 1988), 154–5; Horace A. Ford, *Archery: Its Theory and Practice*, 2nd edn. (London, 1859), 132–3; Jennifer A. Hargreaves, 'Victorian Familialism and the Formative Years of Female Sport', in J. A. Mangan and Roberta J. Park (eds), *From 'Fair Sex' to Feminism: Sport and the Socialization of Women in the Industrial and Post-Industrial Eras* (London: Frank Cass, 1987), 141.

Beauclerk is about to slay him, one of her arrows strikes the dagger from his hand.[46] This sort of archery prowess, employed in the heat of a hunt or a battle, was of a very different sort from that displayed by elegantly clad ladies shooting daintily at targets placed on country-house lawns.

In some cases, Marian's subversion of conventional gender roles was represented in a more literal form, for a plethora of nineteenth-century works feature scenes in which she assumes a male costume. In Marsh's *The Life and Adventures of Robin Hood* she dons the garments of an adolescent youth and nearly defeats Robin Hood in an archery contest. It is not until he attempts to shake hands with the stranger who has very nearly bested him that he recognizes his adversary, crying out her name 'in the greatest amazement'. In a children's book of 1860 the author writes that Maid Marian

dressed herself like a boy, and went into the forest to seek for Robin. At last she met him, but he did not know her in boy's clothes, and with a drawn sword in her hand. Maid Marian would not tell him at first who she was; she attacked him and fought with him, but he soon struck her sword out of her hand. Then she took off her cap, and let her golden hair fall over her shoulders, and Robin knew at once that it was Marian.[47]

On the contemporary stage, some authors took this confusion of gender categories even further, as they assigned all of the parts in the legend of Robin Hood to actresses. The earliest example dates from 1846, when Robin Hood, Little John, and the other Merry Men were all played by women in J. H. Stocqueller's *Robin Hood and Richard Cœur de Lion*. Four years later Robin Hood was portrayed by a 'Mrs. Fitzwilliam' in the Brough brothers' *The Last Edition of Ivanhoe*, performed at the Theatre Royal, Haymarket, and all-female casts were also featured in Sir Francis Cowley Burnand's *Robin Hood; or, The Forester's Fate* (1862); F. R. Goodyer's *Once upon a Time: or, A Midsummer Night's Dream in Merrie Sherwood* (1868); Robert Reece's *Little Robin Hood* (1882); George Thorne and F. Grove Palmer's *Robin Hood and Little John, or Harlequin Friar Tuck and the Merrie Men of Sherwood Forest* (1882); Augustus Henry Glossop Harris's *Babes in the Wood; Robin Hood and his*

[46] John B. Marsh, *The Life and Adventures of Robin Hood* (London, 1865), 37; 'Forest Ranger', *Little John and Will Scarlett; or, The Outlaws of Sherwood Forest* (London, 1865), 60.

[47] Marsh, *Robin Hood*, 83–4; *Aunt Louisa's London Toy Books: Robin Hood and His Merry Men* (London, [1860]), 5.

Men; and Harlequin Who Killed Cock Robin (1888); and Horace Lennard's *Babes in the Wood and Bold Robin Hood* (1892).

Did these episodes of cross-dressing have any significance beyond a desire to titillate their male-dominated audiences with the spectacle of women wearing tight-fitting male attire? In other words, was there a subversive intention on the part of the authors or the actresses? The meaning of gender inversion on the Victorian stage in the second half of the nineteenth century has provoked considerable scholarly contention. To be sure, male impersonators were often sent on stage by impresarios to display themselves before a male audience. It is possible, however, to find individual cases where there was clearly an overt intention to challenge conventional gender categories. Moreover, these figures gradually began to acquire more female than male admirers, suggesting that there was a tacit recognition of the oppression women shared.[48]

By the 1890s Maid Marian was firmly established as a heroine who differed from Victorian gender stereotypes. Even Alfred Tennyson, who used the female characters of the Arthurian legend to reinforce those stereotypes, admitted as much. In his drama *The Foresters* (1892), Marian declares to her father that 'I am none of your delicate Norman maidens who can only broider and mayhap ride a-hawking with the help of the men'. Similarly, in J. E. Muddock's *Maid Marian and Robin Hood* (1892), Marian defies conventional standards of feminine conduct:

She had no fear . . . in venturing into the forest alone, but . . . had she paused to reflect a little, she could scarcely have avoided the conclusion that she was laying herself open to severe criticism; for would not her friends and neighbours declare that she was over bold and lacking in maiden modesty? But she did not pause . . . she gave no thought as to what the villagers might say.

Later, when Robin Hood is captured by the Sheriff's men, she resolves 'that she would not moan and weep while the man she so devoutly loved was in peril of his life'.[49] Instead, she vows to rescue him and

---

[48] Elaine Aston, 'Male Impersonation and the Music Hall: The Case of Vesta Tilley', *New Theatre Quarterly*, 15 (1988), 247–57; Sarah Maitland, *Vesta Tilley* (London: Virago, 1986), 9–10; Laurence Senelick, 'The Evolution of the Male Impersonator on the Nineteenth-century Popular Stage', *Essays in Theatre*, 1 (1982), 30–44; J. S. Bratton, 'Irrational Dress', in Viv Gardner and Susan Rutherford (eds), *The New Woman and Her Sisters: Feminism and Theatre 1850–1914* (New York and London: Harvester Wheatsheaf, 1992), 85.

[49] Alfred, Lord Tennyson, *The Foresters: Robin Hood and Maid Marian* (London, 1892), 11; J. E. Muddock, *Maid Marian and Robin Hood: A Romance of Old Sherwood Forest* (London, 1892), 25, 31.

goes to Nottingham, where she convinces a friar who has access to Robin Hood's cell to pass him a sword which he uses to escape.

This sampling of treatments of Maid Marian in late nineteenth-century literature only scratches the surface, for many similar examples of her assertive conduct and assumption of masculine disguise could be cited. What is most significant, however, is that none of these authors censures her for behaviour that, according to contemporary standards, should have been considered extremely unfeminine. On the contrary, they depict her as a positive character, suggesting that Victorian gender conventions may not have been completely inflexible. This is not to suggest that these authors were in any way endorsing a feminist agenda. Throughout the nineteenth century, those who genuinely believed in the full social and political equality of men and women remained extremely thin on the ground. But the way in which Maid Marian's ability to transgress conventional gender roles was depicted in a wide variety of contemporary literary works indicates that the participation of women in the public sphere was not always perceived in a negative light.

When considered from this point of view, Maid Marian fits into a long-standing tradition in British culture. Although women were generally expected to remain confined to the domestic realm, a few exceptional cases did emerge and take a much more proactive role in public affairs. Antonia Fraser includes in her roster of so-called 'Warrior Queens'—female political leaders who have served as the focus of 'a remarkable outburst of excitement and even awe . . . beyond the capacity of a mere male to arouse'—figures such as Boadicea, Elizabeth I, and even Margaret Thatcher.[50] Maid Marian, although not a political leader in the conventional sense, shares many of the qualities which Fraser identifies as characteristics of the Warrior Queen.

By the end of the nineteenth century, however, Maid Marian's status as a feminine (and possibly feminist) heroine was beginning to alter perceptions of her character. Her intrusion into realms conventionally regarded as masculine implicitly linked her with the so-called 'New Woman' who was frequently ridiculed in the popular press of the 1890s. The label was used to describe a particular type of young, middle-class woman who remained single on principle and eschewed the frivolities of female fashion in favour of masculine dress and a

---

[50] Antonia Fraser, *The Warrior Queens* (New York, Knopf, 1989), 6.

severe hairstyle. Educated to a standard unknown and unavailable to previous generations, she was given to reading 'advanced' books. She earned her own living and was financially independent of her husband or father. Her habits, which might include smoking or riding a bicycle, were in keeping with her progressive views, and she was unafraid to use bold language or ride an omnibus unescorted. In general, she sought freedom from, and equality with, men, an objective for which she was prepared to overturn all convention and accepted notions of femininity.[51]

The New Woman met with considerable opposition from the less progressive elements of late Victorian society. She provided the press with an endless source of amusement, as caricaturists drew her wearing mannish clothes, with hair that was cropped short. And since Maid Marian's brazen conduct often closely resembled that associated with the New Woman, she came to serve as target for similar satirical attacks. In Robert Reece's burlesque *Little Robin Hood*, her predilection for vigorous physical activity becomes a source of ridicule:

> MARIAN: These are the good old days (folks may abuse 'em),
>   When girls have muscles, and know how to use 'em!
> ROBIN: Strong-minded women, as a rule, are hated!
>   You're simple, dear—and yet so-fist-icated!

Later, when a wealthy stranger comes through Sherwood Forest, Marian is eager to subdue him single-handedly:

> FRIAR TUCK: Who'll tackle him? He isn't very tall!
> MARIAN: I will! I'll fight him! Stand by, one and all!
>   One of John's spies! I've not the slightest doubt;
>   Let me cross swords with him! I'll pay him out![52]

Such satirical portraits of Marian, however, can also serve to reveal the complexities of late-nineteenth-century gender roles. In a burlesque of 1900 entitled *Little Red Robin*, by Vivian Matthews and Alick Manley, it is Dame Woffles, 'the lieutenant of Robin Hood's band', rather than Marian herself who functions as the voice of the New Woman:

> Take courage, my sisters! The day is at hand
> When we'll rise through the length and breadth of the land;

[51] Viv Gardner, 'Introduction', in Gardner and Rutherford, *The New Woman*, 4–6.
[52] Robert Reece, *Little Robin Hood: A New Burlesque Drama* (London, 1882), 14, 22.

> Nor will we consider our triumph complete
> Till the brutes who misrule us shall crawl at our feet!
> Then, then will we sing, in the Joy of our hearts,
> The songs of the free (and we'll sing them in parts);
> We'll carry a latchkey, we'll ride on a bike,
> We'll smoke, and we'll wear—yes! We will if we like!

This is clearly intended to poke fun at the New Woman. In other instances, however, the satirical intent of Dame Woffles's strident rhetoric is not so obvious:

> I hereby declare and avow my belief
> That of all living beings THE WOMAN is chief,
> And I hold that in Nature's original plan
> She never was meant to be governed by MAN!
> I freely admit, as a matter of course,
> That THE MAN may be richer in mere brutal force,
> But in all of those gifts which pertain to the mind
> THE WOMAN has left him a long way behind!

This passages gives a far more accurate rendition of the point of view of contemporary supporters of women's rights; upon reading it, it is hard to believe that Manley and Matthews did not sympathize with their arguments to some extent, even if they made light of them. In the conclusion, Woffles's declaration that 'we'll never, no never be anyone's slaves' appropriates the famous 'Britons will never be slaves' from James Thomson's anthem 'Rule, Britannia', thus linking feminist claims with a more conventional brand of patriotism. The characterization of Maid Marian as eager to fight for her country completes the picture, as she joins the male Crusaders in a rousing patriotic chorus:

> Where'er the British clarions swell defeat awaits the Infidel:
> Where'er the flag of England waves there's life and freedom for the
>   slaves,
> A ray of hope their hearts shall cheer, they'll gladly bend a list'ning ear
> To catch the beat of British feet that tread the paths of glory![53]

Her vocal presence in this burst of unabashed jingoism is not questioned; instead, Marian functions as a full-fledged patriot, ready to make an active contribution to her nation alongside her male compatriots.

---

[53] Matthews and Manley, *Little Red Robin*, 5, 11.

The treatment of the female characters from the legends of King Arthur and Robin Hood in the nineteenth century thus suggests that there existed a variety of responses to demands of British women for a more active role in the public affairs of their nation. The conduct of the Arthurian women was subjected to the close scrutiny of those authors who sought to uphold conventional gender roles, as the attempts made by Elaine, Vivien, and Guinevere to intervene in the public sphere met with a negative, reactionary response. The considerable anxiety which this response reveals, however, suggests that some cracks were appearing in the façade of Victorian notions of 'appropriate' feminine behaviour. The treatment of Maid Marian shows that these cracks were not only present but even welcome in some quarters. Despite the fact that she displayed characteristics that were not construed as conventionally 'female', she was not, at least until the very end of the nineteenth century, condemned as an 'unrespectable' woman. On the contrary, her centuries-old, subversive features remained intact and she continued to play an active, assertive role in the governance of Robin Hood's forest commonwealth.

CHAPTER SIX

'Why must we haunt to them foreign parts?': The Legends of King Arthur and Robin Hood and British Imperialism

PLACE-NAMES associated with King Arthur and Robin Hood can be found scattered virtually throughout Britain, but certain regions of the country have traditionally been more closely connected with them than others. The Arthurian legend belongs primarily to the south-west, and in particular the dramatic cliffs of the north Cornish coast. Robin Hood, on the other hand, has long been associated with a very different landscape, the dense forests of Nottinghamshire and southern Yorkshire.[1]

The contrast between these two regions represents a deep-rooted conflict between competing visions of the British nation. On the one hand, Britons have for centuries looked outwards towards their burgeoning empire and territorial expansion. But on the other, they have often favoured a more insular vision which proclaims the dangers of the potentially corrupting influence of the outside world. Nowhere better represents the first point of view than King Arthur's Cornwall, a region in which no point is more than twenty miles from the sea, and nowhere better symbolizes the second than the dark interiors of Robin Hood's Sherwood Forest. Sea versus forest, empire versus isolation, expansion versus insularity—this debate has long raged in Britain, and in the nineteenth century King Arthur and Robin Hood could be found—on opposite sides—right in the midst of it.

---

[1] For Arthurian place-names in Britain, see Neil Fairbairn and Michael Cyprien, *A Traveller's Guide to the Kingdoms of Arthur* (London: Evans Brothers, 1983). For Robin Hood sites, see W. R. Mitchell, *The Haunts of Robin Hood* (Clapham, Yorkshire: Dalesman, 1970).

'A kingdom that shall rule the sea': The Legend of King Arthur and Cornwall

In the nineteenth century, the region of Great Britain most closely associated with King Arthur was the West Country, and Cornwall in particular. This had not always been the case, for in the past other areas had also been linked to the legend. Although it is rarely mentioned in connection with Arthur today, the border region between England and Scotland once enjoyed a strong association with the legend, and its relationship with Wales is even older, stretching back to the early Middle Ages. But although Arthurian sites in both regions were popular with nineteenth-century tourists, they were rarely their primary destination, for most visitors were more attracted by the natural beauty of the landscape. Neither area developed a true Arthurian tourist industry in the nineteenth century, for their associations with legend were a secondary bonus rather than the main attraction.

Instead, by the century's end the south-western part of England had become the favoured destination for tourists specifically desiring to see the places where Arthur's exploits had supposedly occurred. They rarely left disappointed, for there, as the antiquary Robert Hunt observed in 1865, 'King Arthur's beds, and chairs, and caves' were 'frequently to be met with'.[2] Cornwall boasted the ostensible site of Arthur's birth at Tintagel and the ostensible site of his death at Camelford, along with a bevy of other places associated with the legend. According to Sir Edward Strachey:

Arthur's Well still springs from the hill-side, and if Arthur's Hunting Causeway in the field below, Arthur's Round Table and Arthur's Palace within the camp, cannot still, as of old, be pointed out to the visitor, the peasant girl will still tell him that within that charmed circle they who look may see through golden gates a king sitting in the midst of his court.[3]

Before the mid-nineteenth century, however, Cornwall was in no position to exploit its Arthurian associations, for its transportation infrastructure was not sufficiently developed to make a large-scale tourist influx possible. As a result, its Arthurian sites were visited by

[2] Robert Hunt, *Popular Romances of the West of England; or, The Drolls, Traditions, and Superstitions of Old Cornwall* (London, 1865), 204. For Arthurian place-names in Cornwall, see Brenda Duxbury and Michael Williams, *King Arthur Country in Cornwall* (St Teath, Bodmin, Cornwall: Bossiney Press, 1979); C. A. Ralegh Radford and Michael J. Swanton, *Arthurian Sites in the West* (Exeter: University of Exeter Press, 1975).

[3] Sir Edward Strachey (ed.), *Morte Darthur: Sir Thomas Malory's Book of King Arthur and of his Noble Knights of the Round Table* (London, 1868), p. xii.

only the most determined travellers. In 1818 the antiquary Fortescue Hitchens reported that 'in Cornwall we have the castle in which [Arthur] was born, the bed on which he slept, the hall in which he entertained his friends, the path on which he walked to his church, the plain on which he hunted, the impression of his horse's footsteps, and the enormous quoit with which he amused himself'. It was not until the final decades of the nineteenth century, however, that the region's link with the legend began to attract tourists on a large scale. By then, express trains were speeding daily to the west of England, and railway companies, in particular the Great Western, were offering special concessions in fares for the journey. 'A tour through the land which romance has marked out for her own', wrote J. Cuming Walters in his *The Lost Land of King Arthur* (1909), 'and where the fords, bridges, hills, and rocks are called after Arthur or associated by tradition with his exploits, becomes easier every year by the development of railways, little known in the wilder parts until a decade or so ago'.[4]

No single place better demonstrates the growth of Arthurian tourism in Cornwall than Tintagel Castle. Standing on an isolated headland linked to the coast by a narrow neck of land barely four feet wide, the bleak and foreboding ruins of Tintagel seem a sufficiently mystical and remote spot for Arthur's birth. In the early nineteenth century, however, Tintagel could only be reached by a perilous scramble across the rocks at low tide. Thus rendered virtually inaccessible, the site received few visitors. It was not until 1851, when the Revd R. B. Kinsman arrived to take charge of the castle, that Tintagel began to emerge as a tourist site. Kinsman, a local vicar who served as caretaker for the next four decades, rebuilt the path to the headland and made extensive repairs to the ruins. As a final touch, he resurrected the ancient office of Constable of the Castle, and outfitted himself in splendid red and gold robes which he delighted in wearing when guiding visitors on tours.

And visitors there soon were. While on a walking tour in 1865, Walter White observed the new King Arthur's Arms tavern, which he suggested denoted 'the softening influence exercised by visitors'. Soon thereafter the massive King Arthur Hotel was built a short distance from the ruins. Inside, it featured murals depicting famous scenes from the Arthurian legend, along with a facsimile of the Round

[4] Fortescue Hitchins, *The History of Cornwall, from the Earliest Records and Traditions, to the Present Time* (Helston, 1824), i. 396; Jack Simmons, 'Railways, Hotels and Tourism in Great Britain 1839–1914', *Journal of Contemporary History*, 19 (1984), 214; J. Cuming Walters, *The Lost Land of King Arthur* (London, 1909), preface.

Table. In his guidebook of 1899 Frederick Izant referred to the growing number of travellers 'who pay a flying visit to North Cornwall . . . each succeeding season'. Izant had no doubts as to what were 'the irresistible attractions that draw so many people from great distances to this out-of-the-way place'. Although the 'coast views and marine outlook' were 'certainly very beautiful . . . what really awakens the enthusiasm of the stream of tourists who visit Tintagel are the historical and poetical associations which cling to the mighty headland, where . . . are to be found the last vestiges of an ancient castle, which time-honoured tradition connects with the life of King Arthur'.[5] Tintagel's emergence as a tourist destination parallels in microcosm events in Cornwall as a whole in the final decades of the nineteenth century. For centuries, Cornwall's geographical position had preserved its isolation, but by the century's end it was receiving a great many visitors. It was in this period that Cornwall, through the development of a vigorous tourist industry, established its hold over the title 'the land of King Arthur'.

In turn, this geographical identification helped to foster an intimate relationship between the legend and the sea, for in Cornwall the presence of the sea is inescapable. Such a setting inevitably influenced nineteenth-century interpretations of the Arthurian legend. Alfred Tennyson travelled extensively in North Cornwall as he was planning the *Idylls of the King*, and it is scarcely surprising that the Arthurian legend came to be intimately connected in his mind with the sea. In the *Idylls* the word 'sea' appears no less than forty-four times, and 'waves' eighteen. Most noticeable is his setting for 'the last weird battle in the west' between Arthur and Mordred, which takes place 'among the mountains by the winter sea':

> And there, that day when the great light of heaven
> Burn'd at his lowest in the rolling year,
> On the waste sand by the waste sea they closed.

Tennyson's fondness for sea imagery did not go unnoticed by contemporary critics. In an essay on the *Idylls* published in 1878, Henry Elsdale praised his 'power of depicting water and marine effects'.[6]

[5] Walter White, *A Londoner's Walk to the Land's End; and A Trip to the Scilly Isles* (London, 1865), 315–20; Frederick Izant, *Boscastle and Tintagel, North Cornwall. A Souvenir and Guide, with Nine Illustrations* (London, 1899), 43–4.

[6] Robert Bernard Martin, *Tennyson: The Unquiet Heart* (London: Faber and Faber, 1983), 319–20; Henry Elsdale, *Studies in the Idylls: An Essay on Mr. Tennyson's 'Idylls of the King'* (London, 1878), 140.

In terms of pure abundance, however, pride of place among Victorian poets in the use of Arthurian sea imagery must go to Algernon Charles Swinburne. Swinburne's father was an admiral in the British navy, and perhaps because of this family background the sea was a ubiquitous image in Swinburne's poetry. 'Its salt', he once wrote, '*must* have been in my blood before I was born'. In *The Tale of Balen* (1896), Swinburne utilizes sea-imagery to describe the scene when Balen meets Sir Launceor in battle:

> As wave on wave shocks, and confounds
> The bounding bulk whereon it bounds
> And breaks and shattering seaward sounds
> As crying of the old sea's wolves and hounds
> That moan and ravin and rage and wail,
> So steed on steed encountering sheer
> Shocked, and the strength of Launceor's spear
> Shivered on Balen's shield, and fear
> Bade hope within him quail.[7]

Even more prolific in its use of sea-imagery is Swinburne's *Tristram of Lyonesse* (1882), which is filled with ocean voyages and tempests, as well as a bevy of sea-related metaphors. Iseult's eyes, for example, shine 'as the sea's depth', and are the colour of 'the wave's subtler emerald', while her smile moves 'upon her red mouth tremulous | Light as a sea-bird's motion oversea'. Indeed, Iseult and her lover Tristram are throughout the poem closely associated with sea. On the night when Tristram marries Iseult of Brittany, the sea erupts in a violent storm, reflecting the feelings of Iseult of Ireland, who knows she is the one he truly loves:

> And as a full field charging was the sea,
> And as the cry of slain men was the wind . . .
>
> And all her soul was as the breaking sea,
> And all her heart as hungered as the wind . . .
>
> And all their past came wailing in the wind,
> And all their future thundered in the sea.

At the poem's conclusion the lovers are buried in Lyonesse, where

---

[7] Elliot Zuckerman, *The First Hundred Years of Wagner's Tristan* (New York and London: Columbia University Press, 1964), 183; Algernon Charles Swinburne, *The Tale of Balen* (London, 1896), 21, 35.

> over them while death and life shall be
> The light and sound and darkness of the sea.[8]

In other nineteenth-century Arthurian poetry the sea functions as a challenge which separates the knights from the object of their quest. They do not curse the sea as an obstacle in their path, however, but rather celebrate it. In the anonymous *Arthur's Knights: An Adventure from the Legend of the Sangrale* (1859), Sir Galahad declares as he sets off in search of the Grail:

> I will praise the sea,
> While through the darkening waves our vessel sails,
> That break in moonlit sparkles on our lee.
> Doth it not mirror still the heavenly sky,
> Undimmed by shadows of a changeful world;
> Are not its waves, in glorious unity,
> Lulled to a child-like rest, or in wind billows whirled?
> Do not the countless water drops, that ever
> Through earth's dark caves and mountain hollows roam,
> Hasten, through purling brook and rushing river,
> Back to the sea—their home?
> Their home where all earth's changes cease to be,
> The rest of perfect life, the wide and ancient sea!

Similarly laudatory towards the sea is Charles Bruce's *The Story of Queen Guinevere and Lancelot of the Lake* (1865), in which Arthur and his men sail enthusiastically to the Continent, where they hope to extend their domains:

> But up and off! to sea they go!
> The bellying sails gleam white as snow,
> The waters foam beneath the keel,
> While loud the sailors' voices peal:
> 'We love thee, green and glorious sea,
> Earth's ancient mother, wild and free!
> By grief, by woe, no more opprest,
> Thou rockest on thy waves to rest,
> With hoarse but mighty tones,
> Britannia's valiant sons.[9]

---

[8] Algernon Charles Swinburne, *Tristram of Lyonesse and Other Poems* (London, 1882), 11, 14, 22, 90–3, 169.

[9] *Arthur's Knights: An Adventure from the Legend of the Sangrale* (Edinburgh, 1859), 44–5; Charles Bruce, *The Story of Queen Guinevere and Lancelot of the Lake. After the German of Wilhelm Hertz. With Other Poems* (London, 1865), 78.

By emphasizing the love of the sea felt by Arthur and his knights, these authors hint at the brilliant naval future which awaits the British nation, and suggest that the British have been a seafaring people from the time of one of their earliest heroes. They thus use the past to explain the present. In his verse drama *King Arthur* (1895), J. Comyns Carr claims that Arthur's sword Excalibur, which was 'forged beneath the sea' and 'tempered by the waves', was the original source of Britain's dominion over the sea. The 'warrior king' whose 'arm is strong enough to wield it in the fight', Carr asserts, 'shall rule a kingdom that shall rule the sea'. As he accepts the sword from the Spirit of the Lake, the chorus chants:

> Great Pendragon's greater son,
> Arthur, ere thy race be run,
> Thou shalt rule from sea to sea
> England that is yet to be . . .[10]

These repeated references to the sea in nineteenth-century Arthurian literature take on a greater significance when considered in light of the sea's importance to British national identity. In 1878 Robert Louis Stevenson wrote that 'the Sea is our approach and bulwark, it has been the scene of our greatest triumphs and dangers, and we are accustomed in lyrical strains to claim it as our own. . . . We should consider ourselves unworthy of our descent if we did not share the arrogance of our progenitors, and please ourselves with the pretension that the sea is English'. This sense of proprietorship over the sea stemmed primarily from its association with empire, for it served as more than the mere pathway between the nation's far-flung colonial outposts. Instead, it was an integral part of the whole. In their influential book *Imperial Defence* (1892), the Liberal politician Sir Charles Dilke and the popular journalist Spenser Wilkinson declared that it was from the sea that the colonies 'derive their nourishment and their strength'. If the sea were to freeze over or to dry up, they went on to argue, the empire would perish.[11]

Linking the Arthurian legend with the sea in nineteenth-century British culture thus also implied a connection between the legend and the empire, a connection which will be explored below. First, however, we must examine the association between another legendary

---

[10] J. Comyns Carr, *King Arthur, A Drama in a Prologue and Four Acts* (London, 1895), 2, 7.
[11] Cynthia Fansler Behrman, *Victoria Myths of the Sea* (Athens, Ohio: Ohio UP, 1977), 26, 113–15.

hero, Robin Hood, and a very different sort of landscape. For if an essential component of British national identity in the nineteenth century involved reaching out towards the wider world represented by the sea, at the same time Britain's status as an island nation created a sense of distinctiveness and separation. The Victorians took great pride in their empire, but they also revelled in the policy of 'splendid isolation' which kept them uninvolved in global affairs. And nowhere better symbolized this insularity than the dense forests of the English interior, which were seemingly immune to corrupting external influences due to their dense impenetrability. They also served as the setting for the legend of Robin Hood.

'Roving wild and free': The Legend of Robin Hood and Sherwood Forest

'In all ages', wrote the author of *English Forests and Forest Trees* in 1853, 'the forests have been the refuge of the bold, the outlawed, the daring, and the desperate part of society'.[12] Indeed, it is difficult to imagine the legend of Robin Hood set anywhere other than a forest, so necessary does the sort of concealment it provides seem to his activities. The Merry Men depend heavily on the greenwood for their survival against the overwhelming numerical superiority of their enemies. In its thickets and glades it is they, and not the Sheriff's forces, who are the masters.

Much attention has been devoted in recent scholarship to unpacking the mythological function of the forest in western culture.[13] In Britain, it was the myth of 'the liberty of the greenwood' which became the dominant trope. The forest was a place of freedom and equality, a habitat where lord and peasant could coexist in pre-feudal reciprocity— the former exercising his hunting rights with restraint, the latter permitted to use the woods to pasture his swine and to collect wood and other necessities. It was an idyllic landscape in which conventional hierarchies of rank and gender were suspended in the interest of discovering truth, love, freedom, and, above all, justice. There, it was forever green and forever summer, a sylvan paradise in which the normal constraints of everyday life were removed. As such it was a

---

[12] *English Forests and Forest Trees, Historical, Legendary and Descriptive* (London, 1853), 26.

[13] See, in particular, Robert Pogue Harrison, *Forests: The Shadow of Civilization* (Chicago and London: University of Chicago Press, 1992); Simon Schama, *Landscape and Memory* (London: HarperCollins, 1995), chs. 1–4.

perfect environment for Robin Hood. He is, after all, an outlaw, by definition outside of the bounds of society. He belongs to a world in which identity is fluid: a master of disguise, he assumes various costumes with ease. He exists in a nebulous zone between hunter and hunted, taker and giver, enforcer of the law and breaker of it. Like the realm which he inhabits, Robin Hood is inherently liminal: he dwells in an in-between world, in which separate categories are blended.[14] From the beginning, the forest was thus integral to the legend of Robin Hood, serving not only as a setting but also as a symbolic context for some of its most important themes.

In the nineteenth century Robin Hood continued to serve as an exemplar of forest liberty. In his novel for children *Maid Marian and Robin Hood* (1892), J. E. Muddock declares that 'the idea of living a free life in the forests . . . fascinated him; for his love of freedom was inborn, and his hatred of oppression was no less strong'. This motif recurs over and over in contemporary Robin Hood literature. In George Linley's cantata *Robin Hood* (1856), the Merrie Men sing:

> O merry is the Outlaw's life,
> Roving wild and free!
> In the forest chase, or deadly strife,
> Nor care, nor fear have we.
>
> No tribute we pay,
> No monarch obey,
> We eat and drink of the best,
> And sleep as well,
> In our mossy cell,
> As the wild bird in its nest.

To be sure, there were some sceptics. In his review of Alfred Tennyson's *The Foresters*, William Winter wrote in 1897 that 'a man who walks about in a forest is not necessarily free. He may be as great a slave as anybody'. Even Winter, however, fell victim to the lure of forest liberty:

That way, to the tired thinker, lie peace and joy. There, if anywhere . . . he might escape from all the wrongs of the world, all the problems of society, all the dull business of recording, and analysing, and ticketing mankind. . . . In that retreat he would feel the rain upon his face, and smell the grass and flowers, and hear the sighing and whispering of the wind in the green boughs;

---

[14] Schama, *Landscape and Memory*, 140; Joseph P. Nagy, 'The Paradoxes of Robin Hood', *Folk-lore*, 91 (1980), 198–210.

and there would be no need to trouble himself any more, whether about the past or the future. Every great intellect of the world has felt that wild longing, and has recorded it—the impulse to revert to the vast heart of Nature, that knows no doubt, and harbours no fear, and keeps no regret, and feels no sorrow, and troubles itself not at all.[15]

It was not just any English forest in which Robin Hood's exploits took place, however, for one forest in particular was known far and wide as the home of the famous outlaw. 'No one can visit the grand old forest of Sherwood, and ramble 'neath the shadows of its venerable oaks', wrote Cornelius Brown in his *Lives of Nottinghamshire Worthies* (1882):

without instinctively calling to mind the days long ago when Robin Hood and his trusty band roamed, as tradition tells us, at their 'own sweet will' through the forest glades. . . . The man would be strangely unimaginative and unromantic who, in the presence of rugged and venerable oaks which have weathered the storms of centuries, could forget ballad and song, and think only of the England of to-day.

In the late nineteenth century it was all but impossible to mention Sherwood Forest without simultaneously making reference to its most famous resident, so closely associated were the two. And just as in Cornwall an increasing number of tourists were attracted by the region's associations with the Arthurian legend, visitors were drawn to Sherwood by its connection with Robin Hood. In 1893 Ward, Lock and Company's guidebook proclaimed:

For forest scenery, in its most majestic phase of beauty . . . there is no need to travel abroad. The Forest of Sherwood, in the county of Nottingham, has all these charms—and more. Its venerable 'monarchs of the forest,' towering high in rugged grandeur, its ancient monastic houses, its underground palace, and its many relics of the merry outlaw Robin Hood—all combine to make it a veritable fairyland of delight.

As to whether there was any authenticity to these 'many relics' of Robin Hood, the author was coy, for an effort to debunk local mythology might have dampened tourist enthusiasm. On the subject of the so-called 'Robin Hood's Larder', a hollow tree in which the outlaw was

---

[15] J. E. Muddock, *Maid Marian and Robin Hood: A Romance of Old Sherwood Forest* (London, 1892), 68; George Linley, *Robin Hood: A Cantata* (London, 1856), 2–4; William Winter, *Shadows of the Stage* (Edinburgh, 1892), 274.

said to have hung his venison, the author asked: 'Who, at least, shall prove that he did not?'.[16]

Certainly, the blatantly spurious origins of many of these Robin Hood sites did little to deter tourists eager to visit the places where the famous outlaw had ostensibly sat, shot, drank, slept, or stabled his horse. In the 1890s a guidebook reported that a large cave claiming to be Robin Hood's lair had recently opened in Nottingham with an admission charge of sixpence. 'Whether the outlaw, whose name it bears, ever saw it is very much open to doubt', warned the author. He also claimed, however, that it was 'well worthy of examination', although he warned visitors to 'be careful of their head-gear, for in some places the roof is inconveniently low'. Not far away, in southern Yorkshire, the ostensible site of Robin Hood's grave at Kirklees Abbey also received increasing attention from tourists. According to J. E. Muddock, 'the very room in which Robin Hood died, with the window from which he sped his last shaft as his soul was taking flight, are pointed out to the reverent pilgrim who wanders there to view the resting-place of this hero of romance and song'.[17] Indeed, it was so popular in the late nineteenth century that the grave had to be enclosed with iron railings in order to prevent damage from over-zealous curiosity seekers.

By the late nineteenth century the centuries-old connection between Sherwood Forest and the legend of Robin Hood had thus become even closer due to the growth of tourism. Just as the increasing flood of tourists had strengthened Cornwall's claim to King Arthur, the growing number of travellers who included Sherwood Forest on their itineraries helped to cement its claim to Robin Hood. And just as the sea which beat continually against the Cornish coast was an essential part of the Arthurian legend, so the dark forests of Nottinghamshire occupied an equally crucial place in that of Robin Hood. In both cases, the specific cultural conditions of the nineteenth century promoted these topographical associations. The former represented the might of the British Navy, while the latter represented the precious freedom which that navy ostensibly fought to defend.

[16] John Croumbie Brown, *The Forests of England and the Management of Them in Byegone Times* (Edinburgh, 1883), 17; Cornelius Brown, *Lives of Nottinghamshire Worthies and of Celebrated and Remarkable Men of the County from the Norman Conquest to AD 1882* (London and Nottingham, 1882), 8–9; Ward, Lock and Co., *Pictorial and Descriptive Guide to Sherwood Forest and 'The Dukeries' (The Land of Robin Hood)* (London, 1893), 3, 109.

[17] *Pictorial and Descriptive Guide to Sherwood Forest*, 29; Muddock, *Maid Marian*, 326.

But although the sea and the forest symbolized important components of British national identity, those components had very different implications for the construction of contemporary national identity. As we have seen, the sea was inextricably intertwined with the pursuit of empire, whereas the forest was the home of the forces which imperialism sought to contain, control, and ultimately conquer. In their dark and dense interiors could flourish a fierce spirit of individualism which was profoundly antagonistic to the imperial mission of cultural homogenization and political hegemony. In order for its conquest to be successful, an imperial administration had to triumph over the forest; the great sylvan mass had to be denuded or at the very least traversed.[18] Given the nature of this inherent conflict between sea and forest, it is not surprising that the topographical contrast between the legends of King Arthur and Robin Hood evolved into a broader cultural debate between the advocates of further imperial expansion and the critics who wished to see the nation retreat from external entanglements.

'Those who went upon the holy quest': The Arthurian Legend and British Imperialism

Published in 1849, Edward Bulwer Lytton's epic poem *King Arthur* reflects the enthusiasm for empire of a future colonial secretary. Casting Arthur as the ancestor of a long line of British monarchs who will rule an 'empire, broader than Caesar won' and 'a realm where never sets the sun'. Bulwer Lytton compares him to one of the greatest—and most tragic—imperial heroes of the mid-nineteenth century.[19] In 1845 Sir John Franklin, a former officer of the Royal Navy, set sail on a mission to find the North-West Passage, the route to the Far East through the icy waters of northern Canada which had eluded explorers for centuries. Comprising the most lavishly outfitted Arctic expedition in the history of polar exploration, Franklin and his crew of 129 set off amidst great fanfare and little concern for the dangers which lay ahead. Sailing west through Lancaster Sound, the expedition reached Greenland in July. After that, however, Franklin

---

[18] Pogue Harrison, *Forests*, 51, 133 4.
[19] Edward Bulwer Lytton, *King Arthur* (London, 1849), i. 32.

and his men disappeared without trace into the virtually unexplored and unmapped territory to the north and west.

Over the next few years dozens of ships were dispatched by the Admiralty, but there was still no news of Franklin, and by the end of the 1840s concern had reached fever-pitch. It was at the height of this near-hysteria that Bulwer Lytton's poem appeared, and Franklin's still-mysterious fate provided the source for what has become one of the most ridiculed episodes in British literature, King Arthur's visit to the North Pole. First, Arthur fights a fierce battle against a herd of angry walruses with 'flashing tusks', a scene which cannot help seeming highly comical to twentieth-century readers, but which must be considered in light of the relative lack of knowledge which the mid-Victorian public possessed of the polar regions.[20] After the walruses have been fended off, Arthur's ships become locked in the ice, an eerie parallel to the fate which had, unbeknownst to Bulwer Lytton, actually befallen Franklin and his men.

In Bulwer Lytton's poem Arthur's men are ultimately rescued by Sir Gawain and a band of 'Esquimaux', but reality has an unpleasant way of intruding upon fictional happy endings. In 1856, a cairn was discovered containing a note which told of the Franklin expedition's terrible fate. Shortly after leaving their summer camp in 1845 the ships had been beset by ice. After eighteen months the strain upon the hulls proved too great, and they sank without a trace. The surviving crew, numbering 105, set out for the Canadian mainland to the south, dragging boats and supplies with them. A single boat, along with three bodies, was later discovered, but no trace of the rest of the crew was ever found. As for Franklin himself, he had died on 11 June 1847. 'At last the mystery of Franklin's fate is solved', declared *The Times* in September 1859. 'The "final search" has proved that SIR JOHN FRANKLIN is dead. Alas! there can be no longer those sad wailings from an imaginary Tintagel to persuade the credulous that an ARTHUR still lives'.[21]

These words show that, although Franklin may have perished in the frozen wasteland of the Canadian Arctic, the link between empire and

[20] Beau Riffenburgh, *The Myth of the Explorer: The Press, Sensationalism, and Geographical Discovery* (London and New York: Belhaven, 1993), 24–8; Bulwer Lytton, *King Arthur*, ii. 89; Trevor R. Pringle, 'Cold Comfort: The Polar Landscape in English and American Popular Culture 1845–1990', *Landscape Research*, 16 (1991), 43–4.
[21] Owen Beattie and John Geiger, *Frozen in Time: The Fate of the Franklin Expedition* (London: Bloomsbury, 1987); *The Times*, 23 Sept. 1859, 1.

the Arthurian legend survived. This link has existed for centuries. The legend's trajectory, after all, is inherently imperial. Much like civil servants going out from London to administer the colonies under their nation's command, the knights of the Round Table disperse from Arthur's court at Camelot in order to bring the benefits of their ostensibly superior civilization to the less fortunate parts of the world. In return, they receive eternal moral salvation as well as material riches. This vision of Arthur appealed strongly to nineteenth-century Britons, who saw in it a precedent for their own vast territorial empire. '[Arthur's] career', wrote the literary antiquary Samuel Carter Hall in 1842

was one of entire conquest, either upon a huge scale, or in single combats: nothing earthly could withstand the prowess of his stalwart arm. . . . He proceeds from victory to victory; conquering kingdom after kingdom; slaying giants innumerable; rescuing distressed damsels; destroying 'wicked witches;' cutting off whole armies of Paynims and Saracens, and making no more of dragons than greyhounds do of hares.[22]

Historians have previously discussed the broader relationship between the Arthurian legend and British imperialism in the nine-teenth century.[23] This chapter will instead examine one particular element of the legend, the quest for the Holy Grail, in a more specific imperial context: the domestic cultural reaction to the Indian 'Mutiny' of 1857. It has long been acknowledged that the Mutiny had a major impact upon British imperial attitudes. It represented a 'searing trauma' which was the first substantial setback to the slow but steady march whose endpoint was to be the triumph of British civilization throughout the world.[24] It is well known that at the level of government policy the Mutiny produced dramatic changes in the way in which Britain functioned as an imperial power in India. What has been less closely scrutinized, however, is the Mutiny's impact on British imperial culture. This chapter will explore this impact by focusing specifically on the way in which the Grail quest was used to reflect, and in some ways to deflect, the growing anxiety which existed side-by-side with the increasingly vociferous and jingoistic assertions of imperial mastery in

[22] Samuel Carter Hall (ed.), *Book of British Ballads* (London, 1842), 125.
[23] See Victor Kiernan, 'Tennyson, King Arthur and Imperialism', in Raphael Samuel and Gareth Stedman Jones (eds.), *Culture, Ideology and Politics: Essays for Eric Hobsbawm* (London: Routledge, 1982), 126–48.
[24] Thomas Metcalf, *Ideologies of the Raj*, The New Cambridge History of India, III: 4 (Cambridge and New York: Cambridge UP, 1994), 43.

the second half of the nineteenth century. The roots of this anxiety can be traced to the Mutiny, the first in a long series of imperial crises which gradually suffused Victorian culture with doubt regarding the continued viability of imperial endeavour. In this context, the Grail quest became one of a number of cultural mechanisms used to buttress a suddenly vulnerable commitment to empire. In the years after the Mutiny, it was no accident that the image of the solitary, vulnerable knight confronted with one life-threatening danger after another became one of the most frequently employed symbols of the British imperial experience.

In 1864 Ellen J. Millington declared in the *Monthly Packet* that 'many causes have lately contributed to awaken a curious interest in the romantic fictions of chivalry, more particularly those relating to King Arthur and the Knights of the Round Table, with the famous Quest of the Sancgreal'. What was responsible for this sudden surge of 'curious interest'? Previously, the Grail quest had not been a popular motif in literary treatments of the Arthurian legend. Instead, it was generally dismissed as a story which contained far too much superstitious non-sense to be of much relevance in the nineteenth century. The painter William Dyce, who was commissioned to paint a series of Arthurian frescoes for the new Houses of Parliament in the 1840s, rejected the Grail quest as a suitable subject, declaring it to be 'little else than a tolerably intelligible religious allegory, strongly tinctured with the monastic ideas of the thirteenth century, and seemingly to some extent, intended to throw discredit on Chivalric greatness'.[25]

After the Indian Mutiny of 1857, however, the cultural environment suddenly became far more amenable to the Grail quest.[26] To the British, the Mutiny was a terrifying reminder of the virulent obstinacy of Indian barbarism in the face of attempts to deliver the benefits of a superior civilization. It also demonstrated that something had gone terribly wrong with their approach to the governance of India. A new imperial ethos was thus required as the British struggled to recapture

---

[25] Ellen J. Millington, 'King Arthur and His Knights', *The Monthly Packet of Evening Readings for the Younger Members of the Christian Church*, 17 (1859), 253–4; Debra N. Mancoff, *The Arthurian Revival in Victorian Art* (New York and London: Garland, 1990), 122.

[26] See William Morris, *The Defence of Guinevere and Other Poems* (London, 1858); Henry Lovelich, *Seynt Graal, or the Sank Ryal: the History of the Holy Graal*, ed. F. J. Furnivall, 2 vols. (London, 1861–3); Walter Map, *La Queste del Saint Graal*, ed. F. J. Furnivall (London, 1864); George MacDonald, 'The Sangreal: A Part of the Story Omitted in the Old Romances', in *Good Words*, 4 (1863), 454–5.

their former sense of imperial control. In the period after 1857 a new British theory of authority became codified.[27]

One of this theory's essential components was the idea that India was a feudal society which had to be ruled in a feudal mode. Domestically, as we have seen, the British had long since turned to medievalism as a means of counterbalancing the upheavals and uncertainties of the modern world. After 1857 many Britons sought to apply medievalist ideals to the empire as well in an attempt to mitigate the increasing chaos there. India came to be viewed as a society whose administrators should adhere to the principles of chivalry, as the heroism of those who had courageously suppressed the Mutiny had vividly demonstrated. In 1860 a review of a new edition of Malory's *Morte d'Arthur* in the *Dublin University Magazine* declared that 'the tales that lately crowded on us from India restore our belief in the moral power of men who have a cause':

Paladinism has never been more nobly manifested than within the last years of English life. We return to the ancient legends, for the deeds which they relate seem no longer impossible and lying fables. Colonel Inglis at Lucknow [is a representative of] the knight errantry, fostered by the extremes of modern life. . . . The warrior saint Havelock fights his good fight against the Eastern miscreants. . . . The heroic element has been kindled, and we open our hearts to the tales of the Norman past, and find in them sympathy with the feeling which animates our modern literature.[28]

The Mutiny and the fierce retribution which followed generated a cleansing sense of heroism on which took on a specifically chivalric, and very often Arthurian, form. 'Are there not Lancelots in . . . India?' asked the author of the passage cited above. Or, as the historian J. A. Froude wrote to a friend in December 1857, 'we had been doubting, too, whether heroism was not a thing of the past: and what knight of the Round Table beat Havelock and Sir John Lawrence?'[29] To these commentators and many others, the Mutiny became a heroic myth embodying and expressing the central values which explained their rule in India to themselves and to others. Only the supposedly chivalric

[27] Bernard S. Cohn, 'Representing Authority in Victorian India', in Eric Hobsbawm and Terence Ranger (eds.), *The Invention of Tradition*, 2nd. edn. (Cambridge: Cambridge UP, 1992), 179.

[28] Metcalf, *Ideologies*, 72–80; 'La Mort D'Arthur', *Dublin University Magazine*, 55 (1860), 498–9.

[29] 'La Mort D'Arthur', 511; Mark Girouard, *The Return to Camelot: Chivalry and the English Gentleman* (New Haven and London: Yale UP, 1982), 220.

qualities of the British, such as their willingness to sacrifice themselves
to a higher cause, their devotion to duty, and their fortitude in the face
of life-threatening danger, had permitted them to triumph over the
Indians who had threatened the properly constituted colonial authority
and order.

After 1857 Britons thus recognized that there was a connection
between the Grail quest and imperial affairs. But why, more specifically, did the quest come to be perceived as such an appropriate
metaphor for the British imperial experience? On the surface, the
story tells of a brilliant society ruled by a great monarch sending out
its best and bravest knights on a noble mission. Its attractiveness in a
society newly determined to express its political and moral authority in
an imperial context would thus seem to be obvious. But beneath this
superficial reading lies a far darker interpretation. The quest, after all,
leads to the destruction of Arthur's glorious kingdom, as so few knights
return that insufficient numbers remain to defend the realm from its
enemies. In the second half of the nineteenth century this latter interpretation came to be favoured by the increasing number of Britons
who felt that they no longer had the moral right or administrative
ability to maintain their far-flung empire.

In many ways the Grail quest was well suited to representing this
new, less confident point of view. Thomas Westwood's poem *The Quest
of the Sancgreall* was published in 1868 as imperial crises mounted not
only in India but also in South Africa, New Zealand, Burma, China,
Persia, and elsewhere. The poem opens with a 'solemn' and 'sorrowful'
conclave, as Arthur and his knights talk of 'wrong triumphant, power |
Unsanctified, and loss irreparable'. Arthur wishes for a vision of the
Grail as 'a sign | Of benediction, and a hope new-born | To cheer the
darkness of these evil days!' His wish is granted, for suddenly the Grail
appears in their midst. Galahad leaps up and proclaims that he will
seek it 'through the world', and his fellow knights vow to follow him.
But over the next four years the knights trickle back to Camelot,
defeated by their 'hands impure and sinful will'. Only Galahad is
sufficiently pure in spirit to persevere. The rigours of the quest taken
their toll upon him, however, and by the poem's end he is no longer the
naïve young knight who so impetuously made his pledge:

> But wan his visage, withered as with fire,
> And wasted all his strength—like Christ's true knight
> Of Tarsus, much had he endured and known;—

> Perils by water, perils on the land,
> Perils amongst false brethren, hunger, thirst,
> Captivity, the torments of the flesh,
> And warfare with the fiends accursed of God . . .[30]

Westwood's poem is thus no triumphal elegy. It is instead a poignant reminder of the high cost of empire, written at a time when that cost seemed particularly exorbitant. Galahad may be borne off to heaven in the poem's conclusion, but he leaves behind him on earth a broken and dispirited Camelot, filled with knights whose personal and moral deficiencies have been made clear by their failure to achieve the quest.

The following year Alfred Tennyson published the most influential of all nineteenth-century literary treatments of the Grail quest, his poem 'The Holy Grail', which was included in the second instalment of the *Idylls of the King*. Throughout the mid-nineteenth century period of crisis Tennyson evinced an intense interest in imperial affairs. The horrific accounts of the Indian Mutiny affected him deeply, as did accounts of the Eyre crisis of October 1865. It is thus not surprising that Tennyson displays an extremely anxious attitude towards the future of the empire in his version of the Grail story. From the outset, 'The Holy Grail' is suffused with an aura of doom. Instead of focusing on the successful questers, Tennyson relates the narrative from the point of view of one of the many unsuccessful ones, therefore placing failure at the centre of the poem. And this failure is not merely personal, for the departure of Arthur's best and bravest knights ultimately destroys the idyllic society he has worked so hard to build. By the time the knights return to Camelot, the formerly splendid and glittering castle, left defenceless by their absence, has been reduced to a heap of rubble. Only a tenth of those who ventured forth on the quest with such high hopes come back safely. The poem concludes with a despondent Arthur delivering a mournful speech to the fraction of the Round Table that remains:

> And spake I not too truly, O my knights?
> Was I too dark a prophet when I said
> To those who went upon the Holy Quest,
> That most of them would follow wandering fires,

---

[30] Thomas Westwood, *The Quest of the Sancgreall, The Sword of Kingship, and Other Poems* (London, 1868), 6–7, 16–17, 57.

Lost in the quagmire?—lost to me and gone,
And left me gazing at a barren board,
And a lean Order . . .[31]

All of Tennyson's imperial anxieties thus come to the fore in 'The Holy Grail'. In his earlier Arthurian works, written before 1857, he expresses considerable confidence about Britain's imperial future. In these, the empire brings order and peaceful progress to distant lands, as Arthur's ever-expanding kingdom overawes less civilized areas and bestows upon them the benefits of the British way of life. Arthur and his knights bring the light of civilization to the dark corners of the medieval world in much the same way that the Victorians sought to bring it to Asia or Africa. But if in these earlier poems Arthur's realm functions as a symbol of the empire as Tennyson wished it to be, by the late 1860s it increasingly seemed to symbolize the empire as he feared it actually was, or was rapidly becoming. The dark places of the world might still be in need of the bright light of civilization, but Tennyson was no longer so certain that the British would be able to provide it.

After 1870 the focus of literary treatments of the Grail story shifted from the quest to the questers. On one level this transition permitted authors to focus upon the success of individual knights rather the destruction of Arthur's realm as a result of their departure, and in this sense it represented an attempt to assuage some of the doubts and fears which plagued British imperialism after 1857. But when looked at another way, the image of the knight following his solitary and dangerous path was unlikely to inspire much enthusiasm for empire. Before the Mutiny an author like Bulwer Lytton had used the Arthurian legend to depict a more confident and complacent brand of empire, with Arthur as the leader of mighty army capable of defeating any challenger. Now, however, that confidence had eroded away, and it was a very different sort of imperial image—that of the solitary, unprotected knight—that the legend was used to depict. The Grail quest thus was able to represent the dual nature of late-nineteenth-century British imperial culture, which combined a self-confident exterior with an extremely uncertain interior.

---

[31] David Staines, 'Tennyson's "The Holy Grail": The Tragedy of Percivale', *Modern Language Review*, 69 (1974), 747; Alfred Tennyson, 'The Holy Grail', in *Idylls of the King*, ed. J. M. Gray (New Haven and London: Yale UP, 1983), ll. 884–90.

Cultural historians have identified in Victorian literature a new concept of masculinity which reformulated the image of the gentleman as an idealized medieval knight embodying the virtues of bravery, loyalty, courtesy, generosity, modesty, purity, and compassion. When translated into an imperial context, this chivalric ethos served as a code of colonial conduct which functioned to distinguish the British from the ostensible barbarities of the societies over which they ruled.[32] The empire provided a field in which a gentleman could come to the aid of those less fortunate than himself. He could fight the good fight to rescue ostensibly inferior peoples from slavery, superstition, or unjust rulers, and bring them peace, wise but firm government, and the benefits of British civilization.

In the final decades of the nineteenth century imperial heroes were often explicitly compared to medieval knights. Lord Curzon, for example, referred to 'John Lawrence, that rugged tower of strength; Nicholson, the heroic Paladin of the frontier; Outram, that generous and gallant spirit, the mirror of chivalry; Hugh Rose, that prince among fighting men'.[33] This sort of image was deliberately promoted in order to produce a ruling elite for the rapidly expanding empire, and once again the Grail quest was well-suited for use in this context. The Arthurian characters most commonly invoked as exemplars for the modern knight of the empire were Sir Percival and Sir Galahad, the only members of Arthur's retinue sufficiently pure to achieve the quest for the Holy Grail. Like the Grail quest more generally, these two characters had not been particularly popular in treatments of the Arthurian legend prior to 1857. Neither was featured specifically as the hero of a particular work of literature, and indeed they were mentioned only a handful of times. But in the period after the Mutiny the prevalence of Percival and Galahad in contemporary Arthurian literature increased dramatically.

Their sudden burst of popularity was directly attributable to their new role as models for male conduct, men who emphasized moral and spiritual concerns over material ones. In 1864 Frederick Furnivall asked: 'Now what is the Lesson of it all? Is the example of Galahad, and his unwavering pursuit of the highest spiritual object set before him, nothing to us? Is that of Perceval, pure and tempted, on the point

---

[32] Girouard, *Return to Camelot*, 220–30; J. A. Mangan, 'Noble Specimens of Manhood: Schoolboy Literature and the Creation of a Colonial Chivalric Code', in Jeffrey Richards (ed.), *Imperialism and Juvenile Literature* (Manchester and New York: Manchester UP, 1989), 191.   [33] Girouard, *Return to Camelot*, 220.

of yielding, yet saved by the sight of the symbol of his Faith, to be of no avail to us?'[34] As this passages suggests, the purity, bravery, and devotion to duty of Galahad and Perceval made them ideally suited to serve as exemplars for modern knights of the empire. For who better to symbolize the isolated district officer manning his remote post than the brave knights who had ultimately persevered on the lonely and difficult path leading to the Holy Grail?

The extension of the chivalric ideals Galahad and Perceval represented into the realm of colonial politics served to rationalize imperialism as a divine manifestation of Britain's moral and religious destiny to conquer the world for its own good. In her poem 'A Pastoral of Galahad', published in 1899, Elinor Sweetman displays the new model of heroic national service which these knight embodied. Her Galahad declares,

> I am not less a soldier sealed,
> Because in life of filth and field
> I saw the light, I heard the call,
> That God Himself revealed.

G. F. Watt's painting *Sir Galahad*, first exhibited at the Royal Academy only five years after the Indian Mutiny, enjoyed massive popularity in late Victorian Britain, a popularity due largely to its function as an emblem of the commitment of the new Christian knight to sacrifice all in the name of empire.[35] In the late 1890s Watts presented a copy of *Sir Galahad* to Eton College, where it was hung in the chapel in an attempt to inspire generations of Britain's elite.

An ardent imperialist who believed firmly in the superiority of British civilization, Watts clearly hoped that some of Eton's bright young men would dedicate themselves to the imperial cause, a didactic intention which his contemporaries recognized. 'It should not be difficult for us now to understand the purpose of the great artist . . . in presenting this picture to Eton College', the Presbyterian minister James Burns wrote in 1914:

For there are gathered many of the youth of our great Empire who in coming generations are to guide its destinies. In these early and formative days young

---

[34] Furnivall, preface to *La Queste del Saint Graal*, p. ix.

[35] Elinor Sweetman, *Pastorals and Other Poems* (London, 1899), 44; Marilynn Lincoln Board, 'Art's Moral Mission: Reading G. F. Watt's *Sir Galahad*', in Debra N. Mancoff (ed.), *The Arthurian Revival: Essays on Form, Tradition, and Transformation* (New York and London: Garland, 1992), 132–3.

eyes look out upon life with wistful questionings, and young hearts receive their lasting spiritual impressions. It is then that the great decisions are made, and it is upon the nature of those decisions that the future character and stability of our Empire depend.

As a young knight of the empire should, Galahad had wholeheartedly devoted himself to the service of a mysterious power, utterly convinced of its righteousness and necessity. He thus fulfilled the need for an icon who could define national goals and inspire individual heroism.[36]

There was an inherent tension, however, at the heart of the elevation of Galahad and Perceval as role models, for the powers of these men were not so great as to render them invincible. Instead, they were men going out alone to meet the challenge of civilizing distant lands, with no guarantee of a safe return. Moral righteousness was on their side, but that alone did not ensure success. Galahad and Percival thus embodied not only the hopes but also the doubts of British imperialism in the second half of the nineteenth century.

This tension can be seen in J. H. Shorthouse's juvenile novel *Sir Perceval: A Story of Past and Present* (1889), which tells of a young colonial official named Sir Percival Massareen. While on leave from his duties, he pays a visit to his adolescent cousin Constance Lisle, who tells him that he is named after Malory's Percival, 'one of the best knights in the world' and 'one of the very few . . . who saw the Holy Grail'. The modern Perceval is pleased, commenting that 'it is well to have a fellow like that of your name to follow'. Soon thereafter he departs for the west coast of Africa. A few months later he volunteers to go on a dangerous expedition to rescue an English bishop who has been kidnapped by a native tribe. Deserted by his guides, Perceval is captured and killed. Constance is distraught to learn of his death, but also extremely proud that he was granted the opportunity 'to suffer . . . and die, at the divine call of duty and sacrifice'.[37] *Sir Percival* is a story of a brave young man risking his life in the glorious cause of the British empire, much as Malory's Percival had risked his for the Grail. But unlike that of his namesake, the quest of the modern-day Percival ends in a lonely death. This unfortunate fate, the narrative implies, is the

---

[36] James Burns, *Sir Galahad: A Call to the Heroic* (London, [1914]), 20–1; Board, 'Art's Moral Mission', 149–50.

[37] J. H. Shorthouse, *Sir Perceval: A Story of the Past and Present* (London, 1886), 86–7, 276–7.

result of the pursuit of empire rather than the glory of Britain and the salvation of the world.

Following a similar narrative line and raising similar questions about the continued pursuit of empire was Sidney Kilner Levett-Yeats's novella *A Galahad of the Creeks*. Published in 1897, it features as its hero a 'tall, straight, broad-shouldered Englishman' named Peregrine Jackson, who serves as the assistant commissioner of Pazobin, in Lower Burma. Jackson's crusading zeal earns him the nickname 'Galahad' from the two other Europeans in the district. Although he has been told that the local native is 'incapable of progress, a sluggard and a fop', he refuses to believe that a generous dose of the benefits of British civilization will not effect dramatic improvements. Devoting himself to the suppression of the leader of a notorious gang of robbers, he is shot during a skirmish. His last words are: 'Die . . . who says I am going to die? I am young yet—my work is not yet done'.[38] But die he does—yet another tragic but ultimately meaningless sacrifice for the empire.

Beneath their superficially heroic tone, the works of Shorthouse and Levett-Yeats display a pervasive cynicism which reveals the anxieties which plagued British imperial endeavour in the final decades of the nineteenth century. On one level Galahad and Perceval function as idealized models for the young knights of the empire, but on another these authors suggest that their brand of heroism leads to senseless death rather than national glory. Beneath the bluster about the nobility of sacrificing oneself to the great imperial cause lay the unavoidable recognition that in most cases that sacrifice was an empty one.

These works vividly demonstrate that the legacy of the Mutiny had created a fearfulness that could never be completely quelled. The Grail quest became a prominent metaphor for British imperial endeavour in the decades after 1857 because it was able to convey the tensions inherent in the struggle between the effort to regain the level of confidence characteristic of the period before the Mutiny, and the sense that that confidence had been permanently eroded. On the surface the Grail quest inspired hope of a bright future for the British empire, but at its core it revealed the doubts and fears which the Mutiny had awakened, doubts and fears which the British were never entirely able to put to rest.

---

[38] S. Levett-Yeats, *A Galahad of the Creeks and Other Stories* (London and Bombay, 1897), 139–40.

'Mad zeal was gone abroad': The Legend of Robin Hood and Nineteenth-Century Opposition to Imperialism

Although they harboured increasing doubts about Britain's ability to maintain its empire, those authors who deployed the Arthurian legend in an imperial context rarely questioned the validity of the enterprise as a whole. Even if it was doomed to failure, they argued, and even if many brave 'knights' were destined to die in the attempt, the effort must be made. The authors who treated the legend of Robin Hood, on the other hand, were not so certain. Instead of promoting imperialism, they more often attacked it by emphasizing its high cost in terms of the attention paid to more pressing domestic problems. The legend was well-suited to serve as a vehicle for criticisms of external expansion, for just as the trajectory of the Arthurian legend was inherently imperial, that of the legend of Robin Hood was anti-imperial. It looks inwards rather than outwards. Robin Hood and his men are constantly retreating towards a central point—their Sherwood lair—rather than fanning out from it. They do not seek the external world; it, in the form of the forces of the Sheriff of Nottingham and Prince John, seeks—and attempts to destroy—them.

This inherent insularity is reflected in nineteenth-century literary treatments of the legend of Robin Hood. In particular, the domestic chaos engendered by Richard I's absence on the Crusades made excellent fodder for those who argued that governments should focus their attentions at home. Just as Richard had deserted his country and squandered the nation's resources, the British government was in danger of channelling far too much money and manpower into useless imperial expansion. This theme was implicit in a wide variety of treatments of the legend from the beginning of the nineteenth century onwards. 'This king', writes the author of *The History and Famous Exploits of Robin Hood* (*c*.1805), 'transported with a blind religious zeal, ruined himself and almost his whole nation, to carry on a war against the Infidels in the Holy Land, whither he went himself; and during his absence England was filled with intestine troubles, and infested with thieves and robbers'. In his poem 'Sherwood Forest' (1827), Robert Millhouse, too, blames the Crusades for the internal upheavals of the twelfth century, and emphasizes the number of lives lost so needlessly:

> Mad zeal was gone abroad, and ere the flame,
> In frenzied conflict, fanned itself to rest,
> Full many an orphan babe, and widowed dame,

In sorrow's gushing streams their loss expressed,
Which might not fill the void, deep harrowed in the breast.[39]

Robin Hood, meanwhile, appears as the nation's saviour who will assume control in Richard's stead. In Sir Walter Scott's *Ivanhoe* (1820) he joins in the campaign to oust Prince John and his cohorts from power, thereby fighting alongside the forces of order rather than disorder. He is a loyal patriot striving to repair the damage done by a king with confused priorities.

As the nineteenth century wore on, anti-imperialism assumed an increasingly important role in literary treatments of the legend of Robin Hood. J. H. Stocqueller's novel *Maid Marian, the Forest Queen* (1849) opens with a typical description of the problems occasioned by King Richard's departure for the Holy Land. Stocqueller, however, adds a new twist: Robin Hood himself joins the Crusades as captain of the king's archers. When he returns to England he brings with him a Saracen chieftain named Suleiman and his daughter Leila. At first it appears that they are adjusting happily to their new environment, but beneath the surface all is not well. Suleiman is caught attempting to poison Robin Hood, and after his banishment from the greenwood he joins Prince John in plotting to overthrow Richard I's government. Robin Hood foils his evil plan, however, by slaying him with an arrow.

Stocqueller depicts Suleiman and Leila as a disruptive—and overtly evil—influence upon English society. The greenwood is so negatively altered by their arrival as to be scarcely recognizable to those familiar with its traditionally carefree modes of behaviour:

Any one who had been an inmate or visitor of the forest a few months previously, and who had observed the habit of life common to the permanent dwellers in the merry greenwood, would have been much at a loss to comprehend the altered condition of the fraternity. The gay thoughtlessness which characterised the diversions of their leisure, the utter absence of care which their bronzed and good-natured faces evinced, were now exchanged for a partial gloominess and uneasiness, for which few of them could very satisfactorily account.

It is not until after the Saracens' removal that 'life in the greenwood . . . resumed its ancient cheerfulness'.[40] Having spent twenty years in India from 1821 to 1841, Stocqueller was familiar with the conduct of

---

[39] *The History and Famous Exploits of Robin Hood* (Banbury, [1805?]), p. iv; Robert Millhouse, *Sherwood Forest, and Other Poems* (London, 1827), 34.
[40] J. H. Stocqueller, *Maid Marian, The Forest Queen* (London, [1849]), 118, 144.

the native population and, judging from *Maid Marian*, he formed numerous prejudices as a result. Clearly, he views contact with 'infidels' as disruptive and dangerous—a malign infection from without—and believes that it should be avoided as much as possible.

This representation of the impact of 'Oriental perversity' upon British civilization was a prominent strand of Victorian thought. The failure of 'noble' efforts such as Robin Hood's attempt to convert Suleiman and Leila to Christianity was blamed upon the baseness and weak intellect of Asiatic peoples, who were incapable of grasping spiritual truth. When these peoples came into contact with the inhabitants of the metropolis, they therefore represented an infectious threat which had the potential to contaminate British society. In consequence, it was necessary to separate them from the British population as much as possible, as Stocqueller advocates.[41]

Although other mid-nineteenth-century literary treatments of the legend of Robin Hood are less explicitly concerned with imperial issues, they do contain numerous implicitly anti-imperial elements. Richard I continued to be severely castigated for deserting his country in its hour of need. In her children's story *The Boy Foresters* (1868), Anne Bowman writes: 'It would have been well if the soldier-king had remembered a yet more stringent duty entailed on him with his inheritance. While he was engaged in distant war, his kingdom was abandoned to neglect and ignorance, to anarchy and petty tyranny'. Bowman has little regard for the ostensibly ideal objectives of the crusaders. The young Saxon Hubert asks his friend Smith, who has just returned from the Holy Land, about his experience there:

'What a grand thing the Crusade is', said Hubert. 'How I wish I had been with King Richard in Palestine. On that holy ground I should have been ever on my knees praying as if in chapel. Didst thou not feel it very awful, Smith?'

'I can't say as how I ever did that', replied he. 'It wasn't oft that we turned our minds to holy things. Every man's thought was as to whom he was to slay, or what he could get. We thought most on skins of wine, juicy fruits,—which were far beyond our plums and apples—bright sharp daggers, and fine silk sashes. And I reckon as we were all much alike, priests and soldiers, one as bad as another; more for gain and bloodshed than for prayers'.[42]

---

[41] Ruth H. Lindeborg, 'The "Asiatic" and the Boundaries of Victorian Englishness', *Victorian Studies*, 37 (1994), 382–7; Suvendrini Perera, *Reaches of Empire: The English Novel from Edgeworth to Dickens* (New York: Columbia UP, 1991), 108.

[42] Anne Bowman, *The Boy Foresters. A Tale of the Days of Robin Hood* (London, [1868]), 2, 169.

In J. Frederick Hodgetts's *Edwin the Boy Outlaw* (1887), the recurring motif of the neglectful monarch Richard versus the true patriot Robin Hood receives its strongest emphasis yet. Hodgetts depicts Richard as a brutish alien king whose thirst for blood and lust for gold compelled him to undertake the Crusades. Meanwhile, England suffers grievously as 'the treasures of the land were swallowed by his wars, as useless and silly as ever had been waged'. A citizen of Nottingham expresses a negative opinion of rulers who ignore their domestic obligations in favour of imperial adventure: 'If he be England's king why not remain in England, and shed his glory on his people here? What good is done to us by killing infidels?' Other contemporary authors were in complete agreement with Hodgetts's view of Richard's failure to remember his proper priorities. In Edward Gilliat's *In Lincoln Green* (1897), a porter from Nottingham tells Robin Hood that 'it seems to us poor, toiling sons of serfs, that all these fine red-cross knights go out yonder . . . just to show off their own bravery of apparel and feats of horsemanship. Meanwhile, the land suffers at home, the castle goes to rack and ruin, the labourer gets no hire, and the monks grow fat and buy up all the great estates of the broken knights'.[43]

This latent anti-imperialism moves to the forefront of a short story by E. F. Pollard entitled '"Hari Ram," the Dacoit' (1899).[44] The story describes the fictional exploits of Hari Ram, a bandit and 'notorious rascal'. According to a Calcutta police officer:

Rumour runs that he is a sort of Robin Hood. He plunders the rich, and shares his booty with the poor, who consequently protect him in such a fashion that we cannot lay our hands on him; he just slips through our fingers. . . . Caught he must be, and punished pretty severely, or the country won't long be habitable; in its present state it's wholly unsafe.

Efforts to catch Hari Ram prove fruitless, however. When the Commissioner of the district arrives with a full contingent of police, the bandit steals into his tent and carries off his watch, shirt, and money, leaving behind a note conveying his compliments, an episode

---

[43] J. Frederick Hodgetts, *Edwin the Boy Outlaw, or the Dawn of Freedom in England* (London, 1887), 41, 122, 123, 42, 157; Edward Gilliat, *In Lincoln Green: A Merrie Tale of Robin Hood* (London, 1897), 288, 362.

[44] The term 'dacoit' was used by the colonial administration in British India to refer to a gang robber. 'Dacoity' was officially a robbery committed by five or more persons, and was assumed to have political implications.

described by the local superintendent as 'a perfect Robin Hood's exploit'.[45] Pollard thus explicitly compares Robin Hood's resistance to the rule of King John to the criminal activities of a late-nineteenth-century bandit challenging the authority of the colonial government of British India.

Previously we saw in Levett-Yeats's *A Galahad of the Creeks*, also published in the late 1890s, an imperial hero being compared to an Arthurian knight as he attempts to suppress the activities of a local bandit. In contrast, Pollard likens a similar brigand, Hari Ram, to Robin Hood. The implication is clear: in late-Victorian literature Arthur and his knights are the ancestors of the modern colonial servant, whereas Robin Hood and his men are seen as opposed to the growth and administration of empire, staunch individualists who fight against the homogenizing tendencies of the modern imperial world.

Not every late-Victorian author who treated the legend of Robin Hood used it to convey anti-imperial sentiments, however, for there were a few exceptions who employed it to proclaim the benefits of external expansion. In 1897 Major F. B. Toms of the Royal Artillery, Gibraltar, authored a Christmas pantomime entitled *The Babes in the Wood and Robin Hood*, which was performed at the Theatre Royal, Gibraltar, by a cast comprised of British military personnel. Rife with topical references to the life of a soldier in Her Majesty's service overseas, the play abounds with unabashedly jingoistic declarations about the empire. Robin Hood, for example, warbles a patriotic song about Britain's mastery of the sea:

> The wooden walls of England
> Have long since passed away,
> But 'hearts of oak' are beating
> In English breasts to-day.
> And our sons shall tell the story
> Unto their sons again,
> How England held her glory
> In great Victoria's reign!
> And when our children's children,
> Stand lisping at our knee,
> We'll tell them how Englishmen

---

[45] E. F. Pollard, '"Hari Ram," the Dacoit', in G. A. Henty (ed.), *Yule-Tide Yarns* (London, New York and Bombay, 1899), 298–9, 319. I owe my knowledge of this work to Dr Michael Silvestri.

Must ever hold the Sea!
No braggart's boast can guard our coast,
But let them only be
True Sons of Great Britannia,
And she shall rule the Sea.[46]

Even as ardent a promoter of Empire as Toms, however, cannot entirely ignore the increasingly vociferous criticism to which it was being subjected in the 1890s. And once again that criticism found an ideal vehicle in the conduct of Richard the Lion-hearted and his desertion of his realm in order to lead the Crusades. When Richard at long last returns to Nottingham and brings the chaos and corruption which have prevailed in his absence to an end, Blondel the Bard asks: 'I trust you are quite finished with these wars'. Richard, however, states his intention of returning to the Crusades as soon as he can restore some semblance of order to England. 'I dearly like to break the natives' heads, just for religion's sake', he declares. Blondel is dismayed at this prospect, realizing that the King's departure will quickly return his country to the sorry state from which it has so recently been delivered. Moreover, the continuation of Richard's foreign adventures will exact a high price in terms of English loss of life:

'Twas ever thus! The English long to roam
And fight in 'furrin parts', not stay at home.
It is the same in your day, and 'twas in the past,
And will continue doubtless till the last.
In Asia and Africa we've often fought
And victories we've gained, though sometimes dearly
bought.[47]

Thus, even in an ostensibly pro-imperial treatment of the legend of Robin Hood, criticism of continued external expansion can still be heard.

Toms's pantomime demonstrates that, underneath the more vocal flag-waving, jingoistic imperialism of the late nineteenth century there also existed a subtler but equally significant anti-imperialism which saw the nation's future as lying along a more insular path. For every late-Victorian Briton who gazed outwards towards the sea in the quest to maintain and increase national greatness, there was another who looked inwards towards the forest, for no feature of the British

---

[46] Major F. B. Toms, *Royal Artillery Gibraltar Christmas Pantomime: 'The Babes in the Wood' and 'Robin Hood'* (Gibraltar, 1897), 23.   [47] Ibid. 25.

landscape better represented this anti-imperial point of view. And no hero better represented it than Robin Hood, the lord of the green-wood. Like the increasingly vocal Little Englanders, many interpreters of the legend argued that the attentions of the true patriot should be primarily directed towards home, not distant lands. Imperial expansion was simply not worth the high cost. In simple, if ungrammatical terms, Robin Hood's follower Gaffer John sums up the prevailing view in Edward Gilliat's *Wolf's Head: A Story of the Prince of Outlaws* (1899), when he declares: 'God put us in England; why must we haunt to them foreign parts?'[48]

[48] Edward Gilliat, *Wolf's Head: A Story of the Prince of Outlaws* (London, 1899), 161.

'We shall be one people': King Arthur and Robin Hood in the First Half of the Twentieth Century

GEORGE E. ROCHESTER'S *Captain Robin Hood Skywayman* (1935) is a spy novel for adolescents set in the tense period prior to the Second World War. In the opening scene a German agent attempting to obtain details of British military defences is apprehended by a man wearing a scarlet flying kit. Announcing himself as 'Captain Robin Hood', he asks to the spy: 'Do you not realize, you fool, that the soul of England is the mightiest force for good in the world to-day?' He then gives the German his 'card', a small silver arrow with red, white, and blue accents, 'the colours of England's flag'. Inscribed on the arrow are the words: 'This shaft for Merrie England!'[1]

As the novel progresses, it is revealed that Captain Robin Hood is the leader of 'a small and devoted band of Englishmen who . . . were fighting secretly but desperately and earnestly, to save Britain and her Empire from being plunged into a devastating and awful war by those who, since the war years, had been looking with envious and jealous eyes on the might of England and on the richness of her great colonies'. Time after time he foils the efforts of the Germans to sabotage British military preparations. In the final aerial battle he takes on and defeats the German 'Death Squadron', and the novel ends with him vowing to continue the 'fight against these enemies of England'.[2]

In the mid-1930s, as Europe edged closer to war, T. H. White began on the Arthurian tetralogy that eventually became *The Once and Future King*, one of the most famous twentieth-century treatments of the legend. He published the first volume, *The Sword in the Stone*, and *The Witch in the Wood* and *The Ill-Made Knight* followed in 1939 and 1940 respectively. The fourth volume, *The Candle in the Wind*, was finished

---

[1] George E. Rochester, *Captain Robin Hood Skywayman* (London: John Hamilton, 1935), 13–6.   [2] Ibid. 54–5, 164–5, 170.

shortly thereafter, although it did not appear until 1958, when the complete tetralogy was finally published. A pacifist, White was deeply disturbed by the outbreak of war, and his work very much reflects its context. He saw his Arthurian writing as intimately bound up with the war effort, recording in his journal in September 1939 that 'I can do much better than fight for civilisation; I can make it'.[3] In *The Once and Future King*, Arthur's illegitimate son and bitter enemy Mordred leads a 'popular party' called the 'Thrashers' which is clearly intended as an analogue to Nazism. 'Their aims', White writes, 'were some kind of nationalism . . . and a massacre of Jews as well'.[4] When Arthur faces Mordred in battle at the end of the novel, it thus parallels the real-life struggle Britain faced against Hitler's Germany. White would have preferred no war at all, but if one has to be fought, he makes it clear which side is the most just and moral.

These two texts place Robin Hood and King Arthur in the position of defending their nation against the menacing threat of Nazi Germany as Europe edged closer to war in the late 1930s. It is no accident that the authors turned to these two heroes in particular at a time of such dire national need, for this study has shown that they were clearly regarded as national heroes by the beginning of the twentieth century. We have previously seen how, over the course of the nineteenth century, the 'Englishness' of King Arthur and Robin Hood was established in two ways. First, they came to be associated with the rise of the academic discipline of English studies, as both Thomas Malory's *Morte d'Arthur* and the Robin Hood ballads assumed prominent places in the English canon. And second, the ethnicity of the two heroes was altered so as to bring them into line with contemporary racialist notions of the superiority of the Saxon race. In the twentieth century these Victorian contributions continued to shape interpretations of the legends. The Robin Hood ballads were celebrated as examples of the national literary genius in a primitive but robust state. 'Rude these ballads are', wrote the noted literary scholar A. T. Quiller-Couch, 'but nothing in English verse has ever been racier, or more genuine, or closer to the core and marrow of England'. The key text for the interpreters of the Arthurian legend, meanwhile, remained *Le Morte d'Arthur*. 'It was Malory', wrote W. Lewis Jones, Professor of English at

---

[3] Elizabeth Brewer, *T.H. White's The Once and Future King*, Arthurian Studies, 30 (Cambridge: D. S. Brewer, 1993), 9.

[4] T. H. White, *The Once and Future King* (New York: G. P. Putnam, 1958), 628.

University College of North Wales, 'who gave new life to the Arthurian legends, and to him . . . is due the fascination which Arthurian story has had for so many modern English poets'.[5]

The legends of King Arthur and Robin Hood also continued to reflect Victorian racialist notions. Robin Hood remained a Saxon hero engaged in a fierce struggle against the evil Norman conquerors. Published during the First World War, F. Gudgin's *Robin Hood and His Merry Men* opens with an attempt to provide a historical setting for the outlaw's exploits:

In the year 1066 AD Duke William of Normandy crossed the sea and came to England. At Hastings, on the coast of Sussex, he and his followers landed and fought a great battle with the English. In this battle, Harold, the English King, was slain, and the Normans were victorious. . . . Now Duke William became King; and to reward his followers, he took houses and lands from the Saxons . . . and gave them to the Normans. This . . . caused great trouble between the Saxon nobles and their conquerors, and the bad state of affairs lasted for many years.

Robin Hood, Gudgin adds, was among these disaffected Saxons, and 'was always robbing the Norman nobles, and giving their money and goods to the Saxon poor'.[6]

Although, as we have seen, historical probability made it difficult for King Arthur to be labelled a Saxon hero in so blatant a fashion, twentieth-century authors continued to deny his Celtic origins and refer to him as the 'King of England'. In Doris Ashley's *King Arthur and the Knights of the Round Table* (1922), for example, Merlin declares that 'whoso pulleth out this sword from this stone is born rightful king of all England'. Ashley admitted in the preface that the real Arthur had most likely been a sixth-century Celt who had led the fight 'against the invading Saxon', but, like her Victorian predecessors, she justified her reference to his English identity by separating the historical and fictional characters. 'It is not so much as a historic figure', she wrote, 'but as a romantic hero that King Arthur shines forth'.[7]

The twentieth-century work which most blatantly separates Arthur from his historical origins, however, is White's *The Once and Future King.*

[5] A. T. Quiller-Couch, *Robin Hood* (Oxford, 1908–12), 4; W. Lewis Jones, *King Arthur in History and Legend* (Cambridge, 1911), 117–8.

[6] F. Gudgin, *Robin Hood and His Merry Men* (London, 1919), 5–6, 38.

[7] Doris Ashley, *King Arthur and the Knights of the Round Table* (London: Raphael Tuck, 1922), 8, 11.

White establishes a stark dichotomy between the 'Galls' (English) and 'Gaels' (Celts), in which Arthur represents the former and the Orkney clan of Gawain, Agravain, and Morgan le Fay represents the latter. Although the Orkneys are Scottish, their antipathy for Arthur is clearly meant to correspond to the Anglo-Irish tensions of White's day. As the young King Arthur struggles to consolidate his tenuous hold on the throne, Merlyn explains the reluctance of the Gaels to acknowledge his authority, using the foresight he has gained by living backwards through time from the future to the past: 'Look at . . . all that Gaelic crew, fighting against you for the Kingdom. Pulling swords out of stones is not a legal proof of paternity, I admit, but [they] are not fighting you about that. They have rebelled . . . simply because the throne is insecure. England's difficulty, we used to say, is Ireland's opportunity'.[8]

White clearly sees the Gaels as a destructive force. 'The present revolt of the Gaelic Confederation is a process of disintegration', Merlyn declares. 'They want to smash up . . . the United Kingdom into a lot of piffling little kingdoms of their own. . . . I never could stomach these nationalists. . . . The destiny of man is to unite, not divide. If you keep on dividing you end up as a collection of monkeys throwing nuts at each other out of separate trees'. Later, White's hostility towards Irish nationalism becomes even more apparent. Arthur's enemy Mordred symbolizes 'the invincible Gael', who is 'the irreconcilable opposite of the Englishman'. He is an example of

the race, now represented by the Irish Republican Army . . . who had always murdered landlords and then blamed them for being murdered— the race . . . which had been expelled by the volcano of history into the far quarters of the globe, where, with a venomous sense of grievance and inferiority, they even nowadays proclaim their ancient megalomania. . . . They were . . . the hysterically touchy, sorrowful, flayed defenders of a broken heritage.[9]

White thus reverses Arthur's historical identity by transforming him from a Celt into an enemy of the Celts.

Some twentieth-century interpreters of the legends of King Arthur and Robin Hood, therefore, continued to support the racialist notions that had been constructed in the nineteenth century. Others, however,

---

[8] White, *Once and Future King*, 229.   [9] Ibid. 235, 548–9.

began to take a different approach. Although the conflict between Norman and Saxon remained a prominent motif in the legend of Robin Hood, it was no longer universally treated as an immutable biological distinction which made a reconciliation of the two peoples impossible. Instead, there was a return to the position adopted by Sir Walter Scott in *Ivanhoe*, in which the Normans and Saxons had ultimately set aside their mutual enmity in the interest of national unity. In an early-twentieth-century series of fourteen stories entitled the *Robin Hood Library*, Robin Hood declares: 'I would wrest from Prince John and his cruel minions a recognition of equality before the law for every man in this realm. . . . Then would the two races blend together and become a powerful nation'. Similarly, in Alfred Noyes's poem *Sherwood* (1911), Robin states:

> There shall be no more talk of rich and poor,
> Norman and Saxon. We shall be one people,
> One family, clustering all with happy hands
> And faces round that glowing hearth, the sun.[10]

Why did this retreat occur from the strict racialist divisions which had prevailed in the late nineteenth century? As we have seen, the work of Linda Colley suggests that the frequent wars of the eighteenth and early nineteenth centuries created a greater emphasis on the 'Britishness' of the British nation. In other words, the military threat represented by France demanded that the inhabitants of England, Scotland, Wales, and Ireland temporarily set aside their hostilities towards each other and focus on defeating a dangerous foe. And in the first half of the twentieth century we can see a similar process in action. As Britain faced two bloody and destructive world wars, it became imperative to emphasize the similarities, rather than differences, between the ethnic groups who comprised the nation. Furthermore, the fact that this struggle for national survival was now taking place against Germany rather than France meant that the 'Saxons good, Normans bad' paradigm became problematic. In such a context, it was difficult to continue emphasizing the superiority of Teutonic stock and denigrating the Norman French.

The first half of the twentieth century also saw changes in the racial identity of King Arthur, albeit for different reasons. Even as English

[10] *Robin Hood Library*, 9: *Robin Hood and the Wrestler* (London, [1912]), 4; Alfred Noyes, *Sherwood, or Robin Hood and the Three Kings* (London, 1911), 84.

authors continued to de-emphasize his Celtic origins, their Welsh counterparts began to reassert their claim to the legend, a claim which, as we have seen, they had by and large abandoned in the late nineteenth century. In 1913 an Arthurian 'episode' was included in the annual pageant presented in Gwent, which celebrated local customs and traditions. 'The land of Gwent is the land of Arthur', declared Caroline A. Cannon, the organizer of the Arthurian component of the pageant. Cannon criticized those who favoured 'the mystical Arthur' over 'the real historic man', and she added that 'it strikes one as saddening that, as a nation, we are so ignorant of the fact, and care so little for the honour, that to this country belongs the glorious tradition which gave rise to these legends', In the episode, her Arthur wore a 'British . . . royal cloak', and his 'helmet-crown' was 'surmounted with the great Celtic dragon', thus ensuring that there was no confusion about his ethnic identity.[11]

Two decades later another voice protested about efforts to conceal King Arthur's true historical origins. In 1934 an article appeared in the *Maidenhead Advertiser* announcing the forthcoming publication of a one-shilling history of King Arthur. The anonymous author of the volume complained that

the Anglo-Saxon element remains so strong in our Universities and Museums, that it is rare indeed to find any but pro-Anglo-Saxon professors amongst their leading lights or principals. The truly British student is much needed amongst those who seek and accept British chairs of learning and British emoluments. Great is but a relative term, and often misused, or just given to favourites. The Dominies give Alfred this aggrandisement and a prominent place as a Saxon king in historical fact, while hiding Arthur in fiction, giving him merely the hal [*sic*] of an imaginary heraldic visionary, whose trappings they picture from the tournament days of several centuries later than his real period.

He declared that his intention was to restore Arthur's historicity, even though 'to many minds, to reduce King Arthur to the level of a real personage, is to make him both uninteresting and unbelievable'. His objectives were made even clearer in his concluding sentence, which stated in oversized capital letters: 'ANGLO-SAXON IS NOT BRITISH WHICH IS CELTIC'.[12]

As these early examples indicate, the twentieth century has seen a

---

[11] Catherine A. Cannon, *The Arthurian Episode in the Pageant of Gwent* (Gwent, [1913]), 3, 5, 10, 15.   [12] *King Arthur of Britain* (Maidenhead: ABC Publishers, 1934).

growing effort to rediscover Arthur's true historical identity. This has, on the one hand, been motivated by new archaeological discoveries which have dramatically increased our knowledge about the murky period between the departure of the Romans and the arrival of the Saxons. It has become more and more difficult to assert Arthur's 'Englishness' in the face of mounting evidence to the contrary. In addition, however, the emergence of a revitalized Welsh nationalist movement has contributed to the emergence of a new, 'more Celtic' Arthur as well. In recent years the Welsh have not been content, as they were for much of the nineteenth century, to allow their neighbours to the east to maintain an unchallenged claim to the Arthurian legend, just as they have protested against the Anglicization of many other aspects of Welsh culture.

As well as complicating the racial identities of Robin Hood and King Arthur, the twentieth century has also raised new questions about the roles of women and the British empire in the two legends. At first glance, it would appear that women continued to get short shrift in interpretations of the Arthurian legend. Vivien and Guinevere, in particular, were singled out for condemnation. In a version of the legend intended for Indian students, H. Malim, President of Government College, Mangalore, wrote of Vivien that 'her playful ways were like those of a kitten, and a stranger would have thought her the simplest and most innocent girl in the world. But she was bad at heart, cunning and cruel as a cat, and all her playfulness was but a disguise'. Guinevere, meanwhile, was an even greater villainess whose sin reflected the failings of her sex as whole. According to a young maiden at the convent to which she has fled from Arthur's wrath, 'all women must grieve that a woman has overthrown the Round Table'. Other authors agreed that Guinevere's conduct was a result of the deficiencies of the female sex. In his verse drama *King Arthur Pendragon* (1906), Arthur Dillon writes:

> That women err, is it inevitable?
> Like to the lodestone isle that draws a ship
> By the iron stancheons, by that metal within
> That lusteth after kind, these courtly vessels
> Fraught with a kingdom's honour, this allurement
> Pulls from a pilot's course.

Arthur, however, is absolved from any guilt over his incestuous relationship with his half-sister Morgan Le Fay, because:

> Arthur's secret sin
> Is masculine; and a man's heart can die
> Yet leave the mind intact.[13]

The double standard that had prevailed in the nineteenth century was thus seemingly alive and well in the twentieth, as the female characters of the Arthurian legend were condemned for behaviour that was tolerated in their male counterparts.

At the same time, however, there were some indications that this situation was beginning to change. In the first place, after the first decades of the twentieth century gender issues no longer played such a prominent part in Arthurian literature, as fewer and fewer authors dealt with them explicitly. In addition, those authors who did focus upon this theme were often more flexible than their Victorian predecessors had been when it came to assessing the conduct of the female characters. Dillon's Guinevere is no passive victim, but a strong woman who does not grovel at Arthur's feet when confronted with the consequences of her actions. Nor does she subjugate herself to Lancelot. When he begs her to marry him, she resists, asking:

> What is this? What art thou desiring? Paint
> The picture of our commonwealth. Our subjects
> Obsequious, faithful, attendant on us,
> Our peoples would be lamentations; our fields,
> Our cities washed with navigable woe
> For streams whose commerce curses; and all our time
> Stood at a treasury-full of self-contempt,
> Oceans of tears, a firmament of sighs,
> A universe of sorrow without end.[14]

Only Guinevere, Dillon asserts, comprehends what she and Lancelot have done. In the play's final scene she convinces him that there is only one way out, and the two lovers hurl themselves into the sea.

The most complex portrait of Guinevere from the first half of the twentieth century, however, is contained in White's *The Once and Future King*, which depicts her as a fully developed character rather than as a failed feminine ideal. White's Guenever is strong, intelligent, courageous, and forthright, with none of the artificial delicacy and innocence of the Victorian stereotype. She performs her role as queen to perfection, handling her public, ceremonial duties very adeptly.

---

[13] H. Malim, *King Arthur* (Bombay and Madras, 1914), 78, 94; Arthur Dillon, *King Arthur Pendragon* (London, 1906), 50-1, 81.　　　　[14] Dillon, *King Arthur Pendragon*, 192.

White also provides his readers with reasons to feel sympathy for Guenever. Her life is largely solitary, as she is excluded from the male camaraderie of the Round Table. Childless and often husbandless when Arthur is away or preoccupied with political matters, she turns to Lancelot to fill the void. In short, White's Guenever is a tragic figure: a modern woman trapped in a medieval world. His treatment has served as the model for numerous subsequent literary interpretations which have revised the traditional, negative depiction of Guinevere, including those by Marion Zimmer Bradley, Fay Sampson, Sharan Newman, Portia Baker, and Persia Wolley.[15]

In contrast, Maid Marian's character has not required such drastic revision in the twentieth century. As an active, aggressive heroine, she has found it far easier to adapt to the demands of modern womanhood. Marian, writes the anonymous author of *The Adventures of Robin Hood* (1947), was 'no damsel to sit idle in a bower, weaving tapestry and dreaming vain romantic dreams of chivalry; but, clad in buckskins, she would take to the greenwood with her brother and merry men when . . . they went hunting. . . . More boy than girl she was'. To be sure, there were authors who were discomfited by her gender-bending behaviour. In the preface to his *Five Robin Hood Plays* (1932), Ronald Gow declares that 'Maid Marian puzzles me, and so I have left her out. What kind of girl is she to be gallivanting with these forest men? Is she a good cook?' For the most part, however, her behaviour continued to be condoned, and she was allowed to cross conventional gender boundaries without sanction. In Agnes Blundell's *They Met Robin Hood* (1936), she appears before the young Saxon Osmund with hair 'cut short at the neck like Osmund's own' and wearing 'buskins of deerskin . . . and a short, belted tunic'. Astonished, he asks: 'Are you a youth or a lady?' Her reply of 'I am Maid Marian, sweetheart!' reveals that conventional gender categories are insufficient to contain her.[16]

In Chapter 6 we explored the conflict over the pursuit of empire in the second half of the nineteenth century, and how the legends of King Arthur and Robin Hood were deployed on opposite sides of the debate. As these tensions mounted after 1900, Arthur and his knights continued to be depicted as the defenders of a vast empire that brought

---

[15] See Amanda Serrano, 'T. H. White's Defence of Guenever: Portrait of a "Real Person"', *Mythlore*, 21 (1995), 9–13.

[16] *The Adventures of Robin Hood* (London and Glasgow: Collins, 1947), 13; Ronald Gow, *Five Robin Hood Plays* (London and Edinburgh: Thomas Nelson, 1932), p. vi; Agnes Blundell, *They Met Robin Hood* (London: Burnes, Oates and Washbourne, 1936), 66–7.

peace and unity to the world. The second act of Francis Coutts's *The Romance of King Arthur* (1907) opens with a happy scene in which Arthur declares:

> My lords and gentlemen-at-arms, the world
> Has never yet beheld a realm so blest
> As England; full of freedom, full of faith
> In great things yet undone. From shore to shore,
> Against all evil customs ride our knights;
> Peace is within our borders, and beyond,
> We dominate the sea; which while we hold,
> We hold the overlordship of the world.

A similar vision is presented in *The Marvellous History of King Arthur in Avalon* (1904), a satire of the current political scene by one 'Geoffrey Junior', who sets himself up as a modern-day Geoffrey of Monmouth. In one scene the nations of Arthur's empire gather together to proclaim their loyalty and good fortune at being under British rule:

> Through thee we still retain our birthright old,
> And all our diverse lives are one in thee;
> As planets curb their eccentricity,
> And round the sun their steadfast orbits hold:
> Thy realm has many members: each is free:
> How shall the Many to one purpose bind
> The will of each? or how shall each agree
> To bend his will to meet the Common Mind?
> This shall no art, nor system well defined,
> Nor Parliament, achieve; but joint Renown,
> And Mutual Commerce, and the love of Kind,
> That joins in bond of blood both king and clown,
> Shall link a hundred states about a central Crown.[17]

Previously, we have seen how in the late nineteenth century British authors turned to the quest for the Holy Grail, and in particular to the story of Sir Galahad, as an appropriate metaphor for imperial endeavour. Although there were fewer examples of the Arthurian legend being used in this way in the first half of the twentieth century, they did occasionally occur. In 1937 Trevor Wallace published a novel for young adults entitled *Galahad of the Air*. Set in New Guinea, it features a pilot

---

[17] Francis Coutts, *The Romance of King Arthur* (London, 1907), 91–2; 'Geoffrey Junior', *The Marvellous History of King Arthur in Avalon and of The Lifting of Lyonnesse: A Chronicle of the Round Table Communicated by Geoffrey of Monmouth* (London, 1904), 105–6.

named Daniel James who bears the 'responsibility of maintaining law
and order' in the district surrounding a mining camp. As the indigenous population grows increasingly disturbed by the intrusions of the
Europeans, Daniel attempts to prevent a full-scale uprising. In the
process he discovers that the natives are being encouraged by 'a certain
interested Power', clearly intended to be the Germans, who want to
drive the British from New Guinea and claim the colony for themselves. In the end, however, Daniel and the British prevail. The Germans are killed when their plane is shot down, and the native rebellion
is suppressed before it can start.[18]

On the surface, then, *Galahad of the Air* appears to represent a
conventional employment of the story of Sir Galahad to promote
imperial enterprise. A closer look, however, displays a more complex
attitude than can be found in its late-nineteenth-century counterparts.
Throughout the novel, Wallace shows considerable sympathy for the
indigenous population, and recognizes that many of their grievances
are legitimate. Daniel James acknowledges that this

was not the case of a vastly superior white man pitting his intelligence against a
dull-witted inferior race, but rather a bitter struggle between an intruding
civilization and keenly alert brown men at home in their own forest jungles;
resentfully determined to resist every inroad upon the land over which their
fathers had hunted, roamed and fought since times immemorial.

The primary reason for native discontent is that two members of the
tribe of Chief Tupec have been kidnapped and tortured by unscrupu-
lous Europeans determined to 'wrest the secret of a hidden treasure
cave' from them. Although Daniel attempts to quell the rebellion by
dropping bombs upon their village from his airplane, he does feel
sympathy for the New Guineans: 'After all, it was their land that was
being invaded'. Later, Daniel confronts Tupec and asks him why he so
hates the white man:

'Because he destroys my people', he answered simply. 'Is that not enough?'
   'But we don't', James protested. 'We—'
Tupec laughed scornfully, and . . . his prisoner realized the hollowness of his
words, even as he spoke them.

At the novel's end, Daniel's friend Tom declares that 'there is room for
both white and black in this world'.[19] Clearly, it is a message of racial

   [18] Trevor Wallace, *Galahad of the Air* (London: Wright and Brown, [1937]), 7, 81.
   [19] Ibid. 8, 13–4, 40, 248.

harmony, and not one of imperial conquest, which Wallace attempts to promote.

If the use of the Arthurian legend to support imperialism grew more complicated in the first half of the twentieth century, then so did the use of the legend of Robin Hood to criticize it. On the one hand, many of the elements of Victorian 'Little England-ism' remained intact. King Richard the Lion-hearted continued to be castigated for abandoning his realm for the Crusades. In *Told in Sherwood* (1931), Hugh Chesterman writes:

The laws of God and man were being constantly broken by those whose business it was to uphold them. Pillage and robbery were rife. The greed, ever unsatisfied, of the prince and his lawless court preyed upon rich and poor alike. Every day came tales of castles stormed and looted, of land confiscated, of the houses of peasants burnt to the ground and themselves driven into the forest as homeless and beggared outcasts. The king, whose arm should have been strong to protect his people, was in a foreign land, busy winning honours in the Holy Wars. Little wonder that Englishmen began to sigh for his return and to say that a king's place should be with his people.

Also lingering into the twentieth century was the notion that contact with foreigners, especially those of different skin colours, was dangerous. In *For Richard and the Right*, the fifth instalment of *The Robin Hood Library* (1912), Friar Tuck attempts to rescue Maid Marian from the evil clutches of Baron Roystone. At Roystone Castle, however, he is tricked by 'Melchior the Saracen', who uses magic to stun him. As Tuck stands helpless, he sees 'an evil, mocking light' glowing in the eyes of 'the dark-visaged stranger'. Later they engage in hand-to-hand combat: 'The Oriental's eyes flamed with passion, and he made a furious slash with his keen scimitar, which, had it taken effect, would have rendered the friar a fitting subject for a coffin'. Tuck succeeds in giving him a buffet with his quarterstaff, and 'with a loud cry to Allah and Mahomet . . . Melchior . . . went down to earth like a felled ox, to rise no more'.[20] In this scene we have all the sources of contamination with which the empire might infect the Mother Country: malevolent, dark-skinned Orientals carrying dangerous, exotic weapons and practising heathen religions.

The examples cited above could have come from Victorian interpretations of the legend of Robin Hood, so similar are they to passages

---

[20] Hugh Chesterman, *Told in Sherwood* (London, Edinburgh and New York: Thomas Nelson, 1931), 7; *The Robin Hood Library*, 5: *For Richard and the Right* (London, [1912]), 19, 27.

referred to above in Chapter 6. In the nineteenth century, however, Robin Hood served not only as a critic but as a subverter of empire, when he adopted the role of a bandit fighting against imperial authority. In the twentieth century this role was developed further, as he was compared to brigands challenging British rule in a variety of imperial contexts. Conventionally, these stories featured outlaws who disrupted imperial enterprise for a time and then were brought to justice, thus suggesting that, in the end, British imperial might would always triumph. In 1912, for example, Sir Edmund C. Cox published *The Exploits of Kesho Naik, Dacoit*, which describes the exploits of a fictional Indian bandit who behaves in a Robin-Hood-like fashion: 'what Kesho robbed from the rich he distributed . . . to the poor'. In this case the outlaw's activities are overtly anti-imperial. Kesho plans to rob a gold shipment which is on its way from the mines of Mysore to London because he is angry 'that the treasure was sent away to London for the English Sahibs; and he said, "It is not meet that these robbers who have taken our country should also take the gold from the earth and remove it to the islands where all men have riches, while here the land is in poverty and people are crying"'. This statement might engender sympathy from a late-twentieth-century, post-colonial audience, but Cox, a former Indian police officer, makes it clear that Kesho is a dangerous criminal who must be stopped. Unlike Robin Hood, he is clearly a villain, with a 'black' heart and a nature 'of craft and deceit'. He eludes capture for a time, but in the end Kesho is apprehended and sentenced to transportation for life to the penal colony in the Andaman Islands. Good thus triumphs over evil, and imperial authority is maintained.[21]

Very similar is Alexander Wilson's *The Crimson Dacoit*, published in 1933. Wilson's story describes the activities of the 'Young India' movement and its crimson-clad leader Ram Chandra, whose object is revolution against British rule. Attempting to frighten people into supporting their agenda, they raid villages and pillage and murder their inhabitants. Ram Chandra declares to Ian Hunter, the British police officer in charge of the case:

The time has come when you and your race must be driven to your own bloated country—a country inflated and enriched by the blood of the weaker nations you have for centuries ground down in oppression and cruelty. I and others have taken the cue from Mahatma Gandhi, but whereas he dreamt of a

[21] Sir Edmund C. Cox, *The Exploits of Kesho Naik, Dacoit* (London, 1912), 13, 53 4.

nation raised on the impossible foundations of non-violence and pacific intention, we realised that only by war and bloodshed can India attain to its proper
sphere in the world. A great conflict has started in a small way, I am doing my
little bit, but the small way will lead to a conflagration that will shake this
country to its foundations and destroy the power that has for so long misruled
it. . . . Only by utter ruthlessness can we conquer, and by utter ruthlessness we
will conquer. . . . My duty as defined to me by my colleagues is to inspire terror
and desolation among the English, and that I will do. . . . Why, I would hang
the whole of your cursed race from every building you have built in India if I
could!

Hunter responds with a spirited defence of British imperialism:

You can't expect to attain complete independence, when Great Britain has
fought and bled and spent millions to put India in the place she now holds. All
the peace and security, prosperity and advancement which this country boasts
to-day is due to the enlightened rule, and considerate government of Britain.
. . . You know. . . . that if you ever attained independence you would plunge
the country into seething discord and internal chaos, when it would become
the prey of any nation that cared to step in and take it. It isn't ripe for
dominion status yet or even provincial self-government. Heal your own self-
inflicted wounds before attempting to demand concessions.[22]

In the end the rebellion is put down and peace is restored; once again,
the efforts of a Robin Hood-esque outlaw to overturn British imperial
rule thus end in failure.

Other authors emphasized not so much the power of the British
empire in combating banditry as they did its moral and spiritual
authority. In 1930 Amy Carmichael published *Raj, Brigand Chief: The
True Story of an Indian Robin Hood*, which tells the inspirational story of
Raj, a young Indian man falsely accused of banditry. Forced to take
refuge in the forest, he becomes the 'Red Tiger', the leader of a gang of
much-feared dacoits. His activities closely resemble those of Robin
Hood, for he treats his victims with gentleness and courtesy, and he
is described as 'a champion of women'.[23] Finally captured, he converts
to Christianity and decides to cease his criminal activities. His last
illegal act is to escape from prison, but once free he refuses to return to
his old life. His reputation persists, however, and he is accused of
crimes which in fact have been committed by others. Pressure mounts

---

[22] Alexander Wilson, *The Crimson Dacoit* (London: Herbert Jenkins, 1933), 157-8.
[23] Amy Carmichael, *Raj, Brigand Chief: The True Story of an Indian Robin Hood Driven by
Persecution to Dacoity* (London: Seeley, Service and Co., 1930), 40.

on the British authorities to bring this dangerous outlaw to justice, and after an intense manhunt Raj is apprehended and shot.

Eight years later another version of this story was published by Hugh A. Evan Hopkins. Although virtually identical in its narrative to Carmichael's, Evan Hopkins's tale places a far greater emphasis on the conversion of Raj to Christianity:

There are thousands upon thousands in India to-day to whom God is nothing more than that—a vague idea—and who have nothing and no one to worship apart from these stone idols, the work of men's hands, lifeless, dirty, grim and evil . . . Those at home do not realise the power of the devil in a country which for endless years has been given up to him. But we have a God who is stronger, and within a few years Raj had his eyes opened, and his heart was won over by the God of Purity and Love, and he left for ever the 'wretched ways of the abominable devil,' as he himself put it.[24]

In the accounts of Carmichael and Evan Hopkins, it is thus not so much the might of the British empire which results in the failure of these criminal efforts to destroy or at least disrupt it, but the ostensible superiority of the Christian faith. Whatever the case may be, though, the outcome is the same: British imperial authority remains intact.

There is, however, one interesting variation on this narrative motif. In 1939 Edwin Dale published a boys' adventure story entitled *Don Sabre: The Desert Robin Hood*. Dale's tale describes the efforts of a British colonial government in an unnamed Middle Eastern country to bring a dangerous and subversive bandit known as the 'Tiger' to justice. Dale writes that the Tiger 'hated the English who were in his country ruling his people, and he was determined to overthrow them'. In this case, however, it is not the Tiger who is explicitly compared to Robin Hood, but rather Don Sabre, 'the desert Robin Hood', a public-school-educated Englishman with 'bronzed' skin who could 'pass anywhere in the desert for an Arab'. Don Sabre is a T. E. Lawrence-type figure who attempts to protect the local European population from the Tiger's depredations. In the climactic scene the Tiger attacks a caravan of British soldiers bringing food to a starving province. Badly outnumbered and short of ammunition, the British are on the brink of annihilation when Don Sabre arrives and saves the day. At the conclusion of the story Dale declares that 'at last the menace of the Tiger, king of desert bandits, was over! Don Sabre, the Desert Robin Hood,

---

[24] Hugh A. Evan Hopkins, *Raj the Dacoit: The Real Story of an Indian Robin Hood* (London: Seeley, Service and Company, 1938), 25–6.

had triumphed'.[25] Here, then, we have an example of Robin Hood promoting rather than undermining imperial endeavour, suggesting that, as in the case of King Arthur, his relationship to imperialism became more complex in the twentieth century. Perhaps, as imperial tensions mounted in the period prior to the Second World War, Britons began looking for assistance from a most unlikely source. Dale's work suggests that hopes for the future of the empire were coming to rest less on the colonial administration and more on individual heroes like Don Sabre.

For the most part, however, the legends of King Arthur and Robin Hood continued in the first half of the twentieth century to represent points of view which were in diametric opposition to each other. 'Just as King Arthur was the hero of the knightly classes . . . so Robin Hood was the hero . . . among men of a poorer sort', wrote Henry Gilbert in *Robin Hood and the Men of the Greenwood* (1912).[26] That this was the case is not surprising given the traditional political, social, and cultural orientations of the two legends. One is the story of a great and mighty king, while the other is that of a lowly outlaw. One has conventionally been invoked by the elite or those in their employ, while the other has been the possession of the people at large. That two such different figures could simultaneously function as national heroes suggests that British national identity is more complex than historians have often assumed. Beneath its more vociferous and jingoistic expressions lies a plethora of debates over the form the nation should take.

[25] Edwin Dale, *Don Sabre: The Desert Robin Hood*, Champion Library 244 (London, 1939), 4–5, 62.
[26] Henry Gilbert, *Robin Hood and the Men of the Greenwood* (Edinburgh and London, 1912), p. vii.

Bibliography

PRIMARY SOURCES—MANUSCRIPT

Notes of Joseph Hunter, British Library, Additional MS 24480.
Miscellaneous Letters, British Library, Additional MS 38899.

PRIMARY SOURCES—PRINTED

ALEXANDER, A., *Robin Hood: A Romance of the English Forest* (London, 1900).
ALLINGHAM, WILLIAM, *The Ballad Book: A Selection of the Choicest British Ballads* (London and Cambridge, 1864).
ANDREWS, WILLIAM (ed.), *The Derbyshire Gatherer of Archaeological, Historical, Biographical Facts, Folklore, Etc.* (Buxton, 1880).
(Anon.), *A Pleasant Commodie Called Looke About You: A Critical Edition*, ed. Richard S. M. Hirsch (New York: Garland, 1980).
—— *The History of the Robin Hood Society* (London, 1764).
—— *The Famous English Archer; or, Robert, Earl of Huntington* (Monaghan, 1797).
—— Review article on Joseph Ritson's *Robin Hood: A Collection of Poems, Songs, and Ballads Relative to that Celebrated English Outlaw*, in *British Critic*, 9 (1797), 17–21.
—— Review article on Joseph Ritson's *Robin Hood: A Collection of Poems, Songs, and Ballads Relative to that Celebrated English Outlaw*, in *Critical Review*, NS 28 (1798), 228– 9.
—— 'The Life of Mr. John Joseph Merlin', *The Wonderful and Scientific Museum*, 1 (1803), 274–9.
—— 'The Cheshire Enchanter', *Manchester Mail*, 28 May 1805, 3.
—— *The History and Famous Exploits of Robin Hood* (Banbury, [1805?]).
—— *Ancien Ballads; Selected from Percy's Collection; with Explanatory Notes, Taken from Different Authors, for the Use and Entertainment of Young Persons, by a Lady* (London, 1807).
—— *The Extraordinary Life and Adventures of Robin Hood, Captain of the Robbers of Sherwood Forest* (London, [1810?]).
—— 'Vittoria', *European Magazine*, 64 (1813), 146–7.
—— *The History of Robin Hood* (London, [1816]).
—— *The Round Table. The Order and Solemnities of Crowning the King: and the Dignities of His Peerage with Remarks in Vindication of Both* (London, 1820).

—— *Famous Exploits of Robin Hood: including An Account of his Birth, Education, and Death* (Penrith, [1820?]).

—— 'Triads of the Isle of Britain', *Cambro-Briton*, 1 (1820), 201–5.

—— 'Merlin's Cave', *Chimney Corner Companion*, 10 (1827), 223–4.

—— 'Welsh War Song', *Carmarthen Journal*, 9 Mar. 1827, 4.

—— 'Merlin Redivivus: A Dramatic Scene', *Monmouthshire Merlin*, 23 May 1829, 4.

—— *The Celebrated History of the Renowned Robin Hood, the Merry Outlaw of Sherwood Forest* (Glasgow, [1830]).

—— 'Merlin's Prophecy for the Year 1831', *Monthly Magazine*, NS 11 (1831), 1–3.

—— Article on Robin Hood in *Westminster Review*, 33 (1839–40).

—— *The Life and Death of Robin Hood, the Renowned Outlaw* (Falkirk?, [1840?]).

—— *Alderley Edge and Its Neighbourhood* (Macclesfield, [1843]).

—— 'The Knight of the Magic Loom', *Punch*, 9 (1845), 189.

—— *Historical Anecdotes of the Life of Robin Hood; with a Collection of the Ancient Poems, Song and Ballads Relative to that Celebrated English Outlaw* (London, 1846).

—— *General Laws for the Government of the Ancient Order of Foresters* (Manchester, 1846).

—— Review article on Robert Southey's *Robin Hood: A Fragment*, in *Edinburgh Review*, 86 (1847), 122–38.

—— *Old English Ballads, A Selection from Percy, Ritson, and Other Sources* (London, 1848).

—— Review article on Edward Bulwer Lytton's *King Arthur*, in *Illustrated London News*, 25 Mar. 1848, 200.

—— Review article on Edward Bulwer Lytton's *King Arthur*, in *Athenaeum*, 11 Mar. 1848, 262.

—— Review article on Edward Bulwer Lytton's *King Arthur*, in *Examiner*, 27 Jan. 1849, 52.

—— Review article on Edward Bulwer Lytton's *King Arthur*, in *Sharpe's London Journal*, 9 (1849), 373–5.

—— Review article on Edward Bulwer Lytton's *King Arthur*, in *Edinburgh Review*, 90 (1849), 173–212.

—— *The Life of Robin Hood: To Which Is Annexed Robin Hood's Garland* (Dublin, 1852).

—— *Arthur's Knights: An Adventure from the Legend of the Sangrale* (Edinburgh, 1859).

—— Obituary of Sir John Franklin, in *The Times*, 23 Sept. 1859, 1.

—— 'King Arthur and His Round Table', *Blackwood's Edinburgh Magazine*, 88 (1860), 311–37.

—— *Aunt Louisa's London Toy Books: Robin Hood and His Merry Men* (London, [1860]).

—— 'La Mort D'Arthur', *Dublin University Magazine*, 55 (1860), 497–512.

—— *The Life and Exploits of Robin Hood: and Robin Hood's Garland* (Halifax, 1862).

—— *Alderley Edge: A Guide to All Its Points of Interest* (Manchester, 1863).

—— Review article on F. J. Furnivall (ed.), *Arthur: A Short Sketch of His Life and History*, in *Gentleman's Magazine*, NS 18 (1865), 227–8.

—— Review article on Edward Strachey (ed.), *Morte Darthur*, in *Athenaeum*, Pt. 1 (1868), 695.

—— Review article on Edward Strachey (ed.), *Morte Darthur*, in *Notes and Queries*, 4: 1 (1868), 428.

—— 'Mr. Tennyson's Arthurian Poems', *Dublin Review*, 75 (1870), 418–29.

—— 'Malory', *Encyclopaedia Britannica*, Vol. 10 (9th edn., Edinburgh, 1879).

—— *The Story of Arthur and Guinevere, and the Fate of Sir Lancelot of the Lake. As Told in Antique Legends and Ballads, and in Modern Poetry* (London, [1879]).

—— *Six Ballads about King Arthur* (London, 1881).

—— *Second Quarterly Report of the Fifty-Eighth Executive Council of the Ancient Order of Foresters* (Ipswich, 1892).

—— *Third Quarterly Report of the Fifty-Eighth Executive Council of the Ancient Order of Foresters* (Ipswich, 1892).

—— *Robin Hood Library* (London, [1912]).

—— *King Arthur of Britain* (Maidenhead, 1934).

—— *The Adventures of Robin Hood* (London and Glasgow, 1947).

ANSTICE, JOSEPH, *Richard Cœur de Lion* (Oxford, 1828).

ARBER, EDWARD, *An English Garner, Ingatherings from our History and Literature* (London, 1877–96).

ARNOLD, MATTHEW, *Empedocles on Etna, and Other Poems* (London, 1852).

ASHBEE, C. R., *From Whitechapel to Camelot* (London, 1892).

ASHLEY, DORIS, *King Arthur and the Knights of the Round Table* (London, 1922).

AXON, WILLIAM, *Cheshire Gleanings* (Manchester, 1884).

BANNERMANN, ANNE, *Tales of Superstition and Chivalry* (London, 1802).

BERESFORD HOPE, Alexander James, *Poems* (London, 1843).

BEWICK, THOMAS, *Thomas Bewick: A Memoir*, ed. Iain Bain (Oxford, 1979).

BINGLEY, Revd W., *North Wales; Including its Scenery, Antiquities, Customs, and Some Sketches of its Natural History* (London, 1804).

BLAAUW, WILLIAM HENRY, *The Barons' War Including the Battles of Lewes and Evesham* (Lewes, 1844).

BLACKMORE, RICHARD, *Prince Arthur*, 4th edn. (London, 1714).

BLATCHFORD, ROBERT, *Merrie England* (London, 1894).

BLUNDELL, AGNES, *They Met Robin Hood* (London, 1936).

BOWMAN, ANNE, *The Boy Foresters. A Tale of the Days of Robin Hood* (London, [1868]).

BRISCOE, JOHN POTTER (ed.), *Old Nottinghamshire: A Collection of Papers on the History, Antiquities, Topography, &c., of Nottinghamshire*, 2nd series (London and Nottingham, 1884).

BROOKE-HUNT, VIOLET, *Young King Arthur* (London and Edinburgh, 1897).

BROUGH, WILLIAM, *King Arthur; or, The Days and Knights of the Round Table* (London, 1863).

BROUGH BROTHERS, *The Last Edition of Ivanhoe* (London, [1850]).

BROWN, CORNELIUS, *Lives of Nottinghamshire Worthies and of Celebrated and Remarkable Men of the County from the Norman Conquest to AD 1882* (London and Nottingham, 1882).

BROWN, JOHN CROUMBIE, *The Forests of England and the Management of Them in Byegone Times* (Edinburgh, 1883).

BROWNE, FELICIA DOROTHEA, *England and Spain; or, Valour and Patriotism* (London, 1808).

BRUCE, CHARLES, *The Story of Queen Guinevere and Lancelot of the Lake. After the German of Wilhelm Hertz. With Other Poems* (London, 1865).

BUCHANAN, R. WILLIAMS, 'Merlin's Tomb', *The Glasgow University Album for 1838* (Glasgow, 1838), 1–8.

—— 'Merlin and the White Death', *Once a Week*, 10 (1863–4), 251–2.

BULWER LYTTON, EDWARD, *The Siamese Twins. A Satirical Tale of the Times. With Other Poems* (London, 1831).

—— *King Arthur* (London, 1849).

BURGES, JAMES BLAND, *Richard the First* (London, 1801).

BURKE, EDMUND, *Reflections on the Revolution in France* (London, 1912).

BURNAND, SIR FRANCIS COWLEY, *Robin Hood; or, The Forester's Fate* (London, 1862).

BURNETT, GEORGE, *Specimens of English Prose-Writers, from the Earliest Times to the Close of the Seventeenth Century* (London, 1807).

BURNS, JAMES, *Sir Galahad: A Call to the Heroic* (London, [1914]).

BURRAGE, ALFRED S., *The Robin Hood Library* (London, [1901–6]).

BYRON, HENRY JAMES, *Jack the Giant Killer; or, Harlequin King Arthur, and Ye Knights of Ye Round Table* (London, [1859]).

CAMPBELL, JAMES A., *Tennyson's Idylls of the King, Epic and Allegory* (Dublin, 1896).

CANNON, CATHERINE A., *The Arthurian Episode in the Pageant of Gwent* (Gwent, [1913]).

CARMICHAEL, AMY, *Raj, Brigand Chief: The True Story of an Indian Robin Hood Driven by Persecution to Dacoity* (London, 1930).

CARR, J. COMYNS, *King Arthur* (London, 1895).

CHALMERS, ALEXANDER (ed.), *The History of the Renowned Prince Arthur, King of Britain* (London, 1816).

CHAMBERS, ROBERT, *The Book of Days: A Miscellany of Popular Antiquities* (London and Edinburgh, 1864).

CHESTERMAN, HUGH, *Told in Sherwood* (London, Edinburgh and New York, 1931).

CLARKE, ADAM, *Detached Pieces; Including, Critiques on Various Publications, Historical Sketches, Biographical Notices, Correspondence, &c., &c., &c.* (London, 1837).

CONYBEARE, EDWARD, *La Morte D'Arthur: The History of King Arthur, Compiled by Sir Thomas Malory* (London, 1868).

COSTELLO, LOUISA STUART, *The Maid of the Cyprus Isle, and Other Poems* (London, 1815).

—— *The Falls, Lakes and Mountains of North Wales* (London, 1845).

COTTLE, JOSEPH, *The Fall of Cambria*, 2nd edn. (London, 1811).

COUTTS, FRANCIS, *The Romance of King Arthur* (London, 1907).

COX, SIR EDMUND C., *The Exploits of Kesho Naik, Dacoit* (London, 1912).

COX, GEORGE W., *An Introduction to the Science of Comparative Mythology and Folklore* (London, 1881).

COXE, WILLIAM, *An Historical Tour in Monmouthshire* (London, 1801).

CRAIK, DINAH MARIA MULOCK, *Avillion and Other Tales* (London, 1853).

CUNNINGHAM, ALLAN, 'The Old English Ballads', *Penny Magazine*, 7 (1838), 301–4.

DALE, EDWIN, *Don Sabre: The Desert Robin Hood*, Champion Library, 244 (London, 1939).

DARLEY, GEORGE, 'Merlin's Last Prophecy', *Athenaeum*, 14 July 1838, 495–6.

DAVIDSON, GLADYS, *The Story of Robin Hood. Told Simply for the Lower Standards* (London and Edinburgh, [1908]).

DAVIES, HENRY, 'Ode', *Cambrian Quarterly Magazine*, 4 (1832), 544–5.

DILLON, ARTHUR, *King Arthur Pendragon* (London, 1906).

DIXON, FREDERICK, 'The Round Table', *Temple Bar*, 109 (1896), 201–13.

DONOVAN, EDWARD, *Descriptive Excursions through South Wales and Monmouthshire, in the Year 1804, and the Four Preceding Summers* (London, 1805).

DWIGHT, HENRY OTIS, *A Muslim Sir Galahad: A Present Day Story of Islam in Turkey* (New York and London, 1913).

EGAN, PIERCE, *Robin Hood and Little John or the Merry Men of Sherwood Forest*, 2nd edn. (London, 1850).

ELLIS, GEORGE, *Specimens of Early English Metrical Romance* (London, 1805).

ELSDALE, HENRY, *Studies in the Idylls: An Essay on Mr. Tennyson's 'Idylls of the King'* (London, 1878).

ELWES, ALFRED (ed. and trans.), *Geoffrey the Knight. A Tale of Chivalry of the Days of King Arthur* (London, 1869).

EMMETT, GEORGE, *Robin Hood and the Outlaws of Sherwood Forest* (London, 1869).

EVAN HOPKINS, Hugh A., *Raj the Dacoit: The Real Story of an Indian Robin Hood* (London, 1938).

EVANS, JOHN, *Letters Written during a Tour through South Wales, in the Year 1803, and at Other Times* (London, 1804).

EVANS, SEBASTIAN, *In the Studio: A Decade of Poems* (London, 1875).

EVANS, THOMAS, *Old Ballads, Historical and Narrative, with Some of Modern Date* (London, 1777).

FINNEMORE, JOHN, *The Story of Robin Hood and His Merry Men* (London, 1909).

FITZGERALD, PERCY (ed.), *The Life, Letters and Writings of Charles Lamb* (London and Philadelphia, 1895).

FORD, HORACE A., *Archery: Its Theory and Practice*, 2nd edn. (London, 1859).

'Forest Ranger', *Little John and Will Scarlett; or, The Outlaws of Sherwood Forest* (London, 1865).

FRITH, HENRY, *King Arthur and his Knights of the Round Table* (London, 1884).

FULLARTON, R. MACLEOD, *Merlin: A Dramatic Poem* (Edinburgh and London, 1890).

FURNIVALL, F. J., 'Preface', in *Le Morte Darthur* (London and Cambridge, 1864).

—— (ed.), *Seynt Graal, or the Sank Ryal: The History of the Holy Graal* (London, 1861–3).

—— (ed.), *La Queste del Saint Graal* (London, 1864).

GASKELL, ELIZABETH, *The Letters of Mrs. Gaskell*, ed. J. A. V. Chapple and Arthur Pollard (Manchester, 1966).

GASTINEAU, HENRY, *North Wales Illustrated, in a Series of Views, Comprising the Picturesque Scenery, Towns, Castles, Seats of the Nobility and Gentry, Antiquities, &c.* (London, 1830).

'Geoffrey Junior', *The Marvellous History of King Arthur in Avalon and of The Lifting of Lyonnesse: A Chronicle of the Round Table Communicated by Geoffrey of Monmouth* (London, 1904).

GIFFARD, SIR AMBROSE HARDINGE, *Verses* (London, 1824).

GILBERT, HENRY, *Robin Hood and the Men of the Greenwood* (London, 1912).

GILLIAT, EDWARD, *In Lincoln Green: A Merrie Tale of Robin Hood* (London, 1897).

—— *Wolf's Head: A Story of the Prince of Outlaws* (London, 1899).

GLENNIE, JOHN S. STUART, *King Arthur: or, The Drama of the Revolution*, Volume II: *Play the First. The Romance of the Forest: or, The Youth of Arthur* (London, 1870).

GOADBY, EDWIN, 'Who Was Robin Hood?', *Sharpe's London Magazine*, 23 (1863), 307–12.

GODWIN, WILLIAM, *Things as They Are; or, The Adventures of Caleb Williams* (London, 1794).

—— Obituary of Joseph Ritson, in *Monthly Magazine*, 16 (1803), 375–6.

GOLLANCZ, ISRAEL (ed.), *Le Morte Darthur by Sir Thomas Malory* (London, [1897]).

GOODYER, F. R., *Once upon a Time: or, A Midsummer Night's Dream in Merrie Sherwood* (Nottingham, 1868).

GOW, RONALD, *Five Robin Hood Plays* (London and Edinburgh, 1932).

GRANGE, A. M., *A Modern Galahad* (London, 1895).

GUDGIN, F., *Robin Hood and His Merry Men* (London, 1919).

GURTEEN, S. HUMPHREYS, *The Arthurian Epic: A Comparative Study of the Cambrian, Breton, and Anglo-Norman Versions of the Story and Tennyson's Idylls of the King* (New York and London, 1895).

GUTCH, JOHN MATTHEW, *A Lytell Geste of Robin Hode with other Ancient and Modern Ballads and Songs Relating to this Celebrated Yeoman* (London, 1847).

HAIGH, J. L., *Sir Galahad of the Slums* (London, [1907]).

HALES, JOHN W. and FURNIVALL, FREDERICK J., *Bishop Percy's Folio Manuscript. Ballads and Romances* (London, 1867).

HALL, SAMUEL CARTER (ed.), *Book of British Ballads* (London, 1842).

HALL, SPENCER T., *The Forester's Offering* (London, 1841).

—— *Rambles in the Country* (London, 1842).

HALLAM, HENRY, *Introduction to the Literature of Europe, in the Fifteenth, Sixteenth, and Seventeenth Centuries*, 4th edn. (London, 1854).

HALLIWELL, J. O. (ed.), *The Chronicle of William de Rishamger, of the Barons' Wars. The Miracles of Simon de Montfort* (London, 1840).

HAMLEY, GENERAL EDWARD, 'Sir Tray: An Arthurian Idyl', *Blackwood's Edinburgh Magazine*, 108 (1873), 120.

HANSON, CHARLES HENRY, *Stories of the Days of King Arthur* (London, 1882).

HARDY, JAMES, 'Legends of King Arthur and of Sewingshields', in Moses Aaron Richardson (ed.), *The Local Historians' Table Book, of Remarkable Occurrences, Historical Facts, Traditions, Legendary and Descriptive Ballads, &c., &c.* (London, 1843), 45–6.

HARRIS, AUGUSTUS HENRY GLOSSOP, *Babes in the Wood; Robin Hood and his Men; and Harlequin Who Killed Cock Robin* (London, 1888).

HARRIS, WILLIAM CORNWALLIS, *Portraits of the Game and Wild Animals of Southern Africa* (London, 1840).

HARRISON, W., *Ripon Millenary: A Record of the Festival* (Ripon, 1892).

HASLEHURST, GEORGE, *Penmaen-Mawr, and Day-Break: Poems* (London, 1849).

HASLEWOOD, JOSEPH (ed.), *La Mort D'Arthur* (London, 1816).

HASTINGS, THOMAS, *The British Archer; or, Tracts on Archery* (London, 1831).

HAWKER, ROBERT STEPHEN, *The Quest of the Sangraal. Chant the First* (Exeter, 1864).

HAZLITT, W. CAREW (ed.), *Tales and Legends of National Origin or Widely Current in England from Early Times* (London, 1892).

HEATON, WILLIAM, *The Story of Robin Hood* (London, 1870).

HEBER, REGINALD, *The Poetical Works of Reginald Heber*, new edn. (London, 1854).

HENTY, G. A. (ed.), *Yule-Tide Yarns* (London, New York, and Bombay, 1899).

HERBERT, ALGERNON, *Britannia after the Romans* (London, 1836).

HILTON, WILLIAM, *The Poetical Works of William Hilton* (Newcastle, 1776).

HINDLEY, Charles, *Tavern Anecdotes and Sayings*, new edn. (London, 1881).

HODGETTS, J. FREDERICK, *Edwin the Boy Outlaw, or The Dawn of Freedom in England* (London, 1887).

HOGG, THOMAS, *The Fabulous History of the Ancient Kingdom of Cornwall* (London, 1827).

HOLT, ARDEN, *Fancy Dresses Described; or, What to Wear at Fancy Balls*, 4th edn. (London, 1879).

HOPE, HENRY G., 'King Arthur', *Notes and Queries*, 6: 11 (1885), 54.

HOWELLS, WILLIAM, *Cambrian Superstitions, Comprising Ghosts, Omens, Witchcraft, Traditions, &c.* (Tipton, 1831).

HUGHES, JONATHAN, 'Celliwig', *Notes and Queries*, 8: 7 (1895), 90.

HUGHES, THOMAS, *Tom Brown's Schooldays* (London and New York, 1994).

HUNT, LEIGH, 'The Dogs', *The Liberal*, 1 (1822), 246–59.

HUNT, ROBERT, *Popular Romances of the West of England; or, The Drolls, Traditions, and Superstitions of Old Cornwall* (London, 1865).

HUNTER, JOSEPH, *Critical and Historical Tracts* (London, 1852).

IRVING, WALTER, *Tennyson* (Edinburgh and London, 1873).

JAMES, G. P. R., *Forest Days: A Romance of Old Times* (London, 1843).

JOHNSON, R. BRIMLEY, *Popular British Ballads* (London, 1894).

JOHNSON, WILLIAM HENRY, *Sir Galahad of New France* (London, 1905).

JONES, W. LEWIS, *King Arthur in History and Legend* (Cambridge, 1911).

JONSON, BEN, *Ben Jonson: The Complete Masques*, ed. Stephen Orgel (New Haven and London, 1969).

KEATS, JOHN, *Lamia, Isabella, The Eve of St. Agnes and Other Poems* (London, 1820).

KING, CAPTAIN CHARLES, *A Trooper Galahad* (London, 1901).

KITTREDGE, G. L., 'Who Was Sir Thomas Malory?', *Studies and Notes in Philology and Literature*, 5 (1897), 97–106.

KNOWLES, J. T., *The Story of King Arthur and his Knights of the Round Table* (London, 1862).

'L.E.L.', *Poetical Works of Letitia Elizabeth Landon 'L.E.L.': A Facsimile Reproduction of the 1873 Edition*, ed. F. J. Sypher (Delmar, New York, 1990).

LARWOOD, JACOB and HOTTEN, JOHN CAMDEN, *The History of Signboards, from Earliest Times to the Present Day*, 11th edn. (London, 1900).

LAWRENCE, SIR JAMES, 'The Bosom Friend', in *The Etonian Out of Bounds; or, Poetry and Prose*, 1 (London, 1828), 45.

LAWSON LOWE, A. E. (ed.), *Black's Guide to Nottinghamshire* (Edinburgh, 1876).

LEE, SIR SIDNEY, 'Robin Hood', *Dictionary of National Biography* (London, 1891), 258–9.

LEIGH, EGERTON, *Ballads and Legends of Cheshire* (London, 1867).

LEIGH, PERCIVAL, *Jack the Giant Killer* (London, [1843]).

LENNARD, HORACE, *Babes in the Wood and Bold Robin Hood* (Sydenham, 1892).

LEVETT-YEATS, S., *A Galahad of the Creeks and Other Stories* (London and Bombay, 1897).

LEWIS, M. G., *Romantic Tales* (London, 1808).

LEYDEN, JOHN, *Scenes of Infancy: Descriptive of Teviotdale* (Edinburgh, 1803).

LINTON, W. J., *Claribel and Other Poems* (London, 1865).

LLOYD, DAVID, *Characteristics of Men, Manners, and Sentiments; or, The Voyage of Life and Other Poems* (London, 1812).

LLWYD, RICHARD, *Poems. Tales, Odes, Sonnets, Translations from the British, &c. &c.* (Chester, 1804).

LYNN, ESCOTT, *When Lion Heart Was King: A Tale of Robin Hood and Merry Sherwood* (London, 1908).

MACCULLOCH, EDGAR, 'Cornish Folk Lore: King Arthur in the Form of a Raven', *Notes and Queries*, 1: 8 (1853), 618.

MACDONALD, GEORGE, *The Poetical Works of George MacDonald* (London, 1893).

MacNally, Leonard, *Robin Hood; or, Sherwood Forest* (Dublin, 1788).

M'Spadden, J. Walker, *Stories of Robin Hood and His Merry Outlaws Retold from the Old Ballads* (London, 1905).

Maginn, William, 'The Fraserians; or, The Commencement of the Year Thirty-five', *Fraser's Magazine*, 11 (1835), 1–2.

Magnus, Lady Katie, *First Makers of England: Julius Cæsar, King Arthur, Alfred the Great* (London, 1901).

Malim, H., *King Arthur* (Bombay and Madras, 1914).

Malkin, Benjamin Heath, *The Scenery, Antiquities, and Biography, of South Wales, from Materials Collected during Two Excursions in the Year 1803* (London, 1804).

Manners, John Henry, *Journal of Three Years Travels, through Different Parts of Britain, in 1795, 1796, 1797* (London, 1805).

Marsh, George, *The Origin and History of the English Language and of the Early Literature It Embodies* (London, 1862).

Marsh, John B., *The Life and Adventures of Robin Hood* (London, 1865).

Martin, A. T., 'The Identity of the Author of the "Morte d'Arthur," with Notes on the Will of Thomas Malory and the Genealogy of the Malory Family', *Archaeologia*, 56 (1898), 165–82.

—— 'Sir Thomas Malory', *Athenaeum*, 2 (1897), 353–4.

—— '"Mailoria" and Sir Thomas Malory', *Athenaeum*, 2 (1898), 98.

—— 'Society of Antiquaries—June 16', *Athenaeum*, 2 (1898), 827.

—— ed., *Selections from Malory's Le Morte D'Arthur* (London, 1896).

Matthews, Vivian, and Manley, Alick, *Little Red Robin; or, the Dey and the Knight. Original Burlesque Extravaganza* (London, [1900]).

Menzies, Louisa L. J., *Legendary Tales of the Ancient Britons, Rehearsed from the Early Chronicle* (London, 1864).

Meredith, Owen, *Clytemnestra, The Earl's Return, The Artist, and Other Poems* (London, 1855).

Meredith, W. E., *Llewelyn ap Iorwerth. A Poem, in Five Cantos* (London, 1818).

Merivale, J. H., *Orlando in Roncesvalles, A Poem* (London, 1814).

—— *Poems Original and Translated* (London, 1828).

Millhouse, Robert, *Sherwood Forest, and Other Poems* (London, 1827).

Millington, Ellen J., 'King Arthur and His Knights', *The Monthly Packet of Evening Readings for the Younger Members of the Christian Church*, 17 (1859) 253–8, 355–63, and 597–604.

Milman, H. H., *Samor, Lord of the Bright City. An Heroic Poem*, 2nd edn. (London, 1818).

Minto, William, *Characteristics of the English Poets from Chaucer to Shirley* (Edinburgh and London, 1874).

Morris, Richard (ed.), *Sir Gawayne and the Green Knight: An Alliterative Romance-Poem* (London, 1864).

Morris, William, *The Defence of Guenevere and Other Poems* (London, 1858).

Moultrie, John, *Poems* (London, 1837).

MUDDOCK, J. E., *Maid Marian and Robin Hood: A Romance of Old Sherwood Forest* (London, 1892).

MUNDAY, ANTHONY, *The Downfall of Robert Earl of Huntingdon* (Oxford: Malone Society Reprints, 1964).

NEWCOMEN, GEORGE, 'The Lovers of Launcelot (A Critical Study of Sir Thomas Malory's Epic)', *New Ireland Review*, 11 (1899), 44–9.

NEWELL, WILLIAM WELLS (ed.), *King Arthur and the Table Round, Tales Chiefly after the Old French of Crestien of Troyes* (London, [1897]).

NOYES, ALFRED, *Sherwood, or Robin Hood and the Three Kings* (London, 1911).

ODGERS, W. BLAKE, *King Arthur and the Arthurian Romances: A Paper Read Before the Bath Literary and Philosophical Association* (London and Bath, [1872]).

O'KEEFFE, JOHN, *Airs, Duetts, and Chorusses in Merry Sherwood, or Harlequin Forrester*, in Frederick M. Link (ed.), *The Plays of John O'Keeffe*, Vol. 4 (New York and London, 1981).

ORD, JOHN WALKER, *England: An Historical Poem* (London, 1834).

O'SULLIVAN, M. J., *A Fasciculus of Lyric Verses* (Cork, 1846), 63–4.

OXENFORD, JOHN, *Robin Hood: An Opera in Three Acts* (London, 1860).

'An Oxonian', 'Lines Written After Reading the Romance of Arthur's Round Table', *Blackwood's Edinburgh Magazine*, 27 (1830), 705.

PAINE, THOMAS, *The Rights of Man* (Harmondsworth: Pelican, 1976).

PARRY, EDWARD, *Cambrian Mirror, or a New Tourist Companion through North Wales* (London, 1846).

PARRY, Revd J. D., *The Legendary Cabinet: A Collection of British National Ballads, Ancient and Modern* (London, 1829).

PEACOCK, THOMAS LOVE, *The Genius of the Thames* (London, 1810).

—— *Maid Marian* (London, 1822).

—— *The Misfortunes of Elphin* (London, 1829).

PEARSON, CHARLES H., *The Early and Middle Ages of England* (London, 1861).

PENNIE, J. F., *Britain's Historical Drama; A Series of National Tragedies* (London, 1832).

—— 'Richard Cœur de Lion's Arrival on the Coast of Palestine', *Literary Magnet*, NS 2 (1826), 356–60.

PERCY, THOMAS, *Reliques of Ancient English Poetry: Consisting of Old Heroic Ballads, Songs and other Pieces of our Earlier Poets* (London, 1765).

—— *The Correspondence of Thomas Percy and Evan Evans*, ed. Aneirin Lewis (Baton Rouge: Louisiana State UP, 1957).

PORDEN, ELEANOR ANNE, *Cœur de Lion; or The Third Crusade* (London, 1822).

PRIDEAUX, W. F., 'Who Was Robin Hood?', *Notes and Queries*, 7: 2 (1886), 421.

PUGH, EDWIN, *Cambria Depicta: A Tour through North Wales, Illustrated with Picturesque Views* (London, 1816).

QUILLER-COUCH, A. T., *Robin Hood* (Oxford, 1908–12).

RANKING, B. MONTGOMERIE, *La Mort D'Arthur. The Old Prose Stories Whence the 'Idylls of the King' Have Been Taken by Alfred Tennyson* (London, 1871).

RALEIGH, WALTER, *The English Novel; Being a Short Sketch of Its History from the Earliest Times to the Appearance of Waverley* (London, 1894).

REECE, ROBERT, *Little Robin Hood: A New Burlesque Drama* (London, 1882).

RHYS, ERNEST, *Welsh Ballads and Other Poems* (London, [1898]).

—— 'Sir Thomas Malory and the *Morte d'Arthur*', in Charles Dudley Warner (ed.), *Library of the World's Best Literature, Ancient and Modern*, Vol. 17 (New York, 1897), 9645–54.

—— (ed.), *The Book of Marvellous Adventures, and Other Books of the Morte D'Arthur* (London, [1894]).

RIETHMÜLLER, CHRISTOPHER, *Launcelot of the Lake, A Tragedy, in Five Acts* (London, 1843).

RITSON, JOSEPH, *A Select Collection of English Songs* (London, 1783).

—— *Robin Hood: A Collection of Poems, Songs and Ballads Relative to that Celebrated English Outlaw* (London, 1795).

—— *Ancient English Metrical Romances* (London, 1802).

—— *The Letters of Joseph Ritson*, ed. Joseph Frank (London, 1833).

ROCHESTER, GEORGE E., *Captain Robin Hood Skywayman* (London: John Hamilton, 1935).

RODGERS, JOSEPH, *The Scenery of Sherwood Forest* (Worksop, 1898).

ROSCOE, JAMES, 'The Iron Gate—A Legend of Alderley', *Blackwood's Edinburgh Magazine*, 45 (1839), 271–4.

ROSCOE, THOMAS, *Wanderings and Excursions in South Wales, Including the Scenery of the River Wye* (London, [1837]).

RUSSELL, EDWARD, *The Book of King Arthur: A Paper Read before the Literary and Philosophical Society of Liverpool, on the 16th of December, 1889* (Liverpool, 1889).

RYLAND, F., 'The Morte D'Arthur', *English Illustrated Magazine*, 6 (1888–9), 55–64 and 86–92.

SAINTSBURY, GEORGE, *The Flourishing of Romance and the Rise of Allegory* (Edinburgh and London, 1897).

SCOTT, CLEMENT, *From 'The Bells' to 'King Arthur'. A Critical Record of the First-night Productions at the Lyceum Theatre* (London, 1896).

SCOTT, SIR WALTER, *Marmion: A Tale of Flodden Field* (London, 1809).

—— *The Bridal of Triermain* (Edinburgh, 1813).

—— *Ivanhoe*, ed. A. N. Wilson (London and New York: Penguin, 1984).

—— *The Prose Works of Sir Walter Scott*, Vol. 21: *Letters of Malachi Malagrowther on the Currency* (Edinburgh, 1830–6).

—— 'Romance', in *Supplement to the Fourth, Fifth, and Sixth Editions of the Encyclopædia Britannica*, Vol. 6 (Edinburgh, 1824) 455.

—— 'Carle, Now the King's Come!', *Royal Cornwall Gazette*, 10 August 1822, 4.

—— 'Appendix to the General Preface', *Waverley Novels*, Vol. 1 (Edinburgh, 1829).

SEARLE, JANUARY, *Leaves from Sherwood Forest* (London, 1850).

SERVICE, JAMES (ed.), *Metrical Legends of Northumberland* (Alnwick, 1834).

SHORE, T. W., *King Arthur and the Round Table at Winchester* (Hampshire, 1900).

SHORTHOUSE, J. H., *Sir Perceval: A Story of the Past and Present* (London, 1886).

SIMMONS, F. J. (ed.), *The Birth, Life and Acts of King Arthur* (London, 1893–4).

SMIETON, JAMES, *King Arthur: A Dramatic Cantata* (London, [1893?]).

SMITH, GEORGE BARNETT, *Illustrated British Ballads, Old and New* (London, Paris, and New York, 1881).

SOAME, GEORGE, *The Hebrew. A Drama* (London, 1820).

SOMMER, H. OSKAR, 'The Sources of Malory's "Le Morte Darthur"', *Academy*, 37 (1890), 11.

—— (ed.), *Le Morte Darthur by Syr Thomas Malory* (London, 1889–91).

SOUTHEY, ROBERT (ed.), *The Byrth, Lyf, and Actes of Kyng Arthur* (London, 1817).

STERLING, JOHN, 'Richard Cœur de Lion', *Fraser's Magazine*, 39 (1849) 170, 277, and 405.

STOCQUELLER, J. H., *Robin Hood and Richard Cœur de Lion* (London, 1846).

—— *Maid Marian, the Forest Queen* (London, [1849]).

STOKES, HENRY SEWELL, *The Song of Albion: A Poem Commemorative of the Crisis* (London, 1831).

STRACHEY, EDWARD (ed.), *Morte Darthur* (London, 1868).

STREDDER, E., 'Who Was Robin Hood?', *Notes and Queries*, 7: 3 (1887), 201–2, 281– 2.

SWEETMAN, ELINOR, *Pastorals and Other Poems* (London, 1899).

TENNYSON, ALFRED, *Idylls of the King*, ed. J. M. Gray (New Haven and London: Yale UP, 1983).

—— *The Foresters: Robin Hood and Maid Marian* (London, 1892).

The Letters of Alfred Tennyson, ed. Cecil Y. Lang and Edgar F. Shannon, Jr. (Cambridge, Mass.: Belknap Press, 1981–7).

THELWALL, JOHN, *Poems, Chiefly Written in Retirement*, 2nd edn. (Hereford, 1801).

THIERRY, AUGUSTIN, *History of the Conquest of England by the Normans: with its Causes from the Earliest Period, and its Consequences to the Present Time* (London, 1825).

THOMAS, E., 'Briddyn Jubilee, 1782. An Ode', *European Magazine*, 2 (1782), 153–4.

THOMS, WILLIAM JOHN, *A Collection of Early Prose Romances* (London, 1828).

THOMSON, CHRISTOPHER, *The Autobiography of an Artisan* (London, 1847).

THORNE, GEORGE and PALMER, F. GROVE, *Robin Hood and Little John, or Harlequin Friar Tuck and the Merrie Men of Sherwood Forest* (Margate, 1882).

TILNEY, F. C., *Robin Hood and His Merry Outlaws* (London and New York, 1908).

TOMS, MAJOR F. B., *Royal Artillery Gibraltar Christmas Pantomime: 'The Babes in the Wood' and 'Robin Hood'* (Gibraltar, 1897).

TRIPP, Revd HENRY, *A Selection from Percy's Reliques of Ancient English Poetry and from Evans's Old Ballads* (London, 1849).

VERNON, Revd PREBENDARY, 'The Passing of Arthur', *The Sunday at Home* (1896–7), 291–2.

WALFORD, EDWARD (ed.), *Reliques of Ancient English Poetry: Consisting of Old Heroic Ballads, Songs and Other Pieces of our Earlier Poets* (London, 1880).

WALLACE, TREVOR, *Galahad of the Air* (London: Wright and Brown, [1937]).

WALPOLE, HORACE, *The Yale Edition of Horace Walpole's Correspondence*, ed. W. S. Lewis, Vol. 38 (London and New Haven: Yale UP, 1974).

Ward, Lock & Co., *Pictorial and Descriptive Guide to Sherwood Forest and 'The Dukeries' (The Land of Robin Hood)* (London, 1893).

WARNER, RICHARD, *A Walk through Wales, in August 1797* (Bath, 1798).

—— *A Second Walk through Wales* (Bath, 1799).

—— *A History of the Abbey of Glaston; and the Town of Glastonbury* (Bath, 1826).

WATT, ROBERT, *Bibliotheca Britannica; or A General Index to British and Foreign Literature* (Edinburgh and London, 1824).

WESTON, JESSIE L., *The Legend of Sir Gawaine: Studies upon Its Original Scope and Significance* (London, 1897).

—— *Sir Gawain and the Green Knight: A Middle-English Arthurian Romance Retold in Modern Prose* (London, 1898).

—— *Popular Studies in Mythology, Romance and Folklore* (London, 1899).

WESTWOOD, THOMAS, *The Quest of the Sancgreall, The Sword of Kingship, and Other Poems* (London, 1868).

WHISTLECRAFT, ROBERT and WILLIAM, *Prospectus and Specimen of an Intended National Work . . . Intended to Comprise the Most Interesting Particulars Relating to King Arthur and His Round Table*, 2nd edn. (London, 1818).

WHITE, ROBERT (ed.), *Nottinghamshire. Worksop, 'The Dukery,' and Sherwood Forest* (Worksop, 1875).

WHITE, T. H., *The Once and Future King* (New York: G. P. Putnam, 1958).

WILLIAMS, ROWLAND, *Lays from the Cimbric Lyre, with Various Verses* (London, 1846).

WILLIAMS, T. W., 'Sir Thomas Malory', *Athenaeum*, 2 (1896), 64–5 and 98.

WILSON, ALEXANDER, *The Crimson Dacoit* (London: Herbert Jenkins, 1933).

WILSON, F. MARY, 'England's Ballad-hero', *Temple Bar*, 95 (1892), 401–11.

WINTER, WILLIAM, *Shadows of the Stage* (Edinburgh, 1892).

WOOD, WILLIAM, *Tales and Traditions of the High Peak (Derbyshire)* (London and Derby, [1862]).

WOODLEY, GEORGE, *Cornubia: A Poem, in Five Cantos, Descriptive of the Most Interesting Scenery, Natural and Artificial, in the County of Cornwall* (London, 1819).

WORDSWORTH, WILLIAM, *Poems, Chiefly of Early and Late Years* (London, 1842).

—— *The Prelude* (London, 1850).

WRIGHT, G. N., *Scenes in North Wales. With Historical Illustrations, Legends, and Biographical Notices* (London, 1833).

WRIGHT, THOMAS, *Essays on the Literature, Superstitions, and History of England in the Middle Ages* (London, 1864).

—— (ed.), *La Mort d'Arthure. The History of King Arthur and of the Knights of the Round Table* (London, 1858).

WRIGHT, THOMAS, *Some Habits and Customs of the Working Classes* (London, 1867).

YONGE, CHARLOTTE, *The History of Sir Thomas Thumb* (Edinburgh and London, 1855).

PRIMARY SOURCES—FILMED

Programme for *Robin Hood*, Her Majesty's Theatre, Microfiche No. 19, Theatre Museum, Covent Garden, London.

SELECTED SECONDARY SOURCES

AARSLEFF, HANS, *The Study of Language in England, 1780–1860*, new edn. (London: Athlone Press, 1983).

ADAMS, JAMES ELI, 'Harlots and Base Interpreters: Scandal and Slander in *Idylls of the King*', *Victorian Poetry*, 30 (1992), 421–39.

ANDERSON, BENEDICT, *Imagined Communities: Reflections on the Origins and Spread of Nationalism*, rev. edn. (London and New York: Verso, 1991).

(Anon.) *Ladies of Shalott: A Victorian Masterpiece and Its Contexts* (Providence, RI: Brown University Department of Art, 1985).

AUERBACH, NINA, *Woman and the Demon: The Life of a Victorian Myth* (Cambridge, Mass., and London: Harvard UP, 1982).

BALCH, DENNIS R., 'Guenevere's Fidelity to Arthur in "The Defence of Guenevere" and "King Arthur's Tomb"', *Victorian Poetry*, 13 (1975), 61–70.

BALDICK, CHRIS, *The Social Mission of English Criticism 1848–1932* (Oxford: Clarendon Press, 1983).

BANHAM, JOANNA, '"Past and Present": Images of the Middle Ages in the Early Nineteenth Century', in Banham and Jennifer Harris (eds.), *William Morris and the Middle Ages* (Manchester and Dover, NH: Manchester UP, 1984), 17–31.

BEHRMAN, CYNTHIA FANSLER, *Victorian Myths of the Sea* (Athens, Ohio: Ohio UP, 1977).

BHABA, HOMI K. (ed.), *Nation and Narration* (London and New York: Routledge, 1990).

BOARD, MARILYNN LINCOLN, 'Art's Moral Mission: Reading G. F. Watt's *Sir Galahad*', in Debra N. Mancoff (ed.), *The Arthurian Revival: Essays on Form, Tradition, and Transformation* (New York and London: Garland, 1992).

BOOS, FLORENCE S., 'Sexual Polarities in *The Defence of Guenevere*', *Browning Institute Studies*, 13 (1985), 181–200.

—— 'Justice and Vindication in "The Defence of Guenevere"', in Valerie M. Lagorio and Mildred Leake Day (eds.), *King Arthur through the Ages*, Vol. 2 (New York: Garland, 1990), 83–102.

BRADSHAW, BRENDAN and MORRILL, JOHN (eds.), *The British Problem, c.1534–1707: State Formation in the Atlantic Archipelago* (New York: St Martin's, 1996).

BRINKLEY, ROBERTA FLORENCE, *Arthurian Legend in the Seventeenth Century*, Johns Hopkins Monographs in Literary History, 3 (Baltimore and London: John Hopkins Press, 1932).

BROCKLISS, LAURENCE and EASTWOOD, DAVID (eds.), *A Union of Multiple Identities: The British Isles, c.1750–c.1850* (Manchester and New York: Manchester UP, 1996).

BROWN, NATHANIEL, 'The "Brightest Colours of Intellectual Beauty": Feminism in Peacock's Novels', *Keats-Shelley Review*, 2 (1987), 91–103.

BURNS, BRYAN, *The Novels of Thomas Love Peacock* (London and Sydney: Croom Helm, 1985).

BURROW, J. W., *A Liberal Descent: Victorian Historians and the English Past* (Cambridge: Cambridge UP, 1981).

BUTLER, MARILYN, *Peacock Displayed: A Satirist in His Context* (London and Boston: Routledge, 1979).

CASTERAS, SUSAN P., *The Substance or the Shadow: Images of Victorian Womanhood* (New Haven: Yale Center for British Art, 1982).

CHANDLER, ALICE, *A Dream of Order: The Medieval Ideal in Nineteenth-century English Literature* (Lincoln, Nebr.: University of Nebraska Press, 1970).

CHAPMAN, RAYMOND, *The Sense of the Past in Victorian Literature* (London and Sydney: Croom Helm, 1986).

CHRIST, CAROL T., 'Victorian Masculinity and the Angel in the House', in Martha Vicinus (ed.), *A Widening Sphere* (Bloomington: Indiana UP, 1977), 146–62.

COHN, BERNARD S., 'Representing Authority in Victorian India', in Eric Hobsbawm and Terence Ranger (eds.), *The Invention of Tradition*, new edn. (Cambridge: Cambridge UP, 1992), 165–209.

COLLEY, LINDA, *Britons: Forging the Nation 1707–1837* (New Haven and London: Yale UP, 1992).

—— 'Britishness and Otherness: An Argument', *Journal of British Studies*, 31 (1992), 309–29.

COLLINI, STEFAN, *Public Moralists: Political Thought and Intellectual Life in Britain 1850–1930* (Oxford: Clarendon Press, 1991).

COLLS, ROBERT and DODD, PHILIP (eds.), *Englishness: Politics and Culture 1880–1920* (London and Dover, NH: Croom Helm, 1986).

COURT, FRANKLIN E., *Institutionalizing English Literature: The Culture and Politics of Literary Study, 1750–1900* (Stanford: Stanford UP, 1992).

CULLER, A. DWIGHT, *The Victorian Mirror of History* (New Haven and London: Yale UP, 1985).

CURTIS, L. P., Jr., *Anglo-Saxons and Celts: A Study of Anti-Irish Prejudice in Victorian England* (Bridgeport, Conn.: Conference on British Studies, 1968).

—— *Apes and Angels: The Irishman in Victorian Caricature* (Washington, DC: Smithsonian Institution Press, 1971).

DAVIDOFF, LEONORE and HALL, CATHERINE, *Family Fortunes: Men and Women of the English Middle Class, 1780–1850* (London: Hutchinson, 1987).

DEAN, CHRISTOPHER, *A Study of Merlin in English Literature from the Middle Ages to the Present Day* (Lewiston, NY: Edward Mellen Press, 1992).

DELLHEIM, CHARLES, *The Face of the Past: The Preservation of the Medieval Inheritance in Victorian England* (New York: Cambridge UP, 1982).

DOBSON, R. B. and TAYLOR, J., *Rymes of Robyn Hode: An Introduction to the English Outlaw* (London: Heinemann, 1976).

DONATELLI, JOSEPH P., 'Old Barons in New Robes: Percy's Use of the Metrical Romances in the *Reliques of Ancient English Poetry*', in Patrick J. Gallacher and Helen Damico (eds.), *Hermeneutics and Medieval Culture* (Albany: State University of New York Press, 1989), 225–35.

—— 'The Medieval Fictions of Thomas Warton and Thomas Percy', *University of Toronto Quarterly*, 60 (1990), 435–51.

DOYLE, BRIAN, *English and Englishness* (London and New York: Routledge, 1989).

DUGAW, DIANNE, 'The Popular Marketing of "Old Ballads": The Ballad Revival and Eighteenth-Century Antiquarianism Reconsidered', *Eighteenth-Century Studies*, 21 (1987), 71–90.

ELLIS, STEPHEN G. and BARBER, SARAH (eds.), *Conquest and Union: Fashioning a British State 1485–1725* (London and New York: Longman, 1995).

FITZPATRICK, DAVID, '"A peculiar tramping people": The Irish in Britain, 1801–70', in W. E. Vaughan (ed.), *A New History of Ireland*, Vol. V: *Ireland under the Union* (Oxford: Oxford UP, 1989), 623–57.

FOSTER, ROY, *Paddy and Mr. Punch: Connexions in Irish and English History* (London: Penguin, 1993).

GELLNER, ERNEST, *Nations and Nationalism* (Ithaca: Cornell UP, 1983).

GILBERT, ELLIOT L., 'The Female King: Tennyson's Arthurian Apocalypse', *PMLA* 98 (1983), 863–78.

GILLEY, SHERIDAN, 'English Attitudes to the Irish in England, 1789–1900', in Colin Holmes (ed.), *Immigrants and Minorities in British Society* (London: George Allen and Unwin, 1978), 81–110.

GILLIS, JOHN R. (ed.), *Commemorations: The Politics of National Identity* (Princeton: Princeton UP, 1994).

GIROUARD, MARK, *The Return to Camelot: Chivalry and the English Gentleman* (New Haven and London: Yale UP, 1981).

GOODMAN, JENNIFER R., 'The Last of Avalon: Henry Irving's *King Arthur* of 1895', *Harvard Library Bulletin*, 32 (1984), 239–55.

GRAINGER, J. H., *Patriotisms: Britain 1900–1939* (London: Routledge, 1989).

GRANT, ALEXANDER and STRINGER, KEITH (eds.), *Uniting the Kingdom?: The Making of British History* (London and New York: Routledge, 1995).

GREENFELD, LIAH, *Nationalism: Five Roads to Modernity* (Cambridge, Mass.: Harvard UP, 1992).

HARRISON, ROBERT POGUE, *Forests: The Shadow of Civilization* (Chicago and London: University of Chicago Press, 1992).

HILL, CHRISTOPHER, 'The Norman Yoke', in *Puritanism and Revolution: Studies in Interpretation of the English Revolution of the Seventeenth Century* (London: Secker and Hudson, 1958), 50–122.

HILTON, R. H. (ed.), *Peasants, Knights and Heretics: Studies in Medieval English Social History* (Cambridge and New York: Cambridge UP, 1976).

HOBSBAWM, E. J., *Primitive Rebels: Studies in Archaic Forms of Social Movement in the 19th and 20th Centuries* (New York: Praeger, 1963).

—— *Bandits*, 2nd edn. (Harmondsworth: Penguin, 1985).

—— *Nations and Nationalism Since 1780: Programme, Myth, Reality*, 2nd edn. (Cambridge: Cambridge UP, 1992).

—— and RANGER, TERENCE (eds.), *The Invention of Tradition*, new edn. (Cambridge: Cambridge UP, 1992).

HOLMES, COLIN, *Anti-Semitism in British Society, 1876–1939* (New York: Holmes and Meier, 1979).

—— (ed.), *Immigrants and Minorities in British Society* (London: George Allen and Unwin, 1978).

HOLT, J. C., *Robin Hood*, rev. edn. (London: Thames and Hudson, 1989).

HORSMAN, REGINALD, 'Origins of Racial Anglo-Saxonism in Great Britain before 1850', *Journal of the History of Ideas*, 37 (1976), 387–410.

HOSKING, GEOFFREY and SCHÖPFLIN, GEORGE (eds.), *Myths and Nationhood* (New York: Routledge, 1997).

HUTTON, RONALD, *The Rise and Fall of Merry England: The Ritual Year 1400–1700* (Oxford and New York: Oxford UP, 1994).

—— *The Stations of the Sun: A History of the Ritual Year in Britain* (Oxford: Oxford UP, 1996).

HYAM, RONALD, *Britain's Imperial Century, 1815–1914: A Study of Empire and Expansion*, 2nd edn. (Basingstoke and London: Macmillan, 1993).

JONES, EDWIN, *The English Nation: The Great Myth* (Thrupp, Stroud, Glos.: Sutton, 1998).

JOYCE, PATRICK, *Work, Society and Politics: The Culture of the Factory in Later Victorian England* (Brighton: Harvester, 1980).

—— *Visions of the People: Industrial England and the Question of Class 1848–1914* (Cambridge: Cambridge UP, 1991).

—— *Democratic Subjects: The Self and the Social in Nineteenth-Century England* (Cambridge: Cambridge UP, 1994).

KARSTEN, PETER, *Patriot Heroes in England and America: Political Symbolism and Changing Values Over Three Centuries* (Madison: University of Wisconsin Press, 1978).

KEEN, MAURICE, *The Outlaws of Medieval Legend* (London: Routledge, 1961).

—— 'Robin Hood: A Peasant Hero', *History Today*, 8 (1958), 684–9.

KIDD, COLIN, *Subverting Scotland's Past: Scottish Whig Historians and the Creation of an Anglo- British Identity, 1689–c.1830* (Cambridge: Cambridge UP, 1993).

KIERNAN, VICTOR, 'Tennyson, King Arthur and Imperialism', in Raphael Samuel and Gareth Stedman Jones (eds.), *Culture, Ideology and Politics: Essays for Eric Hobsbawm* (London: Routledge, 1982), 126–48.

KNIGHT, STEPHEN, *Arthurian Literature and Society* (London: Macmillan, 1983).

KNIGHT, STEPHEN, *Robin Hood: A Complete Study of the English Outlaw* (Oxford and Cambridge, Mass.: Blackwell, 1994).

LINDEBORG, RUTH H., 'The "Asiatic" and the Boundaries of Victorian Englishness', *Victorian Studies*, 37 (1994), 381–404.

LINEBAUGH, PETER, *The London Hanged: Crime and Civil Society in the Eighteenth Century* (London and New York: Penguin, 1991).

LINLEY, MARGARET, 'Sexuality and Nationality in Tennyson's Idylls of the King', *Victorian Poetry*, 30 (1992), 365–86.

LUNN, KENNETH, 'Reconsidering "Britishness": The Construction and Signifi-cance of National Identity in Twentieth-Century Britain', in Brian Jenkins and Spyros A. Sofos (eds.), *Nation and Identity in Contemporary Europe* (London and New York: Routledge, 1996).

MADOFF, MARK, 'The Useful Myth of Gothic Ancestry', *Studies in Eighteenth-Century Culture*, 8 (1979), 337–50.

MANCOFF, DEBRA H., *The Arthurian Revival in Victorian Art* (New York and London: Garland, 1990).

—— 'In Praise of Patriarchy: Paternalism and Chivalry in the Decorations in the House of Lords', *Nineteenth-Century Contexts*, 16 (1992), 47–64.

—— *The Return of King Arthur: The Legend Through Victorian Eyes* (New York: Harry N. Abrams, 1995).

MANGAN, J. A., 'Noble Specimens of Manhood: Schoolboy Literature and the Creation of a Colonial Chivalric Code', in Jeffrey Richards (ed.), *Imperial-ism and Juvenile Literature* (Manchester and New York: Manchester UP, 1989), 173–94.

MERRIMAN, JAMES D., *The Flower of Kings: A Study of the Arthurian Legend in England Between 1485 and 1835* (Lawrence, Ka.: University of Kansas Press, 1973).

METCALF, THOMAS, *The Aftermath of Revolt: India, 1857–1870* (Princeton: Prince-ton UP, 1965).

—— *Ideologies of the Raj, The New Cambridge History of India*, III: 4 (Cambridge and New York: Cambridge UP, 1994).

MORGAN, PRYS, *The Eighteenth Century Renaissance: A New History of Wales* (Llandybïe, Dyfed: Christopher Davies, 1981).

NAIRN, TOM, *The Enchanted Glass: Britain and Its Monarchy*, new edn. (London: Picador, 1990).

NEAD, LYNDA, *Myths of Sexuality: Representations of Women in Victorian Britain* (Oxford and New York: Basil Blackwell, 1988).

NEWMAN, GERALD, *The Rise of English Nationalism: A Cultural History 1740–1830* (New York: St Martin's, 1987).

PALMER, D. J., *The Rise of English Studies: An Account of the Study of English Language and Literature from Its Origins to the Making of the Oxford English School* (London, New York and Toronto: Oxford UP, 1965).

PANAYI, PANIKOS, *Immigration, Ethnicity and Racism in Britain, 1815–1945* (Manchester: Manchester UP, 1984).

PARRINS, MARILYN JACKSON, 'Malory's Expurgators', in Mary Flowers Braswell and John Bugge (eds.), *The Arthurian Tradition: Essays in Convergence* (Tuscaloosa and London: University of Alabama Press, 1988), 144–62.

—— 'A Survey of Malory Criticism and Related Arthurian Scholarship in the Nineteenth Century', unpublished Ph.D. thesis (University of Michigan, 1982).

PEARS, IAIN, 'The Gentleman and the Hero: Wellington and Napoleon in the Nineteenth Century', in Roy Porter (ed.), *Myths of the English* (Cambridge: Polity, 1992), 216–36.

PERERA, SUVENDRINI, *Reaches of Empire: The English Novel from Edgeworth to Dickens* (New York: Columbia UP, 1991).

PITTOCK, MURRAY G. H., *The Invention of Scotland: The Stuart Myth and the Scottish Identity, 1638 to the Present* (London and New York: Routledge, 1991).

PLASA, CARL, '"Cracked from Side to Side": Sexual Politics in "The Lady of Shalott"', *Victorian Poetry*, 30 (1992), 247–63.

POOVEY, MARY, *Uneven Developments: The Ideological Work of Gender in Mid-Victorian England, Women in Culture and Society* (Chicago and London: University of Chicago Press, 1988).

PORTER, ROY (ed.), *Myths of the English* (Cambridge: Polity Press, 1992).

POULSON, CHRISTINE, 'Arthurian Legend in Fine and Applied Art of the Nineteenth and Early Twentieth Centuries: A Catalogue of Artists', in Richard Barber (ed.), *Arthurian Literature IX* (Cambridge: D. S. Brewer, 1989), 81–142.

RICH, PAUL B., *Race and Empire in British Politics* (Cambridge and New York: Cambridge UP, 1986).

ROBBINS, KEITH, *Nineteenth-Century Britain: Integration and Diversity* (Oxford: Clarendon Press, 1988).

ROBERTS, DAVID, *Paternalism in Early Victorian England* (London: Croom Helm, 1979).

RUBINSTEIN, DAVID, *Before the Suffragettes: Women's Emancipation in the 1890s* (Brighton: Harvester Press, 1986).

SAMUEL, RAPHAEL (ed.), *Patriotism: The Making and Unmaking of British National Identity* (New York and London: Routledge, 1989).

—— and THOMPSON, PAUL (eds.), *The Myths We Live By* (London and New York: Routledge, 1990), 1–22.

SCHAMA, SIMON, *Landscape and Memory* (London: HarperCollins, 1995).

SEDGWICK, EVE KOSOFSKY, *Between Men: English Literature and Male Homosocial Desire* (New York: Columbia UP, 1985).

SHANLEY, MARY LYNDON, *Feminism, Marriage and the Law in Victorian England, 1850–1895* (London: I. B. Tauris, 1989).

SHIRES, LINDA M., 'Rereading Tennyson's Gender Politics', in Thaïs E. Morgan (ed.), *Victorian Sages and Cultural Discourse: Renegotiating Gender and Power* (New Brunswick and London: Rutgers UP, 1990), 46–65.

SHIRES, LINDA M., 'Patriarchy, Dead Men and Tennyson's *Idylls of the King*', *Victorian Poetry, 30* (1992), 401–19.

SHOWALTER, ELAINE, *Sexual Anarchy: Gender and Culture at the Fin de Siècle* (London: Bloomsbury, 1991).

SIMMONS, CLARE A., *Reversing the Conquest: History and Myth in Nineteenth-century British Literature* (New Brunswick, NJ, and London: Rutgers UP, 1990).

—— '"Iron-worded Proof": Victorian Identity and the Old English Language', in Leslie J. Workman (ed.), *Medievalism in England*, Studies in Medievalism, 4 (Cambridge: D. S. Brewer, 1992), 202–14.

SIMPSON, ROGER, *Camelot Regained: The Arthurian Revival and Tennyson*, Arthurian Studies, 21 (Cambridge and Wolfeboro, NH: D. S. Brewer, 1990).

SMILES, SAMUEL, *The Image of Antiquity: Ancient Britain and the Romantic Imagination* (New Haven: Yale UP, 1994).

SMITH, OLIVIA, *The Politics of Language 1791–1819* (Oxford: Clarendon Press, 1984).

STAINES, DAVID, 'Morris's Treatment of His Medieval Sources in *The Defence of Guenevere and Other Poems*', *Studies in Philology*, 70 (1973), 439–64.

—— 'Tennyson's "The Holy Grail": The Tragedy of Percivale', *Modern Language Review*, 69 (1974), 745–56.

—— 'Swinburne's Arthurian World: Swinburne's Arthurian Poetry and Its Medieval Sources', *Studia Neophilologica*, 50 (1978), 53–70.

STALLYBRASS, PETER, '"Drunk with the Cup of Liberty": Robin Hood, the Carnivalesque, and the Rhetoric of Violence in Early Modern England', in Nancy Armstrong and Leonard Tennenhouse (eds.), *The Violence of Representation: Literature and the History of Violence* (London: Routledge, 1989), 45–76.

SWIFT, ROGER, 'The Outcast Irish in the British Victorian City: Problems and Perspectives', *Irish Historical Studies*, 25 (1986–7), 264–76.

—— and GILLEY, SHERIDAN (eds.), *The Irish in Britain, 1815–1939* (London: Pinter, 1989).

—— and GILLEY, SHERIDAN (eds.), *The Irish in the Victorian City* (London: Croom Helm, 1985).

UMLAND, REBECCA, 'The Snake in the Woodpile: Tennyson's Vivien as Victorian Prostitute', in Martin B. Shichtman and James P. Carley (eds.), *Culture and the King: The Social Implications of the Arthurian Legend* (Albany: State University of New York Press, 1994), 274–87.

UNDERDOWN, DAVID, *Revel, Riot and Rebellion: Popular Politics and Culture in England 1603–1660* (Oxford: Oxford UP, 1985).

—— *A Freeborn People: Politics and the Nation in Seventeenth-Century England* (Oxford: Clarendon Press, 1996).

VICINUS, MARTHA, *Independent Women: Work and Community for Single Women 1850–1920* (London: Virago, 1985).

VINCENT, DAVID, *Literacy and Popular Culture: England 1750–1914* (Cambridge: Cambridge UP, 1989).

WALKOWITZ, JUDITH R., *Prostitution and Victorian Society: Women, Class and the State* (Cambridge: Cambridge UP, 1980).

—— *City of Dreadful Delight: Narratives of Sexual Danger in Late-Victorian London* (London: Virago, 1992).

WALVIN, JAMES B., *Passage to Britain: Immigration in British History and Politics* (Harmondsworth and New York: Penguin, 1984).

WEINBROT, HOWARD D., *Britannia's Issue: The Rise of British Literature from Dryden to Ossian* (Cambridge: Cambridge UP, 1993).

WELLS, EVELYN KENDRICK, *The Ballad Tree: A Study of British and American Ballads, Their Folklore, Verse, and Music* (London: Methuen, 1950).

WHEELWRIGHT, JULIE, *Amazons and Military Maids: Women Who Dressed as Men in the Pursuit of Life, Liberty and Happiness* (London: Pandora, 1989).

WHITAKER, MURIEL, *The Legends of King Arthur in Art*, Arthurian Studies, 22 (Cambridge: D. S. Brewer, 1990).

WIENER, MARTIN J., *English Culture and the Decline of the Industrial Spirit, 1850–1980* (Cambridge: Cambridge UP, 1981).

WILSON, KATHLEEN, 'Admiral Vernon and Popular Politics in Mid-Hanoverian Britain', *Past and Present*, 121 (1988), 74–109.

Index